Give us back the
BAD ROADS

First published in 2018 by

Currach Press

23 Merrion Square North,

Dublin 2, Co. Dublin

www.currachbooks.com

Acknowledgements:

The Abolition of Man by CS Lewis © copyright CS Lewis Pte Ltd 1943, 1946, 1978

Impossible Exchange by Jean Baudrillard, Verso, 2001

How the Irish Saved Civilization by Thomas Cahill, Nan A. Talese/Doubleday, 1995

Nothing by Paul Morley, Faber & Faber, 2000

The Case for Working with Your Hands Or Why Office Work is Bad for You and Fixing Things Feels Good by Matthew B. Crawford, Viking/Penguin Books, 2010

Propaganda by Edward Bernays, Liverlight/W. W. Norton, 1928

Propaganda by Jacques Ellul, Vintage Books/Randomhouse, 1973

After the Ball: How America will conquer its fear and hatred of gays in the 90s by Marshall Kirk and Hunter Madsen, Doubleday, 1989

Immortality by Milan Kundera, Faber & Faber, 1991

ISBN: 978-1-78218-901-5

Set in Freight Text Pro 11/15

Cover and book design by Alba Esteban | Currach Press

Printed by ScandBook, Sweeden

Give us back the
BAD ROADS

JOHN WATERS

CURRACH
PRESS

To my wife, Rita Waters

ABOUT THE AUTHOR

Having started his career in 1981 with the Irish Music journal *Hot Press*, John Waters later wrote in *The Irish Times* from 1990 to 2014, when the 'Pantigate' upheaval led to his resignation. His first book, *Jiving at the Crossroads* (1991), about the cultural underbelly of Irish politics at the height of the Haughey era, became a massive best-seller. He went on to write and publish eight other books, including *An Intelligent Person's Guide to Modern Ireland* (Duckworth, 1997) and *Was it for this? Why Ireland lost the plot* (Transworld Ireland, 2012). He has written a number of plays for stage and radio, and currently writes a fortnightly essay for the American magazine of religion in the public square, *First Things*. He is a Permanent Research Fellow at the Center for Ethics and Culture, University of Notre Dame, Indiana, USA.

PROLOGUE:

Probaby

Writing to you in this fashion is what editors call a 'conceit'. Here, the word refers to a kind of literary device – an 'elaborate, fanciful metaphor, especially of a strained or far-fetched nature', according to one online dictionary. I found that funny, since 'conceit' was one of your favourite words – I mean a word you used quite a lot, in a certain context: to pull us back from some self-indulgence or other. Your use of it as a synonym for 'vanity' or 'narcissism' was probably a little out of tune with its true meaning, but had a denunciatory power that neither of those words is capable of supporting.

I bridled at the word here, as much on account of still being able to hear it in your voice as at the subtext: that addressing a father who'd been dead for nearly 30 years cannot credibly be sustained over a whole book. I disagree. There is no 'conceit' involved in addressing you, or any other of the millions upon millions of my dead predecessor Irish men and women. You taught me to see my country as an inheritance held in trust from the dead for the not yet born. That this now seems an eccentric idea is all the more reason to reiterate it with vigour. Its loss is in large part the reason for our situation.

There are two rooms in Ireland now that ought to frighten any sentient person, and these two rooms bespeak a shift in our collective outlook and demeanour that is ultimately against our very selves. One of these rooms is the baby room in the crèche, where toddlers sit on mats from maybe 9.00 in the morning until 7.00 in the evening, while their parents are elsewhere trying to gather the wherewithal to put a roof over all their heads. The other room is, in a sense, at the other end of a corridor defined by a human life, in which elderly men and women, who not long ago were themselves babies, and – more recently – hardworking, up-standing, respected members of Irish society, sit all day in tubular steel chairs around a wall while a 64-inch television set blares from the far corner, rarely speaking to each other except in odd shouts over the din of Mark Cagney. As much as anything, the referendum of 2018 on Article 40.3.3 of the Constitution was about these two rooms, and I mentioned this fact numerous times along my way around Ireland over the past year. For the kind of Ireland we appear to be in preparation for is an Ireland where even the tender mercies of both of these rooms will have been obliterated and replaced with even more horrific realities. This is the na-ture of the fight against 'progress'.

Intermittently, over the six months preceding the referendum, I spoke at meetings up and down the country, usually beginning by reading the opening of Pádraig Pearse's essay 'Ghosts': 'There has been nothing more terrible in Irish history than the failure of the last generation … '. In that essay he invokes the dead generations and reminds us of the debts we owe them, debts that can only be paid to the generations as yet unborn. His ghosts, like mine, have particular faces, his being Tone, Davis, Lalor, Mitchell and Parnell – their invocation, as with my invocation of you, is intended to unleash the spirits of the legions of the dead. In my publicly expressed thoughts, you have, since your death three decades ago, most often represented the dead generations, though sometimes now – since her death in 2012 – I refer to both my parents together, you and Mammy standing for a time and a category of people (John Healy's 'great but anonymous people') incomprehen-sible to most of those living in Ireland today.

In that essay, Pearse speaks of the 'apostolic succession' that is the nation, handed down from generation to generation, a holy and constant thing. The ironies of reading from that in proffering resistance to a pro-longed lethal attack, disguised as 'healthcare', on the very right to life of the coming generations need hardly be spelt out.

To represent the coming generations, or – to be as absolutely precise as we now need to be – to represent the generations as yet unborn, some among them now less likely ever to be born, I invoked also the name of another Tom. This Tom may never be a Tom, but it seemed right to give him this name for the time of our pleading on his behalf.

Before we were long into the campaign, my stepdaughter Sarah (a long story, just wait!) announced that she was pregnant, the sex of her baby then unknown. Her first child, Abigail, the smartest and most effervescent child in the world, was by this time three-and-a-third. When the news broke, we asked Abigail what she might like to call the new baby if it turned out to be another girl. At that moment, she was engaged in drawing pictures while seated on the floor, and, without hesitating or looking up, responded: 'Julia', which we knew to be the name of one of her very best friends. And what – we persisted – if it were a little brother? Again, with no break in concentration: 'Tom'.

It turned out that Tom, too, was the name of one of her friends in the naíonra. The following week she had shifted to 'Alex', another favourite, before finally settling on 'Finn'. Of course, none of these is likely to be her brother's name, but for obvious and other reasons, I stayed with Tom – just as during the time we awaited Abigail she was known as Poppy – using the flesh-and-blood reality of this single human boy in my night-time attempts to articulate the truth about the referendum proposal. What we had to speak of, I insisted, was no foetus, no zygote, no clump of cells. We spoke of Tom.

He comes to me in my dreams, a chubby boy of about two, with a fringe into his eyes. Or perhaps it is a visitation from the spirit of my own boyhood, my life flashing before me in the name of another. I see his likeness everywhere, and when I do, I point him out to my wife, Rita (that long story again!), saying, 'There he is! Look! There's Tom!'

This is the way it has always been – in 1937, which you remember, and 1983, which we both remember. The idea that people, on hearing of a pregnancy, did anything but instantly include the newcomer in their count of themselves is something only a bunch of lying curs such as

< 11 >

have now insinuated themselves as our leaders could come up with. Politicians – and judges responding to their nods and winks, and of course, God help us, journalists – try to tell us that, when the Irish people in 1937 were enacting and giving themselves their Constitution, they expressly intended to exclude from the benefits of citizenship and human protection those beings who were not yet wearing clothes and footwear, on account of being encased in their mothers' wombs. A baby, we are now told, is not a baby until his or her mother says so, and this saying magically turns a 'clump of cells' into a human being. This is what Ireland has come to since you've been gone.

So we took Tom along with us, Rita and I, when we set out on those dark and dismal nights of November and December 2017, and the sometimes more dismal nights of January to April 2018, in an attempt to overcome the doublethink of the present age of Ireland.

Sometimes, in talking through the arguments at public gatherings, I became aware of the issues becoming unaccountably abstract. This was in part because what confronted us in the arena of the battle was a veritable fog of euphemism and propaganda, blurring and dissolving things, rendering them as though theoretical or arcane. The most fundamental and incontrovertible matters thereby became a clash of abstractions, incapable of reconciliation.

But then I had this thought: What if, instead of thinking about all unborn children, we were to think about just one specific unborn child? And imagine that, in a dream perhaps, we had to rush, late in the evening, to a specially convened court to request a life-or-death judgment about that child's right to go on living. Imagine it as something akin to the circumstances of a last-minute application for a reprieve in the case of a prisoner on death row. But here, not only is the subject of the hearing completely innocent of any wrongdoing, he is also completely defenceless aside from whatever protection the court may extend him. And all the while remembering that in this jurisdiction there has never been as much as a half-sentence in any judgment of any court to say that this being, this child, is not a human person from the very first moment, not one sentence to say that Tom was not Tom or Julia was not Julia – what then?

How can it be justified that consideration even be given to the idea that this child – this innocent, defenceless person – might be abandoned by the court, have his or her rights to protection disposed of by some consideration of the will of the people expressed in opinion polls or plebiscites, or the imperatives of some political argument measured as 'social progress' across a span of time? It is unconscionable. It would be wicked beyond comprehension.

Invoking Tom, I tried to confront people with these thoughts, and with the indisputable fact that, although the government and other Yes campaigners sought to duck or fudge every issue and reduce everything to euphemism and circumlocution, it was not possible to provide formal distinctions in law to cater for the duplicity and dualism implicit in the proposal to dispense with the rights contained in Article 40.3.3. Put another way, it was not possible to create a clean set of laws for one category of unborn child – the 'wanted' – and a different set for another category – the 'unwanted' – especially when those children could be deemed to differ only because of their respective mothers' attitudes to them. It was not possible to elevate our hypocrisies to the level of law.

But now we have done exactly that. Tom lives, but we have lost, which means we betrayed all the other Toms, and all the other Julias, not yet born, which means that the debt cannot be repaid to them, which means that, inflated on this account, it will have to be paid in other ways that we are not yet able to fathom.

On 26 May, the day of the count that delivered a two-to-one majority for repealing Article 40.3.3, thousands of young Irish people, more than a few of whom owe their very existence to that article, danced and toasted with cans and champagne glasses their victory over the unborn generations in the yard of Dublin Castle: dancing on the graves of the holy innocents.

I don't exactly know how I got into this. As you well know, I am a rock 'n' roller, by origin and inclination. I started off as a writer in *Hot Press*, writing about bands and songs and gigs. I wrote a book one time that was vaguely about U2, although its subject was really Ireland and what happens when a rich culture is buried for centuries under rubble.

I have always felt that there is a profound connection between the historical sensibility of the Irish and the spirit of the African. And I loved the blues, because that was where the whole thing started: the cry of the slave waking up to the theft of his life. I loved John Lennon and Bob Dylan because they were tuned into that cry and sought to mobilise its power into the modern world. For a few years in my youth I nestled into the cool embrace of modern rock 'n' roll's culture of protest and hope, while driving the mailcar around Roscommon to keep all our bodies and souls in one piece.

As time passed, I began to feel that something was wrong. Rock stars were talking about a woman's 'right to choose' as if, as with the slavery in which their music was rooted, this was a straightforward matter of freedom from oppression, as though the unborn child was somehow the equivalent of the slave master rather than the proxy of the slave. I grew uncomfortable. Driving around in the Hi-ace, I would sometimes listen to Billie Holliday singing 'Strange Fruit' and hear what had to be a different song to everyone else: Scent of magnolias, sweet and fresh/Then the sudden smell of burning flesh.

To say that abortion is the slavery of the present is more than rhetoric, because each of the two in its way involves the purchasing of the convenience of one with the life of another. In Holliday's voice I heard the dying cries of the hanged slaves, strange fruit hanging from those southern trees. But I heard, too, the first/last cries of the children torn from their nests of expectation by an executioner calling himself Doctor, in Graham Parker's unforgettable phrase, 'with talons of steel.' I began to experience a profound dissonance in the face of the idea that the annihilation of these children was part of some agenda of coolness to which I was expected to subscribe. I didn't stop listening to the music – some of it anyway – but I stopped subscribing. I never thought of myself as a pro-lifer – a reductive piety to my ears – but as *probaby*.

A diminishing part of me is appalled at where I've ended up: I can't think of myself as 'right-wing' or 'fundamentalist' or 'reactionary' or even 'conservative', although I have come to accept that these labels will follow me to the grave. I am, of course, a Catholic, and this is frequently proffered by combatants on the other side as an 'explanation' for my perverseness. There is a connection, but it is not as they would have it. I would put it that I come to these positions via the use of reason, and Catholicism, as much as rock 'n' roll, was one of the 'texts' by which I came to learn to think like that. This is not a matter of doctrine or diktat: it is a matter of human empathy and justice. In truth, my resistance to these new ordinances has a constant basis that is less a matter of Catholic doctrine than a determination to preserve particular understandings of law as rooted in transcendent understandings of the human – a perspective now under terminal sentence in Ireland and elsewhere. Of course, these understandings are part of Christian teaching, but I insist on the distinction because I find that, nowadays, people have become oblivious to the fact that these understandings would be necessary and true if Christ had never come

I would love to be cool again, but there is an insurmountable problem: the truth – hard and ineluctable facts that get in the way. Abortion is the killing of the innocent and most defenseless. I have looked at it every which way and cannot find another way of looking. I accompanied my own baby as she grew from a quark to a queen, and today I still see her as nine months older than the world counts her to be. I don't have the choice of seeing or saying it another way.

I know I am against the grain of the culture to which I have subscribed in other ways, and, in a certain sense, it breaks my heart. But it seems to me that, were rock 'n' rollers to be true to the faith from which their music grew, there is only one place for them to stand: on vigil for the baby sleeping inside the most vulnerable place he or she will ever be, condemning the slaughter of innocents, decrying the loss of 60 million American lives since Roe v Wade, 9 million lives in Britain since abortion was legalised in 1967, including 170,000 Irish lives since we introduced the Eighth Amendment in 1983 to block the same kind of legislation being introduced here. I cannot see that there is any other place you can stand and imagine yourself to be to this age what John Lennon was to his – except on the side of little Tom.

A friend of mine says that rock 'n' roll is purely about sex, whereas I've always liked to think it a music of existential truth and justice. There's something in both positions. Rock 'n' roll is the offspring of the blues, and the generic modern western rock offshoot is the prodigal son and grandson of these great forebears, long since surrendered to a false sense of freedom and a vacuous ideological programme.

The blues were born in the plantations where slaves in chains worked themselves to early deaths, hollering out to their brothers over each other's heads on the line, their cries becoming chants, forming songs, unleashing a music that nobody could have imagined or predicted. In time, the blues merged with Negro spirituals and country – itself the offspring of Irish folk songs that had travelled in the hearts of starving emigrants fleeing famine at home – to form rock 'n' roll. The blending of tribal rhythms and melodies with the chords and harmonies of the white world sparked the spastic dance of Elvis, but the pain at the root of it all was soon forgotten in a blind pursuit of hedonism. In the 1960s, rock 'n' roll in the west got mixed up with left-wing ideologies, the spirit and character of the progeny of the blues becoming Marx-saturated in the clubs and cafés and the groves of academe, pumping out an untenable concept of reality to the soundtrack of the Stones and the Beatles. What began as a crying out for pure existential freedom spawned a soundtrack for posturing, selfishness and narcissism, buying into all ten liberal commandments, including Thou shalt kill a child who does not wear cool shoes. The music began to die right there, but everyone was too stoned to notice.

Bands whose music I long to love wear Choice T-shirts and write terrible songs in praise of genocide or duck and dive around the question in interviews. Even the sublime Graham Parker, author of the most

< 16 >

searingly beautiful *probaby* song ever written ('You Can't Be Too Strong') doesn't seem to hear what I hear, repudiating pro-life interpretations of his own composition, usually with some vituperation, seemingly unable or unwilling – or too scared – to hear what his own song is saying: Did they tear it out with talons of steel/And give you a shot, so that you wouldn't feel/And wash it away, as if it wasn't real.

And so I am the sole member of my personal Reformed Church of Rock 'n' roll. People I used to know don't exactly cross the road when they see me coming (most of them anyway), but they do, I notice, squirm a bit when we stop to talk and they examine me for signs of the knuckle-dragging habits they need to identify to justify the gap that must be conjured up between us.

I meet, too, with people I might once have avoided out of prejudice – self-describing pro-lifers, 'traditionalists', 'right-wingers' etc. – and find they are just as personable as the people I used to hang out with. More honest, too, to be honest, these *probaby* people.

Those on the other side of the referendum went all out on euphemism: 'reproductive rights'; the 'right to choose' (choose what?); and the most despicable of all – 'abortion care'. At the heart of the exercise was an immense evasion: the baby, as if the 'living without birth' of the Irish language version of Article 40.3.3 – 'Tom' and 'Julia' by name – as though they were a cancer to be eliminated, chopped off, expunged.

Another word for 'euphemism' is 'lie'. This was a referendum of lies – the lies, exclusively, of those seeking the slaughter of innocents but unprepared to come right out and say so. We on the No side were enjoined to be polite, to keep the debate 'respectful', to avoid 'shock tactics', which translated as 'the truth', just as 'keep the debate respectful' meant avoiding mention of the truth. Politeness in these circumstance would have amounted to a genocidal impulse.

This referendum was about one thing: destroying under Irish law the right to life of a category of human being – the most innocent, defenseless, vulnerable and voiceless category of human being there is. When the euphemisms, evasions and prevarications were stripped away, that is what it came down to.

In those weeks leading up to 25 May 2018, we heard all the elaborate genteelisms and rationalisations, often waiting in vain for the baby to enter the discussion. But the deep meaning of the referendum was that it pitted the convenience of one person against the fundamental right of another ever to breathe and laugh and sing, implying equivalence between the two. 'Repeal' was about empowering the strong over the weak, the strident and demanding over the silent and passive. Only those deluded by hypnotic propaganda – and those who couldn't care less about consequences for anyone but themselves – could buy into such a proposal.

When you look over your shoulder at abortion wherever it exists, it is all and always about killing – killing for convenience, killing for expediency, killing to get shot of, killing as business. It is never about 'compassion', or health, or freedom of any kind worth the name – these being just the weasel-worded pretexts invoked by the vested interests and their paid liars, on a par with defences of slavery that claimed Africans sold other Africans into slavery and protested that other countries had slavery too. In the reality of its everyday existence, abortion is about spilling blood for money, about stamping out innocent but inopportune lives, about pretending there is no Judgement, about the white smoke of death rising from smokestacks on the horizons of normalisation, alien clouds with streaks of the human in them. Strange fruit of the warped thinking of our times.

And abortion will go the way of slavery also, when medical science identifies the child's earliest susceptibility to pain, and posterity will look back in horror at this moment we now stain in the blood of innocents, and every shred of our reputation for human feeling will be in the dumpster of history.

At the heart of the manipulation of Irish people that has been going on for some time is the proposition that, by adhering to such beliefs as the idea of the unborn child's humanity from the moment of conception we are merely demonstrating our backwardness and enchantment by the witch doctors of obscurantism, the Catholic Taliban who bear down upon our every thought and word. These denunciations are soon followed by the equally spurious idea that the rejection of the child's claim to humanity is somehow to be deemed the naturalistic deliverance of history to this moment, a 'progressive' idea. Of course there is nothing 'natural' or 'progressive' about such ideas – on the contrary: by virtue of being delivered by propaganda and censorship they are symptoms of an abuse of power, a false version of reality camouflaged by an elaborate ideology of progress. This is fundamentally why I have withdrawn from Irish journalism. The key function of modern media appears to be to create the correct conditions for the purveyance of the fundamental lie that certain developments are rendered inevitable by the progress of history. This is the essential nature of totalitarianism. The word is not too strong.

The mechanism adopted by the government for replacing the right to life of the unborn child in Article 40.3.3 with a right to annihilate that child using lethal force was to delete the existing text of that article and put in its place what had the appearance of a kind of signpost: 'Provision may be made by law for the regulation of termination of pregnancy'.

This, too, needed translation, for it concealed by a sleight-of-hand what was really going to happen.

In fact, inserting the phrase 'Provision may be made by law for the regulation of termination of pregnancy' was a nonsense in the immediate context in which it was proposed to introduce it. The language of Articles 40 to 44 is quite different from that of the rest of the Constitution. Being fundamental, i.e. absolute, the rights set down in those articles are of a different order and derivation. They contain words that, by and large, do not appear elsewhere in the text: 'antecedent', 'inalienable', 'imprescriptible', 'natural'. These words mean, respectively, more or less: 'pre-existing', 'incapable of being given up', 'incapable of being taken away', 'not made or caused by humankind'. These words ought to alert us to something that is neither minor nor usual.

Just above Article 40 are two headings: 'Fundamental Rights' in large capitals, and, below that, in smaller, bold type: 'Personal Rights', corre-

< 19 >

sponding to other headings above the subsequent articles: 'The Family' above Article 41; 'Education' above 42; 'Private Property' above Article 43 and 'Religion' above Article 44. These headings, as you well know, refer to categories of rights that are distinct and discrete in the context of the dispensations laid down by Bunreacht na hÉireann, the Irish Constitution: they are rights that do not derive from human lawmaking, and therefore cannot be annulled by court, parliament or ballot box. They are the out-of-human-reach rights and, prior to 25 May 2018, they included the right to life of the unborn child.

In striking down the right to life of the unborn child and replacing it with a provision asserting that the Oireachtas would 'regulate for the termination of pregnancy', we were unambiguously agreeing that the hitherto imprescriptible right to life of the unborn child should be supplanted with a right of unnamed others to put Tom or Julia to death. Not merely that, but this right to kill, by virtue of being situated within Article 40 (the first of the fundamental rights articles) would immediately acquire the status of a new fundamental right. It had never happened before in the world that abortion had been accorded the status of 'fundamental human right', but now it was happening in Ireland, once the supposed pro-life capital of the world. Not even the United States, which has had abortion for 45 years – had reached the stage of making abortion a fundamental human right.

This is why I repeatedly said beforehand that Friday 25 May would be perhaps the most momentous day in the annals of Irish history. In the past thousand years, we had travelled a long and bloody journey, with many gory days, from the Battle of Clontarf to the bombing of Omagh. Friday 25 May may now be named the bloodiest day of all.

In seeking to understand how we could even embark upon such a discussion, let alone have it end so appallingly, I would identify three major contributory factors: (1) the normalisation of abortion by virtue of its ready availability in the UK; (2) the indoctrination of Irish hearts and minds by a grossly corrupt and virtually monolithic media, with the help of foreign monies pumped in illegally and surreptitiously; and (3) the virtual disappearance from the 'debate' of the child. Nearly half (43%) of Yes voters questioned for exit polls said that they had voted on the basis of 'personal stories' told via the media. And these stories were invariably the stories of women who had aborted their children. Few, it seems, felt moved to contemplate the most personal story of all: that of the baby cowering in his holding cell while the abortionist sharpened his instruments.

As with the so-called Marriage Equality Referendum of 2015, the impression given by the media afterwards was of an exhaustive, even-handed and comprehensive debate embracing all the issues. Nothing could have been further from the truth. Again, as with the 2015 referendum, the 'debate' was almost entirely one-sided, like a football match in which one team is allowed on the pitch for five minutes at the end, when the other has built up an unassailable lead, and forced to play barefoot. The amount of time given to the Yes side by broadcasters, as with the amount of space afforded by newspapers, was many multiples of that granted to the anti-amendment side. The impression was persistently given that what was at stake was merely a small number of 'hard case' scenarios, when in fact what was being sought, and what was attained, was the most radical evisceration of the rights of unborn children anywhere in the world.

On Thursday 24 May, the day before polling day, I came down with a strange feeling that the day had the atmosphere of a Holy Saturday, a day lifted out of history, on which I have always had a visceral sense of disorientation. Except that here history seemed to have gone into reverse: the Resurrection behind, Calvary in front. The next day, the Irish people climbed Calvary backwards, in the name of progress.

Two out of three of those who voted – 66.4% – said Yes to the removal of the last remaining protection of the unborn child in the Irish Constitution. When you put it into actual words, it is dizzying: just one in three voters – 33.6% – wished this protection to continue. The world's media called it a 'landslide for abortion', but before that it was a landslide for leaving the unborn child – every unborn child – defenceless against assault from outside. When you factor in the fact that roughly one in three of those entitled to vote did not do so (turnout was 64.1%) this unprecedented measure passed with approximately 42.5% of the electorate voting for it. Only one constituency, Donegal, voted No, and this by a tight margin—51.87% for *No* Yes; 48.13% for No. *Yes*

What it rinsed down to was that, for the first time in human history, an electorate had voted to obliterate the last remaining rights of innocents, so that the executioners might do their work without hindrance. And those condemned to die would be the most defenceless, those entirely without voices or words. And this was the considered verdict of the Irish people, not – as elsewhere – an edict of the elites, not tentative but by a landslide.

In my heart of hearts I cannot claim to have been surprised. I had felt the result, or something like it, rising up in my gut for a month or more. The manner and tenor of the contest had been so nauseating that the deepest parts of my psyche had begun to anticipate the outcome long before my head began to compute it. For the final fortnight, I felt as if the cancer the surgeon cut out of my abdomen in February had returned. It was little things: the frivolity of the Yes side: 'Run for Repeal'; 'Spinning for Repeal'; 'Walk your Dog for Repeal'; 'Farmers for Yes'; 'Grandparents for Repeal', which ought surely to have been 'Grandparents for Not Having Grandchildren'. This, like the same-sex marriage referendum of three years earlier, was a carnival referendum: Yessers chanting for Repeal, drinking to Repeal, grinning for the cameras as they went door-to-door on their canvass of death.

On the day of the vote, the self-styled news media gave us a picture of Taoiseach Leo Varadkar, grinningly dropping his vote into a ballot box, over the headline: 'All the lads in the gym are voting yes.'

It might be the epitaph of the country I grew up in, the only one I had to call home, this ancient land, traceable into antiquity by its piety, its valour, and its sufferings. This wretched man, who had entered the last election less than three years earlier as 'pro-life', was seemingly incapable of grasping what he had led us into.

On Wednesday, two days from polling day, Varadkar, with his typical disingenuousness, had called for no public shows of celebration if the vote turned out a Yes. Still, that Saturday evening, the yard of Dublin Castle was filled with thousands of hysterical citizens, mostly young and female, dancing, cavorting, weeping, screaming – and there was Varadkar in the midst of them, cadging every last vote.

That Wednesday also, he had been launching a 'draft National Risk Assessment' of 'the most significant risks facing Ireland', and in doing so declared that the initiative was intended to 'stimulate debate' so as to 'avoid groupthink and have a genuine consultation'. This man, who had utilised every trick of spin and PR to achieve his ends in the referendum, still found in himself reserves of cynicism to warn against the dangers of a phenomenon – groupthink – that he had cultivated with every fibre of his being, as he moved to deny the nature of his wrongdoing like a cat shovelling phantom dirt on the excreta he has delivered to the livingroom carpet.

On Thursday morning, with the pain in my abdomen providing an ineluctable crescendo of prediction, I wrote to a friend: 'The young woman of Ireland have gone stone mad. It is not that they do not know they are talking about human beings – they don't care.'(How right my abdomen was: according to one of the exit polls, voters aged 18–24 voted 87 % for Repeal, with women edging it at 90%.)

She replied: 'It's gaslighting. Pathological. Mad and worse. Selfish. They don't care. And of course lavish ignorance, vapidity and stupidity. This is the result of not teaching people to think and the fact that we don't take responsibility for ourselves. To hear Varadkar – a doctor who a few months ago was for reform, not repeal – say he only takes it now that there are two lives in a pregnancy if the mother says so. That was astonishing. The darkness of it. A baby lives or dies according to its mother's desire.'

Gaslighting: the sowing of seeds of doubt in a targeted individual or group, making its objects doubt their own sanity or perceptions. Yes: the perfect word for what had occurred. A stupefied populace manipulated by amoral cynics and self-serving ideologues who had systematically withheld from them factual information, and pumped them with knowing lies, with the objective of making the objects of the manipulation anxious, confused and unable to trust their own memories and perceptions.

There is a back story, too complex to do more than allude to. The spiritual reconstruction of Ireland that took place after the famines of the 1840s placed mothers at its centre: the moral instruments by which Irish families were to be brought back to the straight and narrow. This placed women on a pedestal, their actions or demands immune from questioning by mere men. Add a dash of feminism, another of Cultural Marxism, and you have an unassailable cultural force, which has now attained its apotheosis. 'Trust women', one of the many fatuous Yes campaign slogans demanded. Trust women to annihilate their children only when absolutely necessary?

Irish women used to be rock-solid, sensible beings, but the recent generations, under the influence of radical feminist distortions, have taken off in the opposite direction, forever babbling about oppression, equality and rights when they are in truth the most privileged beings ever to saunter across an Irish horizon. What do these women want? It is often unclear, but in the spring of 2018 no one could be in any doubt: they wanted nothing less than the right to kill their young.

Of course this is part of a deeper and wider malaise. The cancer at the heart of modern Irish culture is rooted in a profound materialism based on unbelief in anything that is not negotiable in the manner of currency. But that was the diagnosis up until Friday 25 May 2018, the day that will go down as the beginning of the final stage of the disintegration: the carting of the human in Ireland from the spiritual to the material level, with the country that was once the jewel in the crown of European Christianity affirming that a baby is the mere chattel of his mother.

Other factors included the recent corruption of the public conversation, resulting from a journalism almost totally contaminated by leftist ideologies, and the intrusion of external actors operating their bought-and-paid-for puppets in the political and public life of the Irish corporatocracy – the fly-by-night transnationals who came to Ireland on the run from paying their dues and, unable to believe their good fortune, stayed around to tell us how to run our country.

A notable symptom of these ominous new trends were a number of totalitarian intrusions in the campaign by Google and Facebook, seeking to close down the discussion by withdrawing core services as soon as the No side developed a spurt entering the final fortnight. Having more or less wiped out all the opposition and rendered Irish democracy dependent on their services, the new colonists ratcheted up their efforts to turn that democracy into an oligarchy.

And then there were the goon squads stalking the land in search of dissenters to silence. After the stealing of the gay-marriage referendum in 2015, I warned that, in its wake, any group of thugs wanting to impose its wishes on Irish society had a blueprint by which to succeed. So it proved: anti-amendment meetings having to be cancelled because of threats of boycotts and worse, the spurious booking of events in venues that had welcomed No meetings, cancelled later on as though in protest that a No event was being hosted at the same venue, and so on and on.

The Church, with the exception of a sprinkling of pastorals, was tactically absent. This reticence was somewhat understandable in respect of the public realm: the leveraging of antipathy towards Catholicism was a core element of the pro-abortion strategy. What was unforgivable was that this silence extended to pulpits, with some priests actually demanding of their congregations that there be no word of criticism of women who have abortions and no talk of abortion as murder. The Association of Catholic Priests, a kind of theo-ideological trade union bearing no outward indications of a connection with Christianity, intervened to criticise a minor trend of anti-amendment people delivering homilies during Masses. As it happened, this intervention occurred just a few days after I had attracted some hostile (and dishonest) publicity for some talks I gave at Masses in Limerick.

For years, when I travelled in quasi-religious circles abroad, people have teased me about the Island of Saints and Scholars, asking when we are going to send them some more monks. Usually they're only half joking, the scale of Ireland's disintegration being by no means fully understood beyond her shores. On such occasions, it falls to me to disabuse them of any remaining romantic ideas about my country. The outcome of the May 2018 referendum should at least have the benefit of henceforth saving me that trouble.

In his book, *How the Irish Saved Civilization* (Nan A. Talese/Doubleday, 1995), Thomas Cahill tells of Ireland's role from the Fall of Rome to the rise of Medieval Europe.

> Ireland, a little island at the edge of Europe that has known neither Renaissance nor Enlightenment – in some ways a Third World country with, as John Betjeman claimed, a Stone Age culture – had one moment of unblemished glory. For, as the Roman Empire fell, as all through Europe matted, unwashed barbarians descended on the Roman cities, looting artifacts and burning books, the Irish, who were just learning to read and write, took up the great labour of copying all of western literature – everything they could lay their hands on. These scribes then served as conduits through which the Greco-Roman and Judeo-Christian cultures were transmitted to the tribes of Europe, newly settled amid the rubble and ruined vineyards of the civilisation they had overwhelmed. Without this Service of the Scribes, everything that happened subsequently would have been unthinkable. Without the Mission of the Irish Monks, who single-handedly re-founded European civilisation throughout the continent in the bays and alleys of their exile, the world that came after them would have been an entirely different one – a world without books. And our own world would never have come to be.

This is the Ireland of popular imagining in the world beyond her shores. We now know it to be a legend long past its use-by date. The Irish of today are more likely to be among the looters and book-burners, two-thirds barbarians who value nothing but what is expedient, utilitarian and 'cool'. Indeed, on 25 May, Ireland might be said to have put a match to one of its own most sacred modern texts, Bunreacht na hÉireann, of which the fateful Article 40.3.3 was ordered by a majority of voters to be replaced by a fundamental right to kill any unborn child whose mother demanded it. In the throes of a grotesque misunderstanding of freedom, we had progressed to become the eye of the twister of dehumanisation razing the remnants of western civilisation to the ground.

I don't recognise my country any more. I know what's happened – approximately – we've been taken over from without by ideological forces bearing some unmistakable resemblances to those responsible for the deaths of millions across the world in the last century, an outwardly soft and even comical strain of the same breed, but equally ugly in many respects. It's the speed that's troubling. Six years ago, when my mother lay dying in the front room in Main Street, Castlerea, you could say that Ireland was in some kind of continuum that had persisted for centuries. Changing, yes, and not always in good ways, but still vaguely responsive to the wishes of its own people. Within months of her death, this seemed to have changed out of all measurement or recognition. An accelerant of some kind entered in. It was as though an insurgency of indeterminate nature took place under cover of darkness. Mobs invaded the playing area and everyone of decency and principle fled the pitch. It was like some moment that had been prepared from a long time was unleashed at a hidden signal. Mammy died in mid-September 2012; two months later, we had the so-called Children Referendum, in which were snatched the most fundamental rights and protections of Irish families to possess and care for their own children – under the guise of giving rights to those children. In 2015, a smash-and-grab was mounted, superficially on marriage but deeper down on the very definitions of parenthood and family, under the absurd travesty of equating two men and someone else's children with a man, a woman and their self-conceived children. Now we have had the most fundamental attack so far, and in many ways the most basic and essential breaching possible: the voting down of the primary protections belonging to the most innocent and defenceless. And all this has happened in a climate of totalitarian consensus and restrictions, where you could barely open your mouth without being pursued by mobs and menaces.

We live through strange and disturbing times, and things will for certain grow worse rather than better in the time I have left to me. For reasons that are not entirely clear to me, it has fallen to me to be a resistance activist opposing the forces now seeking to ransack our country. Not for the first time, I'm unsure I have anything further to say to the public life of Ireland, but I decided to withdraw once or twice before and found myself conscripted once again by whatever instinct it is that drives me – certainly not self-interest, or even the survival instinct, but some weird impulsion to draw the fire of the darkest forces in any room or space in my direction. By pursuing a series of issues, I seemed to slip into it without really intending to: first the father thing, then the child thing, then the parenting thing, then the family thing, then the marriage thing, then the constitutional thing, then the life thing, and next – perhaps – the death thing.

The cancers afflicting Ireland are of a far more grave and exigent nature than the type that stuck me down in the winter of 2017/8, but I have a fairly educated suspicion that there is a connection between them which may become more obvious when I've outlined the full facts of my life over the past five years.

My own eruption first manifested in the late summer of 2017: I noticed a pain in my lower back when I went on extended walks, but put it down to overdoing it, wearing unsuitable shoes or not walking properly. It felt a little like what as children we knew as a 'stitch in the side'. I had found a new GP after years of medical homelessness, who was pursuing me for the usual things – cholesterol and prostate mainly. He conducted a PSA test and it came back high, so he started on at me to do a physical, not exactly a fun experience. I baulked at first but a further blood test was higher, so I agreed to the physical, which came out all-clear. Still he

< 28 >

wasn't happy, so he sent me to Vincent's for an MRI scan. That too was clear, but a few weeks later they called me and said they'd glimpsed something on my left kidney. There followed further scans and a biopsy, ending in a definitive diagnosis in early December, by which time the pain had become more or less constant. It emerged that I had a golfball-sized carcinoma, which required a laparoscopic nephrectomy, basically a lopping off of part of my kidney, though another few months and I might have lost the whole thing. A year or two later would have been too late.

I had the operation in early February. I had lulled myself into a false sense of complacency, mainly because it was keyhole surgery and the surgeon was happy they had gotten to me early and it didn't seem to have spread. The operation was successful, but it levelled me like I had been run over by a cattle train. Because I had convinced myself it was nothing much, I was up again three weeks later and back on the referendum trail in Blanchardstown. Not a great idea. I think it took me about three months to realise that I might as well have been in an actual train wreck. Even now, I think, I'm only about half right. The official prognosis is good, but I still feel pains and twinges that don't seem to be auspicious at this stage, six months after the operation. Apparently there's an unexplained syndrome whereby the condition sometimes returns to the other kidney. I have a six-month check coming up, so that should clear the air one way or another.

The cancers infecting my country are, as I say, of a far more intractable nature: attacking our very capacity to have conversations about the very things that most matter to our possibility of a future, which means that we no longer have functional conversations about anything but trivialities, which means that the bullies always have their way, which means in turn that our country is no longer our country in any meaningful sense.

Strange the way it happens: you grow up in a place you call your country, assuming the relationship is fixed for all time, then one day you are told in no uncertain terms that your understanding of things has been way off the mark.

Actually, I lied: people do cross the road. It happens when you cross the wrong people. As a result of some of the events I am about to describe, pretty much all those I used to think I knew have turned their backs and walked away from us, including a solid block of those who came to our wedding less than four years ago. Even if I had any remaining illusions, things are converging to leave me in no doubt as to what it means to be a pariah. I have adopted a position whereby I do not impose myself on people in any way, because I have glimpsed the anxiety of certain individuals who fear they may be tarred with the brush used to blacken me. I know how ruthless my enemies are, and have no wish to drag others into the same hole as Rita and I have been shoved into. I know how real it is, and how determined these people are. Consider that, even after victory last 25 May, they were still out demanding the heads of anyone who had questioned their deadly agenda and taking down No posters along with the Yes ones, so that they could put them up again later to draw down fines on the heads of their erstwhile opponents.

So it goes in the new Ireland. The new facts of life.

Still, life, in a sense, I suppose, though not as we had imagined it.

01

The Itch of the Amputated Leg

Since you went away, the country has gone stark, staring, raving bonkers. (I know this sounds like rhetoric – 'The country's gone pure mad!' – but I would like you to read it as in the nature of a clinical diagnosis.) You got away just about in time to avoid going mad in a different way, out of pure rage and frustration at everything.

The seeds of it were there in your time – and I now realise that you were somehow able to detect them, and did. To be honest, I wasn't in the least convinced or concerned by your prognostications of degeneracy and decline when you came in from Ned Rock's giving out stink about that guttersnipe Gay Byrne. I thought of the things you tried to draw attention to as symptoms of a gradual catching up – with what I'm not quite sure; modernity perhaps, or the rest of the world, or the way we might have been if we'd been let alone in the first place. The idea that we were in hot pursuit of some such objective was the prevailing rhetoric of the final three decades of your life, but, at the time, for the most part, I considered myself on the opposite side of the argument, and so tended to dismiss what you said. I was young, after all, so it seemed to make a kind of sense to be in favour of disrupting the old and the fixed.

Now it's probably too late to arrest the drift. The old fixtures have been rooted out, the institutions that provided the bulwarks of the nation and its flimsy civilisation all but demolished. Ireland has ceased to exist in any meaningful sense, has become an indentured strumpet state, sucking the bloated dick of the transnational industrial sector for a meagre and inglorious survival. A century after our founding revolution, we are incapable of anything but a sick mockery of the great thoughts and heroic deeds of the past. We are bankrupt in means, in deeds and in words. We have lost our sovereignty, claiming merely to have lost it in a narrow technical sense and certain that we quickly reclaimed it. But no. We do what we're told and keep out mouths shut other than for spewing forth cant and cliché. Our public conversation is utterly corrupted by cynicism and ideology, our media sector manned by yellowpack halfwits who have been carefully indoctrinated and programmed by the handful of journalism tutors in the various third-level colleges, almost all of whom are followers of either Karl Marx or Leon Trotsky. There's no longer any possibility of reason in the public realm, which belongs not to the people but to our paymasters. We're on the slippery slope to God knows where – except that, in case I forget, there's no God, unless you know different.

Where did it all go wrong? It's impossible to say without starting from some sort of beginning and working carefully through things in a language that tiptoes between the landmines. I'm not sure I know where to begin or how to condense two decades of idiocy and inanity into an account that would make sense to someone who wasn't around for any of it. I'm assuming here that, wherever you are – if you're anywhere at all – you don't have TV or the Internet. But it's not just a matter of raw information. The real problem is that the collective head of the society has been screwed around with to such an extent that nothing makes the same kind of sense now as it did back then, and things have arrived at a state of affairs that would be unthinkable to you or your generation. It therefore requires for its description a new language of the past, the present and the future. The difficulty is not so much with you in reading what I might write, but with me in the act of writing it: finding words that I might still be able to invest with meaning and conviction. I no longer care much about Ireland – I mean the political entity that is Ireland – in any sense related to its present public reality, and am therefore, to begin with, talking of a phenomenon that you could never hope to recognise. The terms that might assist us in describing things have all been undermined and rendered risible or ironic. We are in cultural free fall. Everything has been turned to dung.

I'm supposed to belong to the so-called 'blank generation' that grew up in Ireland between the 1960s and the late 1980s. As we grew, we were constantly being reminded that we were a new breed of Irish people: urbanised and internationalised. Did we not realise, the politicians would inquire, that half the population was under 25? This seemed to mean something, to be more than a mere statement. The notion of youth was hitched to ideas of progress and modernity. We were supposed to have broken away from allegedly rigid notions of Irish identity, such as Catholicism and nationalism. These clichés about my generation were repeated so frequently that I often wonder how people found the energy to state them again and again in tones that suggested they had just thought them up and were astonished by their own insights and radicalism.

In truth, we were a culturally schizophrenic generation, existing in two realities: Ireland and its allegedly insular history, and the Anglophone world, itself rapidly moving towards a state of post-authenticity. We held to both views lightly, yet hold to them we did. In repose, we were both sentimentalists and repudiators: we felt an enormous pride in our country and its history, and yet found ourselves almost viscerally nauseated by the humbug that surrounded it – especially the pretence of separateness from the broader world culture in which we were steeped and by which we were seduced. The most immediately striking thing about us was that we took it for granted that we weren't going anywhere, that we would become the first generation for more than a century not to take the boat to Holyhead or the plane to JFK. In a sense, instead of us leaving to enter the wider world, that wider world came to us, to saturate us with its promises and perspectives. Thus, we became, in a sense, both emigrants working from home and foreigners in our own land. We entered the wider world without leaving where we were.. Unlike the generations that preceded us, we had no occasion to sentimentalise the place we'd come from, but, if anything, tended in the opposite direction, valorising everything that came in from outside precisely because it did. These were among the tendencies that began to trouble me as I grew into adulthood.

Like the countless generations before us, we had that Irish capacity to interpret things in terms of both/and rather than either/or, which allows for the evasion of binary, black-or-white choices. Unfortunately, however, because the thinking up and formulation of ideas concerning the forward movement of Ireland took place of necessity in English – into which the Anglo-Saxon binary view of reality was inextricably folded – the either/or mentality came to dominate, culturally speaking, over the both/and. In public, therefore, most of the cultural and intellectual voices of our generation felt themselves forced to choose one side or the other, and inevitably most took the side of what was called, and appeared to be, progressiveness, an outward-looking globalism that, without the leavening of a comprehending affection for Ireland's journey, tended to lead to excesses of copyism, self-denigration and self-congratulation. And yet, the capacity for grasping such paradoxes, which were embedded deep into Irish history and culture, was fatally mislaid. The ability to speak out of both sides of the mouth became no longer a necessary skill but a symptom of backwardness and native cunning. Even when indigenous elements were taken seriously, the objective was almost invariably to detect the reactionary or substandard factor in the specimen under examination. Thus, the preferred dynamo of Irish progress was deemed to require the jettisoning of as much as possible of existing baggage. Only by a process of unbecoming itself could Ireland move forward.

There's no doubt that what's been happening to Ireland (perhaps more accurately 'what's happened') has a lot to do with the Dublin-based media, in which I worked for 30 years, and in particular with TV, which set the beat, mode and pace for what is called 'progress' over the past few decades. You had that more or less right, and thank you for not allowing us to have a TV in the house until I bought one in 1979.

You might say that the state of Ireland now could be observed retrospectively as a kind of prophecy observable in the TV of perhaps five or 10 years ago. We thought that was 'just TV', or 'telly', as it's now called – a word that in its self-conscious contempt for what is apparently being valorised manages to catch the general drift of things; in reality it was the death rictus of the Irish nation masquerading as a mirthful grin.

I used to think that when you gave out about TV and radio you were merely being cantankerous, in keeping with your age. In your time, TV was inhabited by reasonably sober chaps like Frank Hall, Ted Nealon and Patrick Gallagher, who talked earnestly about the state of the nation and the contents of books that almost nobody would read but a lot of people possibly gained from hearing about. I really couldn't get what you were going on about when you warned darkly of the disintegration that would follow from this kind of thing. You used to drive me as mad as I probably drove you.

If anything, you understated it when you said that those boys above in Donnybrook were out to make a skit of everything. That was only an interim objective, in which they succeeded to an impressive degree. The mistake was in seeing this as being in the nature of entertainment. It was, in its way, entertaining, but we are about to pay a high price for the few laughs we had. You saw something I didn't, some secret quintessence that was not necessarily detectable in the contributions of Frank or Ted or Patrick, but which somehow permeated the entire medium at a deeper, sleeping level. Now that Frank and Ted and Patrick have given way to Ray and Ryan and Miriam, the picture that was clear to you has become clear to me too.

I still believe that TV, left to itself, could have taken a different path. I don't entirely agree with those who hold that it is, of its very nature, a degenerative medium that inevitably drifts towards the gutter. An unexpected variable that entered the equation was the cross-pollination between the Irish media and the British tabloids, devoted as they were to the relentless pursuit of anti-values. In my childhood, UK redtops like *The News of the World* and *The Daily Mirror* seemed to offer an entertaining sideshow to the staid and largely proper Irish media. In fact, up to the mid-1970s or so, *The Mirror*, which featured righteous and gifted writers like John Pilger, Keith Waterhouse and Paul Foot, was a pretty good newspaper. The rot set in with Murdoch and his unspeakable *Sun*, which dragged *The Mirror* after it in a schmozzle to the bottom. From the late 1980s, the Irish press became utterly contaminated with the selfsame mindset, and, at the same moment most of the British redtops started to eye up the prospects of publishing dedicated Irish editions of their scrofulous rags.

We in Ireland have always suffered from the fact that critiques of what is called progress have invariably been couched in moral terms, and have tended to come either from outside or from individuals on the inside who are on the historical back foot, resulting in most people being prepared recklessly to embrace even the possibility of destruction rather than side with characters who give them pains where they never had windows. The true danger is not so much, for example, that television by its nature lends itself to attacks on values, traditions, beliefs and convictions, or even that it is incapable of depicting reality without trivialising it, but that it is possessed of an unacknowledged and quasi-magical power to reduce reality to a mirror image of itself. What you see on TV is, by definition, the future.

Take, for example, the way that people nowadays appear to feel the need to be humorous all the time. I don't mean the wry, gentle humour that occasionally punctuated the conversations you would have with your friends when you brought me around with you and sat me on butter boxes or bags of meal to listen and learn, but a kind of frenetic and constant competition of what I will but loosely call semi-wits, in which each vies with the others to get the loudest laugh by delivering the most cynical encapsulation of whatever is being made a skit of. This competitiveness has leached into the mainstream of culture and is virtually ubiquitous now, certainly in the cities – though you can still catch a little of the old tenor in unexpected moments, usually down the country, perhaps in a filling station or a café, when someone greets you as though beginning a song, and holds the pitch until he has gone out the door, leaving you grinning innocently at the pure music of his personality. This is largely gone from

< 36 >

the public realm, banished by what is called political correctness, pseu-do-sophistication and the self-referentialism of what is laughably called 'popular culture', as well as by the mimicry of imported witticisms and the escalating contempt for what is native.

A couple of years ago, I finally found time to do something I'd been promising for years: record a spoken version of *Jiving at the Crossroads*, the book I wrote a year after your death in 1989. The recording was for the National Council of the Blind in Ireland (NCBI), who supply spoken-word versions of books, magazines and newspapers for people who have restricted vision or none. It was an eye-opening experience. I was, as they say, in a strange place, having withdrawn from journalism six months before, in the wake of the referendum on what is called same-sex marriage. I had stopped reading newspapers, listening to the radio or watching TV programmes other than the odd movie or documentary on BBC Four. I had, for the previous couple of years, been coming down with some kind of virus, of which the primary symptom is a total disgust for politics and politicians. I couldn't have attempted to revisit *Jiving at the Crossroads* at a more testing time, since it's a book that utterly venerates Ireland and Irish politics at some fundamental level.

The experience of re-reading the book, especially reading it aloud for the first time, confirmed for me something I had been living with as a suspicion for more than a year: that I was now utterly and terminally disillusioned, not merely with Irish politics but with the idea that politics might have anything positive or constructive to offer Irish society. Read-ing the various sections about Brian Lenihan, Mary Robinson, Charlie Haughey, Garret FitzGerald, Sean Doherty and the sanctimonious set from D4, I was overcome by an extraordinary torpor that on some days left me in doubt as to whether I would be able to deliver the necessary quality of reading at all. I got through it with some difficulty and after-wards felt that I had drawn a line behind myself, and exhausted the vein of Irish politics as a useful focus for exploring the human condition. In the context of politics as it exists today, the whole thing read like a series of amusing but surreal japes, completely removed from the reality that these politics had delivered us into. At the time I was writing about, I have no doubt, the rituals and games of politics occurred as a backdrop to a real context of power, but that day had long passed us by. Now, the rituals continue, but in the form of charades, concealing the truth that the locus of power has shifted away from politics and therefore even further away from the people.

Essentially, the book was about crossing the road – about looking in the mirror at the blueshirt mentality I had been born into, with both you and Mammy being indisputably of that persuasion. No offence. Among the things I wanted to capture was the way I had grown up taking this fanaticism for granted in myself, and then wandering over to gaze into the fanaticism of the other side. I sought to delve beneath the surface moralism and tribal slogans to excavate some truer sense of what might be going on underneath. It was, I think it fair to say, for its time an unusual book. Combining personal recollection with epic tales from the national political stage, it enabled colossi like Charles J. Haughey and Sean Doherty to become the ambiguous heroes of a story that was really about the relationship between you and me. Superficially, the book's point of view jars with the present mood of repudiation and finger-pointing, but that remains its most valid element: what happens on the surface tends to be misleading as to the swirl of the undertows, and therefore risks untruthfulness as well as injustice. In a way, too, the book contains, in a thin but essential sense, a foretelling of the present moment of unprecedented oligarchy.

Reading to a microphone is something I find tricky at the best of times. The main problem is self-consciousness – the fear of not being polished enough, which causes me to lose my essential self. This fear, married to my growing sense that I probably no longer believed in the possibilities that the book nodded towards, caused me to struggle alarmingly for the first few sessions, some mornings almost deciding that I couldn't go through with the recordings at all. The engineer on the NCBI sessions, which were recorded at their studios in Finglas, was a guy called Karl Browne, who seemed to intuit most of my potential difficulties from the start. He was a generation or so younger than me, but we found a lot of common ground in relation to books and rock 'n' roll. I couldn't help noticing that we spent a lot more time talking than we did recording, which seemed strange at first until I began to realise that this was a deliberate strategy on Karl's part to make me feel more at home in the situation and distract me from both my nervousness and the reservations I might be having about a book that was at that stage nearly 25 years old.

In diagnosing my difficulties, I'm generously prepared to discount the element concerning what I will call my sentences. This seems to me to be an inevitable complication with revisiting things you have written a long time ago. As you grow older, the rhythm of your sentences changes, largely because you grow to understand that words on their own are not the true stuff of communication, that whatever truth you're capable of conveying is largely contained in the rhythms and spaces, which carry most of the irony and humility and lightness that causes a reader to continue believing in you. Mostly, in this regard, the book is okay, but sometimes there's a raggedness that arises from my relative youth when writing it and the appalling fact that it was written in 10 days.

My main difficulty with reading the book aloud onto whatever is the contemporary equivalent of a tape was what, in the light of recent events, I now thought of as its naivety. Reading it again, I was suspended at the point of collision between two opposing ideas: one was the sense I had that the book did manage somehow to achieve a snapshot of its time, the other that this snapshot demonstrated more than anything how inaccessible now was the mood, mentality and texture of those years. Even though, at the time it appeared, I was seen as big on nostalgia, I realised in 2015 that, at the time of writing, I had actually bought into the underlying lie about progress represented by Mary Robinson as a 'character' in the book. Far from defending the 'old ways', what I was trying to do was appease those recalcitrant souls behind the line of modernity to the extent that they would not seek to obstruct our advance towards the Promised Land. The book diagnosed the condescension and incomprehension of the new culture towards the old, but did not take a definitive stance against what was happening, and actually, deeper down, carried that condescension in mutated form. It offered an apologia for the 'left behind' but in doing so sought to reassure them so they wouldn't object to being dragged faster into the future. It left things unsaid or understated about the 'new Ireland' when it ought to have been screaming to high heaven about the stupidity of following a notion of progress that had neither coherence nor a sense of destination. I intuit now that the unravelling I detect in Ireland 2018 might trace its origins to that moment when we crossed that line into what we imagined to be some definitive zone of newness – all fantasy, of course. The period since can be divided into three parts: pre-Tiger, Tiger and post-Tiger, and existentially and historically they are all of a disastrous piece. What should have been a three-part lesson in the meaning of reality became a trilogy of delusions: expectation of affluence, pseudo satisfaction and after-party comedown, an emotional hangover such as nothing in our history appears to have prepared us for.

Still, I think it's a brave book, in its way, in that it says things that were not supposed to be said at the moment I wrote it. It also occasionally veers alarmingly close to sentimentalism. At a quarter century's remove, I detect a few bum notes in it, though they're probably not the ones other people hear. I'm actually very happy with the sections about Doherty and Haughey, which together manage to create an authentic polaroid of the cultural snarl of that moment, catching the duplicities and doublethinks through the personalities of those two emblematic enigmas. It's the sections about you that I have the most difficulty with, because you seem a little implausible. It's not, I hope, that I didn't convey you more or less as you were – I believe I did, more or less – but that, even at this relatively minor remove, even I can see that people who never knew people like you will have some difficulty accepting that you ever existed. The qualities I ascribe to you – indifference to fashion and materialism, auto-didactic brilliance and virtuosity and, above all, unlimited zeal for the good of the entity that was Ireland – will today seem so alien and improbable that I feel I ought to rewrite the book to emphasise and elaborate on some of the factors I tended to glide over. This is a measure of the radical changes that have occurred in Ireland as much as it is of my failure to anticipate their scope and reach. Above all, my sense of the book now is that it may ascribe to you a kind of anorak passion for politics as understood in contemporary terms, which would be grossly unfair. The politics you loved were intimately connected with the human heartbeat in a way that is unimaginable already and will become far more so in the not so distant future. If you were around these days, you would spend your days staring at the wall rather than picking up a newspaper.

Back then, when you were still sardonically hopeful about Ireland's future, we used to decry our smallness and insignificance as an island nation in the Atlantic, beaten down by years of radical interference and abuse. Since then, arising from a combination of increasing globalisation and our openness to it, and a windfall of fortune arising in part from the sheer uselessness and lack of self-belief of our political class, their inability to generate any form of indigenous self-propulsion, and their acceptance of this – things have flipped over. Now, by virtue of our unique position and circumstance, we are disposed to regard ourselves as significant, possibly the worst thing that has ever happened to us. A crucial part of the dynamic of what we call our 'modernisation' has been the influx of an ideological atmospherics from out foreign, which is drummed deep into the culture by means of propaganda disseminated via media and popular culture. This process, by working off the inherited and untreated inferiority complex arising from English colonialism, serves to generate a plastic self-confidence that has enabled a kind of cultural Big Bang, out of which things are emerging that would never have been dreamt of in a culture developing organically by its own impulses.

I seem to have gone from being young to being old, with no clear period in between. Up until my early 50s, I thought of myself as young, but almost overnight I began to notice that I was no longer in tune with the dominant ethos or outlook of Irish society. I may have been especially unlucky in this respect: when I was young, all the emphasis was on age and experience and youngsters were expected to button it and listen up; now, all of a sudden, the only things that matter are the demands and desires of the young and pseudo-young.

I also find that, as I grow older, the past acquires a sort of cubist pattern, whereby distant events seem closer than they should, and more recent happenings morph into a middle-distance confusion of incoherences. I've lost whatever thread I imagined myself to be holding on to, by which I could measure things in the public realm and anticipate what might happen next.

In a dynamic society there is always an unconscious awareness of an ideological backbeat, driving things forward. Sometimes – as in 1990 when I wrote *Jiving at the Crossroads* – this becomes overwhelming: a deep, shared, repeated riff of expectation and certainty. At other times it dies down to the faintest bass arpeggio, as though inviting a handclap to keep it going. But it remains, even when drowned out by background noise: an underlying idea of what might make things 'better'. It is this rhythm that politicians vie with one another for the right to tap out on the national drum kit. The problem now is that the former indigenous rhythm has been overwhelmed by a thudding bass line from abroad, rumbling through the floor as though it were perpetually a Friday night in a three-star hotel in Killarney and the sound mixer of the band two floors down is a little heavy on the woofers.

Back then, it was all very straightforward. We were emerging from the primordial mists of tribalism, traditionalism, clientelism and a dozen other isms that had been repudiated widely enough and sufficiently to create a clear sense of an agenda of progress. Having a woman president was an idea that spoke to these notions. The promise was of 'change', a golden age of Irish life, probably – if you strove to define it – heading in a leftward, liberal, more egalitarian and secular direction. Everything would be different, we promised ourselves, once we shook off the binds of our tribal and traditional past.

By any of the relevant criteria, it is clear that our paths have not in the interim followed the course we might have imagined at that time. We have since seen war followed by peace, subsistence followed by prosperity followed by bankruptcy, hubris followed by loss of sovereignty, a relatively balanced media sector followed by an ugly anarchy. We have also experienced some jarring changes in the driving rhythms of Irish society, not least the baneful effects of coalition governments in which the disproportionate muscle of smaller parties has enabled alien and uncanvassed ideas to be smuggled into the heart of our governing process.

After 1990, the liberal/secular agenda, which had provided the score for the 1980s, the decade out of which Mary Robinson emerged, came to be regarded as more or less unassailable, certainly at the level of the national conversation, to the point where, nowadays, on the face of things at least, everyone is not just 'liberal' but as simplistically and intolerantly so as to bear a striking resemblance to the conservative dinosaurs that seemed finally to be banished in 1990. We had no way of knowing that, at that moment, we were turning the implementation of the social-democratic agenda of equality and fairness over to ideologues with selective ideas about the meanings of words like 'equality', while we got on with enjoying the unscheduled party. While equality became an ideological football, a revolution in credit ensured a redistribution not of means but of debt, creating a time bomb that was soon ticking ominously under our noses.

When we glance backwards, boom, and the inevitable corollary, bust stand side by side as the totems of the quarter century since you left us, their shadows becoming deeper and merging into one. Both conditions have, in differing ways, rendered us more unthinking: prosperity because we didn't need to think any more; its aftermath because the dreaded loss of materialism left us incoherent with irrational rage.

Pádraig Pearse famously rejected the idea that progress and knowledge can be matters of linear growth, insisting that history and human

understanding travel in circles rather than straight lines.: 'Modern speculation,' he wrote in *The Murder Machine*, 'is often a mere groping where
ancient men saw clearly. All the problems with which we strive (I mean
all the really important problems) were long ago solved by our ancestors,
only their solutions have been forgotten.' Thus, things that seem new
are nearly always old, but forgotten, and the future is always a remixed
version of the past.

Harking back to that previous moment of supposedly acute self-awareness 29 years ago, it is possible to perceive the truth in this observation.
We have not progressed along a straight line, but have mostly wended
our way around in a circle. In some ways, things are demonstrably better,
though not in the ways we tend to emphasise; in other matters it is clear
we have slipped alarmingly backwards. But the one thing we are still
missing is the deeper self-awareness that might arise from stepping away
from the 'progress' viewfinder to look closely at other elements of the
fabric of our society: how we might know and describe ourselves now;
what words like 'progress' and 'equality' actually mean; where human
welfare might truly be located.

Our western outlook does not countenance the idea of a circular
pattern in the drift of human understanding. We see progress as linear,
as emerging from the primordial fog and stretching forward into the
dispersible mists of the undiscovered future. To suggest that there will
always be a price to be paid for progress, and that the further science
takes us the higher that price will become, is to join the reactionaries.
To suggest that a necessary balance between the human will and the
unknowable requires us to match each new human discovery or development with its own weight in humility is to surrender to obscurantism
and superstition.

Essentially, we're talking about a country in which the institutions
and offices of power have been hollowed out and had their authority
and influence siphoned off to be used by forces and individuals who
have never been elected to anything. These people operate behind the

scenes, networking surreptitiously among the real power brokers, gaining support from the true governors of Ireland and then conveying their non-negotiable demands to the puppets occupying the husks of offices that briefly offered testament to Irish independence. The charade of democracy continues in the manner of phantom post-amputation sensation. We vote for people who aspire to hold public positions, but know in their hearts that the power will always lie elsewhere, and are happy with that. We know all this also, but it is way too big a disaster for us to admit. The limb itches. We reach to scratch but there is nothing there. We scratch our heads instead.

02

The Hidden Ireland

This article was published in *The Irish Mail on Sunday* on 30 May 2010. It's just one of at least a hundred such articles I've written over the past two decades. As such it speaks for all the others, being perhaps the most comprehensive single account I've written of a form of corruption that had gone metastatic in Irish public culture by virtue of being ignored and covered-up.

A man had called from a 'blocked' number, leaving several messages on my voicemail, imploring me to call him back. Two gardaí had been trying to break into his flat, he said. He sounded deeply agitated, perhaps frightened, but the number he twice carefully enunciated was my own, the one he had just dialled. He said he had sent me an email with details. I checked my inbox and remembered: he had been in touch with me before and we had met once to talk, perhaps a year ago.

He is a separated man, with one son. Easter weekend last was supposed to be his one weekend per month to have his son with him. He had planned what they would do, but at the last minute his ex-wife told him she was taking the boy abroad. Since their son did not have a passport, he did not believe her, but he went to his local Garda station, showed them his access order and asked for their help.

They didn't want to know. He asked them if his wife had been in to have a passport form signed and they said she had not. The following week he discovered that a passport had indeed been issued to his son, without his permission or signature, and therefore illegally.

On discovering that a local Garda had assisted his wife in fraudulently obtaining this passport, he made a complaint to the Garda Commissioner. Now he is receiving threatening visits. The two guards who have recently called to his house claimed to have seen orders preventing him seeing his son. One of them spent 20 minutes with his foot in his front door, making threats of dire consequences unless he forgets about the whole thing.

This is a relatively straightforward example of something that happens every day: a child-related dispute that has escalated because one of the parties has discovered she can do what she likes. The solution is simple: for someone in authority to tell this mother that she has an obligation to behave properly, for her son's sake as much as his father's. Instead, the entire system colludes in her thirst for vengeance or vindication, the forces of the state marshalling themselves against this man because he has dared to insist on being treated as a human being.

When I eventually get to talk to him, there is almost nothing useful I can say. Because he has encountered what is clearly an example of gross abuse of power by local Gardaí, he believes that any newspaper, on hearing about this, will simply make it public and demand answers. Then, he is convinced, things will be set to rights. As gently as I can, I tell him that I cannot write about his case. It is not that I disbelieve him, but it is impossible to write in any meaningful way about what is happening to him, because there is no way of establishing or proving the facts he has outlined and, anyway, I cannot reveal any details that might hint at his identity or location. Moreover, what is happening to him is part of a far bigger picture of corruption and abuse. We talk for a while. By assuring him that I understand how he feels, I manage to calm him down. I tell him to keep in touch.

Such exchanges are part of my daily work. I'm not sure I can call it journalistic work, as almost nothing of it ever gets into print. I have become an involuntary therapist. For a few years during the Celtic Tiger period it seemed to ease off, but now it is back with a vengeance. Every day brings at least two or three new pleas for help, amounting to hundreds every year. Usually I offer to meet the men, even though there is almost nothing practical I can do. It seems to help them just to talk things through, to get their heads straight. Sometimes I am contacted by the sisters or mothers of men, or by their new partners, who tell me scary stories of how these men have been treated by the legal system at the behest of the mothers of their children. They cannot believe that such things can happen in what is supposed to be a free society governed by the rule of law. They cannot believe that the media in general have no interest in any of this.

When I first encountered these problems, 15 years ago, I took to reading up the law, and would advise men about how to fight their cases. Before long I realised the futility of this, since there is no 'law' per se in the implementation of 'family law'. The so-called authorities just make it up as they go along, so 'the law' is whatever the judge says. Sometimes even the judge has no idea what is happening, as court orders are frequently cobbled together by lawyers with the collusion of court clerks, completely contrary to what was agreed in court. This lawlessness has spread to other agencies as well, to An Garda Síochána and the HSE, to 'child experts' and social workers, and now to the media. There is nobody to shout 'Stop'.

Nowadays I rarely mention the law. Instead I try to get these men to think differently about their lives. They are dealing, I explain, with corruption beyond their wildest nightmares. The important thing is to stay sane, to do whatever they can to stay in touch with their children, above all to hold their own lives together. I tell them to keep in mind something I had to discover myself: When your child is 21 or 24, and you are sitting together in a room and the child asks why all this happened and what you did – will you be able to give an account of having done everything in your power to be the best father you could be, in spite of the evil of the family law system? This is all I can offer as a guiding principle. This, I say, is the best we can do, for this is fathering in a world in which justice is an empty word and fatherly love a function to be carried out, as often as not, under the hostile gaze of the state.

What seems to horrify and shock these men beyond anything is that those treating them as non-persons seem often to be 'ordinary people' like themselves, but who have become almost like machines, deaf to arguments or appeals. We talk about who these people are and I stress that they are indeed 'ordinary' people who probably love their own children and remain pillars of their communities. But in this context they have suspended all capacity for empathy, which is why they are prepared to rob and criminalise and dehumanise fellow citizens of a certain category, without scruple or remorse. Sometimes the men I speak to have been accused of the vilest of crimes, and on this account summarily refused 'access' to their children, even though there is not a scintilla of proof of the allegations. We sometimes find ourselves getting into lengthy philosophical discussions about the human condition, how evil works. We talk about the relationship between secrecy and corruption, how everything that is hidden eventually begins to rot.

I try to help these men to see that what is happening to them is not to do with anything they have done, but that there has been a fundamental breakdown in the checks and balances of our justice system. I tell them they must not take on any of the shame or guilt that the system has tried to unload in their direction. The important thing is to understand that their lives have been visited by extraordinary new conditions, to which they must adjust their thinking in order to survive. They need to let go of everything they have believed about justice, equality and democracy, or they will go mad. Only by doing this will they come through the next few years of their lives.

Sometimes, afterwards, I go home and get into bed and cover my head for hours. Sometimes the stories are so unbearably unjust that they cut to the very quick of my being. One man recently told me that his wife had left him and abducted their children to the US, to live with another man. She phoned to say she wasn't coming back and he would never see his children again. He sought to invoke the assistance of the Department of Justice, which is charged, under the Hague Convention, with responsibility for bringing children in these circumstances back to Ireland so that any disputes about their custody can be resolved here. The Department of Justice did nothing. After several months, having repeatedly pleaded to be allowed to see his children, he was told by his wife that he could visit them if he came to the US. When he arrived there he was served with a summons to appear in a US court. The outcome of those proceedings is that he has been ordered by this foreign court to hand over nearly half his salary to his kidnapper wife. If he refuses, he will be deemed a 'deadbeat dad' and rendered liable to arrest and imprisonment, to having his property seized. Just to see what they would say, he contacted the Department of Justice, which had previously refused to help him, to ask them what his position was. They told him that if the US court issued an order against him, the Irish state would be 'obliged' to enforce it.

Incredible? Yes, but it happens every day. There is a man in an Irish prison for nearly a year for contempt because he challenged the right of a court to break up his family. He has been denied his constitutional right to habeas corpus and is being left to rot in jail until he comes to what is called sense. The man has a valid legal argument, which is precisely why he is not being given a hearing, If I write any more about this case, I may end up in an adjoining cell.

It has been going on for a long time, at least three decades now. Last week, *The Irish Mail on Sunday* carried the story of an Irish couple who have recently discovered, five years after having a child together, that they are half-siblings. This is a salutary story of the festering evil that is the Irish family law system. More than 20 years ago, a father went to court seeking access to his young son and was refused. Even though it was acknowledged in court that he was the father, the birth certificate was not changed, so the boy continued to bear his stepfather's name. Thus, years later, this grown-up boy unwittingly developed a relationship with his half-sister, having no way of knowing of their blood relationship. Even when he met his real father, they had no means of recognising one another.

This couple approached me after reading some of my articles about family law on the Internet. They wanted to alert the public to this particular danger arising from a system now completely unaccountable to

< 50 >

democracy or law. I wrote their story in my *Irish Times* column. But, apart from *The Irish Mail on Sunday*, no Irish newspaper showed any interest. No radio programme asked for my help in contacting the couple, although a religious programme on television has been in touch and will do something in due course.

Back in the 1980s, Ireland was rattled by major stories like that of Joanne Hayes, fitted up by the Garda following the discovery of a child's body in Kerry, and Eileen Flynn, fired from her job as a teacher because she had a child with a married man. These stories are now remembered as the defining episodes of a time when various establishments in Irish society bore down on certain women in a way now regarded as deeply wrong. As well as being gripping human dramas, they also involved a range of deeper issues which the Irish media were anxious to prosecute because they exposed aspects of our society that a new generation of journalists recognised as needing to change.

The story of the half-sibling parents is the same kind of story, except that most of the Irish media simply refuse to look at it, despite the fact that it has made headlines from London to New Zealand in the past week. Why? Because it began not with the denial of the human rights of a woman, but of a man. Because it isn't ideologically convenient for those who decide what we should be shocked by and why.

The facts of this case, perhaps more starkly than anything I have written in 15 years, amount to a searing indictment of the Irish family law system. They lay bare how the lives of at least five people have been blighted by the actions of state representatives acting secretly and unaccountably. What entitles these agents of the state to feel confident that they can continue about their wrongdoing, impervious to public comment? Journalists tell us that it is the law – that the in camera rule prevents them from writing about or commenting upon these matters. But would this argument be proffered in relation to allegations of any other form of abuse? It is unthinkable.

If the Irish media, acting together, decided to confront the corrupting

< 51 >

secrecy of the family law system it could call that system to order in a matter of weeks. All it would take is a sustained campaign, such as was run in recent years in England by *The Times*, to have the *in camera* rule abolished and replaced with a provision that would allow the identities of court parties to be withheld while the rest of the facts were made public. This already happens in rape cases.

But it will not happen, because the Irish media are overcome by an antiquated sense of right and wrong, defined by feminist notions of equality and retribution. It will not happen because the pain of men is not an issue that the ideology of modern Irish society invites journalists to be interested in.

When, in the next few days, I sit down in some café and face yet another male victim of the myopia of 'modern' Ireland, I will find myself looking at him in two different ways. In one frame, I will see a man who might be one of my nephews or the son of one of my friends, a fun-loving, intelligent young man who cannot understand what is happening to him. But, across this image will drift another, in which this male figure will answer also to a description that rises up from deep in the sick culture we have created. By this description, the young man is the representative of an oppressive caste, a descendant of the patriarchal regimes that have allegedly oppressed and subjugated the female of the species since the beginning of time. This, rather than as somebody's son, is how our state and society regard this man.

My job is to persuade him to know himself in both ways: to retain his humanity while also understanding what is happening to him and why. And I want him to understand this not so that he will accept his situation and believe it the inevitable and just consequence of a re-balancing of society. No, I want him to accept this understanding so that he may be able to limp back into the warped culture we have created for our sons and find a way of coping with the denial of his humanity by a society that laughably considers itself among the most enlightened in the world.

03

Homophobe!

Smock Alley is a purpose-built theatre on Exchange Street in Dublin, at the furthest end of Temple Bar. It was built in 1662, but began to collapse a short time later due to its poor foundations. It was rebuilt in 1735 and subsequently served for a time as a whiskey store and, between 1811 and 1989, as the Church of Saints Michael and John, where Latin Masses were conducted right up until its deconsecration and closure.. The building reopened as a theatre in May 2012 under the name Smock Alley, with the main space built on the original foundations from 1662.

It was there, I believe, that the final chapter in my life as a journalist kicked off, on 12 December 2013. There was a public meeting that day, organised by the Broadcasting Authority of Ireland (BAI), a kind of public consultation to enable interested parties to join in a discussion about programme standards. I attended, mainly in my role as a member of the BAI board, and to a degree as a journalist with an interest in these matters.

After the introductory speeches, there was a presentation of an Ipsos/MRBI poll on changing public attitudes to broadcasting, which included material about shifts in public opinion of various social issues. The delivery of the poll data struck me as being rather like a weather forecast which predicted that the occluded front of conservatism currently passing over the country would soon clear the east coast, leaving behind long periods of liberal sunshine broken only by occasional intense bursts of fresh enlightenment. This presentation was followed by a discussion in which contributions were invited from the floor. After the first three of four interventions from the various tables scattered around the room, a pattern began to assert itself. Although I had been expecting a bit of special pleading from some of those present, I was a startled to observe that the key demand being articulated by lobbyists for various causes appeared to be for an uncontested run at whatever issues exercised them. Several contributors, including a gay marriage lobbyist and a climate change campaigner, intervened to complain about the fact that people who disagreed with their respective perspectives were being allowed to argue against them. A spin-doctor from Fine Gael, seeing his chance, chipped in to say that the Coughlan judgment (which relates to the achievement of balance in broadcasting content during referendum debates) was hampering the work of the government and should be reversed. Everyone, it seemed, wanted the game rigged his way.

The spokesman for the gay lobby was Ross Golden-Bannon, a board member of Marriage Equality, at the time campaigning for equal marriage rights for lesbian and gay people. He said that what he called 'extremists' ought to be debarred from panels debating gay marriage – it being obvious (from the opinion poll data just unveiled) that public opinion overwhelmingly favoured changing the law. He said that, when debate relating to LGBT issues occurs on radio and TV, 'people of very extreme views are rolled out to challenge' the LGBT position. 'The problem is that the vast majority of people are supportive of marriage equality. If there's a discussion about disability or women, we don't roll out really offensive people to oppose those views.'

In a brief contribution, I pointed out that, since the Irish Constitution at any particular moment represents the will of the Irish people, there is an imputation of responsibility on the part of journalists to go beyond providing uncontested platforms for those agitating for constitutional change. I suggested that it followed therefore that journalism is duty-bound to provide platforms to allow the constitutional status quo to be defended. I also referred to the opinion poll data we had seen earlier, and made some tongue-in-cheek remarks cautioning of the risks of telling a roomful of liberals that conservatism is on the wane. My point was intended ironically, since it had stuck me that the information had been transmitted and received as though to a roomful of liberal activists rather than a gathering convened for the purpose of discussing how to make journalism more objective. In the course of these comments, I referred to us all being 'liberals together', but went on, again referring back to the opinion poll data, to warn sardonically of the dark pall of conservatism that apparently descends when you hit 50.

There were two large TV screens right in front of me, which had rather inexplicably been installed to carry social media communications concerning the day's contributions. As I was speaking, Ross Golden-Bannon, who was seated about 10 feet away from me, tweeted: 'John Waters just described himself as a liberal, oh hang on, just confirmed he's a conservative. Phew.' I had never encountered Mr Golden-Bannon before, but had already gathered that, apart from having no manners, he had a poor grasp of irony.

I made a note to write something of what I had just observed, possibly in *The Irish Times*. I had already filed my *Irish Times* column for that week, however, and was taking some leave over Christmas. Thus it was that I came to write about the Smock Alley meeting four weeks afterwards, on Friday, 10 January 2014. In that column I related some of what had occurred at the BAI event and advanced an argument concerning the Coughlan judgment – more or less to the effect that it would be democratically unsound to pre-empt public debates concerning amendments to the Constitution on the basis that you can presume to understand public opinion from the numbers of Oireachtas members supporting a particular issue, or even from opinion polls. 'While any citizen has a right to propose changing the Constitution,' I argued, 'nobody is entitled to a free run in overturning the settled view of the people as expressed in Bunreacht na hÉireann as it stands. Anyone proposing such a change must make a case in a public debate. The mere fact that an issue excites interest among lobby groups or parliamentarians, or lends itself to fashionable sentiment expressed in opinion polls, should accord an argument no special advantage in the debate proper, which is by definition required to occur in as close as practicable to sterile conditions, with both sides accorded equal respect.'

I argued that the 2012 referendum on the 'Children's Rights Amendment' – which I had taken an active part in opposing – represented a persuasive argument for the equal allocation of broadcast time to both sides of a constitutional dispute. In that debate, I noted, there had been negligible Oireachtas representation for the opposing view, and no appreciable organised No lobby. I might have added that, in the early stages of that campaign, something like 90% of public opinion appeared to favour the government proposal. Yet, in the end, more than two in five voters came down against the amendment.

'There are indications', I warned, 'that we may be slipping into a way of thinking about referendums in which the interpretation of public opinion would in effect – and somewhat prejudicially – be farmed out to mechanisms other than formal democratic processes. ... In formally consulting the people, surely anything we already "know" about "public opinion" must be discounted?'

This intervention, I believe, may have contributed to my being targeted by drag queen Rory O'Neill on the RTÉ TV chat show, *The Saturday Night Show*, the following evening, 11 January. That was one of a tiny handful of times that I had referred to the gay marriage question in my *Irish Times* column, and I had done so here merely because the gay marriage issue had come up in a somewhat wider discussion about the conduct of public debate, and because the tenor of contributions made by gay activists in Smock Alley that day had presented an effective illustration of the attitude of some of the new cultural warriors to the notion of free and open debate. Unlike, for example, members of pro-family lobby group the Iona Institute, which would also be attacked by O'Neill that night, I had not been active in debating the gay marriage issue at all, having turned down innumerable invitations to speak on the issue on both radio and TV, and having disappointed dozens of L&H organisers seeking right-wing bigots – for the reason that my position did not accord with either of the extremes the Irish public was being led to believe comprised the totality of perspectives on the issue. My reasons for dissenting from the by now relentless clamouring for gay marriage derived from my core position in respect of children and parents: that the concept of blood-link should be paramount in all legal considerations relating to children, and that the rights governing this area needed to be reviewed and underpinned before we started to take steps into the unknowable.

Only three or four days earlier, I had declined an invitation from the late-night TV3 Punch and Judy show *Vincent Browne Tonight*, to talk about a statement issued by former president Mary McAleese about homosexuality, the Catholic Church and gay marriage. In doing so, I sought to make clear to the researcher who called me that I was declining to participate because it was obvious that the reason I was being invited was that, because I had been known to take positions on matters to do with Christianity and Catholicism, it was being presumed that I would have a straightforward position in opposition to gay marriage. I did, as it happens, and still do, believe that the purpose of marriage is, ipso facto, to provide for a contract between one man and one woman with a view to protecting any children they may have, but I was aware that the subject was not quite that straightforward. Although I might at various moments have welcomed an opportunity to make some general points from my own rather idiosyncratic perspective, I had long been familiar with the kind of black-and-white discussions the Irish media tend to engineer around such issues, which is why I stayed out of it.

In fact, although I had been a regular guest on Browne's show on RTÉ Radio One up until the mid-2000s, I had only once appeared on his TV programme – this being the debate prior to the Children's Rights referendum at Halloween 2012. One of my reasons for consistently declining to appear was Browne's doggedly aggressive dismissiveness of my long-time arguments concerning fathers and children: virtually every time I had encountered him in recent years he had taken the opportunity to sneer at what he regarded as my obsession with what he called 'fathers' rights'. The researcher who called me that day told me that Browne would be away on the night of this particular debate, and

< 57 >

that Sam Smyth, a journalist who at one time had been a friend of mine, would be filling in. I said that would make little difference to my decision, which really had much more to do with my reluctance to become embroiled in a theological discussion on which I did not hold the position generally imputed to me. I pointed out to the researcher that he had called me on the assumption that I would disagree with Mary McAleese's repudiation of Catholic teaching on homosexuality, and assured him that he was mistaken. Nor, I emphasised, had my views on gay marriage been prompted by Catholic teaching. I said that my position on the matter was complex, but that I did have issues concerning adoption, my argument flowing inexorably from my long-held position on the failure of Irish society to protect the rights of fathers and children. This, I said, was an argument that I had never been given an opportunity to ventilate on any programme presented by Vincent Browne, who had never displayed the slightest capacity for objectivity or fairness on that general topic.

It was the presenter of *The Saturday Night Show*, Brendan O'Connor, not Rory O'Neill, who introduced the word 'homophobic' that evening – and went on to invite O'Neill to name names.

I had never seen or heard of O'Neill. Half doing something else, I idly observed him, in drag, perform some kind of comedy sketch, before joining O'Connor on the sofa dressed as a man. The sketch was unbelievably nonsensical and I paid little attention to O'Neill until he started talking about me.

Up until O'Connor's ham-fisted intervention, O'Neill had used words like 'prejudice', and talked about people being 'mean and horrible'. These assertions were in no way defamatory, although as far as they related to me they were untrue. O'Neill also referred to 'people who make a living writing opinion pieces for newspapers', but at first his remarks were simply annoying in their laziness and prejudice.

It was when O'Connor asked' 'Who are they?' that O'Neill named me and my fellow *Irish Times* columnist Breda O'Brien, and also referred to the Iona Institute, of which Breda was a director. He said: 'Well the

< 58 >

obvious ones ... Breda O'Brien today, oh my God banging on about gay priests and all, like the John Waterses and all those people, the Iona Institute crowd. I mean I just, I just, feck off and get the hell out of my life.' (Here there was sustained applause from the audience.)

He went on: 'I mean, what astounds me is that there are people out there in the world who devote quite a large amount of their time and energy to try and stop people, you know, achieving happiness and that is what people like the Iona Institute are at.'

It's important to stress that, even up to this point, there was no defamation. It's not defamatory to name people who write newspaper columns, even for the purposes of accusing them of harbouring prejudices or writing mean or horrible things – even if you happen to be wrong about this. The defamation came in with the acquiescence of O'Neill in O'Connor's proffering of the word 'homophobic', and this was in only the slightest degree mitigated by the fact that O'Connor's motive appeared to be to defend me against the accusation he detected O'Neill to be making.

'I don't know. I don't know,' O'Connor interjected. 'I know one of the people that you mentioned there which is John Waters. I wouldn't have thought that John Waters is homophobic?' This was the moment things started to go wrong.

O'Neill made some contradictory interventions in the wake of the affair, variously insisting that there had been no defamation and subsequently blaming Brendan O'Connor. In an interview with the gay magazine GCN, he said: 'He [O'Connor] introduced the word 'homophobic'; he asked me a direct question, asking me to name people. He's a professional broadcaster. He knows the rules; he's had the regulations drummed into him over and over again, so it's absolutely reasonable for me, who is not a professional broadcaster, who hasn't had the regulations drummed into me, who doesn't know them, to answer the direct question I was asked. Brendan O'Connor has received quite a lot of stick for it online, and I don't think that's quite fair. He just fucked up. He fucked up on live television and I know that Brendan and the other people who work with him on that show had zero control over how RTÉ addressed it after that. I hold no personal animosity towards Brendan. He fucked up. We all fuck up.'

But, even though the word 'homophobic' had now entered the conversation, there was as yet no defamation, although the conditions had been established to cause every light in the studio to turn red of its own volition. It was still open to O'Neill to employ some device to separate the people he had named from what he wished to go on and say about the general context of homophobia in Ireland, as he saw it. He didn't do so, perhaps because he'd been lulled into a false sense of security by virtue of the fact that O'Connor had blithely introduced the word 'homophobic'. Perhaps O'Neill believed he was on safe ground, having been 'given permission' to continue. That was when he did the damage, elaborating on the now implicit assumption, deriving from O'Connor's introduction of the word, that they were indeed talking about homophobia.

O'Neill: 'Oh listen, the problem is with the word "homophobic", people imagine that if you say, "Oh he's a homophobe", that he's a horrible monster who goes around beating up gays, you know, that's not the way it is. Homophobia can be very subtle. I mean it's like the way, you know, racism is very subtle. I would say that every single person in the world is racist to some extent because that's how we order the world in our minds. We group people. You know it's just how our minds work so that's okay but you need to be aware of your tendency towards racism and work against it. And I don't mind, I don't care how you dress it up if you are arguing for whatever good reasons or you know whatever your impulses … '. At this point, the entire conversation had gone 'live' with the concept of homophobia, which now retrospectively invigorated every word that O'Neill had spoken from the beginning of his rant. This left RTÉ completely without a defence, particularly as O'Neill had cited almost no evidence, and had not indicated, other than a passing reference to that day's article by Breda O'Brien (which amounted to a criticism of homophobia), what he was basing his opinions on.

Here, Brendan O'Connor had a golden opportunity to head O'Neill off at the pass, but he seemed unaware of the danger. He could have said something like, 'Come on, you can't say that without evidence … ', or 'Yes, but what have they actually said that you could claim is homophobic, which is a very serious charge?' He might have asked: What did Breda O'Brien actually write in her column that day? What had John Waters actually said or written that was homophobic? Was O'Neill simply suggesting that to be opposed to or unpersuaded by the idea of gay marriage was itself homophobic? He asked nothing of the kind, did not demand a single item of evidence from O'Neill.

O'Connor then interjected, by way presumably of 'explaining' why people might hold the kind of views O'Neill was complaining of – but only in a manner that dug the hole a little deeper: 'Because it is what you believe, it's your faith or that, yeah?' Here, O'Connor was linking the concept of 'homophobia' – which he had himself introduced – to 'faith' and what people 'believe'. It's as though he had forgotten that people had already been named, that he and O'Neill were no longer speaking of some abstract phenomenon.

I had been a guest on *The Saturday Night Show* several times while Brendan O'Connor was its presenter. One of the things I remarked on was the assiduity of the research process. You got a call perhaps a fortnight in advance, inviting you on. In the week of the programme, you had several lengthy telephone conversations with a researcher, who went through pretty much every nuance of the topics likely to come up in the interview. These experiences led me at first to believe that the 'homophobia' accusations had been 'researched' and therefore orchestrated, with the connivance of O'Neill and some members of *The Saturday Night Show* team, though not necessarily Brendan O'Connor. I subsequently came to believe, having watched the interview and examined the transcript many times, and read the transcripts of some interviews O'Neill gave in the aftermath, that I was wrong in this initial impression. I then tended towards the view that the defamation just popped out, without anyone really expecting it.

The reason it was vital that I respond to this accusation was that I had been here before – both with regard to accusations of 'homophobia' and, before that, similar taunts that, because I was seeking a hearing for men suffering discrimination I was a 'misogynist'. 'Homophobia', of course, is a makey-up word. It has no clear objective meaning, other than the one that has accrued to it in culture. What distinguishes this kind of word from other modes of criticism is that it is a subjectively formulated charge that seeks to label you as something, and in a way that is unanswerable, rather than calling you out for anything you have said or done. It therefore amounts to an assault on your being.

In the weeks that followed, LGBT activists and their hordes of supporters among so-called journalists took up Rory O'Neill's self-justificatory line in asserting that homophobia is something that exists in the eye of the beholder: it is 'subtle'; it's 'on a spectrum'; everyone is 'homophobic' to some degree and if a gay person says something is homophobic that's justification enough for using the word. But this word, like any other, has an objective meaning, which, unless this is subject to qualification, must be taken as the intended meaning. 'Phobia' is defined by the *Oxford English Dictionary* as 'extreme or irrational fear or dislike of a specified thing'. The key words here, from a defamation point of view, are 'extreme' and 'irrational'. The same dictionary defines 'homophobia' as 'an intense aversion to homosexuality and homosexuals'. The word also has strong connotations of an imputed aversion towards homosexuals based on a fear of same-sex attraction, which the person exhibiting the prejudice may detect, and be seeking to suppress, within himself.

Intense aversion to people or phenomena is never 'subtle'; they do not exist on a spectrum. By virtue of being intense they exist only in an extreme condition. If everyone is homophobic, why use the word in a context in which only a handful of people are named?

Variations on the word 'homophobia' are used by gay activists as instruments of censorship, to daub opponents of their arguments or demands with a stain that cannot be eradicated by any form of reasoned response, a stain that scares others into silence. To call someone a 'homophobe' is not merely to demonise and therefore silence them, it is also to dismiss their arguments as rooted only in hatred or fear, and therefore to obviate the necessity of responding reasonably to what they say. Now, paying very close attention to what was happening on the screen, I recognised the attack as an attempt at silencing me, at taking me out of any coming discussion about the urgency or merits of gay marriage by reducing the potential for an understanding of my motivations to the idea that I was simply a hate-monger. This was not something I could simply allow to lie, nor was it something I could respond to as though what was happening was a 'debate'. To simply deny O'Neill's allegation and proffer evidence in my defence would have been to validate the attack as a 'debate'. Oh no, I might be protesting, I have stopped beating my wife!

What puzzled me a little about the interview was why there appeared to be no editorial intervention to redress the situation once it had begun to go off the rails. I recall one occasion I was on the show when Brendan O'Connor seemed to be rushing headlong through the pretty lengthy agenda, skirting over things. He also appeared somewhat distracted during the interview, intermittently losing eye contact with me as though waiting for someone and leaving me talking to his haircut. Afterwards I asked him what had happened, and he said: 'I had a voice in my ear telling me to move on!'

Where was the voice in Brendan's ear during the Rory O'Neill interview? Why did nobody up in the director's box notice that a defamation red light had started to flash from the moment Brendan O'Connor used the word 'homophobic'?

Actually, although much time was expended afterwards in debating the question of whether it is necessarily homophobic to oppose gay marriage, this was actually beside the point as far as O'Neill's defamation of me was concerned. I hadn't opposed gay marriage. I disagreed with it to an extent, and on certain grounds, with certain reservations and caveats, though not absolutely. But whether this actual accusation of itself

amounts to an indefensible defamation depends on both the facts proffered in substantiation and the honesty of the opinion. I believe that the
accusation that it is homophobic to oppose gay marriage is objectively
ridiculous, but that doesn't mean that the opinion cannot be honestly
held by another person. It can – and the honesty of that opinion can
become a comprehensive defence, once the reasons (the facts) on which
it is based have been set out for the audience to consider.

The issue in defamation in the context of opinion is not so much the
falsehood at issue, but the basis on which it is perpetrated. It is not necessary that a defamatory opinion be objectively reasonable – just that it
be honest, a position that a reasonable person might arrive at on the facts
as stated. There is actually a wide degree of latitude provided for in defamation legislation, as well as a high degree of tolerance of subjective eccentricity in arriving at a particular opinion. When someone perpetrates a
defamation, it is not essential that the facts they are relying on be objectively demonstrable as justifying the opinion, but they must be reasonably
accurate and, even more importantly, allow the bystander to decide whether the comment is fair or not. The comment doesn't have to be 'fair' in the
everyday sense of that word – it can, in fact, be quite unfair – but it must be
an honestly held opinion based on ascertainable facts, and it must be such
as a reasonable person might arrive at on the basis of those facts. There is
absolutely no question but that to call someone a homophobe is a deeply
defamatory accusation, one that can be defended only if the basis of the
'honest opinion' is offered to the listeners/viewers/readers for them to
make their own minds up. None of these criteria were met in the interview
with Rory O'Neill on *The Saturday Night Show*.

The defamation was complicated in that it was spread out over an
extended exchange between O'Neill and Brendan O'Connor, but there
is no doubt that what O'Neill said, without evidence or any form of substantiation, was highly defamatory of me and others, and it is clear also
that RTÉ's legal advice confirmed that this was the case. The net point
in respect of the attack on me is that, contrary to what Rory O'Neill

< 64 >

implied on *The Saturday Night Show*, I had not been regularly appearing on TV (or indeed radio) panels with the objective of preventing him achieving happiness.

His core statement was technically and factually untrue. But it was also deeply untrue in terms of the positions that I had taken in public and the motivation behind them. I have never in my life had anything proscriptive to say on any aspect of the personal or sexual life of anybody. I believe such matters are private and should remain so. What people do between the sheets with other consulting adults is none of my business. I have never expressed any negative opinion on homosexuality in any form whatever. I grew up not just listening to the music of Lou Reed and David Bowie, but avidly following their cultural crusades and writing about them enthusiastically on numerous occasions – at a time when the mainstream press in Ireland was befuddled by the spectacle of these freaks.

If, at any time before or after *The Saturday Night Show* of 11 January 2014, you had put my name together with the word 'gay' into the search bar of *The Irish Times* archive, or conducted an honest trawl of my Irish Mail on Sunday columns, you would likely soon have encountered, along with several pieces I wrote about the David Norris 'Greek pederasty' controversy of 2011, pieces that would have confused the lynching party. You might have found, for example, the piece I wrote in 2009 posthumously restoring the reputation of a gay man, Finbar Dennehy, who had been smeared by several newspapers following his murder in 2007. His family had been to the High Court, the Press Council and the NUJ, had pleaded with the various media organisations that had smeared Finbar to publish a correction and apology – to no effect. I had written a demolition of the 'story', beginning my description of what had happened to Finbar Dennehy in a manner that might have fitted seamlessly into an account of my own treatment post-Rory O'Neill: 'The standard "free speech and democracy" argument involves a convoluted reasoning about the dissemination of information in society, demanding there be a right to publish things that are wrong. But if, as a result, we end up promulgating untruth, what is the point? How will the people know whether anything is true? Does the routine valorisation of freedom-of-speech not then become merely the self-serving justification of an industry which has observed that, sometimes, the untrue is more marketable than the true?'

Or the searchers might have come upon a column of mine from March 2013 defending Cardinal Keith O'Brien of Scotland, who had been outed as gay by the British 'liberal' newspaper *The Observer* in relation to several consensual historical relationships with seminarians and younger priests. *The Observer* had asserted that the story was not about the exposure of one man's foibles, but about a Church official 'who publicly issues a moral blueprint for others' lives that he is not prepared to live out himself'. The report asserted: 'The cardinal consistently condemned homosexuality during his reign, vociferously opposing gay adoption and same-sex marriage'.

I argued that there is a difference between the right of gay people to practise their sexuality and the issue of gay marriage: '[a]lthough liberal media persistently insinuate that opposition to gay marriage is "homophobic", many gay men and women themselves oppose this development. A public demonstration against gay marriage in Paris recently included a significant cohort of gays. Some gay people have no interest in gay marriage, not wishing to be absorbed into what they regard as a bourgeois institution. Others fear that unforeseeable consequences of gay marriage and adoption may one day result in a backlash against gays. Some even agree with "traditionalists" that children should, where possible, be reared by their fathers and mothers.'

The trawlers might also have come across one of the pieces I wrote in support of J McD, the gay 'sperm donor' who spectacularly won his case in the Supreme Court in December 2009, vindicating his own standing as a father, but also winning the most emphatic endorsement of the rights of a single father in the history of the Irish state. J McD had become a friend of mine and I had accompanied him through most of his ordeal. He had been abandoned by the gay lobby in Ireland because he found

< 66 >

himself in conflict with two lesbians, for whom he had naively agreed to supply his sperm on the agreement that he would be enabled to have a relationship with his child. The Supreme Court overturned the High Court finding that the father had misled the lesbian couple as to the role he saw himself playing in any child's life. The court had been told that an agreement had been arrived at between the three parties to the arrangement that the two lesbians would become the de facto parents of the child, with J McD mainitaining a relationship with his son in the guise of a 'favourite uncle'.

This is how I ended that article:

> Mr Justice Murray's judgment ... offered an unprecedented reflection on the emotional life of the father: 'In particular it is difficult to see on what basis an agreement or consent of the putative father at that stage as to his future relationship with his yet to be born child could be considered valid and binding. In the High Court it was argued at one point that a father in the situation of McD could give his consent in a way that paralleled the consent which a mother or even a married couple could give with regard to adoption. Even if that were a true parallel, a consent of a mother to adoption prior to the conception or birth of a child could not, in my view, be considered a full or valid consent. The fact is that a person in the position of McD, when faced after birth with the reality of a child, a person, who is his son or daughter, even if biologically in the sense of the facts of this case, may, quite forseeably, experience strong natural feelings of parental empathy and identity which may overcome previous perceptions of the relationship between father and child arrived at in the more abstract situation before the child was even conceived.'

I concluded:

In terms of the usually father-hostile climate of Irish family courts, this is sensational stuff, equating as it does, the emotions of the father to the putative emotions of a mother on holding her own child. This, of course, places in doubt that any man can in future be held to a prior agreement concerning a sperm-donor agreement with third parties, and this is the aspect that has been emphasised in the commentary on the Supreme Court decision.

Far more significant is that it represents, for the first time, an acknowledgment by an Irish court that fathers are actually human. It made me cry. I think it may even have made God cry.

How interesting it is that not one of the 'journalists' or 'social justice warriors' searching my back history on the topic of homosexuality managed to throw up even one of these articles.

< 68 >

04

To See Your Face Again

I remember when you were 60. I was nine. We lived in the house that be-came 'over Beyond' – the house I was born into. That would have been the year you bought Devanny's with the sunrise door across the road, and, being off work after your accident, spent your days working there, fixing it up. You didn't tell until it was almost ready for habitation that it would be ours. We didn't know why you went there every day. After you told us, the idea of moving to a house with electricity and running water was like moving to another world.

I remember the morning we moved. You didn't announce it in advance but simply told us when we got up that we were moving house. I was the first to go, along with Mammy, the first to cross the road. I couldn't believe we were going to live here, in this modern house, with its tubular steel chairs and shiny red linoleum. It seemed like going to heaven: an electric kettle rather than the black kettle on the crook over the flames, light bulbs rather than candles and Sacred Heart lamps, and no more buckets of water to be carried from the pump.

The move was for the arrival of 'Aunt Nora', or 'Norah' – your aunt, not ours. You would grandly refer to her as 'your Great Aunt Nora', which at the time I took to be a matter of rank rather than relationship, like an archbishop of aunts. She was at least 90 then, but sprightly with it. It was to be her first visit since she left for New York, God and you knew how many years before. Her name had changed from Brennan to Feeney, which it remained, although her husband had long since died.

It was supposed to be a fortnight stopover before going on to Sligo, but she cut it short for reasons that were never explained to us young ones. I have to admit that I always believed it had to do with the absence of her customary creature comforts, notwithstanding the modernity that we believed to have suddenly descended on us. Maybe the en suite was not to her liking, the delft jug and basin provided for her ablutions. She was excited to be back in the old country, but there are, I suppose, limits to what a Yank can be expected to put up with.

I can tell you without fear of contradiction that the calling off of the Knock trip was one of the most crushing disappointments of all our childhoods. You were to take a day off work specially to drive us there, we who had never before been further away than Cloonyquin, to visit Granny, or Roscommon to go to the hospital. We endured her for the week in anticipation of this treat.

She was severe, I remember, not very child-friendly. Mammy would take us for walks with her during the day – all six of us trooping down Patrick Street and round the Demesne, putting up with it all in the knowledge that we would be off to Knock come Friday week. And then, with just a few days to go to this treat of treats, she pulled plant, announcing that she had decided to cut short the Grey Castle leg of her visit. Knock was to be knocked on the head. I don't think we've ever really gotten over it.

I never thought of you as old in the way Aunt Nora(h) was old. Neither did I ever know you as young. Having an aunt into your 60s must have made you feel a bit childlike. You were always the same to us, more or less: always just 'Daddy'. I don't think that, for most of my childhood, I even knew what age you were. I remember a few times making calculations in my head after someone dropped some clue or other, and shrinking from the enormity of the gap between us.

I'm not sure whether this is related to my sense of you at that moment, but turning 60 myself in 2015 was an astonishing and dismaying episode. I don't know how it is possible for someone whose whole existence has been so centred in his own childhood to come to terms with the fact that he must at last step across a line to a place where the facts are no longer ambiguous. Being 50 was a bit of a leap, but the problem evaporated in a short time because there was a kind of continuity. There's some truth in the idea that '50 is the new 40'. These days, nothing really changes at 50. But something is changing now. There's a crossing over a line of no return.

Still, inside I don't feel any different from when I was riding shotgun with you in the Thames 800, ALI 240, with its spongy suspensions (no shocks) and the moss growing around the windows. I had it all in front of me then, though I had no idea what 'it' might be. I don't know how I got so old. But I did. I really don't remember you before you hit 60, which would have been the year of Granny's death and Aunt Nora(h)'s visit. You arrived to me in fully fledged agelessness, a man from a different time. I never thought I would become you, inhabit a body afflicted by the phenomena of time and gravity, as I observed yours to have become. Hitherto, inhabiting a dimension of time that you in your turn must have occupied in the years before I really became aware of your presence, I, like many of my generation, found access to a kind of qualified Peter Pan existence, which is now suddenly arrested. Perhaps for reasons to do with the gap between us, I think of maturity as something I managed to escape until the present, but now find it unmistakably and ineluctably plummeting towards me.

Being 60 always seemed to me to be a critical moment when a man definitively becomes an unambiguous adult. There's no fudging it any more, no matter how you dress or try to walk or think. It's not the question of encroaching intimations of mortality – of impending obsolescence followed by obliteration – but something close to the opposite, and I suspect this particular fear comes to me from you: the fear of losing all concern for the world and becoming a child again – at a time when no one else recognises you as such.

The idea of 60, as much as its incarnations, has always scared me, though this part doesn't come from you. Sexagenarians seemed to me the cohort of humanity clinging most assiduously to earthly logic, and no one could ever accuse you of that. They always seemed to carry the weight of the world's importance on their backs, like they had always been here and were always going to be. They were the ones running things, the ones who told everyone what to do. For a long time I read this at face value, resenting them for their sense of proprietorship over reality, until I realised (very recently) that their purposeful truculence was a shield against the thought of obsolescence. There was also about them, I now begin to understand, a sense of urgency arising from their need to get things in order while there was still time. For this one decade, even the most frivolous person became relatively serious. Once they hit 70, the flippancy or irony returned, this time accompanied by a gentle hilarity at the silliness of earthly pursuits. But in that in-between decade, they seemed to immerse themselves more intensely in the logic of this world, as though to deny any former giddiness. Sixty-year-olds always seemed to be indefatigably serious about everything: about politics, pensions, interior decorating, gardening, the state of the nation, the beige they tended to wear as a kind of uniform of their earnestness. But this seriousness towards everything betrayed its true nature in the slightly frantic air that accompanied it. It's as if 60-year-olds – it strikes me now I may be speaking mainly or even solely about men – realised that this, if they were lucky, might be their final intact decade of healthy existence, and so must not be treated frivolously. So they went through it with this air of frantic gravity, in the end capitulating with great relief to the idea that they were still alive and everything from here on out would be in the way of a bonus. I'd sooner be 85, like Willie Nelson, though I am mindful that you were just three months short of 85 when you died.

You didn't go through that 60s phase, as far as I can tell. You were never either young or old but seemed to drift all the time between the two states of being. Just once in my life I saw you riding a bicycle. It was in Cloonyquin, and you were fixing the chain for someone, when suddenly you jumped up on it to test it out and we watched in astonishment. You were always frivolous and always serious – both at once, which I think is what irony really is.

Do you remember when I was a child the way you would bring me around with you on your mail runs, and we would afterwards end up for an hour or two in Dick Nally's saddle-making shop on the Square; or Bill Goggin's garage at the railway station; or Ned Rock's shoemaking work-shop, which dared you to refer to it as a cobbler's; or maybe in Paddy Lavin's, the watchmaker in Ballaghaderreen? (Paddy died not long ago, in the summer of 2016, in his 104th year.)

There would always be some pretext: a quote for a bridle for a man in Castleplunkett, a pair of shoes to be collected for the parish priest of Elphin, a pocket watch belonging to Mrs Carthy from Aughadristan to be dropped off or picked up. I would stand or sit for what seemed like aeons while you and they talked about everything. I don't remem-ber much of the actual discussions, but I do remember the demeanour of all parties: the way it was presumed that the agenda would have but one topic, that that this topic would be 'Ireland', or 'the country' as you called it, which covered just about anything. The way the conversation drifted seamlessly from the personal to the public, from the particular to the general; the sense of proprietorship you had in respect of this entity called 'the country', and the humorous, exasperated affection for it that seemed to be part of all of your personalities. At the time I didn't really give much thought to any of this at all – it was all just there. But now I come to think of it, I recognise that I was a privileged witness at the end of something that would never be seen again.

You had the air of a natural leader, even though you never tried to lead anyone anywhere. People deferred to you, as though instinctively. They waited for your summing up, as though for the closing address of a judge to a jury. What I remember most clearly was the scent of irony that permeated everything, notwithstanding the higher level of gravity. You talked with great seriousness about some recent outrage, some new bu-reaucratic idiocy, some gross incompetence at the civic or national level. All the time you seemed to be experiencing a crescendo of amusement, as though all stories of politics ended in gaiety. The others were like this too, but with you in particular, irony was never far beneath the surface, so that I was hardly ever able to tell whose side you were on. I knew you were on the side of right, of 'decent' people, of what might be called 'the good', but I gathered fairly early on that these were complicated concepts. You could be scarily literal, up to a point, and then dissipate it all with a word or a sudden lapse into laughter, in that way you had of pulling the handkerchief from your breast pocket to wipe the tears of merriment from your eyes.

I still meet people who remember you with a clarity I find unnerving. They remember you carrying them to school, or back home from town. Some remember particular vans or minibuses, others a horse and trap. I met a man once who remembered you doing the runs on a bicycle during the blizzard of 1947. I met another man one day at the ticket machine in the Dunnes Stores car park in Sligo. It was spilling rain and a vicious wind whipped across from Tesco, but this man stood beside me as I put my money in and waited for the ticket and then said, 'Your father used to bring me in to school from Tulsk'. I was impatient and getting wet, so I quickly shook hands with him and asked him his name, and then made to withdraw. As I did, his voice rose to continue the conversation over the roofs of cars and the increasing distance between us. 'They were great times, John. He was some man!' They were, I agreed, he was, with the rain battering me and the wind threatening to lift me into orbit. 'It's a different country now, John'. It is. 'Happy New Year to you, John, and to all belonging to you'. And the same to you, I said, waving and returning to my car with a growing sense of having short-changed this man to whom you meant so much.

Some people who weren't there think it's just me who remembers you, but I hardly knew you half as well as some of these people I still meet. They remember you exactly, not as a 'character' or a functionary but as a clear person. They remember details that I had partly forgotten: the way you would pull your pocket watch out and examine it, whenever you were thinking about something; even the peculiarities of different vehicles, your kindnesses to them. In such moments I realise that immortality is not necessarily confined to a 'next' world, or even to great public deeds in this one, but happens in the private imaginations of people who are moved by what are often no more than moments in the presence of someone exceptional. I'm not sure, in this age when what is called celebrity has become so nauseatingly ubiquitous, that the idea of the immortality of an 'ordinary' person residing in the memories of a multiplicity of other 'ordinary' persons is any longer possible. Everything was always written on water; now it is barely written at all.

You were a square one, I tell you. I wrote *Jiving at the Crossroads* a year after your death because I wanted, I think, to mourn you and acknowledge publicly what you had seemed to represent. Until you died, I didn't think of you as representing much beyond being a father and a familiar figure in a small way. With you gone, I began to realise that you represented much more, that you were emblematic of a certain generation, the one that grew up breathing in the first fresh breaths of Irish freedom after 800 years of slavery. You breathed in the clarity of truth that emanated from the Easter Rising and also the passion that followed from it to grasp this moment and make something of it.

A friend of mine whose parents were approximately the same vintage as Mammy and yourself, proposed to me – after the death of his own mother soon after Mammy passed away in 2012 – that the generation to which you all belonged had formed a narrow band of idealism in 20th century Irish culture, because of having grown up in the background radiation of the collectivised patriotism unleashed by the Rising. Those who grew to adulthood between independence and approximately the late 1960s had imbibed the pure spirit of 1916, he believed, had taken it into themselves and breathed it out again. They took it for granted that the Rising had a profound spiritual dimension – as Pearse had insisted it would. In them – in you – the idea of Irish freedom expressed in the Proclamation had merged with their – your – sense of the sacred, causing you to anticipate its realisation in your own lifetime.

Maybe the four decades of a dirty war in the North put paid to all

< 75 >

possibility of innocence, and the growth of a complacent materialism in the Republic brought your neighbours and descendants to conditions of materialist certitude and self-satisfaction with little visible means of support in any reality you would recognise. Had you lived longer, you may well have watched in dismay as we threw away not just what you had cultivated but even the very words you had used to speak of such things. We absorbed that idealism from you but it did not vivify us because we had already begun to dance to a different drum.

Your life seemed to me to be directed at things other than your own immediate interests, but I have come to realise also that this characterisation risks a misunderstanding of how you saw yourself. You were possessed of ambition, zeal, passion and certitude, but these qualities were directed towards a collective endeavour rather than the realm of personal advancement. It's impossible for us now to conceive of people who thought of Ireland as a personal mission in pursuit of a collective destiny, a work in progress that belonged to them, a genuine republic even before it became one. In this connection, your roots in the west were a critical factor, as was your connectedness with the land, your particular relationship with Catholicism, which is to say Christianity, and your lifelong determination to educate yourself in every conceivable way.

You seemed to come from some place that was neither the town nor the country, although you were closer to the country. In your married life, you lived in the town, but you left it in the early morning and came back towards sundown. In between, you were with your own people again.

You were a strange one, I tell you. I remember thinking that you took pleasure in seeming odd, just so you could embarrass us and teach us something vital. But I say this knowing that you couldn't care less now, any more than you did then. To tell the truth, I was both confounded and attracted by your indifference to styles and conventions. The cap you wore was always a turn out of date, always worn and grubby. I don't think I ever saw you wearing a brand new cap, so now it strikes me to wonder how you acquired them, how you broke them in. Your everyday coat, too, was ragged, though you had a better one for Sundays, and sometimes you may even have worn it of a weekday also, to a meeting with the bishop maybe, which happened just once, or something else out of the ordinary.

Your everyday coat was not like the everyday coat worn by a farmer, which might be tied with a piece of rope. Yours was like an ordinary coat, only very old and very torn, the pockets bulging with the detritus of a life on the road in a vehicle that teetered always on the brink of collapse. The glasses, too, seemed to be part of your personality, unlike anyone else's glasses, apart from John Lennon, though that would be later. When I first started to take in the curious style of your glasses, Lennon still had the moptop.

Although I never thought of you as old, I feared you were going to die at any time from when I was 12, after Johnny Farrelly dropped dead of a heart attack that day after coming in from work. I heard his wife sobbing in the house, five doors away, as, in slow motion, I watched their son Gerry, my closest friend at the time (you called him 'Joad', I never asked you why) walking obliviously up the street with his friends having completed the last of his Primary Cert exams. After that I became obsessed with the idea that you would be next, although you would live for another 22 years.

Because you went to bed earlier than the rest of us, I would sometimes creep into the room just before my own bedtime to check on whether you were still breathing.

I wrote something about it once, for a volume called *The Whoseday Book*, which I dreamed up as a millennium fundraiser for the Irish Hospice Foundation. It was a collection of pieces by 366 artists, writers and public figures, each of whom had been given a postcard-shaped space on a page of a diary for the year 2000. Most of them had to take the day they were allocated, but as the originator of the project I got to choose my own day, so I picked 10 March, which is the day of your granddaughter's birthday.

I called it Raidio Róisín, the baby monitor I used to place near your cot while you slept. It reminded me of your grandfather, who died seven years before you arrived. I wished I had had one back then, to check on him in the night, to ascertain whether he was still breathing, rather than crouching at the bedroom door with my ear to the keyhole, listening for sounds of life. I wished I had had one on the morning he died, so I could have reached his side to say goodbye. Once, while living in our apartment in Colville Terrace, Londing Town, I discovered that there was another baby on the other channel, to whose breathing I had been listening for an hour by mistake. But the first sigh was a bum note that sent me scrambling for the tuner. For a moment I fretted that you might have been awake and calling me. But the moment passed, for in truth I did not need the monitor. Always I would wake two minutes before you stirred, and lie there waiting. There was a time in my life when this might have seemed a massive inconvenience. But, whenever it happened, I'd find myself longing for your cry, so I could see your face again.

< 78 >

05

Greek Chorus

For the record, I am not now, nor have I ever been, a member of the Iona Institute. I say this without the slightest hint of criticism of Iona or anyone connected to it. They are courageous, decent people who do a principled and important job of advocacy on behalf of traditional ideas of family and marriage. I merely note the fact that I am not a member of Iona, although innumerable attempts have been made by journalists and others to imply that I am, or at least to elide the issue and thereby sneakily give that impression to fit their prejudicial purpose.

The defamation of me on *The Saturday Night Show* was actually more serious than the defamation of any of the Iona members – for various reasons. One reason was that, due to the circumstances in which the interview unfolded, and in which Brendan O'Connor clumsily highlighted my name, the brunt of the comments as delivered afterwards appeared to relate specifically to me. These included an implication that not only was I a 'homophobe' but that I was an especially sneaky kind of homophobe who slyly covered his tracks.

There was a bit of a back story here concerning attempts to daub me with the mark of homophobia. These smears began three years earlier, during the early stages of the 2011 presidential election, when retired journalist Helen Lucy Burke went public with her concerns about an interview she had conducted with presidential candidate David Norris a decade before.

One afternoon in June 2011, Burke manifested on the RTÉ phone-in programme *Liveline* to draw attention to the content of the interview in *Magill* magazine in 2002, which she alleged made it clear that Norris was an unsuitable candidate for the presidency. Burke immediately found

< 79 >

herself targeted by LGBT activists and journalists seeking to prevent her airing her concerns about Norris's views on ephebophilia – i.e. sex between adolescent males and adult males. Observing her situation, I wrote about the issue in my *Irish Times* column, recalling the facts of my own involvement in the affair, as I had been a consultant editor of *Magill* at the time the interview was published. The nature of my involvement was in working with Helen Lucy Burke in seeking to persuade David Norris to withdraw from publication some of the comments in the interview.

One afternoon, in early January 2002, I had received a telephone call from Helen Lucy Burke, who at the time was an occasional contributor to *Magill*. I had never, to the best of my recollection, spoken to her before. She was best known as a restaurant critic, and had contributed a number of such pieces to *Magill*. I admired her writing style, although I had never been able to see the point of restaurant reviews. I knew her by reputation: honest and direct to a fault, and fearless when it came to doing her work.

The purpose of her call was to ask my advice. On the basis of a commission from the Editor, she had conducted an interview with Senator David Norris about his life and perspectives, and had been disturbed by some aspects of that interview. I gathered that she was a friend of Senator Norris, a gay man who had been instrumental in the de-criminalisation of homosexual acts under Irish law. At my request, she read me several extracts from the transcript of the interview. I remember being astonished by the content. She read out one quotation, which made references to 'classic paedophilia' in ancient Greece, with Norris asserting that there was 'something to be said' for the approach in which a young man was introduced to sexual behaviour by an older man. Norris said he would have relished such an entanglement when he was younger. In another quotation he proposed that there was a spectrum of child abuse, giving the example of a Christian Brother putting his hand into a boy's pocket, which Norris considered to be at the less serious end of that spectrum. In another extract read out to me by Helen Lucy Burke, Norris suggested that sexually abused children might suffer more from the investigation of their abuser than from the abuse. The thrust of Norris's argument seemed to be summed up in two phrases that featured in the *Magill* article, to the effect that there was 'a lot of nonsense' talked about paedophilia, which he further asserted was the subject of 'complete and utter public hysteria'. Taken in the round, Norris's comments amounted to at least a strong insinuation that Irish society was excessively hung up about paedophilia and that there were other, more laid-back, but perhaps more appropriate positions that might be adopted by societies of a modern disposition.

My first response was to ask Helen Lucy Burke if by any chance she might have misinterpreted Senator Norris's arguments, which suggested he had been engaging in inappropriate casuistry and hair-splitting on an explosive and sensitive subject. There was no sensible reason, in a climate where sexual abuse had already emerged as a deeply disturbing matter, why anyone would gratuitously attempt to initiate such a discussion. He would need to be crazy, I told her, to say these things in public. She was emphatic that she had not misunderstood him, and said that she had taped the interview. She said they'd had a heated argument about it and he had refused to back down. After transcribing the interview, she had called him to read him the extracts she found problematic, but he said, 'Yes, that's fine. That's what I believe'.

In the several years I had known David Norris we'd had some public jousts on various public issues, but I had always found him personable and engaging. He was somebody you could find yourself having real, impromptu conversations with that got you thinking about things – from the nature of eternity to the 'secret' of a great Eurovision song. I felt instantly that the interview had the potential to land him in very hot water, possibly even to bring an end to his political career. I had no wish for such an outcome and felt that he needed to be protected from his own foolhardiness.

I suggested to Helen Lucy Burke that she write up the article with the quotes included and call David Norris again, explaining to him the context in which his remarks would appear and offering him another opportunity to amend or retract them. I also told her that she should tell him she had spoken to me and that I had expressed in the strongest terms that, in his own interests, he should reconsider.

Some days later Helen Lucy Burke called me again and said that she had done as I requested and that David Norris, after proposing some minor amendments – which she had incorporated into the article – had pronounced himself happy for his views to go into print. She was still concerned that the substance of the problematic remarks remained un-diluted, but she said Norris was adamant that he wanted the interview to appear in its revised form. 'So be it', I said.

Although the interview was in my view sensational, in order to reduce the risk of Norris becoming the victim of journalistic opportunism, I advised the Editor that the interview should not be the cover story, as had been intended, but should be allowed to achieve whatever level of attention it achieved without promotion or pre-flagging. He agreed.

For several days after publication, no other media organisation report-ed any aspect of the interview. When the interview was finally picked up a week later by the tabloid, *Ireland on Sunday*, I heard David Norris on radio claiming that he had been misrepresented. I raised an eyebrow but decided he must have been talking about *Ireland on Sunday's* interpretation of his remarks. He contacted neither me nor the Editor of *Magill* to complain about our article, or about any aspect of how *Magill* or Helen Lucy Burke had handled the matter.

I had fully expected an unmerciful uproar to follow on Norris's com-ments. There was no doubt that, had these remarks been made by al-most any mainstream politician, there would have been an explosion of fury and condemnation. But here, not only was Senator Norris not con-demned for his at best flippant and trivialising attitude to child abuse, but for the most part reporters and media commentators looked the other way. And when the story finally emerged into the full light of day nearly a decade later, the same commentators who had ignored it directed their fire at those who sought to ask Norris what exactly he had been seeking to say. Helen Lucy Burke was accused of 'homophobia', of conducting a witch-hunt, of attempting to sabotage Norris's presidential bid. Norris claimed that he had been engaging in an 'academic' discussion, and had been quoted out of context. Nobody asked him to elaborate on the context in which he had intended his comments to be seen, or to say what was 'to be said' for ephebophilia, ancient Greece-style. At the time of her *Liveline* appearance, Helen Lucy Burke said that, although the tape of the interview was still in her possession, she was unable to locate it. Subsequently, she found the tape and extracts were played on *Liveline*. They completely exonerated Helen Lucy Burke's conduct and corroborated her version of events.

Not long after Burke's initial *Liveline* appearance, listening to the radio one evening, I heard a journalist declaiming that Burke's decision to draw attention to her own interview with Norris was evidence of a new 'conservative backlash' emerging from the mists to frustrate the possibility of Ireland having its first gay president. The speaker was a well-known commentator, who for many years had been fulminating about the abuse of children by clerics of the Catholic Church. *The Irish Times* published a disgraceful editorial in which it described the 'revival' of this controversy as an 'implied slur that gay people represent a threat to the young'. If there were any implications arising from this controversy, they arose from David Norris's own words, and nothing else. In fact, there had been no such insinuation, other than in the inferences being drawn by Norris's supporters. If the author of the statements had been a Catholic priest or some gombeen politician, we can safely surmise that the editorial would have taken a different tack. Those who read it may have assumed from the use of the word 'revival' that the newspapers in question had assiduously pursued the issues raised by the *Magill* interview at the time of its publication, in which case those readers would have been wrong; back in 2002, *The Irish Times* had strategically averted its gaze.

Typical of the media hypocrisy was the contribution of a female columnist who dismissed Helen Lucy Burke's 'tired allegations and appalling insinuations'. She then went on to assert that anyone 'with a brain even half the size of Senator Norris's, reading his interview with Burke, would understand that the remarks he made about the ancient Greeks' attitude towards children and sexuality were part of a philosophical, academic discussion'. Again, anyone reading this sentence might be forgiven for gathering that, before rushing to defend David Norris, the female columnist had taken the trouble to read the *Magill* interview. Two paragraphs further on, however, she mildly upbraided Norris for remarks he made on *The Pat Kenny Show* on RTÉ Radio One the previous day, about 'Christian brothers putting their hands into children's pockets'. This, she thought, 'only served to trivialise that grave, criminal offence'. She thought that, in using this example, Norris had done a disservice to the argument outlined in the *Magill* interview: that we tend to lump all abuse in together. What she did not appear to appreciate is that the reference to the Christian brother 'putting his hand into a boy's pocket during a history lesson' was itself part of the *Magill* interview, which clearly she had not even read.

Having written a detailed account of my own knowledge of the affair in *The Irish Times*, I expected that my confirmation of Helen Lucy Burke's memory of events might prove newsworthy. Alas, no. I got just one request for a radio interview about my *Irish Times* article – from *The Eamon Dunphy Show* on Newstalk 106. I had also promised a programme on another station, which had badgered me for several days after my name was mentioned in this connection on *Liveline*, that I would talk on air after my column appeared on the coming Friday. On Friday morning, a researcher from the programme in question told me that my column was 'too factual' and that they had decided not to proceed.

My intervention in defence of Helen Lucy Burke did, however, lead to a scurrilous article in *The Irish Times*, in which I was accused by one of their political writers of being part of a smear campaign against Norris, which in turn led to me being called a homophobe by a guest on the *Tonight with Vincent Browne* programme on TV3. Recognising the use of the word 'homophobe' as an instrument of censorship, I consulted my solicitor Kevin Brophy, who made contact with TV3, and later *The Irish Times*. We asked, in both cases, for an apology and for the allegation to be retracted. *The Tonight with Vincent Browne* programme agreed to broadcast an apology; *The Irish Times* essentially refused to apologise and told me in effect to sue if I wished. I decided not to, on the grounds that I was continuing to write in that newspaper, and TV3 had issued a reasonable and timely apology. In neither case had I raised any issue of damages, nor, in the case of TV3, did I seek even my legal costs.

A few days afterwards, *The Irish Mail on Sunday* carried an interview with Christine Buckley (since deceased), a former victim of abuse in St Vincent's Industrial School in Goldenbridge, and longtime director of the Aislinn support and education group for survivors of industrial schools. Ms Buckley was commenting on the 2002 *Magill* interview with David Norris. Having read an unedited copy of the interview as initially prepared by Helen Lucy Burke, Ms Buckley said that Senator Norris 'does not appear to see the moral dilemma in abusing a child, the psychological impact, the emotional impact, the shattered life'. As a supporter of David Norris in his battles on behalf of homosexuals, she said, she felt a sense of betrayal: 'I'm just terribly, terribly disappointed. There's a huge naivety, I believe, here, and I think that's the issue I have most concerns with. I don't think, for example, that David Norris would ever attempt to abuse a minor, but there's nothing here that would lead me to believe that the whole issue of abuse has actually hit the ventricles of his brain.'

She said that for a presidential candidate to have used what was acceptable – 'if it was' – in respect of the sexual 'education' of boys in classical Greece as an example for today's Ireland was 'kind of disturbing'. She made a connection between the *Magill* interview and Senator Norris's support for the Donegal poet Cathal Ó Searcaigh, who had been at the centre of accusations in 2008 that he had been exploiting teenage boys in Nepal: 'This proves really that [Norris] knew exactly what he was saying [in the *Magill* interview] and that he really continued on that mantra years later.'

'There's no nonsense [talked] about paedophilia,' she said, 'they're monsters.'

Christine Buckley was not accused of homophobia: the interview was simply ignored by all other Irish media outlets. As one of the voices of those abused by clerics of the Catholic Church, Buckley's perspectives had been disseminated far and wide. Until then, it would have seemed unthinkable that any contributions of hers on the subject of paedophilia would be ignored. This one was.

A week after the *Magill* interview resurfaced in 2011, news emerged of another interview given by David Norris to *The Irish Daily Mail* in which he had expressed similar views to the ones he denied outlining in the *Magill* interview, causing something of a sullen silence to fall upon the media. In a car-crash interview on *Morning Ireland*, Norris sought again to waffle about ancient Greece, until he was reminded by the interviewer Áine Lawlor that he was not running for election in ancient Greece, but in 'twenty-first century Ireland'. Even then, many of his supporters did not desist, continuing with their vacuous allegations of 'homophobia' and 'gay-bashing', as if the very act of challenging a gay candidate was an offence in itself. The ultimate destination of this logic was that, unless the Irish electorate agreed to elect gay candidates without question, we were to be deemed a nation of homophobes. And if this sounds absurd, it's because it is: a succinct summary of the Absurdistan in the guise of liberal democracy into which Ireland had fallen.

In the wake of these events, I received an email from a woman who said that she normally disagreed with me, but not here:

> I am a Lesbian and would prefer if the LGBT community would learn from the mistakes made by the Catholic Church in dealing with child abuse scandals. This repeating of the same coping mechanisms when faced with a misdemeanour or some article revealing

< 86 >

some very questionable beliefs from one of your own is just ridiculous. Hasn't anyone been listening, hasn't anyone learned anything? The Catholic Church dealt with its scandals by first protecting their own, issuing denials, asking for proof, pointing to the excellent record of accused clerics, minimising the seriousness of the issue, arguing the finer points of clerical law and finally blaming the victim or the messenger. The Norris case is being handled in the very same way by liberals who would roundly criticise a cleric coming out with the same statements. I know because I would be one of them.

It appears there are many things to be learned about the insidiousness of child abuse and pederasty. The lessons to be learned about abuse are deep and cannot be dealt with superficially, we need to learn how they actually apply in what situations and among which people. These are lessons that need to be learned by both Gay and Straight people, maybe we can eventually learn together. Finding myself in agreement with you I realise maybe I have a lot to learn too, about people I normally dismiss and refuse to listen to.

6

No way, leaba!

I want to tell you something of the way we are, the way we have been, Róisín and I. The idea expressed in the final lines of that prose poem to Róisín from 2000 ('There was a time in my life when this might have seemed a massive inconvenience. But, whenever it happened, I'd find myself longing for your cry, so I could see your face again.') conveys something she unexpectedly gave me, something that, as you well know or knew, would have seemed a tremendous imposition to my pre-existing self, the one you left behind that day in June 1989. It was quite a journey from being that person to being the kind of man who found it a truly wonderful experience to be sitting in a basement flat off Portobello Road at four in the morning, as she bounced, laughing, in her jumpsuit, in a city I was inhabiting for no other purpose but to be with her.

It is strange that there are parts of our life that I cannot tell you about, and not because I am ashamed of them but because I can be put in jail for talking or writing about them. These relate to matters that came before the family law courts of both this country and the jurisdiction of England and Wales, back in 1999/2000. All I can say is that, as the outcome of these proceedings, it was ordered that Róisín live permanently in Ireland in the joint custody of her two parents.

Her mother is a well-known singer, though I doubt if you'll have heard of her. She was not quite famous by the time you went away, but even if she was I doubt if you'd have come across her. I've never discussed anything to do with her in public and won't burden you with any of it now. Suffice to say that we met, had a baby, split up – no: we met, split up, had a baby and eventually got to the point where we were able to get on with life and rearing our daughter without knocking spots off one another.

< 88 >

Strangely, the restrictions that prevent me talking about matters pertaining to our daughter have never appeared to inhibit anyone else. For years, the newspapers of both Ireland and the UK carried gratuitous, invasive, untruthful and vindictive stories about our lives, until I started to get tough and pick them off with my trusty litigation rifle. On one occasion, quite early on, I went to court to take out an injunction against a named individual in order to stop the flow of stories, most of which were one-sided, malevolent and untrue. It cost me 20 grand (punts) to obtain the order, which I presumed would immediately bring the flow of effluent to an end. On the contrary, the stories continued as before, and when I consulted with the lawyers to whom I'd paid the 20 grand, they explained that, 'Oh yes, that's right, Mr Waters, most interesting case, you see, because the order we obtained was issued by a family law court, which is governed by the secrecy provisions of the *in camera* rule, we're not permitted to show it to anyone, so that the editors of the various newspapers haven't actually seen it and therefore can claim immunity from its provisions! Fascinating! A most intriguing case indeed!'

I agreed that it was indeed a fascinating situation but wondered aloud if perhaps there might be any possibility of gaining recognition for the fact that it was also completely bonkers. They agreed that, yes, in a certain sense it was, indeed, yes, a little bit perverse. Back we went to court, this time to take out about half a dozen named newspapers whose editors, this time, not only got to read the order but even had their representatives in court when its provisions were read out. That put the clampers on them for a while, but, of course, in time, they started to chip away at the 'story' again, so from time to time I had to dispatch a solicitor's letter or even a writ to prevail upon them to desist.

Those who are unacquainted with the nature and character of the average journalist find this kind of thing hard to credit. You would think that, once it is clear that something is personal and private, that should be the end of it. You would think, in particular, that if something is governed by a court order, journalists might welcome the opportunity to get on with

< 89 >

other work and dispose of any injunctions from their editors by simple reference to the legal situation. In our situation, at least, this commonsensical scenario did not appear to apply. One factor, undoubtedly, was that the identity of the mother and her fairly determined pursuit of publicity created the impression among journalists that they could publish something simply because she had said it. Another was that, because I had dared to take them on and shut them up, many journalists were waiting to stick the boot into me whenever a chance presented itself. Many of them were especially incensed on account of the fact that, although I never spoke or wrote about anything to do with my relations or interactions with Róisín's mother, I frequently wrote about the extraordinary bias that obtained then, and still obtains, against fathers in family courts. I don't suggest that my own direct experience had absolutely no bearing on anything I wrote in this regard, but the fact of the matter is that I had first gone on record about this phenomenon of prejudice and injustice some two years before Róisín drew her first breath, in my first play for the stage, *Long Black Coat*, produced by Bickerstaffe Theatre Company in Cleere's Theatre, Kilkenny, in the summer of 1994. I had been commissioned to write a play and chose as my theme something that had insistently been conveying itself to me in rumours and whispers for several years.

Long Black Coat, which won the Stewart Parker BBC Award for the best play by a new playwright in 1994, was about how the role of father was been usurped in the Ireland of the time, when increasing numbers of single fathers were being banished from the lives of their children. The play consisted in the main of a dialogue between an old-style father – not entirely dissimilar to yourself – and a 'new-man' father, who might have resembled me at the time. In the course of their arguing, this father and son sought to tease out why it had come about that their grandson/son was no longer permitted to be part of their lives. I found it both astonishing and laughable that, in 1995/96, when the news of my involvement with Róisín's mother first became public, and journalists were trawling around for any bit of tittle-tattle they could lay their claws on, not one of them managed to unearth the script for this play, which contained an uncanny prophecy of my unexpected predicament, aside from the fact that child in the play was a boy and the child in my life turned out to be a girl.

When Róisín came along, you might say, I found myself cast into the dystopia of my own prior imagining. Only some time after she was born did I begin writing as a commentator about the fatherphobia of Irish society and its family courts. In the late 1990s, I wrote a great many columns on the subject in *The Irish Times*. Then, facing a torrent of vitriol and intimidation, and warned from the highest editorial level that I was making myself unemployable, I reduced my output on the subject, eventually confining myself to two or three columns a year.

I'm a different person, writing to you now, than I would have been if Róisín hadn't come along. The 'change' that happens on becoming a parent is like the change of the sapling into the tree, or the caterpillar into the butterfly: It is not arbitrary; it is not a form of renovation; it is not random. It is really a discovering of your essential nature, after a time of growth in curiosity and experiment. It is a coming home rather than a journey to a new place. It is natural, not merely in its effects, but in that it is, or should be, predictable. To the extent that it is not predictable, this unpredictability is a function of our flawed culture, which has a dwindling sense of the meaning of parenthood, and in particular of fatherhood, and so fails to carry very much information on this topic in the conventional channels of popular communication.

For me, becoming a parent brought many things that I did not anticipate. It allowed me to understand you better, for a start. It woke me up to myself and to my true nature and structure. It returned me to a sense of my dependence, mortality, limits, desire. It changed my sense of what freedom is. It pulled me back to the now, jerking me out of the future as though I had been lassoed. It opened my eyes to the specific, to the sense that, at a certain key moment, one must choose one road rather than another, now, or at least after a little thought, and that these decisions are much less vital for their outcomes than for their nowness.

One quality with which Róisín put me in touch was the necessity for particularity. Having been born of the Peter Pan generations that emerged from the revolutionary 1960s, I had acquired a way of looking at the world that to me seemed natural but was actually completely co-opted from the fashionable mentality of the time. This disposition towards reality suggested itself as principled, idealistic, liberal and caring, but in truth was evasive, fragmented, contradictory and confused. Having revolted against authority and truth, our generations had come to believe that we could muddle through life without seeming to take strong lines on anything. We would not be dogmatic, didactic or entrenched in our perspectives. We would be open, tolerant, pluralistic. Everything was relative, after all, and who could say where the truth lay?

But, as you know, this does not work with children. With a child you cannot postpone the necessity for clarity. It is not so much that you have to have an answer, right now, even if it's the wrong one, though you certainly do need to have lots of answers and it is better if most of them turn out to be persuasive. But, more than that, being a parent demands that you reach conclusions. It requires particularity, specificity. Everything is not relative. Some things are good and others bad, and likewise people. Tolerance is fine, but sometimes it tempts danger. Thinking purely for yourself, it is possible to get by without making definite decisions about what you believe, what you stand for, where you are going. But having a child means that you have to start thinking through all the things you spent several decades avoiding reaching conclusions about.

It won't come as much of a surprise to you to hear that for most of my life I had accepted the prevailing idea of freedom as relating to the capacity to do as you pleased, to be liberated from responsibility and 'free' to enjoy yourself. I think this tendency in me was at the back of most of the conflicts between us. Unconsciously, in my life, I had long since been dividing my time into 'unfree' and 'free' time, the former being a price to be paid for the enjoyment of the latter. And yet, as I moved through the years, and occasionally sat back and looked carefully at this division,

I had to admit that the 'free' time I so much looked forward to while I was engaged in my 'unfreedom' never lived up to the promise it held out.

I became acutely aware of this syndrome in caring for Róisín. Because of the huge responsibility involved, I found myself initially dreading the idea of having to spend several days a week taking care of a little baby. And for a while, too, while I was doing so, I would find myself longing for the freedom of the following weekend, when I would be footloose and fancy-free.

But it never worked out like this. Usually, when the Friday of my 'freedom' would arrive, I would find myself bereft, unable to think of anything I wanted to do, now my baby was not here. I would spend the weekends of my freedom wishing her back. And when I looked back over an extended period embracing both 'free' and 'unfree' periods, I gradually began to see that the moments of greatest enjoyment, and thus of freedom, occurred while I was looking after Róisín. Freedom was actually the direct opposite of what I had imagined it to be. When I look back now, it is not the 'free' weekends I remember, but the ones I spent immersed in her existence, cooking her meals, ironing her school shirt for the morning, reading and talking to her in Irish.

In the months before she was due to be born in England in 1996, I returned to school – to a night course in Gael Linn – to recover and revive what little Irish I imagined might be dormant in me. I was surprised to find that there were many pockets of the language still buried in there. Within a few weeks, I arrived at a workable level of communication. I uttered no word of English to Róisín until she was three. At bedtime I read her Irish versions of fairy tales, like Lúidín Ó Laoi and Rapúnsal. She responded in her own version of Béarlachas ('No way, leaba!') but came to love Irish far more than I did. She now has the fáinne óir, and speaks like a native. I'll never forget the exhilaration I felt a few years ago when I listened to her being interviewed with some fellow Leaving Cert students on Raidió na Gaeltachta, and was slain in the spirit by hearing her discourse about hip-hop as Gaeilge before singing in English a blues song she'd written with her boyfriend, 'Ain't Got No Blues Blues'. My Irish has regressed through disuse to a virtual state of nature, although we occasionally makes resolutions to allocate particular days, or times of day, to speaking Irish.

The saddest thing in your not being here over the past 20 years has been that you have not met Róisín and she has not met you. You would not be able to get over her. She's more like you than any of your other grandchildren, in that she thinks everything through from first principles, gathers information, reviews, revises and becomes as emphatically certain of her final position as she was of her first. She recently announced that she and her husband Leo want to go back to Sligo to grow organic vegetables and maybe raise some chickens. It is like some gene that was suppressed for a while is resurfacing and reasserting itself.

7

Tsunami

The idea, subsequently put about by gay rights activists and journalists, that what occurred on *The Saturday Night Show* was a 'debate' about the 'subtleties' of homophobia was risible, as was the idea of any kind of equivalence between my role as a commentator and O'Neill's fulminations – the usual 'if you dish it out you ought to be able to take it' line. If, during my 24 years as a newspaper columnist, I published anything potentially defamatory of someone, I was likely to be sued, and as a result liable to lose my employment. I had one or two close shaves, but nothing I wrote ever caused *The Irish Times* to have to admit liability for a defamation perpetrated by me – despite being enthusiastically at the heated centre of Irish public debate with that paper for 24 years. There is a difference, in other words, between 'debating' and peddling untruths, smears and slurs, and maintaining that distinction is one of the things that make debate possible. Thus, there was indeed a 'free speech' issue at stake in the 'Pantigate' affair: the right of people to engage in public debate and avail of a presumption of good faith, free of assertions or innuendoes of malice or hatred. Unless these conditions are available, there is no freedom, and therefore no debate.

No one was suggesting that Rory O'Neill should not be allowed to criticise anything said or written by me or any member of Iona; nobody said that he should not be entitled to describe and critique the culture of homophobia he perceived to exist in Irish society; nobody said that he should not be free to state his honest opinion about anything that had been said or written about gays in general or himself in particular, by me or anyone else. What I and others said, through our lawyers, was that he was not entitled to suggest, without evidence, that I or any of the other defamed parties, were motivated by hatred or dislike of homosexuals, or that our arguments about any matter in which the gay community has an interest are not legitimate views which citizens of a free democracy are entitled to hold without being pilloried or demonised on that account.

RTÉ, having been given an opportunity to make amends, started to faff around and trivialise the issue. In the beginning, as in previous instances, all I had asked for was an apology, to be broadcast at the first available opportunity, which would have been the following Saturday night, 18 January.

In fact, I had made contact by text with Brendan O'Connor before the end of the progamme on 11 January, informing him that the item had been defamatory. Later that night, both O'Connor and his producer Larry Masterson texted me to tell me I could come on the show the following week to respond to what O'Neill had said. Since this would have amounted to me going on to protest against an accusation based not on something I had said, but against my very person, and which had been made without substantiation or evidence, I would have been reduced to responding by, for example, listing my gay friends, or telling about the numbers of gay people whom I'd supported as a journalist etc. – putting myself right in the firing line for the sneers and further attacks of an increasingly ugly LGBT lobby. On the Sunday following the interview, my lawyer, Kevin Brophy, wrote to RTÉ asking that urgent attention be given to removing the defamatory content from the repeat of the programme to go out that evening, and also that the programme be taken down from the RTÉ Player. He received an automated response from the email address supposedly made available for critical editorial communications – and nothing else. The programme remained on the RTÉ Player, unedited. On Monday, he again wrote to RTÉ on my behalf, requesting an apology and now, on account of the non-response, a nominal donation to a charity, the Society of St Vincent de Paul. I specified a €15,000 donation; RTÉ subsequently indicated a willingness to pay €5,000.

On Monday also, I texted Larry Masterson expressing disappointment that, despite my communications with programme personnel, the programme had been repeated unedited. I told him it was not a right-of-reply matter. I took a telephone call from him on the following (Tuesday) evening, in the course of which it emerged that he (and undoubtedly others) had spent the previous couple of days trawling the Internet in search of evidence to validate retrospectively what Rory O'Neill had said. He made a reference to an interview with a college magazine, but in general appeared to believe that the trawl had not been a great success. (It was interesting that, in the wake of the interview with O'Neill, RTÉ and gay lobbyists were able to dig up only a handful of fleeting references to gay marriage in my columns, usually passing references at that.. There was also an interview which I'd given two years previously for the online edition of *College Tribune*, a magazine read by perhaps a couple of hundred students. For the previous six years, I'd been writing weekly columns in two national newspapers, so if I had been setting out to obstruct the progress of gay rights, I was making a pretty poor fist of it.) Masterson again invited me to come on the following Saturday's programme, pointing out that I had been on the show several times. (In fact, I had been a guest on the original pilot, which had resulted in Brendan O'Connor winning a contest to present *The Saturday Night Show*, against some formidable competition, including the late Gerry Ryan. I had appeared on the show at least once per season since then.) Masterson then pointedly asked me if I was prepared to go to court on this and I said that, unless I received an adequate apology, I was most certainly prepared to go to court. The matter, I said, was entirely in RTÉ's hands.

The following day, in consultation with Kevin Brophy (who for historical reasons having nothing to do with me, was also representing several members of the Iona Institute, a factor that was to cause some people to jump to conclusions with no basis in fact), I helped draft an apology which was sent to RTÉ's lawyers that same day. This apology, having been agreed with all the injured parties, read:

On last Saturday's show comments were made by Rory O'Neill stating that John Waters, Breda O'Brien and everyone associated with the Iona Institute are homophobic. RTÉ accepts that these allegations are completely without foundation, and would like to apologise for any upset or distress caused to the individuals so named and identified. We accept that it is an important part of democratic debate that people must be able to hold dissenting views on controversial issues without characterisations of malice, hatred or bad faith.

When a controversy broke out some two weeks later about the payment of damages, RTÉ claimed that this apology had been 'too long'. However, they did not raise this objection at the time. What they said is that they could not refer in the apology to Rory O'Neill, offering no explanation as to why. In due course it became clear that they also had a mysterious difficulty with the final sentence of the apology, which for me and the others was crucial to the issue of proper redress. Over the coming 10 days or so, Kevin Brophy was to submit several variations of this apology, all of which were rejected. All wordings proposed by RTÉ, apart from being lame and laden with weasel words, notably excluded any approximation of that final sentence. This was puzzling, since the sentence amounts to no more than a summary of RTÉ's public responsibility – being a sentiment that might plausibly be posted over the front door of the RTÉ building in Montrose.

RTÉ's first draft of a proposed apology arrived after 5.00 pm on Friday 17 January. It amounted to no more than an expression of regret that we had taken offence. There was no mention of Mr O'Neill, but merely an assertion that RTÉ did not share the opinions he had expressed. RTÉ indicated that it would issue this 'apology' on the following night's show, whether or not we agreed. I instructed my lawyer to tell them that, if the 'apology' were broadcast in that form, it would make things worse. Thus did RTÉ fritter away a full week in which the matter could have been disposed of with minimal cost.

The following day, Saturday 18 January, I texted Bob Collins, Chairman of the Broadcasting Authority of Ireland (BAI), of which I had been a member since its inception in 2009. The text stated:

> Bob, I wish to resign forthwith from the BAI in order to pursue a legal action against RTÉ on foot of an outrageous libel and attack on me on last Saturday's Brendan O'Connor show for which RTÉ refuses to provide an adequate apology or retraction. The result is a blizzard of hated directed at me, which makes it dangerous for me to walk the streets. For several years, I have sought to draw the attention of my colleagues on the BAI to what was happening to free speech in this country, to no avail. We have failed to address the issue in our work as regulators, so now it falls to me as an individual to pursue it and do something to ensure that this society is able to retain some right to dissent without citizens with different views to powerful lobbying muscle being demonised in this manner …

Bob was in bed with flu at the time and asked if I could hold off a little to allow him to consult with Michael O'Keefe, CEO of the BAI. He had not seen the programme and did not want to lose me from the authority. I provided him with further details by text and a few days later spoke by telephone both to him and Michael O'Keefe. In due course it was agreed that my resignation was the best course in the circumstances, and I then submitted my letter of resignation to the Minister for Communications, Pat Rabbitte.

I was not exaggerating in informing Bob Collins that I now regarded it unsafe for me to walk down the street. I had never in my life seen anything like the unmitigated venom to be encountered online, the utter lack of perspective in the mainstream media, the hysteria of certain politicians – all converging in a sense of menace that seemed to pervade every space or street I entered. Because I chose after a couple of days not to venture into certain areas, the number of face-to-face incidents in which

< 99 >

I was personally confronted or abused was at that stage no more than a handful, and yet the anxiety they provoked, in the absence of any channel by which to put out some truthful account of what had occurred, created a sense of helplessness that I had never before experienced as a journalist or public figure. The main problem was that I was up against just one word — 'homophobe' – albeit a word with a deliberately cultivated demonic aura and a capacity to strike fear into bystanders lest they too be daubed with its nauseous meanings and innuendoes. The condition I found myself in seemed to arise almost by something like 'appointment' of Rory O'Neill, by virtue of some odd form of ordinance within his remit as a gay man. He could call me a homophobe and did not need to proffer evidence. All I could do was deny it, but I would, wouldn't I? I decided not to – to remain more or less silent, except for a brief conversation with a journalist from *The Sunday Business Post* and one slightly ironical statement issued to *The Sunday Independent*, in which I proposed that, in view of the impossibility of a fair and balanced debate about gay marriage, Enda Kenny might bypass the requirement for a referendum and simply introduce gay marriage by legislation 'on Tuesday morning'. (This resulted in a further 'debate' online about why I was now calling for the legalisation of gay marriage!)

On Monday 20 January, when one might have expected RTÉ to be even more contrite in view of their failure to issue a decent apology at the first available opportunity, it became clear that their attitude had hardened somewhat, probably emboldened by the torrents of hatred and abuse being directed at the Iona people and me via Twitter, Facebook and the mainstream media. In a brief further exchange of letters, RTÉ's lawyers demonstrated a tendency to engage in crypto-philosophical debate about the rights and wrongs of the issue, offering trite arguments about the definitions and value of freedom of speech and so forth. Their prevarication concerning the apology continued also. It looked like another week would be frittered away with this nonsense, so I instructed Kevin Brophy to inform RTÉ that, if they wished to debate the matter,

< 100 >

they could do so in front of a judge and jury. It was at that point that they began to take the matter seriously. They agreed an apology and settlement with Iona and I was asked if I was prepared to accept the new apology as drafted. Kevin Brophy was in effect conducting two sets of negotiations with RTÉ – one on my behalf and one on behalf of the several Iona members who had been defamed. On Friday 24 January, he called me to say he believed the Iona members were on the point of agreeing a settlement, including a much improved apology. I considered the new apology, which I found still fell a long way short of what we had requested. I discussed it with David Quinn of Iona, who was anxious to dispose of the matter in advance of the funeral of his colleague Tom O'Gorman, who – in a bizarre and gruesome occurrence in the hours immediately after the O'Neill interview – had been violently murdered by a tenant at his home in Castleknock. I called Kevin Brophy and said that I was prepared to agree the new apology, but that, in view of RTÉ's behaviour, I was not now prepared to agree a settlement without damages. I said I was not entirely happy with the new wording, but in deference to the Iona members agreed that it could go ahead provided adequate damages were paid. RTÉ at first made me an offer of €30,000, and, following a brief negotiation between the lawyers, it was agreed that I would be paid a sum of €40,000. I was informed that a total of €45,000 would be paid to the members of Iona, including Breda O'Brien, whom O'Neill had also referenced by name.

Damages are the way this society has ordained as a means to compensate citizens for damage to their reputations. There is no other measure of the gravity of an established unwarranted assault on a person's reputation except the wholeheartedness of an apology and the quantum of money paid in damages. Still, if RTÉ had behaved with courtesy and good faith from the beginning of the negotiations, the matter would have been settled a week earlier at a fraction of the cost. I would have received no damages, nor, as on several not dissimilar occasions in the past, would I have asked for any.

< 101 >

In the wake of these events, a major storm persisted on the Internet and, gleefully mirrored in the national press, continued unabated through February and into March. In the course of this tsunami of outrage, it was as if all of the wrongs suffered by homosexuals in Ireland in living memory and before were the responsibility of those named by Rory O'Neill. Innuendo-laden articles and editorials were carried in the national press. Email campaigns of the most virulent character were pursued against those named by O'Neill. Gay public representatives made tearful speeches in the houses of the Oireachtas. International celebrities, including Madonna, Stephen Fry and Graham Norton intervened to issue tweets of support for 'Miss Panti'. Major international newspapers like *The Guardian* and *The New York Times* carried one-sided accounts of the saga. 'Miss Panti' was allowed to address the audience from the stage of the National Theatre in Dublin lamenting his experience of homophobia in Ireland, a speech that one breathless commentator described as the greatest since Daniel O'Connell.

Generally speaking, the role of the media in these matters was pretty disgraceful, befitting a culture in which uncritical concurrence with the gay agenda is regarded as the only acceptable position. Journalists sought to demonstrate their correctness by lining up to kick me and the various Iona people. Although I was not a member of Iona, an impression to the contrary was widely conveyed. Sometimes the same journalists who attacked us on this basis took the opportunity to prosecute another of their vested interests and 'liberal' hobby horses by attacking us for using the defamation laws – for the purpose they were intended to serve – which journalists anxious to gain brownie points with their paymasters are frequently at pains to do. The intervention by the Minister for Communications, Pat Rabbitte, in which he denounced us for, apparently, demanding that 'Queensberry rules' should apply to public debate, was unprecedented for a communications minister. What our response had demanded was that people who engage in public debate do not tell untruths about us, or seek to demonise us because (they believed) we were in disagreement with them.

< 102 >

In my own case, the most immediate and arresting aspect of the cascade was the deluge of emails that started to arrive in my inbox, growing in intensity over the course of a fortnight or so, and then tailing off. The following is a random selection. It captures the general level of venom, illiteracy and imagination-deficit. Rather than extend these communications the consideration of separate paragraphs, I've run them together, separating discrete emails with asterisks.

> You're a fucking homophobe.*You are a HOMOPHOBIC AS-SHOLE. Have the decency to apologize to Panti, and then drop off the face of the earth.*Fuck you, you worthless piece of shit. And, fuck, you are damn ugly too. Cut that dirty long hair, you HO-MOPHOBIC ASSHOLE.*John Waters is a HOMOPHOBIC AS-SHOLE. Take your stringy, greasy hair and shove it up your hateful ass, douchebag.* You sir are a Bigot. and i would ask you to kindly KILL YOURSELF.* Fuck off and die you horrible Bible bashing twat, the youth of this country will forever remember your ideological hatred and your prancing around a bigoted institute. As a straight young man you turn my stomach with your pompous superiority complex. Don't forget that you have to down your underwear and take a shite like the rest of us greasy head.*Hi John Just wanted to tell you everyone in Ireland thinks youre a bastard. Sinead O'Connor is better off having nothing to do with you. You are a piss stain.* I hear you're a homophobe now John. Any chance of a few bob please?*Can you justify for me in a reply why you think you deserve more rights under our laws than a gay couple, can you? I've met bigoted taxi drivers who had at least the courage to admit they were racist, You sir are a not just a bully but a coward.*Dear John, You are entitled to your views however archaic and displeasing they are to the masses. However you are not entitled to our money. Grow a set of balls and return our money or donate it to a good cause. Kind regards One of many disgusted Irish people.* Fuck you.* You're some

bollocks boy. Go away and get yourself a bottle of cop on.* Bye bye career, homophobe!* you are a fucking homophobic wanker :)*Dear John, I am a great fan of your works. You write exactly like a bigot. I would like to invite you over to sniff my panti(es). Love, Ms Delightful*Please do progressive Ireland a favour and quit journalism, you are an embarrassment to my country.*If you have any shame at all, you'll donate that taxpayer money to a worthy charity. Preferably a gay rights charity, and not a sham like the Iona Institute. Luckily, I am confident that you and your homophobic ilk will not hold Ireland back against the wishes of the majority of its population for much longer.

And so on and on.

I used to get critical emails all the time, sometimes offensive ones, but never anything like this deluge. Generally such correspondents tend to make some point about something I've actually written or said, even if, as frequently occurs, they've misunderstood me or heard something secondhand. These emails, however, consisted entirely of abuse. They tended to come in waves, after dark and into the early hours, at a rate of 20 or 30 per day. Rarely did any arrive before midday, and sometimes the weight of the day's consignment would come after 10.00 pm. Then something even more peculiar emerged: some days there were no emails at all, and I would think it had stopped. Late next afternoon, however, another lone email diatribe would arrive and I would think: wouldn't it be interesting if there were 20 more of these before midnight? And, invariably, so it would come to pass. This happened several times: on a Wednesday there would be 20; on Thursday none at all; on Friday 30 more – even though the level of related activity, commentary and invective in the public arena had remained constant over the full three-day period. I formed this image of a room somewhere in the depths of the city of Dublin, full of heated LGBT activists, all churning out poison emails to the alleged enemies of their happiness, perhaps pausing occasionally to exchange ideas for new phrases and insults, a veritable cottage industry of toxicity and, yes, hate-mongering, working feverishly in the cause of justice, equality and fairness in the world.

8

The Vitality of the Particular

It took me some time to recognise that, in acting out the role of father, I was drawing on your example and guidance all the time. Fatherhood is poorly understood in our societies, if at all. Motherhood we get: nurturing, cuddling, feeding, changing. In so far as fatherhood gets to be discussed as a method of parenting in the world now, it tends to be depicted as a kind of male mothering. In so far as we allow for a different role for the father, we seem to think of him as some kind of supervisor/coach/security guard, rather than the one who provides the existential accompaniment to the child in the initial walk towards the horizon, which was the role you played for me.

The most beautiful description I've come across of what fatherhood means was by the American poet Robert Bly in his foreword to *Society Without the Father*, a book by the German psychoanalyst Alexander Mitscherlich. Bly said that the father had been destroyed – accidentally, he believed – by the Industrial Revolution, which removed him from the home and made his powers invisible to his children: 'Industrial circumstances took the father to a place where his sons and daughters could no longer watch him minute by minute, or hour by hour, as he fumbled incompetently with hoes, bolts, saws, shed doors, plows, wagons. His incompetence left holes or gaps where the sons and daughters could do better'.'

I've come to regard myself as lucky in this regard – in the fact that you were much older than me and had your roots in a pre-industrial era. I remember how you would teach me and my sisters things without appearing to be teaching anything, how you would get us to help you – to find a tool for you while you bled the brakes on the van, or to clean the spark plugs in paraffin oil and hand them to you, one by one. I thought of these things as chores, but they were really lessons in the vitality of the particular. In this way we were taught that reality is entered into through the specific – the actual things and problems that are right now in front of your eyes and ears, and the very thingness and challenges they present.

I remember one summer when I was 12 or 13, and you put me to grinding the valves in an engine you had acquired to replace the one in BZC 648, which was on its very last, last legs. The 'new' engine came out of a Thames you'd found somewhere 'up the country'. I don't remember the full reg number of the donor vehicle, but the prefix was ELI. The Thames had been clumsily hand-painted in canary yellow, and was held together by the moss around the windows, but you were certain the engine was basically sound. You asked me if I would grind the valves and, thinking it an easy job, I rashly agreed. You set me up in one of the sheds and explained the general principles at the back of the endeavour. I gathered that the objective was to restore the cylinder head to something like its original condition. You showed me the valves and their seatings and explained their function and how some worked in conjunction with the camshaft to regulate the flow of the mixture into the cylinders and others to let the spent gases escape. You explained why it was vital that the carbon deposits be cleaned away and the matching, subtle ridges in the valve heads and seating be restored to their original pristine condition. You showed me how to do it, using a rubber suction cup at the end of a short stick to twist the valve rapidly and repeatedly in its seating, using a rough paste for lubrication.

You said it would take a few days, at maybe a couple of hours a day. Yeah, right, as Róisín might say. It seemed to go on the entire summer, with no appreciable progress until the very end. I would dutifully put in my couple of hours most days, and you would return at evening time and immediately lapse into inspection mode.

You had this way of weighing everything up, very methodically, looking at things from all angles. I still sometimes imitate the way you would push your glasses up on your forehead and peer closely at things. You would do it as we walked along the street. Catching sight of a recent piece of work – a new shop window or a plastered wall, you would go over, shove up your glasses and begin rubbing your fingers along the woodwork or plaster, sometimes getting down on your knees to eye up the line of it. It drove me mad but now, sometimes, I have the urge to do it myself.

You would peer at the valves, one by one, for a long time, fingering them lightly. Sometimes you would take the stick with the rubber suction cup and give it a go yourself for a minute or two, carefully noting the outcomes. Then you would straighten up, contemplate for a half-minute or so and pronounce: "More grinding!"

This went on for weeks and then months, with occasional breaks when you were feeling unwell and I was required to come along on the run to help with the mailbags and the newspapers and the day-old chicks and the 80-year-old passengers. This was a welcome relief from the grinding, and yet I remember going back to the task afterwards with a new zeal. The progress on any given day was so infinitesimal as to be undetectable. Yet, gradually, I began to observe a change in the surfaces I was address-ing. I began to notice that the rim of the valve had a pattern of grooves, not unlike a gramophone record, which corresponded to a similar pat-tern of grooves in the head. As the grinding took effect, the result was gradually to clean away the carbon that had formed on both surfaces, which first broke down into spots and then revealed tiny pits which grad-ually faded away under the attrition of the grinding stick.

But even towards the end, as I was beginning to note the fruits of my somnambulant exertions, you were relentless. Every evening you would return, shove up your glasses, peer expectantly at the valves and their seatings and pronounce: "More grinding!" Encouragingly, you became a little more selective as time went on, picking out particular valves for special attention and pronouncing one or other "almost done".

Then, one magical evening, you stood up and said nothing for a minute or more, as though engaged in some profound calculation. You wiped your hands on a greasy cloth and declared: "I'd nearly say they're fit."

< 108 >

That Sunday, we reassembled the engine, restoring the block with its new gaskets and the other reconditioned parts you had prepared. I remember watching as you wired in the battery and connected the jump leads. The engine burst into life with a thunder of protest and a ferocious belching of smoke. It spluttered for a few moments, then found a rhythm and calmed down to a purr. We stood there listening to it, without speaking, each paying attention for any telltale irregularity. There was none. You nodded. "It might be not so bad," you said. I don't think you ever praised me so highly. To be standing there together in the balm of that noise, knowing what it signified and what it has arisen from, we were united in a way that could never be erased.

At the time, I did the grinding for you to gain your favour and your affection. You had a way of equating work with goodness, and idleness with the opposite, so we always felt wicked unless we were doing something 'useful'. To be honest, I thought you were just giving me an awkward job to keep me off the streets. Now I see more clearly: you were doing what Robert Bly said fathers had always done.

When I look back on that summer today, it becomes the most glorious of them all. That was the summer I learned about resolve, application, determination, perseverance, postponed gratification, cause and effect, effort and reward, about how the impossible is not impossible. I learned a little about engines as well, but this was a minor collateral benefit. That engine lasted for years afterwards, and every time I heard it running I was taken back to those moments together, conscious of my part in it, and your part in teaching me things that will always be intimately connected to the sound of internal combustion engines.

One of the things I unconsciously adapted from your personality was the idea of reconstructing myself to cohere with some unfocused 'moral' paradigm for the benefit of my growing daughter. It's strange to think how easily I fell into this without thinking about it, becoming pious and solemn and serious-minded, without knowing what purpose this might serve.

I remember the day I first said 'fuck' in front of Róisín. It was an accident, because, by whatever mechanism, I had never come close to doing it before. When I say it was an accident – I don't mean me saying 'fuck', but the fact of her hearing it. I said 'fuck' all the time to other people – still do – but up to that point I had never used such language in front of her, which is probably related to the fact that I never used it in front of you either, not as long as you lived. My friends all said 'fuck' in front of their fathers, without as much as a 'pardon my French', indeed with a kind of gleeful bravado that seemed enhanced because they knew I was listening and that I would never say 'fuck' in front of you.

I'm not proud of saying 'fuck' all the time, and neither am I boasting about not saying it in front of Róisín, which at the time seemed to me the least I could do for her, although I couldn't for the life of me explain why I thought this. In fact, I recognise two conflicting absurdities in my use of the word 'fuck', which I find myself unable to decide between in terms of their burden of silliness. On the one hand, I possess this fairly common sense of puzzlement that a word, any word, can become so powerful as to be unutterable in any context, even a four-letter word beginning with 'f'. I think about 'flip' or 'fake', or 'fact', and wonder if they would ever become so robust and fierce as to deliver shock waves simply by virtue of being spoken. But on the other hand, I think it is right that, most of the time, for most of my life, I managed to refrain from saying 'fuck' in front of you, Mammy, nuns, priests and teachers. I once said 'fuck' in front of a priest – just to see how he would react, but he didn't react at all, which opened up all sorts of new and relativistic speculations in me. That was some time after I was caught by my daughter accidentally saying 'fuck' while she was within earshot, and was probably triggered by that event, perhaps distantly related to the way they say it's easier to kill the second time.

As far as I know, you never said 'fuck' in all your 84 years and nine months of living in this dimension, even in the deepest recesses of yourself. I could be wrong about this – it's one of those questions I wish I'd taken up with your old friend, The Gentleman, when I had the chance, but it never occurred to me, and now your secret, if any, is safe. In fact, if he had told me that, even once or twice, he heard you saying 'fuck', I think I would have become convinced that everything he told me was lies. I can't imagine you saying 'fuck', and if you ever did I don't want to know about it.

And this was certainly a factor in my never saying 'fuck' in front of Róisín – until one day I did.

She was seven years old at the time – old enough, as it turned out, to understand that 'fuck' was too robust and incendiary a word to be said by fathers in front of their children; yet young enough to be shocked by hearing it, which implies some understanding of the significance, if not the meaning, of the word, or at least of its cultural power.

I was on the phone talking to someone who was obviously neither my mother nor a priest. Róisín had been in another room, but then she returned, quietly and unexpectedly, in the middle of my telephone conversation. I looked up from just saying 'fuck' and suddenly there she was, looking at me with her saucer eyes out on stilts. I recognised immediately the significance of what was occurring. I terminated the telephone conversation as quickly as I could and waited for her to say something. Eventually, she said, 'Daddy said a bad word' – half innocently and half ironically. It struck me instantly that she obviously knew the word and also 'knew' that it was 'bad'. I wondered if this was because she had heard other people saying it all the time and, because she had never heard me saying it, put two and two together: words that other people say but Daddy doesn't must be 'bad words'. I don't remember knowing the word 'fuck' when I was seven, and certainly don't think that, if I had heard it then, even from you, I would have recognised it as a word to be shocked by.

One of my favourite authors is the British rock 'n' roll writer Paul Morley, who started out in the 1970s with the *New Musical Express*, and has since written a couple of the best non-fiction books of the third millennium. In *Nothing*, an exquisite memoir about the suicide of his father, Morley described the one and only time in his childhood he heard his

< 111 >

father say 'fuck', and the effect this had on him. He remembered that, at the time, he had been old enough not just to know the word but also to note that, the way his father said it, he must have said it all the time. His father, too, had been on the telephone, speaking to someone to whom he said 'fuck' as a matter of course. Morley remarked, too, on noting how skilfully his father had hitherto refrained from saying 'fuck' in front of his children. As he said it, Morley wrote, 'he sounded freer, looser, not as still and caged as he seemed to be to me. He sounded like somebody else, maybe like somebody I might have got to know if he was still alive'. It slightly scared him and slightly thrilled him to hear his father say 'fuck'. It showed him in four letters how much his father had hidden from him about himself, about how his father had isolated different parts of himself and kept them always separate. 'He didn't give the whole of himself to anyone, not even himself. Until he died, when he brought all the parts of himself together.'

I have thought many times, in many different ways, about that moment when Róisín heard her daddy say 'fuck', but for a long time didn't dare mention it to her. One day, a long time afterwards, some signal would trip between us, after which we began saying all manner of words in one another's hearing. But for a long time we carried on the pretence that the word 'fuck' did not exist, or that, if it did, we did not know it, or knowing it, knew also that it signified something dark or unwholesome and therefore did not wish to revisit the moment when this darkness or unwholesomeness had suddenly erupted between us. More recently, we've taken to saying 'fuck' quite a bit in each other's presence, and I'm not particularly proud of that either, though neither am I as perturbed as all this palaver may be suggesting. Saying 'fuck' is not such a big deal, no matter which of us says it. And yet, something is lost by its utterance, something precious and irreplaceable, something beautiful and delicate and pure. I don't dwell on it in any state of moral discombobulation. I don't think my character, or indeed Róisín's character, is somehow reduced or sullied because of a word with four letters. But, still, something

< 112 >

is lost. What is it? Innocence? Childhood? Shelteredness? Do you know? Do you know even now?

Whenever I say the word, something happens within me which is related to you: deep down, I still don't think it's a suitable word for a father to be saying in front of his daughter, or even for a father to tolerate from his daughter, but it seems too late to go back and erase all those 'fucks', starting with the first one. I hope you're now in a place where saying 'fuck' is seen in some kind of perspective, as something neither to be avoided nor indulged in but simply something that happens from time to time because in certain situations there just isn't any other word that adequately substitutes for 'fuck', which is presumably why the word is so ubiquitous.

I haven't yet gotten around to asking Róisín about that moment, if she remembers it and, if so, in what way? Did she, like Paul Morley, feel both slightly scared and slightly thrilled? Or was the experience entirely of disillusion? A little of her little world must have crumbled in that moment, along with a sizeable chunk of the literalism I had constructed to protect her. The pious mask I had borrowed from you and donned for her benefit slipped for a moment, long enough for her to see that the piety was just a figment of her father's father-image. Did she see the mask? Did she see that it was slipping? Did she understand that this slipping thing was a mask, and therefore that what was happening was something that could never be undone? For a time, whenever I thought of it like this, I would go into a dizzying kind of emotional freefall, surveying the fragility of the father image and the scariness of how something on which so much depends can be dispersed in an instant. I don't think there were ever moments like that in our relationship – except perhaps when I would sometimes wander into the sorting office in the evening and discover you pretending not to be amused by some obscenity uttered by one of the postmen or clerks.

I wonder how much of my daughter's earliest understandings were collapsed in that moment, how much it delivered her from absolutism, how much she lost of certainty by hearing that one word. Was it like the moment she heard someone say something worrying and incredible about Santa Claus? Did it begin some opening up to possibilities that might otherwise have remained closed? Did it generate the germ of some otherwise avoidable relativism? Or was it simply the necessary precursor of a more realistic engagement with the world? Are these questions relevant or useful? I'd love if you were around to answer them for me, or even to talk them through. I feel a great sadness that we never got to this point of potential understanding, of facing each other across a table, not as father and son but as two fathers comparing notes..

9

Buggering Brothers

In July 2014, six months after the eruption of the events on *The Saturday Night Show*, and several months after I had departed *The Irish Times*, the drag queen who had started the whole thing off by attacking me gave an interview to VIP magazine in which he responded to a question concerning what he might say to me if he 'bumped into' me some time. Rory O'Neill responded: 'Probably nothing. There's no point. John has said a lot of things that I strongly disagree with. However, I will agree when he says that he hasn't set out to campaign against gay people. And he's a columnist, or he was a columnist, and he had to fill a column every bloody week, so he probably ended up getting into areas he probably shouldn't. So I feel I can put John aside.'

While it was gratifying to learn that I could now be 'put aside' by Mr O'Neill, and while I pondered for a time the concept of areas I 'probably shouldn't have been getting into', and while I admit I spent a moment or two reflecting on the meaning of all those 'probablys', which had the look of the weasel about them, I did find it astonishing that, six months after claiming to have been hard done by, O'Neill was now apparently admitting that he had made a mistake, that I hadn't been seeking to deny him happiness at all. I might have saved myself all that reflecting and puzzling: no more than three months later, O'Neill published a book in which he dusted down his original allegation, using as 'justification' a couple of lines that purportedly came from a UCD students' magazine interview I'd given two years before, and which were already in their highly selective orbit of circulation at the time O'Neill gave his interview to VIP. In February 2014, this interview had been produced by the then editors of UCD student magazine *College Tribune*, as their contribution to the tsunami of character assassination and dishonesty that followed O'Neill's Saturday Night Show interview.

I had given the interview at the end of July 2012 to James Grannell, one of the two joint-editors of *College Tribune* at that time. Grannell had merely asked me to contribute to a series of articles he was writing on gay marriage. The interview with me was to be one of six, all conducted around the same time, three from what he characterised as 'either side' of the argument. The editors had decided to run these interviews in their online edition of *College Tribune* (they never actually appeared in print) because the Students Union had decided to campaign for a Yes vote in the imminent referendum. As a student newspaper, they were conscious that there might exist a plurality of views on the issue that were not being given attention at the time within the university. The six articles, one based on each interview, were an attempt to present some of these different perspectives in a dispassionate and non-confrontational manner. Although individual students had told the editors that they opposed same-sex marriage, none were willing to go on the record and, as a result, James Grannell told me, there was an anxiety at editorial level in the magazine concerning lack of balance. It was especially worrying, in his view, that such an absence of balance had manifested in a university, where it might be thought a matter of principle and honour that vibrant discussion should occur on all contentious issues.

When we met, in a rather noisy Starbucks in the Dundrum Town Centre, James Grannell related these fears and difficulties to me. There followed a lengthy, freewheeling conversation between us, some of which Grannell recorded to provide background for his article, quite separately from the quotes he wished to obtain from me as to my precise position and general perspectives on the matter. He would tell me afterwards that our conversation was by far the longest of all the six interviews and ventured into areas that didn't really have much to do with the gay marriage debate per se. We discussed abortion, fathers' rights, family courts, the high incidence of male suicide, children's rights, and what it means to be

< 116 >

'human', among other topics. Only a fraction of our conversation was used in Grannell's written piece.

I found Grannell a pleasant and straightforward fellow and he gave me no reason not to trust him. He seemed relieved that I was prepared to engage in an open and unrestricted conversation with him on a topic concerning which many people had seemed to be terrified to speak.

When the six articles were first published in 2012, they received no attention whatsoever from the national or international media, nor did any journalist raise anything to do with any of the articles at any subsequent time while James Grannell was an editor of *College Tribune*.

Grannell's article contained a sample of opinions I'd expressed on the gay marriage topic – mostly sceptical ones, but largely concerning the child-related difficulties I saw arising from the kinds of changes being proposed. I was quoted as saying: 'In a certain sense it's not even gay marriage that I'm opposed to, it's the idea of gay adoption.' I asked what was going to happen to the parents of the children absorbed into gay families who were not part of those units? I pointed out that the champions of gay marriage had 'nothing to say on this question at all'. I spoke about the inversion of the purpose of adoption, which had originally been conceived to ensure that a child who had lost his or her parents could be placed in a family situation which might replicate, in as far as this was possible, the security and well-being that had been lost. Now, the child was being treated as a commodity, to be supplied to 'alternative families' in response to the needs and demands of adults. I also talked about the dangers of people jumping to positions because of a desire to be fashionable rather than on the basis of reason, logic and fact. I warned that politicians were cynically treating the gay marriage issue as a means to burnish their 'liberal' credentials and to obtain credits to cancel out failures in other contexts. I pointed out that 'conservative' politicians were often prone to this tendency.

I said (a quote that, interestingly, did not get regurgitated after the O'Neill interview): 'The way this is being set up, there's almost a blackmail clause involved, whereby if you don't support it you're a homophobe. This bullying is actually silencing people and it's preventing any kind of open discussion. … You're sneered at and ridiculed.'

I expressed further reservations about what the gay lobby was really after. 'This is really a kind of satire on marriage which is being conducted by the gay lobby. It's not that they want to get married; they want to destroy the institution of marriage because they're envious of it and they feel really that it's an affront to their equality. … This is the interesting thing: when they were fighting for civil unions I raised the question that what they really wanted was marriage, that what they really wanted was adoption, and they all denied it – "That's complete paranoia. We have no interest in marriage at all, this is about our civil rights." … But the next day [after civil partnership was passed into law] they got out of bed and started to campaign for marriage.'

We then proceeded into a deeper question about the function of religion in society. I spoke of the destructiveness of what is called liberalism, the contemporary Irish version of which seemed intent upon pulling down everything. I predicted that gay marriage would be introduced: 'It's going to happen because we don't have any intellectual basis in this society any more to fight it. … Sometimes you have to allow things to happen for the consequences to become obvious.'

It is interesting that none of the material that was actually included in the published interview was deemed sufficiently helpful to Rory O'Neill's case for it to be cited in the wake of *The Saturday Night Show* interview. Yet, when the recording and alleged transcript of a section of my conversation with Grannell emerged in February 2014, 18 months after the original publication of the interview, this came to be spoken of as 'the interview'. The juiciest of the quotes – judging from the number of times it was reproduced – was my rather clumsy parable of the Buggering Brothers, related by way of constructing an analogy with which to make clear a particular very pertinent point.

My point here was that, if two bachelor brothers attempted to adopt

< 118 >

a little girl, society would come over all squeamish. Why was this different from two gay men? Could it be, I pondered, that to qualify as suitable parents they needed to be buggering one another? My intention and purpose was to provide an instance of one of the many absurdities surrounding the notion that gay couples, by virtue of being married, might acquire parenting rights equivalent to those of a married man and woman, especially in the context of the outright indifference of both politicians and journalists to the denial of the rights of father and children to enjoy protection for their natural rights under Irish law. What was most interesting about the outrage directed at this analogy was the deliberate efforts to misunderstand or misrepresent it, rather than deal with its substantive point: some activists tried to suggest I was equating homosexuality with incest, others took strategic offence at the use of the word 'buggering', which my dictionary defines as 'penetrating the anus … during sexual intercourse'. Since this is a definition of what gay males call 'having sex', I have been unable to grasp how the word denoting it could be problematic.

On 6 February 2014, at the height of the firestorm of hatred being directed at me after *The Saturday Night Show*, I received an email from the then editors of *College Tribune*, Ronan Coveney and Amy Walsh, proposing that a full transcript of the interview ought to be published and requesting my permission to release it. The email contained the very interesting construction: 'We think it is in everyone's interest to publish the quotes used in our article in the original context of the transcript.' I responded immediately – a little more than an hour later – declining categorically to give permission: 'I do not give my permission for you to publish anything of any interview conducted with me in any form whatsoever. I trust this is clear.' Ignoring this, the editors published the transcript, and also apparently released portions of the recording of some of the conversation between me and James Grannell. The sound quality of the recording was very poor, with a great deal of background noise, but some doughty keyboard warriors extracted a handful of half-sentences in

< 119 >

an attempt retrospectively to justify O'Neill's accusation, including a totally de-contextualised presentation of the 'buggering brothers' reference.

The fact of the matter is that what the recording contained – a barely audible exchange in an extremely noisy location – was a free-flowing and general conversation between me and James Grannell, with a view to exploring the background issues surrounding the gay marriage question. This is something I had done for students many times in the past, talking them through issues so as to provide background and assist them in teasing out whatever issues they were proposing to write about, either for magazine articles or for their dissertations. I do not recall asking Grannell to treat any particular sections of our conversation as off-the-record, though some such arrangement was clearly understood between us. In the context of the pell-mell descent of academia down the same chute as journalism, this may seem to have been a rather naïve thing to do, but I was convinced by Grannell's disposition and assurances, and afterwards had no reason to be disappointed or dismayed by anything he included in his article. Had I known what was going to happen – that his successors at the magazine would get hold of the original tape and use it in a selective manner to assist forces lined up against me – I would have been a great deal more careful, and indeed would have been a great deal more careful in 1,001 other interviews I gave to students over the years. In all my experience of co-operating with students in various ways as a journalist and public figure, it had never occurred to me that we might have entered a new era in which regard for protocol, convention and implicit agreements was to be set at naught.

Subsequently it emerged that the recording and transcript of the exchange between Grannell and myself had remained in the *College Tribune* offices and was regarded by the 2014 editors as the property of the magazine. The release of the material was perpetrated without reference to James Grannell or, as far as I know, the other editor at the time of the interview, with whom I had had no dealings at all. Grannell was the person whom I had trusted implicitly to treat our exchange in the spirit in which we had entered it, which he duly did. His article was comprehensive in respect of the agreement we had entered into and he behaved decently and competently throughout our dealings. Neither of us had any way of anticipating that the tape would subsequently fall into the hands of individuals who would seek to use it to damage me, or indeed him. The leaking of this conversation, in my estimation, had a precedent in Irish academia only in the publication in 1990 of a recording of an interview given (to a UCD student as well) by Brian Lenihan Senior, which similarly breached all agreements and protocols and ended up destroying Lenihan's candidacy for the presidency of Ireland after *The Irish Times* – departing from its role as a newspaper and entering the political fray – held a press conference to unveil it.

10

Love and Bad Turf

The weirdest thing of all, perhaps, is that I chose the very mid-point of this horror story to get married myself. My wife's name was, or used to be, Rita Simons. Now she's Rita Waters, the addition of the merest 'R' to my mother's married name, although she has yet to get around to changing it on her passport, since we've been away so much over the past couple of years, in Europe, America and Sligo. Her people, on her father's side, come from Roscommon town. Her late grandfather, Frank Simons – Rita refers to him as 'Pop' – was involved in the patriotism business way back and had a leadership role in the Scramogue ambush carried out by the IRA during the War of Independence, when two British Army officers were killed along with a driver and an RIC constable when a patrol lorry was intercepted and fired upon. The IRA men discovered two Black and Tans in the lorry, who had been placed under arrest by the soldiers, and they shot them to avoid being identified. Frank Simons was in on that assignment, by all accounts. I'd say yourself and himself would have had things to say to one another. Maybe you did already.

I'm not sure I could have come through it without Rita; actually, I'm pretty sure I wouldn't have. To be honest, I was fairly surprised myself, waking up on 20 December 2014, on my honeymoon in Ardmore.

We're very happy. She's a smart, gorgeous and, above all, sensible woman. We have a lot to say to one another, and even after six years together our conversation shows no signs of drying up. We also have the same kinds of memories of important things like Kimberly biscuits and the fascinating usefulness of the yellow transparent paper that once came wrapped around Lucozade bottles. You used to use it to turn your headlights into fog lamps.

< 122 >

It was a slow burner. We ran into each other years ago when she was still married, and didn't connect again until about ten or 12 years ago, when I ran into her in a café in Dublin. We spoke for a couple of minutes and I got the distinct impression that she was on the loose, so I made enquiries and confirmed that it was the case. Next time we met was a couple of years later, outside the Bank of Ireland on Stephen's Green, where she worked as an assistant manager. We walked up as far as Grafton Street together and I got her phone number. I left it a bit late to ring her and, by the time I did, to invite her to a poetry reading in the National Gallery, she was otherwise engaged. As with a lot of things in my life, I had given up and then received a nudge from some place. A year later, I got an email from her asking if I'd fancy a cup of coffee. We met in Starbucks in Blackrock in the middle of the heaviest snow for years. We went to Sligo a few weeks later and it was still snowing (maybe it stopped in between). It took us about six hours to get there but when we did, Ben Bulben was resplendent in white. An omen, I suppose.

Rita quit her job in the bank just before we got married. How's that for old-fashioned? The interesting thing is that she gave her job up for pretty much the same reason I've given up journalism: disgust with the way things had been going. Once she'd loved it, and was the public face of Bank of Ireland in their adverts, but now she hated going in to be harangued by some wagon half her age about targets and the like. Banks, which used to exist to serve customers, have latterly seen themselves as being involved in the speculation game, more interested in flogging 'products' than in preserving the goodwill that kept them going in good times and bad.

Rita and I seem to spend our whole lives gallivanting around places, laughing our heads off at our good fortune, only occasionally finding ourselves at home. Everyone loves Rita, including Marian, Teresa and Margaret. She lights up every room she walks into. She has a teeming family of sisters and their husbands and children, who are a tremendous bonus of fun and affection.

I think if you were to come back now, you'd disown me and adopt Patrick, her brother. Despite your best efforts to turn me into some kind of craftsman, or even handyman, I just don't seem capable of sustaining my interest beyond the level of emergency interventions directed at making things function at the bare minimum level, then going back to whatever I'd been doing when the emergency broke out. Still, all my life, I've envied men who could make and build things, and manipulate the earth the way it's meant to be. Patrick is one of those, and you were another.

I don't know if I ever confided to you that, when I was a child, I had a Swiss Family Robinson fantasy – a deep yearning to end up in some extreme (but undefined) conditions and have to survive entirely on my own ability to exploit what Providence put there. Maybe just for a week, mind. At the age of eight and nine, I read Johann David Wyss's book and have never quite gotten over it. I wanted to be shipwrecked and have to grow stuff and discover things in the wild and fashion things from all kinds of improbable materials, like arrows made from bamboo and candlesticks from dried reeds. You could have been the father in the story, always fixing things and building things and planting things, though you had a tendency to leave things half-done for years on end while you went around complaining that you hadn't time to finish them.

I was deeply affected for a long time by the idea of growing things. I remember the first time I came upon a stalkful of potatoes in Roddy's dump, that spot behind the wall along the back road where they used to chuck everything and let it rot or rust or remain. I found all kinds of stuff in there: discarded books and magazines, decrepit but useable toys, a broken-down electric heater that I used for a make-believe fire in a tree house, a carpet that did service in the same cause, bedsteads that I used to hold up the nets behind the goals in Hackers Lane. But one day I noticed something that reminded me of the potato stalks I'd seen on Granny's farm in Cloonyquin: that luxurious verdant vibrancy that I'd always thought of as announcing, like a rainbow, the riches underneath. I pulled it up and out popped about a dozen of the biggest, whitest spuds I'd ever seen. They really were astonishingly large: the potash in the dumped ashes from Roddy's living room fire had blown them up into beauts. I took them in to Mammy and we had them for the next day's dinner, and from then on I was hooked. That was when I started to tame our garden, first planting spuds and then cabbage and onions. I remember you watching me thoughtfully and then coming home with stakes and wire to make a fence. You also had some baby trees you wanted to nurse at home for a while before planting them out in Aughaderry for the Haw's cattle to munch on. I made a kind of pen in the middle of the garden to accommodate the trees and give me enough space for a few drills of vegetables. I made a hames of putting in the stakes, which had to be set in concrete, and which ended up even more unruly looking than the trees – being just about solid enough to hold the wire up. But I couldn't believe how easy the gardening part was, not to mention fun. Later on, after poring over your gardening books for weeks without respite, I tried my hand at carrots and turnips, but with rather less success: too many stones in the daub underneath. My pride and joy was a rhubarb crown I got from Ned Rock.

My favourite part was building a compost heap, a science all to itself: grass cuttings, eggshells, potato peelings, used teabags, horse dung from Roddy's stables, all metamorphosing into the most beautiful jet-black humus. I think I got about two seasons out of it before Uncle Martin, bored with laughing at my incompetence, took over and turned it into the most amazing vegetable garden I've seen to date.

At various points in my life, I've embraced the obsession in different ways. Not long after I came to Dublin in the mid-1980s, I rented a house just off Grand Canal Street and tamed the wilderness out the back. The first year was a huge success, but in the summer of the second year I got notice to quit, and lost nearly everything. My cottage in Dalkey had a garden the size of a tea towel, so my survivor fantasy had been in hibernation in the meantime. A few years ago, I rented an allotment from a guy who was managing an experiment they were conducting in the park behind Rita's house in Booterstown. For the first time in a quarter century, I had a plot of potatoes – King Edwards mainly – as well as carrots, turnips, cabbages, lettuce, curly kale, onions and, briefly, a couple of broccoli plants. Altogether it was only about enough for a fortnight of dinners, but in my head I was Robinson Crusoe. The plot was just about big enough to bury a baby giraffe. But, since it had never been cultivated before, there was as much work preparing it as I invested in the far larger spaces I'd worked back at home. The plot was dry, with heavy soil and not much light due to overhanging trees. But a few weeks of taming it rebooted my frontiersman bug. For a while I was at serious risk of becoming one of those gardening bores who ring in to ask Gerry Daly about carrot fly.

Shop-buying Muggles will never understand, but gardening draws you into yourself in search of your secret inner-Adam. There's no meal quite like one for which you've cooked something you've grown yourself. It's not so much a matter of making one carrot grow where none grew before, as it is having a role in the miracle of creation and realising how small that role is. Within a day or two of starting, I'd reverted to childhood and was looking forward with enthusiasm to the collapse of the euro (this was 2013), which would enable me to realise my fantasy of self-sufficiency at last.

As well you know, virtually everything about growing stuff is counter-intuitive to someone who hasn't done it: the fact, for example, that 90 % of a plant is generated from the carbon dioxide emanating from the soil, but otherwise frittered away in the air. I have always been fascinated to know you can overdo the hard labour, that the best approach is to leave things as much as possible in the hands of whatever force or god you think responsible for making this strange planet of muck and soul and enabling it to spin around under its own steam for the past 13 and three-quarter billion years.

My favourite gardening book is one you got from your gardening book club, *The Lazy Gardener's Guide*, by Geoffrey Gilbert. It arrived around the time I started my first plot at home, and hit precisely my level of competence and application, a veritable philosophy of horticulture. There's a chapter, for instance, entitled 'How to Keep Soil in Good Heart', which describes the role of worms in digging the garden. In an average-sized suburban vegetable garden, perhaps about one-tenth of an acre, the worms sift, fertilise and bring to the surface a ton of soil every year. A clever gardener, instructs Gilbert, lets the worms do the work.

The book also offers succinct and beautiful potted explanations of things like photosynthesis, aeration and the workings of chemicals in the growth process – answering questions like, 'Is the ammonia we smell in the stable any different from that manufactured in the factory?' (No.)

But still, because our allotment was on the outer fringes of Dublin 4, I wanted to be as 'organic' as possible and avoid pesticides and artificial fertilisers. Another tip Gilbert offers is to provide decoy food for slugs and other pests, rather than take on the impossible task of elimination. I've discovered that, by planting cabbage at both ends of the plot, you lose only those at one end. The snails and slugs converge on one batch and stuff themselves stupid, never thinking of looking further afield. My Savoys were riddled but the curly kale was untouched.

Naturally, I had a scarecrow, a Bart Simpson lookalike constructed of a sweeping brush, an alligator mask and a Dunnes Stores windcheater. I'm not sure he earned his keep, but he looked the part. Certainly I know he stood idly by when someone came along one evening with a sharp knife and chopped away my broccoli heads – one of the downsides of having your allotment in such a disreputable area. That experience is probably what mostly led to me not taking the allotment a second year. My aim has been to start up a proper garden in Lislary, now that I have time on my hands, but now Róisín and Leo seem like they're going to save me the heavy lifting.

As I say, Rita's brother Patrick is more focused and capable in these matters. He works in computers but at weekends goes west to Mayo, where he grows stuff and keeps chickens. He has a workshop in a big shed, with drills and welders and vices of the iron variety. He's built an impressive-looking trailer with engine, transmission and steering, for use on the bog. The locals think he's for the birds, but get enormous delight from observing his style of frontiersman adventuring.

He cuts turf – by hand. He may be one of the last dozen or so people in the country using the sleán, which I need to explain to people in Dublin is like a spade with a knife-edged wing, which cuts the sod. The first year we started going down there, he gave me a bag of his turf, and, in keeping with tradition, I promised him 'a couple of days on the bog'.

Although I am, of course, a jumped-up bogger, from a town left down in the middle of a bog, I hadn't been 'on the bog' for 40 years. I remember the experience of going to the bog with you like it was yesterday: Lisananny, a blaze of purple in late summer; the precise flavour of ham sandwiches and TK Lemonade, a taste I've never found again; the quiet tumult of curlews, cuckoos, pheasants and sudden breezes: the bog cotton, lichens, the overwhelming yellow of the whin; the sunshine, which seemed eternal. I remember submitting to the expanse of the day before me, caught in that peaceful, unearthly place, and no choice but to surrender to work and weather and your notions of when to call time.

Patrick won't mind me saying his turf is 'only middling'. There are good veins to be found, but mainly it's light and spongy, good for kindling a quick fire, but in need of support from heavier artillery for the cold winter nights.

Working in Dublin during the week, and consequently ill-placed to exploit sudden benevolences in the weather, Patrick has constructed what at first sight appears an over-elaborate method for drying his turf, a system of stacked pallets which allows the wind to sweep through the turf and dry it in no time. It eliminates several of the 'traditional' stages of turf-harvesting – footing, clamping and stacking – reducing the process to two stages: cutting and palleting, which sounds almost sacrilegious. The pallet method at first created great merriment among neighbours, but now they watch more carefully as Patrick bags his turf in late summer, while theirs rots on the bog. It's all perfectly legal, since Patrick's bog, near Kilmaine, is unaffected by EU habitat directives. As far as I can see, he's the last man around there cutting by hand.

A couple of times, as we were working away – him cutting and me filling the pallets –the Hopper machine came and cut, it seemed, every other plot in the bog. 'Cut' is the wrong word. An excavator comes in firstly to dig a deep hole, and then the Hopper sucks the turf up from below, mixes the good stuff and the only-middling stuff and lays it down in straight lines of impressive blackstuff. But such methods leave holes, which fill with water, pock-marks after six million years of ecological osmosis. I've also noticed that the Hopper can't avoid mixing bits of chalk or limestone in with the turf, which causes outbreaks of spitting when it comes to the burning stage. The very first morning we tackled it, we filled 10 pallets in about two hours – enough for a month of winter weekends.

James Kilbane from Achill came by to inspect our progress. Kindly, he declared our turf suitable for bedding down the fire at night, enabling it to smoulder like Gabriel Byrne until morning when it was raked over and rekindled. He explained the method of the turf meitheal down Achill way, where four men might work in harmony, 10 minutes apart, cutting differ-ent layers, one man throwing the turf up onto the bank, another casting out onto the cutaway section or 'hollow bog'. Gently, he hinted that vir-tually everything we were doing was wrong. We've been cutting too wide – 20 or so sods at a time. Six or seven is about right, he explained. "Or is it a motorway ye're makin?" We'd been cutting two spits deep, but James said to go at least another spit down, maybe two. "By the fourth spit you're into the Bronze Age," he declared. "That's where ye'll find the best stuff."

Not long after James left, we espied two men tottering over the hori-zon – neighbours of Patrick's down there, a father and son, John and Michael Maughan, come to check on our progress.

John, in his late 70s, cut turf on this bog 40 years before, though now-adays they 'get' their turf with the Hopper. He's one of those great but anonymous Irishmen you might sometimes think extinct, but who live still out there in the countryside: deep wells of wisdom, memory and quiet irony. Their intelligence of things comes from way back, an absolute knowing with little scope for being added to now.

John was torn between his amusement at our incompetence and nostalgia for his own time. He waved his hand up the vague, overgrown line of an ancient bank. He would have cut that in a couple of days, he said, all 200 hundred yards of it. He showed us how to cut the turf inwards rather than down, to go with the grain and avoid the sods breaking. He gazed towards the horizon, scanning for a church steeple he remembered. They would come here at 9.00 am, he says, and work all day, with half an hour for lunch, when they would talk and play and laugh. 'Our only time would be the Angelus bell from the chapel beyond.'

He had a way of making us laugh at our own expense, without any hint of insult. His amusement seemed to simmer inside him, emerging only as understatement and gentle drollery. His only concession was for the pallets, which he allowed were an excellent innovation. Then it went downhill. He surveyed the sods on the topmost pallet. "Jayes that's bad turf!" he exclaimed. "It's like loafeens of bread. Ye'd want to wrap that stuff in paper bringing it home in case it'd get wet with a shower!"

Then he thought to go deeper into the question of the pallets, picking one up. "Was that a bit of a chicken coop?" he dryly enquired. Patrick said he'd made them specially. "Jayes," declared John, "you're an awful man!"

"Would ye not get the Hopper in?" his son Michael asked. I got the feeling that they were a little bit torn between us and the Hopper, as though by a bad conscience. Patrick explained that we'd prefer to do it the old way, keep the tradition going. John gazed dreamily towards the horizon: "Yah, yah, yah … keep the tradition going, yah." The chuckles threatened to burst out of him. Tradition, I gathered, is a luxury in those parts.

Those days with Patrick on the bog were a kind of awning, not just into the past but into the continuous moment that is infinity. On the bog I felt time collapse in me and the world rearrange itself around me. There was no past or death or presence or absence. Everything you had been to me remained, as did you, as real as if you were standing beside me.

I am unable to convey to you, at least to my own satisfaction, the sense I have of the wealth of legacies you have given me. In a world disintegrating at every seam, I find that my sense of the integrity of reality intensifies as I grow older, so that, as the political and media-described worlds disintegrate into incoherence, I find myself in a solid and continuous place that is both infinitely greater than those artificial and mendacious constructions and contained like a sparrow's nest within them. I know no other father could have given me this capacity to walk through the world so lightly.

I was just into my 40s when, one evening in the late summer of 1995, I came to realise that you had not raised us to live in the constructed world, but to alert us to its falsity and give us the means to survive even after we had seen through it. Everything you taught us was directed at this intention. I was driving home to the Grey Castle, with Mammy, my sister Margaret and her two boys, Barry and Ben. It was coming dusk as we travelled the ten or 12 miles from the Douglas Hyde Centre near Frenchpark, where I had been speaking about the effects of the 1840s famines on Roscommon, it being the start of the 150th anniversaries of those calamities. It had been a long and tremendous summer, day after day of scorching sun, maybe a match for the summer of 2018, when I finally got to finish the present book. If I live to be a hundred, I shall never forget that evening, the five of us driving in pure silence from Mullen to Cloonarragh, across a landscape that might have been the plains and bogs of heaven, glancing off Fairymount as our heads swivelled to stare at the radiant gorse, purple as the lining of a bishop's coat, the whin yellow as a virgin yolk, the colours intensified by weeks of heat and light and silence. Through Cloonfinglas and Cloonsheever, by the bog of Lissannany where we had footed turf as children, and then on to the town, a road you had travelled in the evenings, six days a week, for more than 50 years. I remembered us sitting on the turf bank, drinking our cold tea from Guinness bottles, you instructing us in the fine arts of footing and clamping. I could feel the abrasiveness of the turf on my fingers, searing and tickling at once. I was at the time going through a minor purgatory due to the publicity surrounding the imminent birth of your granddaughter, and I knew that Mammy was silently sharing that place of fire and learning with me. Nothing was said in that car that evening, nothing of beauty or tradition or Hyde or you, but we knew by the time we hit town that we had that evening crossed no earthly estate. And I knew that this was the estate you had reared me to live in, and that everything would therefore turn out all right. I had this strange and, in some ways, unsettling insight: that I could never accommodate to a false idea of this world, or the Irish part of it, no matter how powerful its proponents, no matter what the cost.

11

My Dog

I don't recall us ever discussing it, but I had wanted to be a writer, or, if not that, a journalist, from the age of 11 or 12. I've never considered journalism to be 'proper' writing. It's pretty much all reactive and ephemeral and occurs more out of the need of the space to be filled than the need in the writer to fill spaces. I think that, at the beginning, I saw journalism as a stepping stone to the real thing, but it tends not to work like that, for two reasons. One is that journalism takes you over, body, mind and spirit, drawing you eyeball-to-eyeball with a superficial image of the world. The other is that, in a certain sense, journalism is the opposite of real writing, in that it happens in a different part of the head. I think of it as happening immediately behind the forehead, whereas proper writing happens way down the back, mostly while you're asleep. If you keep doing stuff that holds you in the forehead zone, it becomes almost impossible to get to the real stuff.

I had no plan for my life and still don't. To be completely honest with you, I believe that, of the two of us, you were the only one thinking of my future around the time I left school. There was something strange in the air then – perhaps some new agitation in the hearts of the young brought about by the aftershocks of the 1960s, which hit Castlerea, the Grey Castle, round about 1972. I have no idea how I picked this up, but it never for a moment occurred to me that I might have to do anything 'ordinary' for a living. It wasn't so much that I rejected such an option in favour of pursuing some more exotic lifestyle or profession: I rejected it in favour of doing nothing and not giving the slightest thought to what I might do with my life. Any ambitions I had were of the vaguest kind: I wanted, I think, to be George Best and John Lennon combined in one body, doing songs like David Bowie's. Whatever was in the air then, we really did think that something enormous was going to happen to us, and were therefore poorly adapted to reality when it hit us later on.

The trouble was that I wasn't much of a musician or a singer, and, as our late neighbour Peiler would from time to time remind me, I couldn't kick snow off a rope. Writing was about the only thing I had any talent or aptitude for.

I think it helped a great deal that I managed to avoid going to school more than the odd day. Lying home in bed, while you were out on your runs, I read a lot, sneaking into that roomful of books you'd picked up at auctions, while you were out of the house. I don't know if you ever went through those books, but they didn't amount to a bad selection: everything from Tolstoy to James Bond, via Dickens, Shakespeare and Tales of the Arabian Nights. I read as many of them as I could find my way into, as well as lots of children's books Marian would bring from the library for me: Just William, Enid Blyton, Billy Bunter, Jennings and Darbyshire, Biggles. I remember reading *Little Dorrit* when I was seven or eight, though I took it up recently and couldn't remember a thing about it. The book I most loved was, as I've said, *The Swiss Family Robinson*, but I tried reading it for Róisín a few years ago and it just didn't seem to ignite – for either of us.

You never let us go to the cinema, thinking it a bad influence or something. I used to watch enviously the other lads playing Cowboys and Indians on the way home from the matinées at the Castle Cinema, which you may be pleased to hear is now in ruins. The first picture I saw was Ben Hur, which we went to from school. I couldn't make head nor tail of it. I remember going to see *The Greatest Story Ever Told* and coming out confused as to why it was called a 'story'. The first picture that really inspired me was *Let it Be*, a kind of requiem for the Beatles, the first movie I went to because I wanted to.

In all the 14 years I theoretically spent there, I learned nothing at school except how to avoid it and how to be afraid. I was fortunate in having that famous bad chest, which was good for about two weeks out of every month. Because of my bronchitis, you were hyper-cautious about letting me go outdoors, in case of a relapse. The two most frightening words I ever heard you use were 'relapse' and 'pneumonia', which in my head I spelt 'newmonia', but otherwise I was happy enough to be unwell. I don't believe you were aware of the extent of my talent for summoning up totally convincing illnesses in myself. At the end of a fortnight AWOL from school, and facing Mammy's implacable resolve that it was time to get back to 'normal', I would awake at dawn on a Monday and concentrate like Uri Geller until I conjured up a pain in my stomach. Once, after I was dispatched to school after several weeks in which I had exhibited symptoms of more than half the entries in your medical dictionary, I reluctantly set off about three yards behind one of my sisters, I think probably Teresa, I knew you were due to come back into town from your morning run around that time, so I walked as slowly as I could until I saw the mailcar come into sight on the Post Office hill. As you drove on to one end of the bridge and I came on to the other, I started to speed up and at the same time dragged my feet, toes first, until I succeeded in tripping myself. I did quite a bit of damage, enough to be put in the mailcar and carried back to Mammy, good for another fortnight of bed and books.

On the rare occasions when I ran out of symptoms and had to face another week or two of the routine brutality and sarcasm of the Brothers, I found myself pretty much bored with everything. Although I hadn't been following any formal programme, and allowing for a couple of blind spots that resulted, I was mostly light years ahead of the level my classmates had reached. I was reading Tolstoy; they were learning about the cat that sat on the mat. Although my attendance record improved marginally when I went to secondary school, I don't think I chalked up a full year's worth of schooldays during all my time with the Marist Brothers. At the end of third class, Brother Terence sardonically congratulated me for breaking all previous records: 20 days' attendance in a single term.

Of the days I actually attended, there was hardly a day that I didn't get a few belts of some implement or other. One Brother had a league table for corporal punishment, awarding penalty points for failures or misdemeanours, dishing out the punishments over the following week. You might have 100 'slaps' to get over the course of a week, but the interesting aspect was that you could take a few whenever you felt like it and he would knock them off your score. Several of the most infamous developers in Ireland were past pupils of his, which must tell something or other about the value of education. I remember one time that brother telling us that, if we didn't want to get slapped, all we had to do was bring in a note from home – in which case he would decline to have anything further to do with us: we could sit over at the periphery of the class and rot for all he cared. The interesting thing here was that the lads who brought in notes were all from Arm and Church Road, the 'cottages' as you used to call them. Some of those lads were pretty thick, but one or three of them were at least as bright as anyone else. After they brought in the note, they were left to their own devices, so long as they kept quiet, which generally they did. The rest of us, reluctant to broach the issue of the note with our parents, continued to take our chances with the league tables. I'll be honest: I've always thought that, if I'd come to you looking for a note like that, you'd have ran me.

On the other hand, that selfsame Brother, the one with the league table, was also responsible for me starting to write. One day, he held an impromptu contest for the pupil with the best sentence in his essay. He gave us 15 minutes to perfect our most promising sentences. I forget most of mine, but I do recall it was about a swallow and finished with the words 'invisible to the naked eye'. The Brother praised it so much that it occurred to me that this might be something I could do with myself.

Two or three years later, in secondary school, I achieved a dead heat with Enid Blyton in an essay competition. Because the other guy was younger than me, it was decided that he would get the first prize of five guineas, and I'd get a 'consolation' prize of two guineas. But the worst of it was that it was his essay that would be published in the school

< 136 >

magazine, which was, fairly appropriately, called *Guff*. It was later discovered that he had cogged his entire essay from one of Blyton's adventure series stories and hadn't even bothered to change the name of the parrot – Kiki. My essay was about road accidents. It was pretty pedestrian, to be honest, but what riled me most of all about the incident was that, because the culprit was a Big Shot, they didn't blow the whistle on him, but waited until the next year to cast a cloud over everyone by saying that, since the dispensation of trust had been betrayed, we would have to write our essays in class that year. (The previous year we'd been allowed to write the essay at home over a weekend.) Determined to win this time, I wrote my essay over the weekend, learned it off by heart and came in on Monday morning and wrote it straight out from memory. To take the piss, I decided to write under the title My Dog, a rite-of-passage essay from senior infants. This time I won first prize and made it into *Guff*, where they changed the title to Dogs and printed my name upside down. I often think that that episode prefigured my entire career as a journalist.

I think if my life had depended on the Leaving Cert, it would have been over before it began. But it took me some time to come to this conclusion, and for a good few years I had something of a complex about my academic failure. I don't need to tell you that I barely scraped the Leaving first time out, and made two further half-hearted attempts that got me nowhere.

The first attempt at repeating – in the immediate next year – I abandoned after a row with a priest who came in to teach us Christian Doctrine. I got a job then as a railway clerk, and decided to put the academic life behind me. But, after a few months sorting the consignment dockets covering the bacon going out from Claremorris Bacon Factory, I started having nightmares about, of all things, the Leaving Cert. I would wake up in a cold sweat having failed it again in my nightmares, and ruined my life on that account. This went on for several years, despite my waking hours' resolve that I was better off without it. Eventually, as you know, I left my 'good job' with CIE and joined a pirate radio station, which

< 137 >

folded within months. For this brief period, I was Station Manager and Head of News at Mid-West Radio, Castlerea, one of the earliest pirate radio stations outside the main urban centres. The station closed after about six months due to insurmountable technical difficulties (we were attempting to broadcast on AM, which was at the time overloaded with stations). It subsequently re-opened in Ballyhaunis, County Mayo, broadcasting on FM, and went on to become one of the most successful local stations in the country.

After a few months as a band roadie and a petrol pump attendant, the nightmares grew worse and worse. My worst job offer was as petrol pump attendant and tyre changer at a garage in Goatstown, for 20 quid a week. It would have been slavery. Later that day I got word I'd got a job in Murphy Chambers of Dundrum, just filling petrol, no tyres to change. I even had a little hut with an electric kettle, and 70 quid a week. I stuck it out for a few months but eventually decided to abandon Dublin and head back to the Grey Castle.

That was when I decided to give the Leaving another go, with a view to getting into Trinity as a mature student. I set about it with great seriousness and application, taking English, economics and, I think, history. I was provisionally accepted as a mature student by the English Department in Trinity, and had an interview with someone in the Philosophy Department, which was inconclusive. He asked me to write an essay entitled, 'Can we have objective knowledge of right and wrong?' I told him, 'If I knew that, I probably wouldn't need to study philosophy?'

I spent three years trying to get into *Hot Press*, having been staggered when it emerged in the summer of 1977, brimful of the kind of stuff about music and life and everything that I felt I might write myself if I could escape from what I was becoming. I was a clerk in the railway station in Westport when the first issue came out. When I saw it I had this weird feeling that I wished it hadn't come out, that my world would be easier to live in if it didn't exist, that now this magazine, coming out every fortnight, would accuse me as I curved towards orthodoxy and normality.

< 138 >

I was spending most of my time polluting good paper with meaningless recordings of inconsequential consignments going out and coming in, the rest selling train tickets in the box office, or 'booking out' trains, as it was formally described. I was quite capable of living in that world and convincing myself in my head that I was some kind of artist or pop star, wearing my hair long, dressing up in bomber jackets and loon pants at the weekend, shaping around the dance halls (you were right about all that). *Hot Press* put it up to me to make the transition from fantasy to reality. Writers like Bill Graham, Declan Lynch, Liam Mackey and Dermot and Niall Stokes really got me wired. They were so good I didn't think I could ever measure up, and yet so inspirational that I needed at least to try.

The value of *Hot Press*, in my view, was that it helped open up a new frontier in Irish journalism to enable a celebration not just of rock 'n' roll but of the things rock 'n' roll was about. It tried to do this in the language of rock 'n' roll, with the attitudes of rock ' n' roll, which was really something very strange and unexpected when it first appeared over the horizon in the 1970s. The main attraction in the music for me was that it contained sounds that seemed already to exist within me, but nobody had previously thought about making audible. It was the first phenomenon, I think, that suggested itself as offering an exclusivity from the world immediately around – from you, Mammy, the house, the street, the town. I guess it was part of some 'burgeoning youth culture', as the sociologists put it, but the point about it was not the idea of that culture but the nature of that culture. The music had arisen, via a series of unexpected impregnations, from the meeting of various roots music – blues, gospel, skiffle, rhythm 'n' blues, country and even jazz. It had gone off into a multiplicity of exotic directions, but at its heart it was a music of things fundamental: a kind of coded way of talking about stuff that you couldn't say straight out because you thought you were the only one with weird shit like that going on. It was also, among its fundamentalisms, about sex – sex in all its exotic variations and possibilities. This seemed to be the main energy behind the music, though as you listened to some of the older artists as they grew even older, you could hear this energy morph into something else: into questions about everything, including fundamentalism and sex.

I dabbled a bit in the guitar and songwriting. I wasn't shaping up to be much of a musician, although I had a bit of a talent for writing songs, having collaborated (writing the words, mostly) with Tiger Taylor (he'd played with the Eire Apparent, who played support on several tours with the Jimi Hendrix Experience), Mick O'Hagan (brother of Johnny Logan), and my friend from the Grey Castle, Tommy Moran. Now I had the possibility of a different way of combining words and music.

My first attempt to get published actually succeeded, which was both a great and a bad thing. It was a review of a Horslips gig in the Midnight Club, Ballaghaderreen, on New Year's Eve 1977. It was a fairly run-of-the-mill gig but I spiced it up with a spot of creative writing, after a drunk lad found himself on the stage and bassist Barry Devlin gave him a playful shove with his shoe and sent him back where he came from. I put the episode at the centre of my review, took a liberty with the drunk lad's crewcut and called him a punk, and scolded Horslips for doublethink: on the one hand nodding to CBGB's by playing 'Blitzkrieg Bop' and with the other foot kicking punks off the stage. I came to know Devlin later on and was relieved to discover that he was confused between myself and another John who used to write for *Hot Press*. Years later, launching a book for the band's former drummer Eamon Carr, I checked the room for Devlin and, confident of his absence, related this account of my sensationalist entry into Irish journalism. Immediately there was a whoop from a dark corner and Devlin emerged shaking his fist.

After that initial triumph, there was a long lean period – more than a year – when nothing I submitted made it into print. Then I had a couple of snippets published in quick succession, then nothing else as the 1980s trundled towards me. With my 25th birthday in the offing, I thought my goose was cooked. It didn't once occur to me to simply make contact with the Editor of *Hot Press*, even though it might be said

< 140 >

that, having had some pieces published, I had the necessary standing to do so. I pondered long and hard the reasons why some of the pieces I'd submitted had not been used. They seemed good enough to me, better than a lot of the stuff in the paper. In the end, I came to the conclusion that the problem was that I was writing everything out in longhand when the conditions of the modern world demanded typewritten scripts. As it would turn out, I was completely wrong about this, since, when I eventually went to work full-time in *Hot Press*, I found that nobody there used a typewriter, except occasionally Bill Graham.

I decided to give it one final lash. I would learn to type and submit one review in typescript. I spent the autumn of 1980 with the qwerty card propped up in front of me at the kitchen table, after you went to bed. When I had achieved some middling competence, I wrote a review of a band called Bagatelle when they came to play at the Fountain Blue in Longford. They were big at the time, a slightly R&B-ish MoR band who'd had a few radio hits over the previous couple of years and were turning into quite a phenomenon out in the country. I spent days composing the review, and several further days carefully typing it up. I was happy with the result and felt that I had overcome the final obstacle to regular publication. A week or so later I bought *Hot Press* and nearly collapsed when I saw the review of Bagatelle. Yes!

Actually, no. The review was by Bill Graham, their star writer. It had all been for nothing.

After the Bagatelle heartbreak, I actually gave up, deciding the fates or the gods were against me. I concentrated on studying to repeat my Leaving Cert with a view to getting into Trinity. But, three months later, the day I returned home from my stalemated interview in the TCD Philosophy Department, I received a typed letter from Niall Stokes, the Editor of *Hot Press*, saying how much he'd liked the Bagatelle review and regretted he'd been unable to use it. Would I like to write some reviews and interviews for the paper?

In *Hot Press* we were trying to replicate in print the spirit of the music we loved. We were, to a degree, heavily influenced by UK music papers like the *NME*, *Melody Maker* etc., but really our objective was to produce a music paper that, unlike the ones that preceded *Hot Press*, was not shite. *Hot Press* was quintessentially an Irish paper – most of the time anyway – seeking to promote and celebrate local music, and there was a strong sense of the inter-connectedness of roots Irish music and rock 'n' roll. Bob Dylan never made a great secret of the fact that he had lifted most of his earlier tunes from folk songs he heard sung by the Clancys and the McPeakes.

So *Hot Press*, essentially, was the end of my formal education. I again abandoned the Leaving Cert. I thought the nightmares would come back, but they never did. The sense I have, meeting people who've been educated to third level, is that, generally speaking, they've been immunised against the subjects they've studied. It's like we teach them a little dangerous thinking to make sure they don't pick up the full-blown condition. I meet people with Masters in Philosophy, and they don't appear to be able to use the things they've learned in any useful way. Similarly with economics. I learned more economics listening at the back of an Inter Cert class that I wasn't even part of than most Irish economists seem to have encountered in the totality of their educations. Going around Irish universities, participating in L&H debates and so forth, the thing that strikes me most often is the absence of a genuine diversity of ideas and opinions. I was unaccountably glad when Róisín finally made it to Trinity, and I sometimes feel nostalgia for the university life I never had, but I rarely meet anyone who makes me feel I missed out on something by not going. My sense of things is that, in order to become a full citizen and a free human spirit, you have to overcome the attempts of the education system, on behalf of society, to turn you into another cog for some wheel of theirs. I've always told Róisín that the purpose of the education system was to make her turn out like everyone else, and her job was to make sure they didn't succeed.

12

The Plot Thickens

On Monday 6 January 2014, five days before the interview with Rory O'Neill on *The Saturday Night Show*, I received an email from Una Mullally, who had recently become a regular columnist with *The Irish Times*. I had never met or spoken to Mullally, though I had been aware that she had engaged in frequent attacks on me while a columnist with the doomed *Sunday Tribune* some years before. I had never actually read any of these attacks, but had been told the approximate gist of them. Mullally was an arch feminist and also a gay activist and, as would later emerge, a close ally and confidante of Rory O'Neill.

In her email to me, Mullally wrote:

Hi John,

Happy New Year! Hope you're keeping well.

I'm getting in touch because I'm currently writing a book about the movement for marriage equality in Ireland. It's an oral history and will be published later this year by the History Press.

At the moment, I'm gathering interviews from as broad a spectrum as I can, across politics, LGBT groups, media, and so on. I'm also keen to have dissenting voices in the oral history as part of the narrative as told by those who impacted on the movement in a major or minor way in their own words. I'm hoping that my approach in casting the net wide will give a fair, detailed and representative account of the legal, political, campaigning and media discourse on the issues of civil partnership, same-sex marriage and so on over the past decade or so.

I was wondering if I could grab a half hour or so of your time over the next few weeks for an interview. I'm keen to include as many diverse opinions as possible on the issue.

Let me know what you think, I'd really appreciate your input.

Best wishes,

Una

On the following day, 7 January, I responded as follows:

Dear Una,

I'd be happy to help, but I'm not sure that my voice will necessarily service by way of balance or ballast.

In principle, I'm not really bothered about what's called gay marriage. I do happen to believe that marriage is, ipso facto, something that happens between a man and a woman, but this is a position in principle, and in reality what is nowadays called marriage has long since moved beyond this. My remaining issues relate only to children, which is to say adoption. I believe we have inverted the pyramid of adoption logic from a provision designed to provide a child who had lost his or her parents through death or other calamity with a home situation approximating to a normative family, to something that is really calculated to commodify the child for the benefit of couples who wish to 'have a family' though they cannot have children of their own. My objection to this sustains regardless of whether the couple in question is heterosexual or homosexual. I believe that drifts in this regard are leading to unprecedented evils in a world in which, in the future, the idea of honouring the biological link between a parent and a child may come to be regarded as weird and puzzling. That troubles me. The State will be the parent of all children, and day-to-day parenting carried out by nominated parties on the basis of an ideological programme. I'm glad I won't be around for most of this.

You may be surprised to hear that I don't have any theological objection to gay marriage. I have disappointed many's the TV and radio researcher in this regard. I've refused almost all requests to become involved in this debate, partly because my position is not what people expect and partly because of the bullying which has characterised the discussion from the beginning. It's not that I mind being called names, but there needs to be a prize worth winning or preserving in order to justify running such gauntlets, and I'm not sure that this is the case here.

My argument is fundamentally (as it were) about the maintenance of the blood link between parent and child, which is really transcendent of the marriage issue per se. I have a child but am not married, and I have never accepted any suggestion by anyone or by society that I have an inferior right to a relationship with my child on this account. I've won this argument at the personal level and I'm happy now to leave it at that. In fact, now that I think if it, I'm probably better suited for filing under 'Anti-marriage' than under 'Anti- Gay Marriage' ...

I certainly don't make these arguments from any of the conventional positions, least of all a Catholic one – although it's no secret that I am a Catholic. I suppose that, deep down, there is a metaphysical basis to the insistence on the primacy of a biological connection between a child and parent, but I don't see the necessity to couch such arguments in metaphysics when there is still just about enough common sense about to sustain them. And I know all the 'what about' arguments here – about exceptions and de facto situations, but my position on these is that, in virtually any argument about virtually anything, this tactic can be used to disintegrate the normative approach in favour of laissez faire. I believe that arguments should be made in principle and then reasonable arrangement made to deal in a human way with exceptions, rather than having the exceptions dictate the norms.

Actually, I haven't been impressed by Catholic objections to gay marriage per se, and even less so concerning recent Catholic protests about the rights of children to know both parents. My interest in this subject has stemmed naturally from my work over the past

< 145 >

18 years or so in trying to convince the world that there's a purpose to fatherhood and that it's damaging to children to banish fathers from their lives. In as far as I've been exercised on the issue of gay marriage (and I probably haven't been nearly as exercised as people might think – I've written very sporadically, and usually elliptically, on the subject) it's probably most often to ask why those who claim marriage equality as the 'most important civil/human right of the age' were completely silent on the issue of fathers and children. Check out Eamon Gilmore's contributions under this heading, for example – it won't take long.

But I have been equally dismayed by the attitude of fellow Catholics to this subject, and don't remember meeting many Catholics on the barricades either. Nor can I recall a single priest, bishop or pope in the past 18 years uttering a single sentence that I could even elliptically have interpreted as supportive of the rights of fathers and children to enjoy protected relationships in this (or indeed any) society. I believe that this is down to a rather distorted ideological position arising from the anachronistic na-ture of the Holy Family in the Christian narrative – the fact that St Joseph was the stepfather of Jesus, rather than his 'biological' father. Catholics, in talking up 'family values' have traditionally had to elide this factor, which requires a little diversion from the normative path. (I've written that a few times and managed not to get excommunicated, which just goes to show that the Church is far more tolerant than most liberals believe.) Anyway, when Catholics come looking for me to man their barricades against gay marriage, I find myself torn between remembrance of two silences: theirs and that of the liberals they seek now to face down in the name of protecting families and children.

But nor am I convinced by conventional arguments about the ef-fect gay marriage will have on the 'institution of marriage' as we know it. I don't buy the idea that gay marriage will of itself be so-

< 146 >

cially destructive. Apart from the issue of children, I can't see how it could have any effect whatsoever. Were it not for the adoption issue, I'd possibly have no interest in the issue at all, and my interest in that regard is dwindling also, because I think that what's happening with adoption is part of a far wider agenda concerning children. I believe we're on the cusp of an era of state-trafficking on a massive scale, under the cover of 'child-protection'.

Absent the children aspect, indeed, I don't believe there would be any such thing as marriage, since the sole purpose of marriage was to maintain fathers in close proximity to their children. This is the only interest society has had in poking its nose into the private relationships of citizens. Otherwise, people might do as they pleased within the law, and that's my position also, by and large.

Actually, I believe that marriage has already been fatally undermined – not by gays but by heterosexuals, who have reduced it to a temporary contract with one permanent provision only: the responsibility of one partner to maintain a dependent spouse until death, regardless of any moral principle. In Ireland, what was intended by the electorate, (and voted into law by the smallest of margins) as a last resort remedy to irretrievable marriage breakdown has been delivered as, in effect, divorce-on-demand, with one spouse unilaterally able to approach a court and seek a separation/divorce. And this is typical of what happens all over the world, rendering marriage a meaningless institution – a big day out and little else.

This, sketchily, is my position. I'm not sure it qualifies me as impacting on the gay marriage debate. But if anything in the above strikes you as interesting, I'd be happy to meet up for a chat or to expand on it in further email exchanges.

Best of luck with the book.

Kind regards

John Waters

About lunchtime on Monday 20 January 2014, two weeks after that email exchange and 10 days after Rory O'Neill's appearance on *The Saturday Night Show*, I received a call from a friend who suggested I immediately get hold of a copy of *The Irish Times* and read it. He was referring, he said, to an article by Una Mullally. I went to the home of another friend, where I read the piece online. I was stunned by the content of the article, which included my name in reference to the allegations made on *The Saturday Night Show* by Rory O'Neill, and also put me in the frame with a range of acts and statements of homophobia in past and recent history, including extreme prejudice, oppression and murder. There was a reference to a recent statement by the Russian president Vladimir Putin, to the effect that gays were welcome to come to Moscow for the Winter Olympics, but should 'leave the children alone'.

Mullally's column continued:

In Nigeria, gay men are being rounded up, arrested, tortured and whipped because of their sexuality. We need to fight homophobia internationally and at home.

And later on:

Teachings of the Catholic Church on homosexuality are homophobic. Hopefully these teachings will evolve, as other teachings have. Most of the prominent voices in the Irish media who oppose marriage being extended to same-sex couples represent a Catholic point of view, organisation, or the Church itself. At the time of writing, the performer and businessman, Rory O'Neill, has received four solicitor's letters from associates of the Iona Institute objecting to a brief discussion of subtle homophobia in Irish society on Brendan O'Connor's *Saturday Night Show* on RTÉ. RTÉ also received legal correspondence including a letter on behalf of columnist John Waters leading them to remove the programme from the RTÉ Player.

< 148 >

I was troubled by this on a number of grounds, not least the fact that Mullally had given no indication of her exchange with me of less than a fortnight before, in which I had outlined a very precise and detailed position and, inter alia, made clear that Catholic theology played no part in any issues I might have with the topic of gay marriage or adoption.

I immediately called Denis Staunton, the Deputy Editor of *The Irish Times*, and said I had been alarmed by the splenetic and defamatory context of the Mullally article. I said it repeated *The Saturday Night Show* defamation and lumped me in with Putin and some of the most egregious episodes of anti-gay activity in the history of the world. He said he had not been on duty the previous night and had not yet read the article. He then proceeded to do so as I waited on the phone. Having read the article, he appeared genuinely shocked and said that he would not have published the article had he seen it beforehand. He said he believed the word homophobia should be used 'sparingly'. I said that the word had a 'demonic aura' about it and he agreed. He said, 'Of course it's open to you to take the legal route but naturally I'd much prefer if you didn't.' He proposed that I write a letter to the Editor, for publication on the Letters page. I replied that it might look odd if a columnist in *The Irish Times* was reduced to responding to an attack by another columnist by means of a letter. He said it was now *Irish Times* house policy that columnists not be seen to be 'sniping' at one another in their columns. I said I had heard such a policy being mooted before but found it odd that it only ever came to be mentioned after some other columnist had attacked me. I then told him about the exchange of emails I had had with Mullally and he asked me to send these emails to him, which I immediately did. At about 3.30 pm he called me back and said he had spoken to Mullally, who had told him that she hadn't named me in her submitted copy. Staunton said that it appeared that a sub-editor had added my name. It was unclear at that point whether this happened with Mullally's knowledge or without. Denis Staunton then sent me her original copy, as submitted, which I confirmed did not mention me. I considered the matter and de-

< 149 >

cided that there would be no point in trying to convey even the essence of what had occurred in a letter to the Editor of *The Irish Times*, which would at most amount to about 500 words. I therefore decided to place it in the hands of my lawyer, with a view to obtaining a published apology in *The Irish Times*. In pursuing this course, I had in mind also the desirability of not feeding the frenzy of online commentary by then in train in the wake of *The Saturday Night Show*. Over the next couple of weeks, however, *The Irish Times*'s lawyers responded with the utmost tardiness and prevarication to Kevin Brophy's efforts to resolve the matter, and in due course came up with a 'clarification/retraction' which was even more derisory than the one initially offered by RTÉ.

This was but the beginning of what proved to be a long saga, with many twists and noises in the night. It ended, three years later, with *The Irish Times* paying me a six-figure sum in damages, and almost the same again to cover my legal costs. Like the RTÉ dispute from which it had arisen, this matter could have been resolved in a couple of days, with either a proper retraction and apology or the offer of a half page in the paper to adequately put my side of the story. Instead, the newspaper for which I had worked for nearly a quarter of a century employed every trick in the manual of shoddy journalistic practice in an attempt to deter me from pursuing the matter, including the tactic used to such effect by the national broadcaster: stirring up an online mob against me. For three years they refused to admit that what had happened was wrong, persistently seeking to intimidate me rather than concede that I had never done anything except what I was paid to do, while others who ought to have been my colleagues in that endeavour sought to turn me into their enemy. They stood by while I was savaged by the mob, while I was forced to walk away from my job, and then tried to present me as the villain. For three years, they feinted, threatened, prevaricated and argued as though they had a case. A casual observer might have gathered that they held a hand of aces. Then, seeing that to go to court in such circumstances would have exposed several of their personnel to a process of international shaming, they threw in their cards. In this, yet again, *The Irish Times* demonstrated the dishonesty of journalists and editors seeking to use their privileged access to the instruments of public communication to present to the public an untruthful sense of how defamation works, how they do their work and, above all, their attitude to admitting error and wrongdoing when these occur. From listening to journalists lamenting the 'draconian' libel laws, the uninitiated observer might well be forgiven for thinking that defamation proceedings were always brought against hapless, innocent media organisations, powerless in the face of such an unjust and unbalanced instrument wielded by a plaintiff seeking nothing but to impose silence on these crusaders for truth and decency. As had been demonstrated many times before, the opposite was closer to the truth. What they sought was the right to lie and inflict damage with impunity on someone to whom they were determined to deny any possibility of reply, or any other form of redress, even though either or both could be extended in a form that would cost them nothing but a temporary and merited loss of face.

< 151 >

13

Mau-maus

I hardly need to say that there is no single Sligo landscape. Perhaps the reason for its largely undiscovered condition is that it contains a multiplicity of distinct landscapes. Of these, Maugherow is perhaps both the wildest and the most subtle. It is a strange collision of farmland and wilderness, seeming to persist on the very extremity of civilisation. I have never heard anything like the roar of the Atlantic here in mid-winter, like an awareness factory owned by God. I hardly need to tell you; you were born here. Now I've come back to the place you left nearly a century ago.

The people of the Maugherow peninsula understandably oscillate between a desire to shout the glory of their place from the top of the mountain and an equal but opposite determination to keep to themselves all knowledge of this quintessence of the unspoilt and untamed.

What I love most about this place is that it feels like it is haunted by everything and everyone that ever passed through it, including you. I have been coming here for nearly 20 years, having bought a cottage in a hollow just before the Celtic Tiger found her stride. It was your ghost that brought me here, and the house I bought is no more than a half dozen fields away from your home place in Mount Edward.

As a child, I heard you many times recite the names of places in this locality as though a litany: Ahamlish, Grange, Cliffony, Lissadell and, with a clearing of the throat to give it its full resonance, Maugherow, or 'Mock-her-ow!', the final syllable pronounced to rhyme with 'cow' and with a kind of built-in reverb that caused the name to rattle in your head for a while after you'd heard it.

Strictly speaking, our house is in Lislary. But when I say this to Sligo people, most of them look at me blankly. Our postal address is Ballinfull and our electoral ward is Lissadell North. Maugherow is actually the tiny village up on a hill to the south-west, with a steeple, a school, a huddle of houses – all together a cluster of lights after dark, like a township from a Western directed by Sergio Leone – but the entire locality is known to locals as 'Maugherow' and the name seems to claim everything from Grange to the north, to Drumcliffe on the eastern side.

I find it strange to have ended up here, almost as strange as the fact that we never came down here until we were adults. I'm not sure why. Perhaps you couldn't bear to go back to such a beautiful place, having been forced to leave it? In any event, I spend a lot of time here nowadays, perhaps to make up for all the times you missed.

In the dim and distant past, Maugherow or Machaire Eabha (the plain of Eve) was the name given to the strip of land between the mountains and the sea. Much later this large area was divided into the civil and religious parishes of Drumcliffe and Ahamlish. Maugherow had been part of Drumcliffe since at least 1900, but was made an in-dependent parish in 1972. Apparently, although geographically part of Maugherow, we're in the parish of Ahamlish, which is, for all intents and purposes, Grange.

The house where I now live about half my time is the birthplace of the developer Tom Gilmartin, whose lethal Maugherow memory caused the establishment of the Mahon tribunal. Down the road, an ethical half mile away, is a house once owned by Charles Haughey. It was left to him by a long-time supporter in the 1970s, and there is some dispute locally as to whether he ever actually visited it, although his family spent many a summer there, according to unsworn local testimony. I have heard of the Haughey boys coming there in the summer months, being seen heading up the rocks and over the hill to Ellen's pub, and Charlie's mother Sarah sometimes sitting outside the front door.

The surfing thing is big here. The rugged coastline to the west is a much-favoured haunt of water warriors from all over the world. I have heard it claimed that only Hawaii offers a more challenging swell. This

< 153 >

can seem like an exaggeration until you've spent an idle hour watching these guys dice with a watery grave.

Walking from 'Haughey's house' on the lip of the foreshore, towards what I am gradually coming to call 'home', I am watched from a distance by the beady eye of Ben Bulben, sitting like a slumbering tiger in the distance, gazing across the fields as though precisely in our direction. Ben Bulben has become, by dint of genius and opportunism, the spirit of Yeats, which surveys Maugherow as though it always has, infusing everything with meanings from the socio-patriotic to the metapsychic. I think this is why the area is destined to become, more and more, a magnet for artists and writers – as well as surfers. I suspect the appeal is that people can find here a place that seems to be as Ireland once was, before we lost the plot.

There is a legend around Sligo about the people of Maugherow, who used to be known as 'Mau-maus'. It is said that, on their way into town, they would wash their necks in a drinking trough at Duck Street. A man called Jim Jennings once relayed this slur in The Sligo Champion, referring to the trough as 'the Duck Street mirror'.

We come from a line of people who can be traced back 200 years within this general locality. On my way from SuperValu in Grange, I pass the forge where your mother's father, Thomas Brennan, plied his noble trade. I'm intrigued to find your people are mostly buried in Ahamlish cemetery, in what appears to be a communal grave: it also contains the remains of another family of Waters, and one of Watters, to neither of which do we appear to have been closely related. I have mixed feelings about your being buried in the Grey Castle, where you ended up, somewhat for lack of planning, I think... To the best of my knowledge, you left Mount Edward some time in the late 1920s or early 1930s and, as far as I know, never again went home to the eight-acre farm on which you and your four brothers grew up. There's a story here that remains unexcavated.

Trying to enter the life of another time is a futile exercise – like attempting bi-location by force of will. It is tempting, in seeking to understand the past, to adopt a deterministic position, looking for patterns and reasons by the light of the present, whereas such matters are surely governed by different patterns and reasons existing only by the lights of the distant and unrecoverable moments themselves. I'm not trying to do anything like that here, but simply setting things out and making comparisons and contrasts between different moments with a view to provoking frissons of realisation in myself.

So it's in a matter-of-fact way that I inform myself, and remind you, that you grew up on eight acres two roods and 34 perches in the townland of Mount Edward (also known as Drangan) in the civil parish of Ahamlish, in the Electoral Division of Lissadell North, in the Union of Sligo, on a wet hill overlooking the sea and guarded by the world's most aesthetically pleasing mountain, near the north-west coastal tip of County Sligo. The homestead was a standard long cottage, returned in the 1911 census as a house of the 2nd class. The walls were built of 'stone/brick or concrete' and the house consisted of three occupied rooms, with three front windows, a perishable roof [thatch], and three out-offices [a stable, cow-house and barn]. These three rooms were shared throughout your childhood and adolescence by your parents, your brothers and yourself.

Your father's name was John Waters; your mother had been Anne Brennan, the daughter of the blacksmith on the road to Grange. According to the 1901 census, your father was illiterate but spoke Irish. He was to get married later that year. He would have been born in 1858, little more than a decade after the Great Famine. You were the second eldest of their five surviving boys. Two of your siblings died within hours of birth: an unnamed boy, who was born in 1908, when you were four, who lived for just eight hours, was weakly at birth and died 'with no medical attention'; and a girl, born in 1903, the year before you, christened Bridget, who was recorded as being 'weakly at birth' and as having died without medical attention within hours of her birth.

In the research for a TV documentary I did about 10 years ago, we established with the help of genealogist Nicola Morris that our family lived in Mount Edward at least as far back as 1855, when your grandfather, James Waters, was recorded as leasing a house and 6 acres 2 roods (approximately 6½ acres) from Captain J. Jones. By 1892 his lease had increased in size by 2 acres. In 1894 the lease was transferred to your father, John Waters, following the death of your grandfather. In 1915, John Waters was recorded as having finally purchased his landholding from the Jones family under the Land Purchase Acts. The occupation and ownership of this landholding was transferred to your mother, Mrs Anne Waters, in 1925, following the death of your father.

On the Brennan side, we found a similar pattern. The 1901 Census recorded five siblings living with their mother, their father having died some six years before, aged 59. Born in 1842, your grandfather, the blacksmith, would have been a child in the worst years of the famines. In that 1901 Census, Anne Brennan was recorded as being 25 years old. The Brennan farm was recorded as occupying just over 15 acres.

The 1911 Census recorded the presence of one Norah Brennan, aged 19, who had not featured in the enumeration of a decade before. She was the 'Aunt Nora(h)' who would come to visit us from New York, more than a half century later.

Your father died in 1922, when he was 63 and you were 17. Your mother lived for another 29 years, to the age of 80. The Waters family were still recorded as residing at Mount Edward in 2000, although my last surviving uncle, your oldest brother, James Patrick, had died about 20 years before. That year, 2000, strangely, is when I bought my house in Lislary, which means, I suppose, that some continuity of tenure has been maintained by a force of will that transcends mere human planning.

Between 1845 and 1850, the population of Sligo fell from 180,000 to 128,000, or roughly 30% in five years. In 1841, the parish of Ahamlish had a population of 3,236 living in 555 houses; by 1851 the population was 2,431 persons, living in 421 houses, a decline of about 25%.

In researching our documentary, which traced both lines of my background back to the Famine, we discovered some salutary contrasts exist-

< 156 >

ing in the same moment, in the same place.

An editorial in *The Sligo Champion* during the Famine period described the 'balls and parties hosted by public officials where all the markets of Sligo could not furnish sufficient articles for their groaning supper table, so that expresses were sent to the city for wines, fruits and other luxuries … showing the gross vulgarity of underbred people making ostentatious displays of their wealth while not subscribing a single sixpence to the relief of their poor.'

I came across a letter written to *The Sligo Champion* in February 1847 by a Fr Noone, recording a death by starvation of a John Watters, aged 18, from Mount Edward. This is likely to have been a grand-uncle of yours, the brother of James, my great-grandfather. Before the Famine, I gather, Mount Edward was settled according to a system known as the 'Clachan', which meant that extended families evolved in close proximity to each other, leading to clusters of a single family name. This is why there are so many Waterses and Watterses in the area, even still, and also, I presume, why the family grave in Ahamlish cemetery is shared with another family of Waterses and one of Watterses. I gather the 't' business was a moveable feast: some people chose to have two, others stuck with one. After you died, going through your books, I noticed that you had inscribed special volumes with your name and a date. From that I gather that you had used the double-t until you came to County Roscommon, when you changed to the more conventional option.

Another editorial in *The Champion*, three months earlier, in November 1846, had observed:

> It is an awful thing to have to record the loss of a human creature by the most horrible of all deaths – starvation … We have this week to [add] another name to the list of victims of famine. On Wednesday week a man named Patrick Murray fell down dead from actual want while working on the road between Collooney and Ballymote. He had been fasting from three days and although worn to the bone

with hunger be still compelled to work upon the road to endeavour to procure subsistence for himself and his family. At the time of his death ten days wages were due him by Government and to all the labourers using the same line of road. We implore of the Authorities to pay labourers twice a week; indeed, they should if it were possible receive their wages every night. We cannot hold those who kept back Patrick Murray's money guiltless of murder.

Two months later, in January 1847, the newspaper chronicled the drastic escalation in the situation:

The condition of the people is becoming every hour more deplorable. Deaths from starvation are now so numerous that they are looked upon as a matter of course and have ceased to cause alarm, or horror in the public mind. The mortality has fearfully increased in the locality of Sligo and this increase is solely attributable to a need of a sufficiency of food. We are, indeed, but at the beginning of the horrors – the land is untilled, the peasantry have no means to sow the seed nor time to dedicate to that purpose. The home supply of grain is fast diminishing. The supply brought in from foreign countries is wholly inadequate to meet the demand. The price of food is hourly increasing and judging from the aspect of things we have not one, but many years of famine before us.

When I get out of bed in the morning and open the front door looking out at the Atlantic, I think of these people, the lives they lived and the deaths they met. I think of you and speculate again on the reasons you left this place, never to return, and know there is a connection, if only I could fathom it. These are not random or trivial things, but heavier than anything we can imagine now: the burden of a malevolent history bearing down upon you; upon me too, though perhaps not so noticeable by virtue of being – temporarily – snagged on something in the dark matter of the invisible, so its weight does not impose upon the present. Can this be guaranteed? For how much longer? It is unresolved, unaccounted, unspoken, but it will not be denied its own resolution, soon or beyond the deceptive horizon of the knowable.

14

A Boy Called Don't Sue

It is interesting to observe how the gay marriage bandwagon has been joined by a number of high-profile self-styled liberals who, as far as I know, are not themselves gay. Invariably this category of individual is one with which I have come into conflict in the past, as these were among the loudest voices of excoriation and silencing I encountered when I tried to raise the issue of the rights of children and fathers to have legally protected relationships. This work, to be sure, is one of the key factors that put me in the sights of people like Rory O'Neill.

To my mind, there were actually four relevant factors in what I will call O'Neill's thinking in including me in his assault. One is that I had for some time in my *Irish Times* column been exploring religious questions from the position of arguing for the necessity that Irish society become mindful of what it might be losing in jettisoning its Catholic/Christian heritage. I was also getting deep into some questions about the functionality of religion in both the life of the human person and the life of society. I had published two books on these themes, *Lapsed Agnostic* and *Beyond Consolation*, and had attracted a high volume of splenetic responses as a result of pursuing this kind of topic in my *Irish Times* column. A second and more immediate factor, as I've described, was my attempt to outline the basis on which discussions concerning changes to the Constitution should proceed. A third, undoubtedly, was my intervention in the 2011 presidential election campaign to defend Helen Lucy Burke and call David Norris to account.

Perhaps the most critical factor had to do with my writings over many years about parenthood and children and, perhaps more specifically, my

< 160 >

involvement in the 2012 so-called 'Children's Rights Referendum', when I was among those who unsuccessfully resisted an attempt to include a specific provision for children's rights in the Constitution, arguing that children already had robust constitutional protections, largely exercised through their parents, and warning that this measure was clearly a power grab by the government to appropriate and transfer these rights from parents to the state. We came within an ace of winning that referendum, against the ranked forces of government, media, Oireachtas and state. In late October 2012, just three weeks before voting day, an opinion poll put the Yes side at 80% and the No side at 4%, with 16% describing themselves as 'Don't Knows'. The outcome of the referendum on 10 November was 58% in favour, 42% against. In this referendum we had a situation where all parties in the Oireachtas, along with the media, the Catholic Church and innumerable NGOs and other groups were behind the amendment, with only a handful of people – literally five or six of us – campaigning against.

A critical factor in the rapid turnaround was undoubtedly the last-minute exposure of governmental criminality in attempting to persuade the public to give up their own and their neighbour's parental rights. Seeking to conceal its ill intentions behind the pretence of an interest in children, the Fine Gael/Labour coalition overplayed its hand and ended up being exposed in one of the most insidious breaches of trust ever perpetrated by an Irish government. Using public monies to promulgate propaganda in an attempt to confuse and bully the electorate, the politicians set out to cancel rights that existed before the Irish State came into being.

Just two days before polling day, the Supreme Court unanimously ruled that the government's 'information' booklet, advertisements and website advocating a Yes vote in the referendum were in breach of the 1995 McKenna judgment governing the use of public funds in referendum campaigns. The improper financing of the government's 'information' campaigns had been successfully exposed in a legal challenge by Mark McCrystal, a case in which I was involved as a witness. In handing down his judgment, Mr Justice O'Donnell of the Supreme Court said that I had 'conducted a careful, detailed, and in my view illuminating, analysis of the passages in the [government's] website … '.

The judgment exposed and indicted the by then habitual attempts to undermine the Irish Constitution going back to the Lisbon Treaty referendum of 2008 and continuing with the dictatorial re-running of that referendum question a year later.

When I first began writing about family law and its injustices and corruptions, more than two decades ago, I naively imagined that what I was saying would result in the immediate rectification of what I assumed to be an oversight in public policy. Instead, I came under sustained attack from people describing themselves as 'feminists' and 'liberals' – attacks often couched in the most personal terms, but rarely engaging with the substance of what I was actually saying. Whenever I responded I was accused of attacking them and their 'achievements' for women. Ivana Bacik, for example, who was to become a highly visible participant in the gay marriage debate, regularly attacked me on this front by trying to shift the argument back to the alleged rights of women to exclude fathers from the lives of their children, inaccurately claiming that I failed to speak concerning the rights of children. In fact, the idea that father-child rights were conjoined was at the core of my argument.

Of course, when I responded to such less-than-liberal fulminations, they accused me of being 'angry', as though this might be either surprising or exceptionable. Indeed, on one occasion, the then CEO of Amnesty Ireland told me that his organisation would have supported me had I not been 'so angry'. I asked him if there were any other recorded instances where Amnesty had rejected a potential client on this ground. I never heard from him again.

Another of those who regularly and splenetically attacked me was my fellow *Irish Times* columnist Fintan O'Toole. In 2001, O'Toole broke a long silence on the issue of fathers and children with an Irish Times column in which he fingered those who had raised the issue of injustices against fa-

< 162 >

thers in Irish family courts with responsibility for some of the most egregious crimes imaginable. O'Toole used a tragedy of the previous weekend, in which a man killed his child and himself, to condemn those who have highlighted the unjust treatment of fathers in the family law system.

The problem, he declared, was not the arguments raised by those who had criticised the system and culture, it was 'that these rational arguments often come wrapped in a hateful rhetoric that feeds the kind of paranoia, rage and infinite resentment that, in a deranged mind, can seem to justify horrific violence'.

Having previously not criticised the system that inflicts great pain on fathers and children, the social attitudes that force men to suffer in silence, or the secrecy of the family courts system that renders all this invisible, it was to say the least interesting that O'Toole's first intervention was to attack those who had spoken out – by demonising them for the crazed actions of a solitary, desperate and disturbed man. Having suggested that those who protest about systematic denials of human rights had in doing so been in some arcane way responsible for the killing of children, he then claimed not to have said this. 'It would be absurd', he wrote, 'to suggest that rhetorical distortions about the nature of Irish society cause anyone to kill children'. Having made his allegation and withdrawn it, O'Toole then repeated it. 'What they [rhetorical distortions] do, however, is to feed into an already unstable mentality a picture of a world in which there is a vast conspiracy to deny men any kind of domestic justice. If you put wild resentment together with a paranoid sense of hopelessness, the result is bound to be explosive.'

It did not surprise me, then, that O'Toole took the opportunity afforded by the Rory O'Neill-prompted 'homophobia' controversy to stick the boot in again.

Although the Deputy Editor of *The Irish Times* had indicated to me on 20 January that my options in responding to Una Mullally were limited to (a) going 'the legal route' or (b) writing a letter to the Editor for publication, no such limitations appeared to have been conveyed to Fintan

O'Toole, who, on Tuesday 11 February 2014, published a column that was flagged on the front page of *The Irish Times* under the headline: 'Why I don't sue'. This, interestingly, was a full month after the Rory O'Neill interview, some three weeks after the Mullally article, and – perhaps most relevantly – a week or thereabouts after my solicitor had written to *The Irish Times* asking for a retraction and apology.

Inside, under the heading 'Columnist's position comes with obligations', Fintan related a ludicrous story about once having been libelled in *The Sunday Times*, which, in an anonymous profile (he seemed to regard this as especially egregious) had outrageously suggested that he drove away from an engagement – as MC at an Irish Congress of Trade Unions rally against the bank bailout – in a BMW 5 Series. 'The implication,' he wrote, 'was pretty clear: I was a hypocritical, champagne socialist, stirring up the masses from a position of wealth and privilege.' O'Toole went on to demonstrate how wrong the story was: he didn't own a BMW 5 Series, or any kind of BMW, or any kind of car. He couldn't drive and had gone home that evening, as always, on the number 13 bus.

The profile, he declared, was a gold mine. 'I had hit the libel jackpot. *The Sunday Times* couldn't possibly go into court to defend an article that was so sloppily written and badly researched. Even the most aggressive lawyer would tell them to stuff my mouth with gold and make the whole thing go away fast. I have to admit that for about five minutes I was intoxicated on the potent brew of greed and revenge that I imbibed to soothe my hurt feelings. I thought how lovely it would be to get Rupert Murdoch to buy me an actual series 5 BMW and pay for the driving lessons and a lifetime's supply of petrol. I would call the car Rupert and every time I turned the key in the ignition I would give a mad cackle of glee.'

But then he remembered something: he was a national newspaper columnist, who occupied 'a position of enormous privilege'. He was 'allowed to take part in what we might call the semi-official national discourse'. He was allowed to be robustly critical of all sorts of people, 'to

< 164 >

enrage some of those people and upset others' (though he didn't set out to do so!). He was given these freedoms because 'there is a working assumption that free and open and robust debate is not just permissible in, but essential to, a democracy. If you benefit from these freedoms in the extraordinary and highly privileged way that newspaper columnists do, you have to be very, very careful about the way you conduct yourself.'

At this point I began to wonder what Fintan might be getting at. I began to get the distinct impression that he might actually be talking about me, although my name appeared nowhere in the piece. Could he be equating his little anecdote about the egregious Beamer allegation with the accusation against myself and others that we had been guilty of hate-mongering against gay people?

O'Toole actually appeared to be somewhat confused as to what point he was making. Was he saying that journalists shouldn't sue at all – ever – or was he saying that journalists should take every other conceivable course and sue only as a last resort? It was unclear. In his own case, he recalled that, instead of hiring a lawyer and suing *The Sunday Times*, he had talked to the paper's Irish editor, who agreed 'pretty quickly' that the article was 'inaccurate and indefensible'. The article was taken off the paper's website and a retraction was published the following week.

That was all right, then. O'Toole was spared the terrible conundrum of having to decide what to do if the editor had told him to go take a running jump, or sought to initiate a philosophical debate about the gravity of being accused of being able to drive. O'Toole did not say what he would have done then, or what he might have done if the editor had drafted a derisory retraction, refusing to acknowledge the significance of the defamation, procrastinated and missed the opportunity to right the wrong at the earliest opportunity, i.e. the following Sunday. What would have happened then? O'Toole didn't say.

And yet, he appeared to be satisfied that this episode was sufficiently illustrative of his total and definitive attitude to defending, or not defending, his good name. That, he declared, 'was the end of it. The record

< 165 >

was put straight. No money changed hands. No lawyer's school fees were paid. I still don't have a BMW.'

Yet, in a somewhat contradictory paragraph a little further down, O'Toole appeared to acknowledge that the decision about whether to proceed with a legal action for defamation could depend on the nature of the response to the initial complaint: '... the threat of a possible libel action is implicit in these affairs but it has always seemed to me that for a newspaper columnist it should be an absolute last resort'. Oh! In other words, if my translation of this typical O'Toole sophism is correct, he appeared to be implying that if the Editor of *The Sunday Times* had not been so accommodating, events might well have taken a different course.

It seemed clear that O'Toole was insinuating that myself and Breda O'Brien, his *Irish Times* colleagues, when accused without a shred of evidence of being hate-mongers, should simply have sucked it up – that the 'privilege' we enjoyed as newspaper columnists came with responsibilities. Or was he? He was also, it appeared, not saying this: 'I'm not suggesting that being a newspaper columnist means that you don't have the same rights to protect your good name as every other citizen. People have to exercise their own judgment about how they react to public comment they believe to be inaccurate, unfair and damaging.' So journalists might, after all, be entitled to take legal actions in defence of their reputations against lies? It was all a little confusing. As I've noted before, sometimes, with Fintan, it can be difficult to establish a distinction between what he says he is saying and what he says he is not saying.

'But there's a price to be paid,' he continued, 'for the considerable privilege of being granted an especially loud voice in the national conversation. With the megaphone comes a duty to protect freedom of expression and a vested interest in keeping it as open as possible.'

Actually, I agree with him about the journalist's duty to protect freedom of expression. That's why I believe that, when necessary, journalists as much as others should exercise their full legal entitlements when nothing else offers the means of counteracting a lie. Sometimes only a

< 166 >

legal action offers the possibility of protecting one's voice from bullies and liars who seek to take advantage of the alleged 'privileged' positions of their opponents by claiming a right to demonise and defame them with impunity.

Then O'Toole arrived at what revealed itself as his purpose:. 'If, for example, you want to be free to call the National Women's Council "feminazis" or suggest that atheists are not fully human, you need a robust sense of where the limits of acceptable polemic lie.'

Ah! It was here that I became pretty certain that Fintan was talking about me. I recognised a dim simulacrum of both of the accusations contained in that last sentence as referring to me – not because I actually said the NWCI were 'feminazis' or that atheists were 'not fully human', but because these entirely spurious suggestions had been made numerous times in the past – mainly in anonymous posts from 'readers' at the end of my *Irish Times* column.

O'Toole, in other words, was relying on his 'memory' of second-hand accounts of certain things I was alleged to have written. Perhaps a decade before, Fintan and I debated on radio my occasional use of the word 'feminazi', and afterwards I decided to stop using the term because I realised it gave my opponents on the father/children rights issue too ready a stick to beat me with while avoiding my actual argument. This, however, did not stop O'Toole from bringing the word 'feminazi' up at every available opportunity, as he was now doing yet again, many years later.

Some people seem to think I invented the word 'feminazism'. I sometimes wish I had, for it captures rather beautifully something of the man-hating venom of a great deal of modern feminist rhetoric. In fact the word is still widely used in political discourse elsewhere, not infrequently by anti-feminist women, though in recent times – clearly in response to the kind of disingenuous censoriousness exhibited by Fintan O'Toole – it has been substituted with the word 'feminasty'.

In fact, a survey of my *Irish Times* column reveals that I used the word 'feminazi' twice in total, and the word 'feminazism' once, each time in

< 167 >

a general context to summon up a particular kind of man-hating feminism and its impact on culture. On 12 January 1999, I wrote: 'It is time
for men to confront the sources of the propaganda which makes possible their marginalisation from home, family and society, to challenge the
bully-boys and bully-girls, the misandrists and the feminazis who, while
berating the inhumanity of 1950s Ireland, are quite comfortable with the
inhumanity of the present.'

On 12 February 2001, I wrote (in a column about the TV cartoon Bob
the Builder!): 'But perhaps we had better not draw attention to Bob, lest
the feminazis go after him. If you think this implausible, consider Babar
the Elephant, targeted by the custodians of political correctness on account of the dangerous messages he is transmitting to the young.'

On 8 June 1999, I used the word 'feminazism' in quotation marks in an
article criticising some politically correct initiative by the then Minister
for Justice John O'Donoghue. I wrote: 'No greater tribute can be paid to
the achievements of "feminazism" than that a man as unreconstructed
as Mr John O'Donoghue is able to stand up in public, make such a statement and cause nobody to blink an eye.'

Equally wearisomely familiar, and equally unfounded, was O'Toole's
accusation that I had described atheists as 'less than human'. This is
something that frequently happens when I write something critical of
secular-atheism: some statement of mine becomes instantly reduced to
a caricature of itself, then turned inside out and tied up in a neat but deceptive little bow, then re-presented in its adapted form as the word-for-
word 'recollection' of what I wrote or said. This had become the almost
unvarying pattern in the comments thread at the end of my *Irish Times*
columns, where a rabid collection of genuine hate-mongers congregated
every Friday to attack every aspect of my work, personality and appearance. It was not enough for me to have said what I'd said, or written what
I'd written, and for them to criticise me for that; they seemed to need
to twist what I'd said or written before proceeding. Next time out the
distortion would have become hard fact, until eventually what they were

talking about in the name of talking about me was nothing like anything I'd ever said or written, but some distant cousin of a fractured interpretation of what someone thought he half-remembered reading somewhere about something I once said about something.

The 'atheists are less than human' 'quote' is a typical example. It never happened. Nothing even vaguely resembling it was ever written or uttered by me. Yet it is 'remembered' so well that even the Literary Editor of *The Irish Times* had become certain that I said or wrote it.

It is, of course, based on something, and by recalling this genealogy, we can gain an insight into the integrity of those who 'remember' things I've said, and therefore claim the right to describe what I stand for.

In my *Irish Times* column on 20 November 2009, I wrote as follows:

Religion, rather than just another 'category', is the guiding hypothesis that makes sense of the whole, the public expression of the total dimension of human nature. No other channel has the capacity to convey the broadest truths about man's nature and his relationship to the universe. Secularists do not like this characterisation of the situation, but it has long been obvious that they have nothing to offer society as an alternative source of ethics, meaning or hope. It is, of course, possible for an individual to survive without any overweening means of reconciliation with reality, but such values are culturally incommunicable other than as opposition to religion. The collective presents a particular problem not addressed by personal objections to particular religions. A society without a cultural consciousness of the absolute, such as we are in the process of creating, is like a lawn laid on top of a concrete yard: it may briefly give the impression of health, but eventually, for obvious reason, it withers away. What is called secularism, therefore, strikes not merely at specific religions, or even religions in general, but at the very capacity of humans to be human.

Is this the same as stating that atheists are 'less than human'?

This was not O'Toole's first onslaught on me after I had sought to defend my reputation by recourse to the libel laws. Back in 2001, when I sued *The Sunday Times* for a scurrilous attack by its gossip columnist Terry Keane, O'Toole wrote that 'like most people who know John Waters', he was 'very glad' that I won the libel case. He then went on, in his hallmark large-print-giveth-small-print-taketh-away style, to say that I should never have taken the case in the first place. Side-stepping the core of the matter – that the attack on me was of the most insidious personalised kind – he recycled the hackneyed journalistic argument against libel laws that seeks to conceal special pleading behind humbug about the public interest

> A simple fact of this business is that journalists occasionally make mistakes. It is very easy for a passionate argument to cross the line that separates necessary polemic from unfair attack. Even when the writer is trying to be careful, an implication or allegation that ought not to be made can slip through the net of caution. This happens from time to time to every columnist, including John.

The effect of this kind of thing, it appears, is that the 'most important victims, moreover, are not the journalists, but the public who are deprived of information they need'.

It was strange: O'Toole did not appear to be suggesting that any of this logic might be applied to Terry Keane's article about me. He did not seek to suggest that she had simply 'made a mistake'. Nor did he claim that Terry Keane had been trying to be careful. Nor did he suggest that what she had written was simply an implication or allegation that had slipped though her 'nets of caution'. Oddly, in the light of what appeared to be his overall argument, O'Toole described the Terry Keane article on foot of which I took action as 'nasty and indefensible'. He might well have added 'malicious', but perhaps he was being careful. He did not seek to point to any information in Terry Keane's article the public needed to obtain. He seemed, in short, to be suggesting that a public commentator has no right to sue, no matter what the potential damage or scale of the provocation.

The last time I checked, the word 'indefensible' meant 'not justifiable by argument'. Indeed, in this case the word was quite literally valid, since the judge in the trial had thrown out *The Sunday Times*'s defence of justification (truth!), leaving the jury to decide only on the level of damages I should receive. *The Irish Times* had managed to exclude this part of the proceedings from its coverage of the trial, thus, by O'Toole's logic, depriving the public of information vital to forming any understanding of what the case was about.

O'Toole conceded: 'The implication [the Keane article] contained that he would be an unsympathetic father to his daughter was, as anyone even slightly acquainted with John would know, so far from the truth that it did not even occupy the same galaxy.'

Actually, this is bogus. People 'only slightly acquainted' with me would know virtually nothing about my role as a father other than what they had read in the newspapers. This had been – at that stage for some six years – such a constant farrago of lies as to make it forgivable for someone to have long since decided that being an unsympathetic father to my daughter was the least of my faults. O'Toole himself might well qualify as someone who was 'slightly acquainted' with me, and he had never once sought either to correct this impression or question those who sought to promulgate it. Nor was there any reason why he should have done so: How, after all, was he to know that I was not as the press had portrayed me? Moreover, even if he had been moved to defend me, he, in common with myself, would have been constrained in what he might say by virtue of the fact that virtually everything to do with my fatherhood of my daughter was circumscribed by the *in camera* rule. And this exposes the raw truth of the matter: I had no way of defending my reputation against attacks rooted in my relationship with my daughter other than by recourse to the libel laws. This is why these laws exist, and why citizens have a right to avail of them when nothing else succeeds. And ironically, it was only after a lengthy libel trial, albeit one only partially reported by the so-called press, that Fintan O'Toole felt himself sufficiently informed to come out and acknowledge that I was a sympathetic father to my daughter. My strategy of suing *The Sunday Times* had done the trick after all!

15

Tempory Jobs

Remember how you used to tell us, when you had completed some emergency operation around the house or the garden that it was 'a tempory job'? The idea was that you had no time to do a permanent job, and so improvised a solution with whatever tools and materials were to hand: sticky tape, cardboard, wire, old tin cans. This became a family joke, because the tempory job invariably remained untouched until the next breakdown. And the joke was double-edged because, though we laughed in full knowledge of the postponement involved in your temporary intervention, we also laughed because we knew your tempory jobs tended to remain because they were executed with the utmost skill and ingenuity. I remember yellow sheets of Lucozade paper standing in for window panes; electric cable doing duty as a clothesline and crumbling floorboards braced with dismantled orange boxes. Once so designated, a tempory job was entitled to kid-glove treatment – lest the repair be undone. Orange box repairs were, where possible, to be tiptoed upon; a Lucozade window was for letting in light, not for pressing your nose against.

Although I didn't inherit much of your talent for practical things, I have to tell you that I'm a dab hand at the tempory job. I've become known for it. There are few delights in life akin to discovering, when a toilet no longer contrives to flush when its handle is turned, that the bracket linking the handle to the plunger inside the cistern can be adapted with the aid of a knife to operate at a somewhat shorter but still functional span. Usually, what's happened is that the plastic bracket has worn due to the repeated use of the handle, but, with a scalpel and a small file you can cut a new hole that works with about 75% of showroom efficiency. You carry out the repair with the express intention of visiting the hardware shop as soon as practicable to purchase a new bracket, but secretly you intend to leave it as long as you can to see if it lasts.

It may be necessary to circulate detailed instructions in conjunction with the repair. In the case of the flushing mechanism, for instance, you may need to conduct short training sessions to show all those potentially implicated that, if they follow through on the flushing motion, rather than simply jerking the handle and expecting it to operate normally, they will learn to operate the tempory mechanism without thinking, turning it as though it were a gym machine designed to develop wrist muscles rather than a functional instrument for flushing the toilet.

My favourite among my own collection of tempory jobs is a fridge handle I installed at home when Mammy was ill. Through use or abuse, the handle, which was an inbuilt part of the door, had cracked, making imminent a serious rupture to the door. I cut up an old cassette case and glued half of it on top of the crack, holding the whole thing together and enabling the handle to function again without undesired repercussions. Six years later, in spite of the band-aid plastic having cracked due to untrained usage, the repair remains in place. I could fix it again, but that would spoil the fun of it. The whole point is that the job lasts as long as possible: only when it breaks down completely should it be patched up again.

I see this tendency in myself as part of a larger inheritance that relates not so much to technical skill but to a more existentially grounded inclination. It is connected, I believe, to a quality of impermanence I had long intuited in our life as a family. I think of your journey east from Sligo as a kind of biblical passage, perhaps a retreat. I think of you as having settled, but only temporarily, in Roscommon, of not so much intending to return to Sligo as acting always on the presumption that you would eventually leave, perhaps to go back, perhaps to go on. Scattered throughout the Bible are mentions of the correct habitation for man in this world being a 'tent' – the better to avoid becoming excessively attached to this existence. The home I grew up in for my first 10 years, I feel, aspired to fulfilling such an injunction for living. It was a shelter

< 174 >

from the elements, but no more: two functional rooms, no electricity, no running water, lit by paraffin lamps and candles, our water drawn from the 'pump' (really a public tap) up the street. You never worried much about any of this, although I think it troubled Mammy somewhat and certainly created no end of embarrassment for us as children. And yet, in a different sense, it was no more or less than normality. Like your vans, both houses we occupied at different times were held together with string and wire and insulating tape.

We were never what you might call 'settled' people, our homes really no more than temporary encampments, in which we lived as refugees from something that never became clear – some conflict, perhaps, some catastrophe, some upheaval. This was the part of your personality that it was most essential to appreciate in order to understand you: you never intended to remain. I think of this in both physical and metaphysical terms, because in you these seemed to be inseparable. You were here with a total and constant understanding of being in transit, and you gave this to us, or you gave us its antithesis. My sisters are all homemakers, keeping beautiful houses with stylish, elegant furniture and sparkling windows. I have both this tendency and its opposite: an indifference in the face of domestic order that sometimes reminds me of Mammy's judgment on you: that you didn't care what state the place was in provided you could make your way to the chair in the corner. This is me, too, punctuated by bursts of hammering and painting. I remember the way you painted up the house we moved to in 1965: working assiduously for months on end to meet the deadline of Aunt Nora(h)'s arrival, and afterwards leaving the job precisely in the unfinished state it had attained at that moment for many years to come. I have this tendency too: I plunge in for as long as there is a focus, and afterwards abandon the project and enter a different mode of being.

I believe this has left me with a rather unusual attitude to everyday reality. Although I always took the fact of my existence very seriously, I don't believe I have ever totally embraced it as a definitive and final state. Like you, I walk lightly through it, ever watchful for signs.

When I look back from here at my teenage years and young manhood, I realise I gave you a lot of heartache and trouble. Most of it was inevitable: we were at cross-purposes. For a long time, I analysed our confrontations in the conventional way: new ideas versus old. I thought of you as trying to put me into a conformist box, to make me become something clear and safe and nameable, when I hadn't a clue what I wanted to be. This was the pattern I saw for a long time, but lately I've begun to see a different one.

First you tried to pack me off to agricultural college. I mean to say: Did you really think that was going to work out? Maybe it was my dabbling in the garden that got you thinking along those lines – understandable, I suppose; it was an odd thing for a young lad to be interested in, but my interest was existential, not vocational.

It's strange that I've never before made this connection to myself, but now it seems obvious: you thought I had green fingers. I hadn't. I used to think I was operating off some kind of weakening inherited instinct, but now Róisín seems to have caught the full-blown condition, which would have to have jumped the gap to get to her. Among my peers, I was a weirdo fond of getting dirt under his fingernails; alongside Uncle Martin and Granny and yourself, I was a dilettante. My Swiss Family Robinson fantasy was really a kind of partially realised daydream, doomed to evaporate on contact with the real world. So I suppose it's not surprising that you got the idea that I might be interested in horticulture. I realise now that parents are always looking into their children's fascinations in search of clues that might help to render them safe and secure. I confess I went along with it too, succumbing to your pressure to pursue my application to the regional tech in Sligo, and pretending to be pleased when I was accepted. I remember you getting me digs with the conductor of the Castlerea to Sligo bus, whose name will come back to me in a while. I led you on, engaging in all the preparations to go away, and then pulled plant at the last minute. It was months afterwards before we exchanged a word.

But that was as nothing compared to the schism that occurred when

I left CIE after four unhappy years as a Clerical Officer, Grade 3. You must have been beside yourself with relief when I got that job after so many disappointments. It was respectable – somewhere on the upward scale between a post office clerk and a bank official – and pensionable too. It was also near to home: in the four years I had three postings – Claremorris, Westport and Galway – all in counties neighbouring Roscommon, which might have seemed like a dream come true for many's the emigrant of the previous 125 years. It occurs to me now that your acceptance of me in this role must have amounted to a surrendering of your ambitions that I might turn out even a little bit like yourself. For this was at the opposite end of the spectrum from farming or any kind of skilled-working: a penpusher, a clerk sitting at a desk in a warm room doing the kind of work a woman could do just as easily and as well. The tiny goods office was an anthill of activity, with a constant flow of locomotive engineers, lorry drivers, forklift operators, milesmen, checkers, shunters, and inspectors – invariably muscular, perspiring males who carried their ill-kempt clipboards with something between nonchalance and disdain. And then there were the clerks, of whom I was one, nominally in supervision of the chaos, but in reality remote from the dirty and sometimes dangerous work of packing, stacking, counting, booking, charging, discharging, wagon decoupling, gantry-unloading or cleaning up after pilferage and damage-in-transit.

I hated it from the first moment. There were some good people working there, especially the Chief Clerk, Michael O'Reilly, who in his spare time collected and fixed clocks, but I couldn't get out of my head that this job was totally alien to everything I felt about myself. Money-wise it was at the lower end of the pen-pushing scale, but it offered enough for me eventually to buy a second-hand Mini. The work was excruciatingly tedious: writing up outward consignments from Claremorris Bacon Factory and tracking the deliveries where necessary, processing claims for lost packages and engaging in humdrum 'correspondence' with various pains-in-the-posterior from inside and outside the organisation. I just couldn't believe that I'd ended up doing this. It was about as far from whatever I'd been dreaming of as to turn my mirror reflection into someone completely different.

The trouble was that I hadn't a clue what exactly I'd been dreaming of, or at least my dreams were so far from being concrete schemes that it amounted to the same thing. I wanted to be something meaningful and glamorous, like a footballer or a musician or a writer. Problem was, I was no use at football, couldn't play in time or in tune and had no idea what I wanted to write about. So here I was, surrounded by men who, unbeknownst to me, suggested themselves as women, not because of any characteristic of femininity in them but because they were running around the place with sheaves of paper in their hands, and in this sense struck me as completely unlike the kind of men I'd known growing up. Although we pen-pushers were technically 'superior' to locomotive drivers, signalmen and shunters, I now realise that these all seemed to me to be real men, whereas the office staff were like eunuchs in their midst. The sole exception was Mick O'Reilly and his redemptive clocks. He had started off collecting antiques, rapidly zeroed in on clocks – wall clocks, grandfather clocks, mantelpiece clocks – and taught himself to be a master clockmaker, lovingly restoring wrecks that had been written off by the world to the most beautiful timepieces you'd ever seen. Sometimes, when one of his mates with some similar fixation called into the office, they would talk for hours about tracking down the missing parts for one of their clocks, how they'd released bound-up springs or got the chimes to ring again.

I came to realise that, in a sense, you had written me off. You had shifted your expectations of me from one end of the scale – farming – to the other – pen-pushing. I was in a job leading nowhere and didn't even have the saving grace of a skill or a craft to boast of. I could lay claim to neither the sense of dignity I'd observed in you and your fellows nor some new calling with the merest claim to stand alongside these ways of life. But I had a respectable job.

< 178 >

Shifts to the goods office in Westport and subsequently to the school bus office in Galway did little or nothing to change either my heart or my mind about my non-vocation as a railway clerk. Eventually I had to quit. I know you were greatly put out by this, but I have to tell you that I was always going to give it up at the very earliest opportunity. I understood your feelings: this was the 1970s, when jobs of any kind were hard to come by. For a while I knuckled down and counted my blessings. But in 1978, when Paul Claffey offered me a job as 'station manager' at his newly opening pirate radio station in the Grey Castle, I left the railways behind with hardly a backward glance.

If you'll bear with me a minute, I'd like to offer a slightly deeper analysis of what happened with the CIE business that may surprise you. It certainly surprised me when it came to me. It's broadly this: once you realised I wasn't going to become a farmer, you settled for me being a pen-pusher. I think what you were trying to do was, because you couldn't figure me out any better than I was able to figure out myself, was boot me up out of the stratum of society you'd belonged to, where working with the hands had become devalued and disparaged, to a stratum in which I'd be 'working the head'; whereas, in spite of my own equal indoctrination in the idea of the 'progressive' path of man, what I was doing was emitting a desperate metaphysical scream at the very idea of this. I didn't know that this is what I was giving expression to. I thought I was simply bored, that the work was beneath me, that a machine could do it much more effectively. All that was true, but these were symptoms rather than the 'thing-itself' of my objection.

This was at an early stage in a general process of transferring worth and esteem from physical to sedentary occupations. There was this new idea that education was the thing, and that education meant stuff you learned from books and lectures rather than at a bench or at the top of a ladder. The problem was that the jobs we, the clerks, did were almost entirely pointless, useless and dispensable. If I didn't show up for a month, there might have been a pile-up of paperwork, but there wouldn't have been a crisis. If the signalman failed to show up (which happened from time to time!), the trains were left blowing for the road at the outer home signal. I used to wonder how they were able to justify paying us even the pittance they did – less than half the lower end of the scale for those categories we were supposed to be 'supervising'.

Essentially, what was in train, so to speak, was the beginnings of a social shift from manual to office work. Even though I was supposed to be among the beneficiaries of this shift, I found it offensive, largely because I recognised the value of skilled work as a result of working with you for those few years of my adolescence. I had disdain for the idea that, because I was called a 'clerical officer', I was automatically entitled to respect. I knew a few guys in the job who took a contrary view, who relished their status and authority, but for me it was a humourless joke. I hated the idea that I was supposed to check up on locomotive drivers when they came on duty, to make sure that they had consumed no alcoholic beverage. To me, these men were gods, and that too was your influence.

One of the central elements in this general shift was the absorption of women into the public workplace. Factory work, in which formerly human skills had been mechanised, coded, tabulated and redistributed as a set of mechanistic functions, could be carried out by physically weaker and relatively unskilled personnel. In this context, the idea of the 'supervising officer' made sense: her or his functions were simply to note the efficiency of the production line and report up. The idea of a skilled man as 'someone to be' was becoming increasingly tenuous, if not culturally ludicrous. The wages of skilled employees, including locomotive drivers and signalmen, were forced down, while the salaries (the distinction was critical) of the pen-pushers went up. It was as if those who had become 'educated' were entering into a conspiracy to render themselves relevant and worthy by redefining reality to downgrade those who actually did things and valorise their own 'supervisory' functions. This process foreshadowed another: the shift from an economy of needs to an economy of wants, in which an artificial concept of growth based on appetites fostered by advertising was sold as a true and functional model of collective human existence. And, of course, all these processes were emanating from the city, from the rows upon rows of joined-up buildings in which the new claims to ownership over reality were being asserted.

These phenomena were by no means disconnected from the evisceration of family and community sovereignty in the same period. Loyalties were being remade, identities put in flux and individualism becoming the preferred mode of freedom. In reality, freedom was being surrendered: the ability to govern your own space and time by means of skills and capacities that actually belonged to you was being quietly set aside – and this seen as a sign of progress. What you lost in human dignity and identity on the treadmill, you bought back in the boutique or the motor showroom. Consumerism supplanted personal creativity to become the new brand of freedom. To achieve this freedom, it was necessary to suggest to the screen slave or cubicle hostage that the work he or she was doing was part of a vast new model of communal creativity. Thus, a false idea of creativity became synonymous with a false idea of freedom, in which the 'creative' element became the capacity to operate various systems, processes and technologies and switch between equally mundane and unsatisfying functions under the illusion of mastery. The machines needed to be 'clever' to carry out their allotted functions, so their operators, even though no more than button-pushers, were enabled to feel even smarter. This, together with the even deeper illusion of 'autonomy' conferred by individualism, convinced the post-1960s generations that they were not merely the most free, but the most creative generations ever to grace the planet. In truth, creativity had been surrendered with the skills, trades and crafts that had once belonged to those, like you, who practised them. You and your fellows had pursued a line of instruction in order to become first competent, then adept in your own lines of work, and thereafter capable of sustaining yourselves by means of vocations that belonged to you and became a central part of your public identities. A man who was a carpenter was more than a man. A woman qualified

< 181 >

and skilled as a dressmaker was someone from whom an opinion emanated in a new way, seen to be born of a depth of endeavour and application to reality that made her worth listening to.

Relieved of the necessity to absorb the logic and feel of an entire dis-
cipline – such as mechanics, or stonecutting or weaving – the individual
was 'freed' to float in a world increasingly dictated by technologies created by unseen actors. The sense of a societal intelligence became fractal,
with apparently no human entity guiding it.

Familiarity with technologies, in personal as well as professional contexts, creates an illusion of fluency, but it is a superficial fluency born
of a deceptive familiarity. In truth, few people know anything about iP-
hones apart from turning them off and on again when something seems
to go wrong. But, more than that, the 'need' for an iPhone, though it may
suggest itself as absolute, is itself manufactured. Forty years ago, I could
be out in the wilds of Loughglynn for a day or more and not even notice
that I was uncontactable; now it seems unthinkable. These personalised
technologies fulfil a need, but it is an artificial need created by the alienat-
ing processes of modern society. In such a place it is necessary to ignore
the deep call from within that insists on understanding things. Meaning
remains elusive, hovering behind the veil of mystery presented by the
technology. Our fathers – you included – accessed meaning through their
manipulation of meaningful objects; we handle objects that must, surely,
have meaning, but this remains encased in plastic and chrome, tantalis-
ingly present, even observable, but utterly inaccessible to us.

The modern obsession with individual identity is a further stage in
this process. Even modern consumerism has its limits in affording the
mechanised citizen a means of escape from treadmill or cubicle slavery.
New means of personal differentiation are needed, hence the idea that
there are (already, but still counting) 72 different 'genders', as well as
innumerable 'lifestyle choices' which the enlightened modern citizen is
expected to endorse, applaud and give due consideration to as possible
options for himself. The loss of the true forms of individuality, which

once men carved out with knives and chisels, has ushered in new options in the form of self-reinvention that often involves denial of natural laws or limits. It is important, then, to observe that these developments are not naturalistic modes of 'progress', defined according to unfolding enlightenment or maturity, but the offshoots of an aberrant process of mechanisation, consumerism and alienation. They are symptoms not of growing illumination but of late-capitalist degradation.

Consumerism introduces to social relationships bonds that come without responsibility or compulsion. They are matters of choice and buying power – rather than, for example, blood, geography, duty or patriotism. So long as the consumer has spending money, he or she is 'free'. Advanced mass production has arrived at a level of customisation capable of conferring on every individual the illusion of total uniqueness. The modern 'republican' – the apparently autonomous individual – is someone who defines his own identity, fashion-wise, taste-wise, gender-wise and sexually. He is a consumer of illusory choices, masquerading as an autonomous being.

This is the meaning of the otherwise inexplicable appeal of the 'Like' button on blogs, posts and newspaper articles online. For an elderly man to sit in his cottage in Maugherow, browsing through the Farmers Journal and marking each article in green biro with the words 'like' and 'dislike' would be seen as a qualifying characteristic for immediate transfer to the nearest mentler. Yet, many people nowadays spend large portions of their day doing something similar, electronically speaking. Devoid of expression through real work, the human being is being led back into forms of play that would scarcely keep an eight-year-old contented for more than a few minutes.

I inherited a few of your talents. I could plant a drill of spuds, paint a gate, or set the contacts in my car, but was not what you would have called a tasty worker. I often look at rows of buildings on a street scape or motorway and think that all this, one way or another, is the outcome of interventions by other men. (In general, I use the word 'men' in its

generic form, to indicate both men and women, but here it's intended to indicate, overwhelmingly, men: human beings with testicles.) Each
piece – building, bridge or flyover – is perhaps the conception of one or
two men, but has been executed through the interventions of dozens or
hundreds of other men working together towards a common goal. Sometimes, walking down a street, I am overcome by shame that there is no
place on the face of the earth, aside from the occasional library shelf, that
contains any analogous contribution of mine. Something in me believes
I have a duty to make some kind of contribution to the construction of
the world. Perhaps this is the true 'god particle', some ineradicable and
unacknowledged element in my humanity that insists on being useful, on
building and making and doing, on leaving a mark on the world that others
can stare at, or walk upon, or drive across, or shelter under.

For the past 40-odd years as a journalist and writer I have felt myself part of, and complicit in, an increasingly unreal world, in which the
means of my existence are generated by others, while I simply observe
and makes notes, a hurler on the ditch. I have felt myself not merely
drifting away from the concrete world you inhabited, but actually from
any kind of reality I might once have recognised as such.

Most of the people I meet these days resemble me in this respect.
We live in cities and thereby judge ourselves superior to those who get
their hands dirty out in the sticks, but really we are slaves of a new kind:
indentured to technologies which steal our time, creativity and imagination. Every so often, in a café or restaurant in one of the great cities of
the world, I have that same sensation I had in those railway goods offices
in Claremorris and Westport 40-odd years ago. I look around and realise that all those present, male and female, make their livings from secondary or tertiary economic activities, unproductive in any fundamental
sense – you might even say parasitical on the main business of wealth
creation. Yet, invariably, these people – young, well-to-do, fashionably
dressed – convey an air of indispensability. If you drive 50 or 100 miles
out into the country, and visit a diner or fast-food restaurant, you will

< 184 >

be struck by the fact that the very different clientele to be seen there – labourers, tradesmen, factory workers – have about them an air of humility, if not defeat. These, who continue to, yes, man the real world on the wrong side of history are the ones facing obsolescence in an era in which the real is no longer what it says in the dictionary. At the same time, most of the paid work available to the growing generations exists in a crypto-totalitarian climate of dissociated authority, standardisation of processes and mandatory guidelines. In a culture in which human skills and judgment have been siphoned out of all human context, patented, codified, tabulated and reduced to algorithms, there is a deep suspicion of human discretion. Expertise belongs to the system, and ever fewer human beings are empowered to interfere.

Hannah Arendt wrote in *The Human Condition* (University of Chicago Press, 1958): 'The reality and reliability of the human world rests primarily on the fact that we are surrounded by things more permanent than the activity by which they were produced, and potentially even more permanent than the lives of their authors'. Arendt, of course, was talking both about physical craftsmanship and what we call art, which includes great books as well as great buildings. But a strange thing occurs when you're the first, as I am, to come off the end of a line of practical men and seek to make your living in a sedentary activity, even if it aspires to the same kind of longevity as a cathedral or an archway. It's hard to take it seriously: I mean that it's hard to convince yourself that anything you do is real work. Unless it's breaking your back and skinning your hands, you think of it as play,. Several times, writing books or plays, I've made myself seriously ill because I refused to accept that I had reached a point where I was doing an adequate day's work, even when I wrote for 10, 15 or even 20 hours. Only outright collapse was enough to satisfy whatever strange gene inhabits me and nags me in this way.

Indeed, far from writing becoming a substitute for 'real' work, perhaps what it pursues is a compensatory doodling to occlude the absence of a true intervention, as the oyster clothes the sand grain in pearl because it

< 185 >

cannot think of anything more useful to do. Perhaps this is what art and literature amount to: the late mutations of the craftsman's compulsion to build and mould and weave, a kind of existential clerking that seeks to compensate for a life bereft of any truly worthwhile contribution?

A shoemaker is a kind of poet. There are few things in the world as strange, when you get right down to looking at one, as a shoe. It captures, as though in a photograph or a poem, the frailty, the conceit, the absurdity and the ingenuity of the human person. To make one, therefore, so that it fits a particular person, is to become a poet of that person's humanity, a photographer of his journey, a sculptor of her little pomps and circumstances, heels and toes. Making things, fixing things, takes a man out of his self-absorption and renders him answerable to the logic of the world and the rest of its inhabitants. It is the enemy of narcissism and self-will.

< 186 >

16

Thomas59

The 'homophobe' cascade might have been bearable if *The Irish Times* had behaved with a scintilla of integrity during it. Instead, it joined gleefully in the witch-hunt, sending out its attack dogs to assist the LGBT mob, publishing a series of outrageously one-sided articles directed at both me and the Iona Institute, sometimes carrying splenetic or sarcastic asides in articles that had nothing to do with the controversy. There were also frequent attacks by my *Irish Times* 'colleagues' on Twitter, most notably the Consumer Affairs Editor, Conor Pope. On 7 February 2014, a movie review by the paper's film critic, Donald Clarke, included the following sentence: 'Given recent, unhappy developments in domestic discourse, there could hardly be a better time for a film about a homophobic jerk – partly fictionalised and entirely dead, so he can't sue – who, after getting a hint of what it's like to be at the crappy end of the stick, gains some degree of empathy and understanding.'

My decision finally to resign from *The Irish Times*, on 26 March 2014, was the culmination of these events and others, some of which were themselves the culmination of issues going back many years. I didn't see a choice, given the unwillingness of the editors of the newspaper to do anything other than sit at their desks waiting for me to cave in. In a previous era, the Editor would at an early stage have intervened to put an end to what was happening by outlining my long record of constructive contributions to Irish debate – 24 years of columns and other pieces in *The Irish Times*, in which I had fearlessly set out my positions and stood to fight my corner without resorting to personal abuse or invective. But the Editor was nowhere to be seen, did not communicate in any way with me and did not utter one public word about the matter.

At all times in my role as a columnist for *The Irish Times*, I had sought to carry out my work without fear or favour, and had as a result gained the respect of many people in Ireland and elsewhere, not just for myself but for *The Irish Times*'s stewardship of its responsibility to provide free and open debate on matters of importance to Irish society and beyond. In certain areas, I had often had to carry alone the burden of executing this democratic responsibility, as the newspaper's personnel – sometimes right to the very top – seemed to be operating against the alternative voice. For many years, I had been subjected to a campaign of bullying, intimidation and ostracisation within *The Irish Times* because of taking positions on issues that were uncongenial to the consensual ideology of the bulk of the newspaper's journalistic staff. Now the nightmare was re-curring, with this latest, most lethal fire being stoked and coaxed into the broader public arena by those the outsider might understandably mistake for my colleagues.

For many years, I had written my columns in *The Irish Times* and never allowed myself to be fazed by the abuse my views invariably provoked in some quarters. For instance, although I have tried to make the point to my line managers in the paper that the kind of online commentary they had been cultivating of late was as damaging to the reputation of the newspaper as it was to me, I would never before have woken up in the middle of the night to the thought of a mob outside my window. Now, I had been presented to Ireland and the wider world – with the conniv-ance of people who knew better – as in effect the face of homophobia in Ireland, and *The Irish Times* was silently nodding its head and winking at those who attacked me.

Even though the existence and content of my exchange with Una Mul-lally was by now known about at the highest level of the newspaper, noth-ing was done either to set the public record straight or discourage or inhibit the attacks. These people knew me and knew how far off the mark was the depiction of me by Rory O'Neill, someone who, at best, hadn't bothered to reach beyond his own prejudices in selecting his targets.

< 188 >

I had never attacked gay people on the basis of their sexual orientation or otherwise, in *The Irish Times* or elsewhere. I had not even taken an active stance against gay marriage, yet, everyone sat there enjoying the spectacle of me being savaged by the LGBT lions. I understood and accepted that columnists were fair game for those who disagreed with what they wrote, but this did not give an open licence to those who disagreed with someone to say or write what they liked, regardless of truth. To say that, because I was a 'controversial commentator', I was not entitled to protect my reputation or to deserve a basic level of civility and truth-telling was like telling a cyclist who has been deliberately run over by an articulated juggernaut that, since he had at the time been using the public highway, he has no reason to complain and no prospect of redress.

Moreover, to the extent that it was relevant that I had a role in public commentary as a 'controversial journalist', a relevant factor was surely that *The Irish Times* employed me with precisely this end in mind. The idea of the newspaper allowing its journalists to now join in with such relish in the attacks on me, publishing articles in which I was named and defamed, and refusing to acknowledge any possibility of there being another side to the story, was beyond hypocrisy.

It seemed clear to me that if, for example, I were to return to work in *The Irish Times* and seek to embark again on a critique of social workers, the family courts, local authorities, gardaí, judges, secularists or feminists – or, indeed, to address any of the menu of contentious topics that I'd previously sought to present in the face of the implacable hostility of my colleagues and other unseen and often anonymous actors – the invective would crank up again; the anonymous underneathers would begin pumping out their hatred with a new vengeance; the online edition of my columns would carry up to 1,000 unmoderated 'comments' weekly, mostly of unspeakable bile; and I would be told, in effect, to 'suck it up'.

Having indicated in February that I intended to leave the paper, I had agreed, following a discussion between the Deputy Editor, Denis Staunton, and my solicitor, Kevin Brophy, to put my resignation on ice and continue with a five-week leave period I'd negotiated to work on a book I was writing. At that point I remained open to the idea of eventually being able to withdraw my resignation, as Denis Staunton indicated he wished me to do. I believe I would have done so, were it not for what happened next.

Perhaps the most sinister development over the course of the entire saga was the unearthing of Thomas59. This individual was first brought to my attention by two friends, a lot more internet-savvy than I am, one of whom has a detailed understanding of social networks and their secrets. Somewhat into the controversy, they came across a particular Twitter account, which seemed to belong to someone with a high degree of knowledge of events inside *The Irish Times*. His Twitter moniker was Thomas59, obviously a pseudonym. At that stage he had just five followers.

Thomas59 had a lot of pretty unflattering things to say about me, Breda O'Brien and the Iona Institute, and was a follower – and also seemingly a strong supporter – of PantiBliss, which was Rory O'Neill's Twitter handle. On 18 January, as the story of our dispute with RTÉ emerged, he texted @PantiBliss: 'don't worry Panti ... the same crew do it all the time. It's about intimidation ... can't win the argument? Send a solicitor's letter.'

On 26 January he tweeted: 'Let's face it folks. Neither blacks, Catholics or gays should be allowed marry. And I'm not a racist, a bigot or a homophobe. Just reasonable.'

On 1 February Thomas59 became involved in a brief exchange with another tweeter called 'liam driver', who was commenting on that evening's *Saturday Night Show* debate on the homophobia controversy, in which I had declined an invitation to participate. Liam driver referred to one of the panellists on the show, Susan Phillips, who had put forward a traditionalist viewpoint on marriage, tweeting, '#satnightshow Suzan – model middle class white catholic Irish snob. Fucking whore burn in hell, you and your church.'

Thomas59, revealing himself as a stickler for accuracy, tweeted back: '@DriverLiam liam she's Church of Ireland and all the above.'

On 3 February Thomas59 responded to a tweet from Paul Duane, tweeting under the name MrPaulDuane, who had announced: 'Well, I just got an email from John Waters – the gay one, who makes movies. He knows ALL about our John Waters. "I get his Google alerts."'

Some hours later, Thomas59 rejoined: '@MrPaulDuane Is he planning to change his name?'

That same day, Thomas59 tweeted Colm O'Gorman, the gay activist and head of Amnesty Ireland, who had been on radio debating the issue with Breda O'Brien and others: '@Colmogorman Colm, why do you engage with these assholes?'

On 4 February he tweeted Mary Kenny, the *Irish Independent* columnist, who had had the temerity to call for a little restraint: 'O for God's sake Mary. Your lot have decades of experience in doing that, Now you employ lawyers to do so same as against abused.'

Thomas59 appeared to be a close follower also of certain current affairs programmes on television and had on 4 February tweeted the *Tonight with Vincent Browne* programme on TV3 to tell them that I had sent a solicitor's letter to *The Irish Times* about Una Mullally's article of 20 January.

On 5 February he tweeted: 'Breda O'Brien. Prey for us. J Waters. D Quinn; J Murray, P Casey, R Mullen, M Steen. Prey for us … on homophobic gays. (Sponsored by RTÉ).'

Also on 5 February he tweeted: 'Panti in Wednes Indo. Won't happen in Times. Complaints from Breda O'B and legal action by J Waters over Una Mullally Panti article January 27 (sic).'

The same day he tweeted: 'Iona Institute and J Waters denounce UN for anti Catholic 'bigotry'. 'Disappointed' at its condemnation of child abuse and Magdalen laundries.' This was a reference to a UN statement condemning the abuses in Magdalen laundries, and calling on the Pope to investigate them. The tweet was presumably an attempt at satire.

On 6 February, after a debate on the issue on *Primetime*, Thomas59

< 191 >

tweeted the programme attacking one of the participants, a gay man who defended the Iona Institute's position on gay marriage: 'Paddy Manning? Well every minority has its Uncle Toms… #rtept'

On Friday 7 February, obviously watching Senator David Norris on *The Late Late Show*, he tweeted: 'Let's face it – David Norris is a national treasure. Let's celebrate him while we have him. That 'satire' quote he read was by John Waters.'

That same evening, he tweeted: 'Panti for President in 2018?'

On 9 February, in what appeared to be a reference to the recently published recording and transcript of my conversations with James Grannell in *College Tribune*, he tweeted: 'By the Waters of Babble-on-and-on..... I lay down and wept...and wept...and wept...floodwaters...'

The following evening he tweeted in response to an emerging controversy involving the Garda Siochána Ombudsman Commission (GSOC) which had become embroiled in allegations concerning espionage at its offices in Dublin: 'Oh no. More buggers. Where's John Waters when you need him? And them about to subvert the State. Could be satire. But feels like farce #Vinb.'

Shortly afterwards, he came again: 'It must have been Sean Doherty/ Haughey again...but? Or maybe one of John Waters bug-gers? Trying to subvert society. Of course. That's it…'

He seemed to have a particular interest in me and Breda O'Brien, though with apparently a poor grasp of the ironic shadows cast by his own pseudonymous status.

On 12 February he tweeted: 'So it's the O'Brien children who are now fronting for the Iona Institute. See letter by B Conroy - Breda O'Bs son - in Times today. Cowardly.'

Shortly afterward, he corrected this tweet (he felt moved to do this rather frequently, since his initial efforts often contained errors of fact or serious misspellings): 'Apologies. That's Breda O'Brien's husband. Her son batted on Saturday Night Show. Dishonest. Public should be told.'

Once my Internet sleuths began to take a close interest in Thomas59, his identity was not long emerging. They followed his tweets back to the point when he initiated his Twitter account on 28 May 2013 (my birthday!!). There they found that, in the immediate aftermath of setting up his account, he had either carelessly or naively given away his true identity in several different ways: signing off one tweet with his real first name and referring in another to his nieces and nephews by the family name; mentioning his occupation as a correspondent in a particular area, and supplying his work email address for someone he requested to contact him. He had also neglected to disable the GPS facility on his mobile device, which meant that, every time he tweeted, he revealed his precise location, which was sometimes his flat in southside Dublin, sometimes his local pub, Goggins of Monkstown, and sometimes the offices of *The Irish Times* on Tara Street, Dublin. Thomas59 was revealed in all his ingloriousness as Patsy McGarry, Religious Affairs Correspondent of *The Irish Times*.

You knew his father, actually called Thomas. I remember the way you used to refer to him – humourously – as 'that blackguard'. I remember those lengthy confabs between you and Tom, sitting in the front of his brown and battered Mercedes, outside the front gate of Lynchs at Aughaderry, the 40 acres of which McGarry had 'taken' for his cattle. These summits would usually follow yet another atrocity of tree-eating or fence-razing by said cattle, who seemed to have absorbed by osmosis something of McGarry's disregard for convention and boundaries. But despite the persistent argy-bargy, you continued to hold one another in high affection. We all liked the McGarrys. I always found myself smiling when I saw Tom coming, even though I knew of his reputation as an incorrigible rogue.

They called him 'the Haw', although with you it was always 'Tom', or, when you were vexed, 'McGarry', or 'that blackguard'. He was witty in a laid-back way and teased people relentlessly. His wife, who sometimes accompanied him when he came to 'look at' the cattle, was a beautiful woman in every way – kind, gentle, friendly. You had known her also for years, having carried her people in and out from Castleplunket. There was a history between you all of which I had only the dimmest outline.

By all accounts he got the nickname 'The Haw' when he was working as a 'male nurse', as we used to call them, in the 'San' – the mental hospital – in Castlerea during the 1940s, before he became a health inspector. It was a play on the nickname of the Second World War pro-Nazi propagandist William Joyce, 'Lord Haw Haw', who, like McGarry, was known for his anti-British diatribes.

He had a tongue fit for stripping paint. There was a legend about when, as a member of Roscommon County Council, he argued for a swimming pool in Ballagh on the grounds that there were a lot of people in the town who hadn't had a wash since the midwife signed off on them. His family appeared to regard him with a mixture of irony and trepidation, not least because of his loose attitude to fencing. His cattle were the most travelled in Roscommon, along the main roads or through other people's lands. As a result, the path to his door was reportedly well trodden by sundry complainants who were invariably sent away with a witticism to chew on. Once a woman came to complain his cattle had eaten the cabbages in her vegetable plot. "It's all right, Noreen," said Tom. "It'll do them no harm."

On 14 February I sent a comprehensive portfolio on Thomas59 in an email to the Editor of *The Irish Times*, Kevin O'Sullivan, and his deputy, Denis Staunton. I drew attention to the implications of Thomas59's behaviour for the reputation of *The Irish Times* as a voice of diversity and balance in Irish society, revealing the identity of the individual in question, and demonstrating beyond doubt that he was tweeting aggressively on virtually a nightly basis against colleagues and people he was expected to write objectively about in his job. I supplied texts of his numerous tweets and indicated the identities of several of his 'followers', including *The Irish Times* Assistant Editor, Literary Editor and columnist, Fintan O'Toole. Had I been Editor of *The Irish Times*, I would have been keen to put these questions to Fintan: What interest did he have in the twitterings of Thomas59? Was he aware of the true identity of this individual? If so, what did he have to say for himself? If not, why was he one of

Thomas59's followers? After I had sent him several reminders, Staunton sent me a bad-tempered acknowledgement. I never received any kind of response from O'Sullivan.

Although I named McGarry in an article I wrote about the matter for *Village* magazine in April 2014, he did not, then or since, come out to defend himself, although a number of other journalists lined up to do so and he himself was occasionally to be heard muttering about not being the kind of journalist who sues people. It was asserted by some of those seeking to bat on his behalf that the fact that he had failed to cover his tracks meant that he was being open about his identity. This is bogus, as was to be revealed by Thomas59's response when he came to realise that I knew who he was.

One radio presenter and self-confessed friend of McGarry tried to suggest that since one element of his Twitter 'handle' included what turned out to be the landline number of his flat, it was quite obvious who Thomas59 was. All nonsense. The full Twitter handle was given at the top of the feed as 'Thomas59 @Thomas2805607'. The number 2805607 was, or had been, McGarry's landline number at his flat in Monkstown, but could have been the number of the Man in the Moon for all you would know unless you happened to recognise it as McGarry's from having used it yourself. For McGarry or anyone speaking on his behalf to claim that his identity was transparent would be akin to me setting up a Twitter account with the handle MickeyJoe99 @MickeyJoe2350909 and claiming that this made clear who was tweeting.

It is obvious that McGarry had no idea he was leaving a trail behind him as he tweeted, perhaps imagining that tweets were like emails, that historical tweets were visible only to the user. Only by tracing the thread back to its beginning were my sleuths able to track down the culprit, and they had a very particular interest in so doing. It is difficult to imagine the circumstances in which anyone else would have been prompted or disposed to do that.

More effectively than any case I had been able to make to date, Thomas59's tweets established the existence of a highly toxic climate of illiberal antagonism towards particular viewpoints at the heart of *The Irish Times*'s editorial operation, and towards me in particular. The Thomas59 tweets also left no doubt that this supposedly objective correspondent was encumbered by an outright ideological bias which ought to have disqualified him from writing as a reporter on the matters he was required to cover for the newspaper. Moreover, Thomas59 had been tweeting in full view of at least one senior editor at the newspaper, who must be assumed to have been aware of the true identity of the account-holder he had elected to follow. There could scarcely be the slightest doubt that the culture of the newspaper was utterly repugnant to the supposed historical ethos of *The Irish Times* as a liberal newspaper with a commitment to diversity of opinion on controversial issues.

If I imagined that my email to Staunton and O'Sullivan would be the end of Thomas59's Twitter career, I had another shock coming. Thomas59 continued to tweet. On 20 February: 'So Breda O' B says says marriage is about bonding parents and biological children. What about adoptive parents? Like David Quinn of Iona.'

And ...

'O dear. New poll says 76% Irish people favour same sex marriage. Breda O'Brien, John Waters, Iona Institute heading for Uganda.'

On 21 February, having received no replies to two earlier communications, I again emailed the Editor and his deputy, asking that they take steps to have the material removed and to convey to its author that this was not appropriate behaviour for a senior *Irish Times* journalist. Denis Staunton emailed me curtly to say that he had spoken with the Editor about the matter.

The following day, 22 February, Thomas59 tweeted the 16 words which would put paid to the defence that he had been open about his identity: 'One has been rumbled by H2O. ... but does one care? Non. Who wants such cruel friends?'

Rumbled? A quick search of an online dictionary throws up the following definition: 'discover (an illicit activity or its perpetrator).' So much for those who claimed Thomas59's identity was intended to be an open book. McGarry clearly imagined that his sneaky character assassination would remain undetected.

Shortly afterwards, the ever-punctilious Thomas59 'corrected' this tweet: 'Should have been H2Os in previous tweet.'

Most disturbing about all this was that I had imagined for a long time that McGarry was a friend of mine, as his father Tom had been a friend of yours. We had met not long after I went to work in journalism in Dublin, he being a friend of a then girlfriend of mine. At the time he was working in radio, and also in some capacity with *The Irish Press*, doing, among other things, theatre reviews.

In fact, it was I who, after *The Irish Press* closed down in 1995, tipped him off that *The Irish Times* was looking for a Religious Affairs Correspondent and that it might suit him.

He had not been a casual acquaintance or a mere work colleague, but someone whom I knew well and had associated with both professionally and personally for many years. When I was editing *Magill* in the late 1980s, he wrote regularly for it. He even put me up in his flat for a couple of weeks one time when my house was flooded by a burst pipe. To add to the piquancy of the Thomas59 saga, at the time we discovered who he was, I had been in communication for some months with a male relative of McGarry's, who was having some difficulty in the matter of gaining access to his child. I had spoken to him a number of times on the phone, recommended someone from whom he might be able to obtain legal advice, and made a number of attempts to meet with him without success. On one occasion, he contacted me expressing intentions of committing suicide, but after a number of exchanges between us, he thought better of this plan. This unfortunate individual, blithely unaware of what was happening, actually called me in April 2014, just after I had exposed Thomas59's identity in *Village* magazine – to ask for further assistance with his ongoing problem. Somewhat taken aback, I nonetheless again tried to advise him as best I could. We spoke for a few minutes; he thanked me and hung up. I did not hear from him again.

< 197 >

In recent years McGarry and I had seen less of one another than in the past, but I had no clear-cut cause to feel that our relationship had deteriorated – save for one incident in the middle of 2012 when he attacked me verbally at Croke Park on the final day of the Eucharistic Congress. That was actually quite a shock, coming without warning just after we had appeared together on a BBC radio show, during which he gave no indication that he was personally displeased with me. He stormed at me across the press room, accusing me of disloyalty to my colleagues – I presumed on foot of an article I had written in that day's Irish Mail on Sunday criticising the inaccurate and hostile media coverage of the congress.

In the meantime, he had attended Mammy's funeral in September 2012, following which we exchanged friendly emails and even met for a coffee just before Christmas. After that, we had no engagement for about nine months, when we had a brief and, I thought, reasonably cordial telephone conversation, during which I asked him if he would be available as a guest lecturer at a forthcoming course in journalism I was booked to conduct in the new year. He said he would be happy to accept – and that was to be the last contact between us. Weirdly, I had been about to call him up to fix an exact date for the lecture when the Thomas59 stuff erupted.

At Mammy's funeral in 2012, McGarry embraced my daughter Róisín, my girlfriend – now my wife – Rita, my sisters and me, and briefly, with considerable apparent piety, touched my mother's hand in her coffin. Afterwards we engaged in an exchange of emails in which he spoke very movingly about her and about you:

> I have always regretted missing your father's funeral. I knew him since I was a child when he would pass our house [...] every day at 6pm on the button. He marked out my childhood day. He used also give lifts to my mother's uncle and aunt [...] and he and my father had that frequent experience – where my father was concerned - of starting out as enemies over land and politics before ending up fond of one another.
>
> May your mother rest in peace, as I am sure she will. Seeing her in the

< 198 >

coffin was to be reminded of my own (maternal) grandmother, another woman of great faith who died in her 80s after a difficult couple of decades with arthiritis [sic]. My paternal grandmother was dead before I was born. There was a tremendous stoicism about such women.

We discussed, too, the comfort there was to be gleaned from the extended country ritual of publicly sympathising with bereaved families at the funeral. We agreed that we hadn't really understood the power of this until it became directly relevant in our lives. He said that his sense of this had motivated him to come to the funeral, regardless of our recent differences. 'Some things are more important than those,' he wrote.

In the interim between those emails and the Rory O'Neill-instigated controversy, no fresh difference of opinion had arisen between McGarry and me. We just hadn't seen each other or spoken, apart from the two exchanges I've mentioned.

I had been aware of a certain intermittent coolness from him in recent times – mainly, I thought, because, as Religious Correspondent of *The Irish Times*, he had a bee in his bonnet about the evils of Catholicism, whereas I was more interested in exploring the indispensable elements of religion. There would, from time to time, be certain barbed references in our writings to things the other had written, but this was no more than the normal attrition of public commentary.

Certainly, he had no reason to be suddenly surprised by anything concerning my views on gay marriage or the parenting of children. Indeed, I had never gathered, over the course of our relationship, that he had any interest in these matters at all, apart from an odd intervention in the wake of the 2012 referendum on 'Children's Rights', when he was heard on radio complaining that the No vote was boosted by 'scare tactics'. This was a guy who had never before had anything much to say about children's rights, family rights, family or marriage, and who had never, to the best of my knowledge, written a single sentence in favour of gay marriage up to the time Rory O'Neill appeared on *The Saturday Night Show*.

< 199 >

Since it was clear that Thomas59's attacks on me did not arise from any recent personal or professional difference between me and their author, the only alternative explanation is that they were provoked out of the deeply noxious atmosphere of antagonism that had been allowed to fester towards me for many years inside *The Irish Times*, worsening dramatically in the years after Kevin O'Sullivan became Editor. The tweets were their author's calculated contribution to a campaign contrived by a powerful lobby group with the clear aim of disabling me as a commentator by inflicting on me grievous reputational damage and inciting extreme public odium towards me, perhaps with the added objective of demonstrating to all concerned what these lobbyists were capable of doing.

In the wake of the extraordinary discovery of the true identity of Thomas59, I reflected deeply on whether I should reveal what I knew. I had some reservations about doing so, not least because I believed, perhaps naively, that McGarry was acting out of character, having come under the sway of stronger personalities within *The Irish Times*. For two reasons I decided that naming him was the more honest course. One was that, in order to spell out the full implications for *The Irish Times* I needed to give such a degree of detail about him that his identity would become obvious to virtually anyone who was familiar with the newspaper. In this context, my failure to remove his coward's cloak of anonymity would have seemed somewhat coy. Even worse was the possibility that people might jump to the wrong conclusion about the identity of Thomas59.

The second reason is that I had come to believe that such pseudonymous activity was by then a fairly widespread pursuit among *Irish Times* journalists, and that this needed to be exposed, where possible, for the protection of those who carry out their journalistic work in an open and straightforward fashion.

Once it became clear that the editors were not going to do anything about Thomas59, I resigned from *The Irish Times*, after 24 years of service as, variously, a columnist, reporter and feature writer. I did so with many regrets, but nevertheless certain of the importance of protesting the ominous drift of the newspaper under the influence of a poisonous ideological orthodoxy that threatened its role as an esteemed journal of record and a bulwark of Irish democracy.

< 201 >

17

The Mechanic's Heart

I came across a remarkable book in an Oxfam shop that's nearly having as much of an effect on me as *The Swiss Family Robinson*. It's *Shop Class as Soulcraft*, by Matthew B. Crawford, who's both a motorbike mechanic and a philosopher, and equally serious about both disciplines. The book was published in America in 2009, and subsequently this side of the Atlantic under the unwieldy and death-kissing title *The Case for Working With Your Hands, Or Why Office Work is Bad for You and Fixing Things Feels Good*. It was published in Italian under the title *Eulogy to the Carburettor*, which better captures the poetry of it.

I don't want to do an injustice to Crawford's thesis by pinning it down too neatly, but it's along the lines that something fundamental, indispensable and non-replaceable happens when a human being uses his or her hands to make or fix something. He quotes the philosopher Alexandre Kojéve on the 'man who works', by which he means the man who takes a task from the beginning to the end through a set of skills that he's spent some time acquiring and perfecting, and in doing so intervenes in the world in a way that leaves a mark behind: 'The man who works recognises his own product in the World that has actually been transformed by his work; he recognises himself in it, he sees in it his own human reality, in it he discovers and reveals to others the objective reality of his humanity, of the originally abstract and purely subjective idea he has of himself.'

Crawford writes about working on his motorcycle, about being 'drawn out of oneself and into a struggle, by turns hateful and loving, with another thing that, like a mule, was emphatically not simply an extension of one's will'. You had to conform your will and judgement to certain external facts of physics that still presented themselves as such. 'Old bikes don't flatter you,' he declares, 'they educate you.'

But fixing things, unlike making things, has another facet that, as a by-product of the process, can be beneficial for society. Like the doctor, the 'temporary jobsman' does not fix things for good and so becomes guarded against conceit. I remember that in your lexicon the word 'conceit' also stretched to naming something that seemed to be among the worst of sins: the tendency of certain people to big themselves up, to overstate their talents or achievements. 'You could go into that fella's house and not find as much as a hammer,' you would say. I thought it a vanity of your own, but now I see something else. For you, fixing things was compatible with a modest ambition to adhere to the laws of reality, not to set yourself above it, or drag it down. You'd like Crawford. He says: 'The experience of failure tempers the concept of mastery; the doctor and the mechanic have daily intercourse with the world as something independent, and a vivid awareness of the difference between self and nonself'.

This familiarity with limits and fragility serves to moderate any tendency to claim either omniscience or omnipotence, and is clearly nowadays missing from our cultures, where the illusion of having mastery – by virtue of possession over a machine that someone else has designed and built – is enough to send people into a permanent orbit of self-importance. The involvement of the doctor or the mechanic, Crawford stresses, is an ethical one – the mechanic's perception is not that of the spectator, but an active process rooted in his bank of knowledge of root causes and telltale patterns. It is driven not by an abstract quest for clues or symptoms but fundamentally by the fact that he cares about his 'patient'. And this caring is related in turn to a deep pride in the calling and its responsibilities and demands.

A repairman of the old kind, Crawford reminds us, needs to develop a relationship with objects that involves a real understanding – not ownership or a claim of dominance, but a sense of how these objects fit into the logic of the world. 'For this very reason,' he writes, 'his work

< 203 >

also chastens the easy fantasy of mastery that permeates modern culture. The repairman has to begin every job by getting out of his own head and noticing things; he has to look carefully and listen to the ailing machine.' The repairman, then, represents a threat to the modern narcissist: 'The problem isn't so much that he is dirty or uncouth. Rather, he seems to offer a challenge to our self-understanding that is somehow fundamental. We're not as free and independent as we thought.'

I think of Matthew Crawford as being essentially you with a philosophy degree. He strikes me as being, first of all, a tradesman, a mechanic, but then as someone who isn't satisfied that what he's engaged in is just doing things with his hands: he has to understand where the urges come from, why it feels good, where it takes him in himself, and after that the place of these processes of doing in human culture. He sets out an impressive stall of philosophical thought, which he had investigated with the same assiduity you might bring to the conundrum of an overly rich mixture in a set of twin carburettors. I think of your thinking as being grounded in the experiences you gleaned from kneading and planing and filing reality into a more congenial shape for the purpose you intended. All your thoughts, great and small, about the big questions and the little ones, had this characteristic about it. I suppose you would call it common sense – the presumption of coherence that must accompany any exploration of the world – scientific, spiritual, artistic or otherwise. Crawford brings his mechanic's heart along in pursuit of the idea that this coherence can be traced backwards in thought-time as well as forwards, at arm's length, under the bonnet, the sink or the cistern, that it is bedded in a concrete frame of seeing and speculating that once invaded our patterns of thinking without our having a clue about this. Like all great thinkers, he takes the view that there is more to the obvious and the axiomatic than meets the eye. He is alert at all times for the repetitive rattle in reality that indicates a problem of timing or understeer or the possibility of an elusive looseness in the universal joint. He needs to know not merely what is to be known, but what it means to know and how this knowledge relates to the texture and mixture and shape of real things, their true purpose, their mode of operation, the way they communicate a slippage from full functionality. This is fundamentally a moral endeavour. 'For humans,' Crawford says, 'tools point to the necessity of moral inquiry. Because nature makes only ambiguous prescriptions for us, we are compelled to ask, what is good?'

To practise a trade or craft is to enter into a relationship with a world that exists independently of yourself. To get better at something is to be drawn closer to an understanding of how the world works in practice. To be an apprentice to a master is to be guided along a path of learning. A carpenter is bound by the evidence of his level, an electrician by the irrefutable witness of the circuitry he has assembled. Do the lights work or not? The individuality of the tradesman is expressed in his engagement with a world he shares with other similarly engaged beings, a world of which understandings are stored and exchanged. The defining spirit is a sociable individuality based on mutual passions. It's not the same as autonomy, which Crawford says denies that we are born into a world that pre-existed us. 'It posits an essential aloneness: an autonomous being is free in the sense that a being severed from all others is free. To regard oneself in this way is to betray the natural debts we owe to the world, and commit the moral error of ingratitude. For in fact we are basically dependent beings: one upon another, and each on a world that is not of our making.'

Forty-odd years ago, when I left the education system, such as it was, I thought nothing of the fact that I was coming away without a tradeable skill or craft. Had I considered this at all, I would probably have regarded it as close to a virtue. In this sense I was pretty typical of the late 20th century generations of school-leavers. I sensed I was missing something, yet had no idea what it might be. I now understand what it was I lacked: your capacity to integrate your view of reality with the objects you manipulated and the things you did with your hands. In you, the processes of thinking and doing were fully integrated; in me they were not, or at least not entirely. Your view of politics and economics was rooted firmly

< 205 >

in your sense of how a door frame should be mortised together, how a valve should be ground, how a tree should be pruned.

I often watched you examining your own work or someone else's – the attention you paid to the feel, the action, details, finish. You used the same head for politics, and that was why your thoughts exhibited a coherence that is nowadays missing from almost everybody. This is where the senselessness of modern political life arises from: when everyone is allocated just a tiny discrete part in a process, it is unreasonable to expect them to contemplate the entire systems. Each thing is merely its own narrow self: democracy, equality, free speech, compassion, rights. The idea of an interconnected apparatus, such as is implied by the idea of a constitution, is, by definition, completely alien to such a culture. The idea of the republican – an autonomous yet dependent man (I mean a human being) who governs himself in accordance with a clear view of his createdness, his givenness, who lives in full awareness of being dependent, who looks askance on anything that threatens to steal his freedom – such a human being is anathema to such a culture.

In this context, Crawford speaks of what he defines as the true republican man, who is both creature and creator: possessed of given gifts and talents, he follows their logic in search of the new. He masters his own hands so as to become the servant of something that is not simply another man, or other men. He is the artisan of ideas, the craftsman of culture and the journeyman of the truth. Without him, ideals wilt, culture atrophies and the truth disappears from plain sight.

18

A Question of Loyalty

In April 2014, when I published my 7,000-word response to the 'homophobe' saga for *Village* magazine, I probably expected to be inundated with calls from journalists, as I had been in January, February and much of March. I presumed that some of those journalists who had hounded me for three months would now follow the logic of their apparent zeal in pursuing this 'story' by reporting what I had said in response.

I got a couple of nibbles and three significant bites. One of these was an interview I rather stupidly gave to a journalist with *The Sunday Independent* who had been ringing me almost weekly for the previous two months, and now did so again. The other two were radio interviews, one with Matt Cooper on Today FM, the other on *Today With Seán O'Rourke* on RTÉ Radio One. In January, when the controversy erupted, O'Rourke had contacted me personally to invite me on his programme. At that point, anxious to avoid fanning the flames, I'd declined, but we agreed that he would get first refusal if I decided to speak publicly. I kept my word, and sent him and his producer advance copies of the *Village* article. The sharp intakes of breath from Montrose could be heard in Belmullet. There was an extended delay while the programme consulted its lawyers. Eventually it was agreed that an interview with me could be pre-recorded. At the outset of the interview, O'Rourke, by way of a declaration of interest, announced that he was a friend of Patsy McGarry's, and what followed was entirely predictable on that basis.

Apart from these three take-ups, I got no communications or enquiries from anyone seeking to tease out what I had written, in print or on air. Had there been holes in what I said in response, I have no doubt that the

< 207 >

agitators in the media would have found them and zeroed in. Instead, tellingly, they looked the other way. There were a few half-baked online attempts to twist things I'd written, in the hope of starting the whole circus up again, but these rapidly petered out. A couple of Sunday newspapers carried brief references to my exposure of McGarry, but invariably in a manner calculated to get him off the hook. As for the rest – nothing, providing definitive evidence of the advanced corruption of most of the Irish media, which had now ceased to be interested in reporting what actually happens, but instead were almost universally devoted to ensuring that particular kinds of things happened and others did not, stymieing anyone who dared to see things differently. It is also reasonable to speculate that the reason for the silence around my article was that, with the same-sex marriage referendum on the way, the proponents of the proposal were determined not to let go of a convenient scapegoat merely because the facts were not in harmony with their objectives.

I did, however, receive a number of informal communications in the wake of the *Village* article from journalists, including some from inside *The Irish Times*. These were highly instructive in different ways, not least concerning the unwillingness of people to say publicly what they were prepared to confide to me sotto voce.

For me, the kernel of the media corruption I speak of resides in the inability of journalists to comprehend that a newspaper is not the property of any individual or individuals, no matter what positions they may hold within it, or any ideology to which they may subscribe. A newspaper, especially one like *The Irish Times*, is a conduit for divergent views on reality, and as far as possible for the conveyance of uncontaminated information concerning events, trends and perspectives on matters relating to public and collective life. If it falls into the hands of any singular perspective, to the point where other outlooks are made to feel uncomfortable or unwelcome, it will have ceased in effect to be a newspaper in any meaningful sense of the word.

And this, in respect of *The Irish Times*, was the tenor of the comments

< 208 >

I received from the few colleagues who responded privately to what I wrote in *Village*. One former *Irish Times* colleague wrote: ' … a short word to say I just read your lengthy piece in *Village*. It's a stunning piece of writing, not least the fascinating deconstruction of what I agree is now an obsessive, even aggressive "liberalism" at the heart of *The Irish Times*, it has really been transformed in a negative way as a newspaper since Geraldine Kennedy retired.' Another senior journalist wrote to me to express, he said, his solidarity in the light of what had occurred. He had intended to write earlier, he said, to convey his hope that the recent turmoil would not result in my leaving the newspaper, but now saw it was too late for that. He had been meaning to say that he too had been finding the 'New Establishment' within the paper 'hard to take at times', but that there were still 'shades of oul' decency within the paper'. Now that I had left, he worried, who would seriously challenge that tyranny? He mentioned having raised at a senior level concerns about the direction of the paper, but being rebuffed. 'It's the Orwellian nature of some of the language and the sheer anti-intellectualism of some of the new house style that galls,' he wrote. 'It seems to me that at the moment the pseudo-liberal righteousness that prevails is totally blind; that it is so smug that it can't bear any proper self-reflection. A disputatious paper is a good paper, I feel, and I always loved that about the IT, but an oppressive paper isn't. … I think some clear, sharp direction from the top would solve problems and allow all voices to be reasonably politely heard, but so far that's not happening.'

As regards the recent controversy, he felt that it was 'generally better that journos don't sue', but in the face of a gratuitous defamation, in which a rapid apology had been withheld, it was 'reasonable' to take such action. He mentioned the acrimony between myself and Fintan O'Toole, which he said reflected the battle-lines within the country, and wondered if this might have been diluted or ameliorated had we been in the practice of conducting vibrant in-house debates about contentious matters. The strange thing here was that, from my perspective, the 'acrimony' between O'Toole and me had been entirely one-sided. It was true that he had launched a number of extraordinary attacks on me in his column, and that I had responded to these in robust terms, but it was also true that, whenever we met, we maintained an extremely cordial relationship. For my part, although I found some of his commentaries cutting and unfair, I had never held a personal grudge about anything he had written, considering it part of the attrition of the commentator's calling. I had known O'Toole from my days as Editor of *Magill*, when I had several times commissioned him to write articles. In 1992, when I did a series of programmes about Irish life and politics for BBC Radio Four, I had interviewed him and included several of his contributions. On one occasion we met accidentally boarding the same Ryanair flight to Stansted, and had an intense and highly enjoyable conversation all the way across and on the train into Liverpool Street. Some years later, I was somewhat perplexed by a response of O'Toole to an interviewer who asked him about me. In an earlier interview, asked about my personal relations with Fintan, I had described these as 'friendly'. When asked about this, O'Toole responded that I had never been a friend of his, a gratuitous and disingenuous remark. It was true that we had not been 'friends', but we had indeed been 'friendly'. There is a difference.

A former *Irish Times* journalist captured the core of the issue when he wrote to relate an incident in which he had spoken very recently to a 'very senior *Irish Times* person', who had told him: 'Waters keeps criticising the media, by which he obviously means *The Irish Times*, and yet he expects some personal loyalty.' My correspondent thought this 'revealing of the loss of perspective and slipped categories of institutional groupthink there'.

This is the point. The rot centres on misconceptions of loyalty, with many people in the newspaper now seemingly regarding loyalty as being due to themselves or each other, rather than to the spirit, history, traditions, values and ethos of *The Irish Times*.

The role of *The Irish Times* in the aftermath of *The Saturday Night Show* attack was especially troubling to me, since I'd been with the paper for nearly 24 years, a columnist for 23. Those years, it's true, were not without difficulty, though nothing on the scale of what happened in 2014. Because my outlook on reality had in general been different from the mainstream view of the paper's journalists, I had incurred a great deal of disfavour from my colleagues there, especially since I started writing in the mid-1990s about the impact of family law discrimination on men and fathers. Luckily, for the most part, the Editor at that time, Conor Brady, had a reasonably robust approach to diversity of opinion. He took seriously the injunction in the Memorandum and Articles of Association of *The Irish Times* Trust document that the newspaper should accord 'special consideration ... to the reasonable representation of minority interests and divergent views'. I don't claim that interactions and communications between Brady and me were entirely unruffled – they certainly weren't – but I always had a sense that, on his watch, *The Irish Times* was, as he used to say, a 'broad church', and that my dissidence was, if not exactly cherished, at least protected.

Almost five years after the events of early 2014, nobody in *The Irish Times* has emerged to respond to any of the things I had said publicly about those events and the paper's role in them. From time to time, people who've been in contact with me unofficially have referred to what appears to be the justification being offered inside the newspaper for this treatment of me: that I have persistently criticised the paper and people who write for it. This is bogus. It's true that, in criticising the media, I have never sought to exclude or exonerate *The Irish Times* in the context of general comments that I felt might apply to it as much as any other media outlet. But I have never launched personal attacks on any of my colleagues, even though several of them have used *The Irish Times* to attack me, sometimes in quite splenetic tones. I have been told by former colleagues, for example, that Patsy McGarry had felt 'stung' by some of the things I'd written about him. The thing is: I never wrote anything derogatory about Patsy McGarry. Sometimes, it's true, I wrote general commentaries about the lamentable coverage of religion in Irish media, and it is possible that something in this may have annoyed him. But I never once referred to him either by name, title or office.

In my column, I had occasionally adverted, usually in quite oblique terms, to what I saw as the increasingly ideological nature of Irish journalism, in particular in its manifest hostility to the Catholic Church and its determined pursuit of an agenda diametrically in opposition to Catholic teaching and values. Over several years, I'd written on this theme in relation to several specific episodes, including the contorted and selective coverage of the Eucharistic Congress in June 2012 and the extraordinary bias exhibited by almost all reporting of the Savita Halappanavar saga that began later that year. These columns of mine appear to have gone down badly among some of my supposed colleagues, who apparently recognised themselves in what I had imagined to be extremely generalised commentaries. I received several irate emails from *Irish Times* journalists, one from a senior editor, denouncing me for 'disloyalty'. This was precisely the same charge levelled at me face-to-face by Patsy McGarry when he attacked me on the final day of the Eucharistic Congress at Croke Park in June 2012.

In my column in that day's Irish Mail on Sunday I'd published a trenchant critique of the media coverage of the congress, but without naming any particular journalist or instancing any of the dozens of malevolent pieces about the congress that I might have listed. That column began:

'The commandments for most of those covering the Eucharistic Congress seemed to be: 1. If there is an empty chair, we must photograph it. 2. The time to do your live-to-camera report on the congress is when the pilgrims are at lunch; then you go into the empty arena and talk about empty chairs and child abuse.'

On Sunday, the first day of the congress, one of the leading 'religious' correspondents from a national newspaper looked up from his computer screen and declared to a colleague sitting nearby: 'It's all a bit too much, isn't it?'

Translation: 'Who are all these people and why are they so anxious to persist in their obscurantism? Do they not know that the narrative has already been written? Do they imagine that they still matter in this secular, pluralist Ireland that we are busily hammering into existence?

I admit it. The 'religious' correspondent I referred to was indeed Mc-Garry. I had been told the anecdote by the colleague he had made the remark to.

When, earlier that morning, McGarry and I participated in a BBC radio discussion broadcast live from an adjoining room; I noted McGarry's rather cool demeanour towards me, but thought nothing of it until he came at me, ranting and raving, a short time afterwards. For me it was a mildly entertaining episode, but Rita, who was with me, being unfamiliar with media dogfights, was quite alarmed. Some weeks later, I referred to this occurrence in oblique terms in a column I submitted to *The Irish Times*, writing about having been attacked by a colleague but without naming McGarry. Before publication, I received a call from the Opinion Editor, who asked me to whom I was referring. I told him it was McGarry and he said that he would 'have to clear it with Patsy' before he could decide whether to leave the reference as it was. He reverted to me a short time afterwards saying that McGarry had 'requested' that the section be removed from my column, and that he, as Opinion Editor, was acquiescing in this. I didn't argue, having by this time grown weary of *Irish Times* double standards.

19

A Workers Republic!

I believe there was a true republic in Ireland, for a while, though it coincided neither with the actuality of the period from 1948, after the Irish Republic was formally declared, nor with the fantasies of the Provisionals or any of their progenitors. I believe the republic came about by osmosis, the collective actualisation of energies and actions and imagined possibilities in the minds of men and women, one by one, two by two, groups of four or six at the most, who brought the republic into being by virtue of their playing out in reality of the ideal of a human person – functioning, living, dreaming and intervening in reality by virtue of their own skills and ideas, putting their imprints on the world through the mediums of shoemaking, welding, knitting, weaving, sawing and screwing (in the older, original sense of the word).

This was the republic to which you belonged, the one that knew itself intimately by virtue of the mutualised sense of work to which you and others like you pledged your allegiance by daily practice. This was a republic without leaders, though not without leadership. All the men and women who belonged to it drew their power and their majesty from the skills they had honed in themselves, and the mastery over objects and fabrics that it gave them. A republic, yes, and a kingdom too. You were kings and queens of an Ireland that belonged, at least in potential, to its people.

I remember you and your fellow republicans: walking around from shop to shop, comparing your works and your wares. I remember the way you, my father, could not pass a newly completed piece of joinery without getting down on your knees and rubbing your hands along the planed timber, feeling its lines and smoothness. I remember you pushing the glasses to the top of your head and wondering why you did that. Why was the work of yourself or others the only kind of thing you would examine without your spectacles?

I remember you and your comrades using the word 'worker' not as an ideological designation but as a term of acclamation. Although you earned your living driving a mailcar, you were skilled or semi-skilled in a variety of crafts and trades, including carpentry, bricklaying, plastering, car mechanics, electrical work and horticulture. Your friends, as I've remarked, all seemed to be craftsmen: a shoemaker, a saddler, a watchmaker, a fellow mechanic. For you and your contemporaries to describe someone – male or female – as 'a great worker' was the ultimate praise, an acknowledgment of a quality that negated almost every flaw. Implicitly, such analyses assumed that the virtuous 'goal' of work related to its communal, that is its economic, dimension. But work was also an intrinsic aspect of personality. To say that someone was 'a good worker' was to describe not his usefulness but his character.

All this is gone now. In its place is a new dependency, exhibiting many dimensions of slavishness, narcissism, self-importance, helplessness and disconnection. We no longer make or fix, but simply consume and spectate. Matthew Crawford observes that this reorganisation of the human personality must of necessity affect our political culture, but he does not pursue the matter. His intuition is correct: even politics now has become something unmoored from the rational world of things and doings. It has become simply a matter of the citizen observing and the politician acting in accordance with the willed requirements of these spectators. I do not say 'voters', because voting is no longer really an essential element. Politics, a technology of the public space, has come to seem as opaque and impervious to democratic intervention as an iPhone. It is strange to think now that the shift, perhaps half a century ago, from practical work to intellectual attainment has rendered men and women far less engaged with their societies and the ideas that drive them than were previous societies, which to the casual eye seemed to impose the thoughts of a few on to the lives and works of a relatively uneducated many. We in our time have acquired the name of increased cleverness, but this enhanced intelligence is limited, it often seems, to the storage of information, or increasingly to the capacity to track information down when we need it. There is no governing intelligence, one that automatically sifts and sorts each detail in search of its place in the overarching scheme of things. There is, in other words, no sense of meaning, which explains why reason, logic and even facts are often nowadays regarded as instruments of oppression. A craftsman is by definition less susceptible to falling for lies or bullshit because his instinct is to place every received piece of information into a paradigm or grid or jig wherein he requires it to find its place and make sense. Once a whole generation of men and women loses this instinctive insistence on coherence, demagoguery and propaganda have fertile soil to work with. The republicanism I remember, therefore, is a republicanism of the hands and of the mind working together, a republic of the five senses. And this is a rather different way of stating why the Easter Rising of 1916 was essentially a drama of true republicanism: it was an event based on action as much as on words. The guns became tools, which left their marks on the world, and these marks would never be undone.

Work has become much degraded in our modern cultures, an activity oddly regarded as both an entitlement and an imposition. We claim for ourselves the 'right' to work, and yet appear to resent the demands work makes on our time, energy and freedom. Many of us do no more than struggle out of bed, slouch towards our places of employment, and remain there for the minimum hours, all the time watching the clock, listening for the signal of release. The disc jockey on the piped radio station keeps us going with the promise of the weekend, which seems to start on Wednesday and continue, at least as a happy memory, until Tuesday.

There is something to consider here about our understanding of what it means to be free. In our conventional idea of freedom, life is always moving ahead of us, out of the present moment towards something else, some other, future moment, a moment that resonates with a promise

< 216 >

lacking in the instant one. The demands of this present moment, there-fore, are something to be endured, tolerated, moved through. Somehow, the desiring mechanism of the human has switched to 'project' – project as verb – skimming over the moment that actually exists and seeking its satisfaction and justification somewhere in the future – 'going forward'. Our economic systems tend to mimic this tendency, or perhaps it is a refraction of their logic. They offer us a reward for our labour which is only marginally a means of subsistence or living – really, it is a system for compensating us for the 'inconvenience' we have suffered by virtue of having our energies diverted from something called 'life' to something called 'work'. And, even as we project ourselves forward in anticipation of something better, we recoil in fear of the same future and seek to store up our security against its dangers.

Work and life are not opposites, but intimately connected if not actu-ally coterminous. Man's duty to subdue the Earth is not a one-way street: man is also the subject of this undertaking. The call to engage in the ac-tions amounting to work is a directive to him to realise the total humanity that is his destiny by reason of his very existence. It is not incidental that Jesus trained as a carpenter.

The sources of the dignity of work are to be sought primarily in the subjective dimension. The basis for determining the value of work is not the type of work being done but the fact that the one who is doing it is a human being – being. This means that the purpose of work is not merely its apparent objectives, but also – even more so – the functioning of the human person who performs the task, no matter what it is. Work is good for man; it corresponds to his dignity. In intervening in the world, man achieves a form of fulfilment that renders him more human.

But something about the nature of work as it is organised in the modern world appears to tyrannise man more often than it fulfils him. The rise of individualism and increasing specialisation in the workplace means that workers have but a diminishing understanding of their place in the general picture, knowing little or nothing of what their colleagues are doing up the production line. Each function is discrete and self-justifying, leaving each worker with the feeling that he is unimportant and dispensable. The individual man/woman finds more and more that work is a source of stress and dissatisfaction. For many, too, the blurring of boundaries between traditional male/female roles leads to increasing confusion: men in particular cannot escape the awareness that their continuing relevance is no longer guaranteed. Man becomes more and more anxious about the future he can't stop thinking about, and this anxiety seems to increase in tandem with his apparent success in meeting the challenge to 'subdue the Earth'.

In some respects, this has arisen because man has allowed the technologies that were ostensibly developed to relieve him of the tedium of work to steal some of the intrinsic satisfactions that work holds out. Man has a knack for creating Frankenstein technologies that threaten to become his enemy, to supplant him in the world and steal his genius, creativity and independence.

Nowadays, the virtue and joys of work are subordinated to the economic function, which becomes the sole means of measurement and assessment of our working lives. And this implies that what any of us contributes to the world is ultimately negligible compared to the interventions of the banker, the economist and the stock-trader. Instead of honouring the meaning of work, we shifted the emphasis to banks, stocks and markets, elevating the jargon of the marketplace to a sacred tongue by which we think to access the pure nature of reality.

Our societies came to believe not merely in the endless weekend but in the notion that wealth could be magicked out of the air. The emphasis of our economies moved from effort-and-reward to a process not unlike gambling, with workers being offered cheap loans instead of proper wages, and money treated as the ultimate commodity, itself the measure of all intrinsic value. The process of modern 'money creation' might even be deemed a form of priestcraft – the manipulation of money systems by designated, ordained bankers, who generate power and wealth for themselves and their accomplices at the expense of social functioning and human security. The chief mechanism of this process is a kind of ex nihilo substantiation of the symbols of exchange and wealth retention. The money system is owned and controlled by privately owned banks, which create money in the form of debt, tying each worker to a process of enslavement which, by default, becomes the 'purpose' of his work.

We have been experiencing, then – in the meltdown of our economic systems – the inevitable culmination of years of increasingly disturbed thinking. We thought we could catch the future, grab a little more than we needed from each day of working, so that one day we would achieve the 'freedom' of a workless life. To define the meaning of freedom as residing only in leisure is to surrender to a concept destined to confuse and frustrate, but also to reduce the working life of a man or woman to a burden entered into for the sole purpose of earning income. We have lost the idea of work as something valuable of itself, as an expression of human desire and identity, as the grit around which the pearl of human life is formed.

You knew and lived all your life the truth that work is but in small part a burden, a cross to be carried. It is also resurrection. Its 'death' is accompanied by a promise of life – not a life of leisure 'at the weekend', but a life of peace and fulfilment that flows from having responded to the challenge it poses.

Matthew Crawford also touches on an interesting use of the word 'liberalism', invoking one of the earliest uses of the word as a way of contrasting the 'liberal arts' with the 'servile arts'. The liberal arts were those activities befitting a free man; the term 'servile arts' speaks for itself, relating to mechanistic, repetitive processes. He talks about 'illiberal' work, by which he means trumped-up office jobs or treadmill clock-watching, jobs that make you feel, despite yourself, like some kind of machine that simply augments the technologies you're supposed to be operating. It would be unsurprising if people who buy into the delusion that this kind of work amounts to a progression from times past were not susceptible to thinking themselves more liberal than their parents while barely understanding the meaning of the word.

What we encounter here, then, is a 'liberalism' that emerges from a kind of unacknowledged servility. The worker does a job he hates, which bores him. He is moderately well paid, but he doesn't feel he deserves even this level of remuneration. Nothing of what he does belongs to his own spirit or imagination. He carries out perhaps a single meaningless and dissociated function in a process he does not comprehend, that is, quite literally, none of his business. His life, of itself, at least as expressed through his work, has no meaning or purpose other than to gather the wherewithal for his continuance. His only semblance of meaning arises from the connection with a brand, an organisation, which epitomises a certain notion of modernity. He has an iPhone. He even works for Apple! Yes, he is modern! This alibi of modernity becomes everything and ties him to the corporation in a kind of self-indentured slavery. The compensation is that he feels entitled to express himself, to pontificate, out of this sense of 'modernity'. He is part of the modern world, at the cutting edge of it. No one need know the precise nature of his participation, only that he is there at the heart of things. Apart from this, his only possibilities for carving out meaning from his life reside in religion (unlikely), leisure, fashion, personality, identity and lifestyle. Far from offering him a coherent meaning, his life lacks even a rudimentary sense of integration. Hence the importance of his Twitter or Facebook account, which provides him with an illusion of contributing something to the discourse of his society, affording him a functional public identity that he feels incapable of forging in any other way.

In these situations – in the offices and corporations, in the universities where these automatons are turned out – a new illiberalism has emerged to mimic the nature of the activities described as 'work'. These are the sources of the diversity programmes, the gender quotas, the speech codes, the affirmative action protocols. These are the breeding grounds of what is called political correctness. As far from manly work – from actual creativity – as it is possible to imagine, hyper-regulation is required to keep the stopper in the bottle of human desire and aspiration. Crawford explains all this as the necessary safeguarding against the breakdown in social relations that arises from the absence of clear goals and concrete tasks. 'Maintaining consensus and preempting conflict become the focus of management, and as a result everyone feels they have to walk on eggshells. Where no appeal to a carpenter's level is possible, sensitivity training becomes necessary.'

20

Argy-bargy

The latter-day tendencies I have identified in relation to the toxic ideological atmosphere of *The Irish Times* were present in latent form more or less from the time I joined in 1990. I experienced at first a mixture of hostility and condescension of a general nature, probably because I wasn't an '*Irish Times* type', was 'up from the country' and not particularly bothered about admitting it. I had words early on with the then Political Editor, Dick Walsh, after he tried to spike a column of mine one night while the Editor was on leave, because he didn't agree with what I was saying about Charles Haughey. After that, even though I'd had a best-selling book about Irish politics, I was blocked from writing about politics or elections for several years. The hostility went full-blown after I started to write about family law, feminism and the treatment of men in modern society, topics that many *Irish Times* people seemed to regard as the antithesis of the newspaper's agenda. When they sought to reprimand me for my treachery, as they sometimes would, I invariably directed them to the 'principal objectives of the editorial policy of *The Irish Times*' as laid down in the Memorandum and Articles of Association of *The Irish Times* Trust. These included:

- that news shall be as accurate and as comprehensive as is practicable and be presented fairly;

- that comment and opinion shall be informed and responsible, and shall be identifiable from fact;

- that special consideration shall be given to the reasonable representation of minority interests and divergent views;

Some months after Róisín was born in 1996, I began writing in my column about the disturbing things I had been discovering first-hand about the absence of legal protections for the rights of single fathers and their children, which I had first stumbled upon some years earlier when researching my play *Long Black Coat*, and was now confirming in my own life. When I began to write about this, I found myself inundated with stories from other men – about being badly treated by the family courts, about being robbed, cheated and having had their children stolen. It was clear that some people in *The Irish Times* were deeply unhappy about these articles and I found that attitudes towards me were chilling detectably. On a couple of occasions, the then Opinion Editor, Seán Flynn – a decent guy who has since died – warned me off the subject. I recall one occasion when, clearly under instructions from on high, he brought me into *The Irish Times* boardroom and said that the Editor was 'heartily sick' of me writing about the same subject every week. I said that this was not the case. Seán had with him a folder from the library containing cuttings of all my recent articles. I asked him to open up the folder so we could have a look, but he refused. I then picked up the folder and began to go through my recent columns. I said I would go back three months – 13 columns. I found that one of these columns was about fathers – the rest covered a range of subjects, 12 in all. Poor Seán made his excuses and left.

But the hostility continued and soon I found myself running foul of the newspaper's lawyers virtually every time I wrote about fathers or related issues. I also learned that several of my female colleagues had been making frequent trips to the Editor's office to complain that I was being given a platform 'to attack women'. On a number of occasions, the Editor spoke to me about the men-related themes of my column, but in a roundabout way, without openly asking me to cease writing on this subject. Instead, he encouraged me to go back to feature writing, which he said I had been 'very good at'.

I noticed that an increasing number of highly critical – sometimes quite malevolent – letters were being published about me on the Letters Page. I recall one particularly odd episode, in October 1999, after I wrote an article comparing the low state spending on men's health with that on women's health. Some days later, the following letter, submitted by a US-based academic, was published:

> Sir, - John Waters (October 26th) contends that 'all serious conditions which are capable of affecting both genders tend to strike down men much earlier in life.' Mr Waters is himself a case in point. Chronic, virulent misogyny (CVM) is a disease that has adverse affects on more women than men, in general. However, if his worsening symptoms are anything to go by e.g. the violent, raging fulmination's against women, which appear like clockwork with every column deadline, then it looks as though Mr Waters's nasty dose of CVM may soon give him a heart attack. - Yours, etc.,

That afternoon, when I arrived at *The Irish Times*, I found that enlarged copies of this letter had been made on a photocopier and mounted on every noticeboard in the building. Upon making enquiries, I learned that the protagonist was a senior female sub-editor.

The Irish Times had been operating an online website, ireland.com, since the mid-1990s. One morning, around the turn of the millennium, I received a phone call from a friend who said that he had seen a reference on the Opinion page of the online edition to the fact that I was on holiday. I confirmed this and added that I was pleased that they had added this line at the end of the replacement column, which sometimes they omitted to do. He said: 'Would you like to know what else it says on there?' I asked him what he meant. He said: 'It says, 'John Waters is on leave. Phew!'

I made an immediate complaint to the then Opinion Editor, Peter Murtagh. Later that day I received a call from Conor Brady, who said that he had tracked down the culprit – one of the online operatives who had put the comment in 'for a laugh' and forgotten to remove it. He said

< 224 >

the individual had been given a stern talking to, whatever that meant. I suggested that the episode appeared to indicate the prevalence of an atmosphere of hostility towards me in the paper, when a staff member could do something as blatant as that and not expect to be sanctioned for it. He didn't agree, insisting that it was a one-off incident.

On another occasion, a year or so later, I was approached in very odd circumstances by a fellow columnist, Vincent Browne, with whom I was quite friendly at the time. He said that he was coming to me 'as a friend' and wanted to advise me that I would render myself unemployable if I did not cease writing about men and fathers' rights. He said that he had been in *The Irish Times* offices a few days earlier and had overheard a very ominous conversation about me between two senior members of the editorial management, whom he declined to name. The tenor of the conversation was that my days in *The Irish Times* were numbered. Some years later, when I gave him a lift home to Dalkey one night after his radio show on RTÉ, Browne confided that he had, on that occasion, actually been requested by Conor Brady to approach me and warn me off certain topics which he said were proving very unpopular with some of my colleagues.

I had, it appeared, stumbled upon the hard centre of Irish 'liberal' journalism, which existed, it was clear, not to advance issues of interest and importance to Irish society, but more precisely to educate Irish society in the singular outlook of a particular cadre sharing a particular view of history, humanity, equality and justice.

In 2002, a change of Editors occurred, with Conor Brady being replaced by Geraldine Kennedy. The new Editor and I had previously had a good relationship, having shared a desk in the newsroom when she was a political correspondent. Now, however, she proved distant and uncommunicative. In fact, I did not hear from her at all until about six months after her appointment, in March 2003, when she called me after I had written a column about Islamist extremism. She said that there had been a complaint from a reader who had accused me of incitement to hatred and said he

< 225 >

was reporting the matter to An Garda Siochána. She said that it was a very serious matter, and that of course the newspaper could not stand over any columnist who was found to have engaged in incitement to hatred. I asked her if a legal opinion had been obtained. She said that it had. I asked her what the nature of this opinion was. She replied that the lawyers were of the view that the charge had no reasonable basis. I asked her if this was not then the end of the matter. She replied that there was more to it than simply a matter of law – there was also the issue of 'public perception'. This seemed to suggest that, if the charge were levelled, I would be regarded as guilty regardless of the law or the facts.

There followed a bit of argy-bargy, during the course of which I got the distinct impression of someone for whom power had been a life-changing experience. It seemed clear what she was saying: if someone came after me, I would be on my own. In the event, the complaint fizzled out, so we would have to wait a while to test the quality of liberalism available under the new Editor.

Towards the end of that same year, a controversy erupted within the newspaper concerning the remuneration of senior executives, including the Editor and managing director, both of whom were being paid more than the taoiseach, the British prime minister and a host of editors of UK newspapers enjoying several multiples of the circulation of ours. The matter was being covered in other newspapers but not in *The Irish Times*. One day, I received a call from my then friend and colleague Patsy McGarry, the religious affairs correspondent, who said that he had just emerged from a meeting of the paper's members of the National Union of Journalists (NUJ), who had agreed that it was shameful that none of the newspaper's columnists had written about what was going on in the paper. He said he did not wish to pressurise me but was simply passing on the information. I asked him if he wanted me to write about the matter, and he said that he would certainly be pleased if I did. 'Fine,' I said, 'in that case I will!'

At that time, my column appeared on Mondays, and on the following Sunday afternoon I submitted, for publication as my column the following day, a trenchant critique of the behaviour of *Irish Times* management. A short time later, I received a call from the Opinion Editor, Paddy Smyth, who rather ruefully said that he would like to go through some issues raised by the newspaper's lawyers concerning the column. He said the Editor had read the column and had agreed to its publication provided the changes suggested by the lawyers were made. He took me through the piece line by line, discussing and debating each sentence with me. I agreed to a number of changes and in the end he pronounced himself satisfied and said that the piece could now be published. A short time afterwards, I received a call from Geraldine Kennedy, who told me that she had changed her mind and that the piece would not now be published after all. I asked her why and she cited 'legal issues'. I said that I understood that these had already been addressed and asked if she could be more specific. She declined to elaborate and asked me to write a replacement column. I said that, since I had already submitted my column as I was contractually required to do, and had been told that it had already been passed for publication by the lawyers, I had fulfilled my obligations. She said that she was refusing to publish the column. I said that this was her prerogative as Editor, just as it was mine to stand over what I had written.

I informed Patsy McGarry of what had happened and said that I believed I had done my part to try to expose what was happening and was now done with the matter. He said he would discuss these developments with his colleagues. The following Sunday morning, we awoke to find that a number of national newspapers had obtained copies of my column and published extensive extracts. These had clearly been leaked by someone within the editorial department of the newspaper. I did not leak them and had not forwarded my column to anyone else, not even McGarry. I received no communication from Geraldine Kennedy that day. The following day, I agreed to appear on RTÉ Radio One's *News at One* programme with Sean O'Rourke, who interviewed me about the episode. At the end of the item, during a commercial break, he said: 'You did well there. But I'd be a bit worried about your use of the word 'compromised' concerning Geraldine.' I had simply suggested that the Editor had inherited a particular remuneration culture, which had left her 'compromised'.

The following Saturday evening, about 9.00, I received a hand-delivered letter to my home from the Editor of *The Irish Times*, informing me that, since I appeared to be dissatisfied with working in *The Irish Times*, I should seek work somewhere I might find conditions 'more congenial'.

It was interesting that it took the Editor five days to act on such a straightforward issue, which suggests that there may have been extended discussions. It was also suggested to me that a factor in the decision may have been a belief around *The Irish Times* newsroom that I was no longer a member of the NUJ, and that no industrial relations issues would arise from my dismissal. I had in fact, some time before, resigned from the NUJ following an episode where they had pursued the publisher of one of my books for compensation on behalf of a woman who had taken a photograph of me that had been used on the dust jacket. In fact, under Irish law, the image belonged to me, as it was categorised as a family photograph, but there was a grey area because my publisher was based in London and English law was somewhat different. In protest, I resigned from the NUJ and was therefore unrepresented at the time I wrote the column criticising *The Irish Times* management and when I appeared on the radio to discuss it.

On hearing me on *The News at One*, a retired colleague rang me and said that the interview had been 'very interesting' but was I a member of the NUJ? I explained why not and he responded that I should rejoin as soon as possible. I interpreted this as a typical trade union sanctimony but said I would maybe think about it when things quietened down. No, he said, I should rejoin right away. He said he would come immediately from his home, on the opposite side of the city, collect the relevant forms from the NUJ HQ, and be at my home within two hours. He would then have the forms countersigned and submitted by close of business that day. That ex-colleague saved my job – as, arguably, did the individual who countersigned my NUJ application form: Patsy McGarry.

Suddenly the powers-that-were in *The Irish Times* discovered that they were dealing with an NUJ member after all. There followed several days of intense publicity, and then a series of negotiations between the Editor and Seamus Dooley of the NUJ, culminating in a joint statement and my reinstatement as columnist.

Over the years, I had many other exchanges and correspondences with other *Irish Times* journalists and senior editors, usually on the basis of general criticisms I had made in my column of the behaviour of media and their treatment of various matters relating to Irish public life. On each occasion, when I sought to pursue the factual bedrock of these questions, my interlocutors chose to retreat rather than answer the points I made.

For example, in May 2013, the Opinion Editor, Chris Dooley, emailed me to challenge a claim in my column that journalists had sought for many years to ignore or misrepresent the nature of the suicide crisis in Irish life, seeking to gloss over the fact that it was an overwhelmingly male phenomenon. He wrote:

> You routinely accuse your colleagues of taking an ideological approach to their work – not a slur to be taken lightly, because week after week you cast doubt on their fitness for the job they do, in my opinion, with great professionalism and dedication – but it seems to me that in this case, at least, you have attempted to fit the facts into your own ideological position, and you have come up with something that isn't true, and is demonstrably not true, i.e. that the mainstream media prefers to use constructions such as 'young people' in order to avoid telling the truth, i.e. that young people who kill themselves are predominantly male. And that we (I say we, as I am not long out of the newsroom myself) do this for some bizarre ideological reason.

Dooley sent me a number of links to *Irish Times* articles which he claimed disproved my thesis.

I replied:

I've been writing about suicide as an issue in *The Irish Times* for more than 20 years. The first time was in the summer of 1990, just after I joined the newspaper, when I wrote a series of articles on the subject. I have returned to the topic at least once or twice a year, and have sought always to underline not just that the problem was, by definition, a male one but that the kinds of analysis being offered by media or supposed experts were not the full story.

I have therefore been in a position to observe things fairly consistently over that time. I stand over what I said in the column: 'For many years, the media's approach to the suicide issue was blandly to report the figures while ignoring the hippopotamus in the hallway. Almost invariably, if the deeper nature of the problem was adverted to at all, it was in terms that served to divert into general questions concerning the mental health of 'young people'. Other analyses, especially those seeking to focus on problems specifically relating to males, were suppressed or dismissed.

This was 100% my experience 'for many years' – both of observing the way media were reporting the issue and watching in frustration as every conceivable attempt was made, in the specific context of suicide and more generally, to avoid exploring the precise problems men might be having.

There is a great deal of difference between reporting the figures and delving into the meaning of them, and it is in this latter context that I had been seeking to draw attention, for many years, not just to the nature of the issue of men and suicide, but to the reality of the widespread media avoidance of it. There has been no attempt WHATSOEVER to look at the particular difficulties which men may have, which have led to the catastrophic disproportionality of male suicide.

Uniquely in Irish media I have sought to place the suicide issue in a wider context, both in terms of asking 'why men?' and what, beyond the tautological factors adduced as explanations (depression, failure to express feelings etc.) might be at the back of this issue. For 20 years I was a lone voice on this subject in *The Irish Times* or outside it. I cannot access all of the pieces you sent me links for (I don't have access to the archive anymore) but none of the pieces I've opened do any more than 'blandly state the figures' or, at best, trot out the same old 'mental health' analysis, which at the level of global thinking is regarded as a mask for the real problems.

About three years ago, I spoke at the opening of a men's centre in Limerick. Among my fellow-speakers was Joan Freeman, founder of Pieta House, an organisation which has recently been making a remarkable contribution to our understandings of the suicide problem, and has done much to change the terms of the media discussion in the last three or four years. Before the event kicked off, I was approached by a female reporter who told me she was there representing *The Irish Times*. She said she might be called away during the speeches and wanted a few lines from me about what I proposed to say. I told her I was going to talk about male suicide and gave her a line which, in any other context, would have been a sub-editor's birthday present headline: 'Young men are dying of Irish society's indifference'. In fact, the reporter remained in the venue for the entirety of my speech and appeared to be writing assiduously as I spoke.

When Ms Freeman spoke, she addressed the Pieta House experience of the problem. Her comments were at the time remarkable in that they flew in the face of the conventional analysis relating to mental illness. She said the Pieta House experience of suicide indicated that inability to cope with loss, rather than mental health issues or communication skills, was the primary issue. Relationship breakdown, loss of home and family and such issues were the most noticeable common factor in cases coming to their notice. Single and separated men – men living alone – were far more likely to seek help from Pieta House than married or co-habiting men. She also referred to the abuses of men in the family law courts. For many men, she said, the breakdown of a relationship means also the loss of home, friends, extended family and, most importantly, she stressed – loss of spontaneous access to their children.

Next day, I looked for the report of the event in *The Irish Times* and found that not a word uttered by either Joan Freeman or myself had been reported. The headline and report focused on something that had been referred to peripherally at the launch, and indeed had been a media talking-point for a couple of years: that couples whose relationships had broken down were forced to stay living under the same roof because they couldn't sell their homes.

This episode was typical of the attitude I encountered in *The Irish Times* towards my writing about men. While masquerading as a 'liberal' news-paper dedicated to the promotion of equality and rights, *The Irish Times* is in truth nowadays a highly ideological protagonist in Irish life, dom-inated by left-liberal ideas in general and feminism in particular. There was a determined effort across the board, from the very time I began to write about men, not just to suppress or dismiss my perspectives and to discourage me from writing on these subjects, but actually to deny that the hostility I had been experiencing had been happening at all.

Something ominous began to happen to the paper when Conor Brady left in 2002. In part the change arose from the financial crisis that precipitated his somewhat premature retirement, and especially from the departure on redundancy or early retirement of large numbers of senior journalists and editors as part of the rationalisation programme that followed. His successor, Geraldine Kennedy, was ostensibly as committed to diversity as Brady had been but lacked his octopus-like engagement with every section of the newspaper. Kennedy was a polit-ical groupie, whose chief attributes as a journalist were her encyclopaedic knowledge of Irish politics and a dogged commitment to enforcing accountability and probity in public life. She had no interest in subjects like sport or theatre or religion per se, and so tended to leave these areas of the newspaper to the tender mercies of whoever happened to be running them when she arrived. Hence, although Kennedy had a far more autocratic personality than her predecessor, her tenure as Editor somewhat ironically brought about a sudden departure from the uno duce, una voce culture of editorship that had been a hallmark of the newspaper throughout most of its history. The result was the emergence of a federation of fiefdoms, with not just the various departments drifting towards autonomy, but most correspondents, apart from the political correspondents, being more or less left to their own devices. As *The Irish Times* had tended to attract a highly ideological brand of left-liberal journalist, this meant that the paper shifted radically away from its 'broad church' ethos, with dissenting voices coming to be regarded as eccentric, irksome and undesirable. Although Kennedy and I had our differences, this would probably not have been her own view of my contribution, but the effect on *The Irish Times* of her personality and narrow range of interests was such as to hand the newspaper over to the highly motivated ideologues who lurked in every corner and crevice, giving them the impression that the editorial ethos could be remade in whatever way they wished. By the time Kevin O'Sullivan came to be appointed Editor in 2011, the damage was pretty much done. Department heads and correspondents were operating to their own agendas, more or less unconstrained by editorial direction.

A complicating feature was that, during Kennedy's editorship, the newspaper industry was hit by both a crisis and a revolution arising from the effects of the worldwide web and the shift to online editions. Following the purging of older heads that occurred after the departure of Brady, it became obvious that the online edition of the newspaper was being given its head to make its own direction, almost independently of the newspaper per se. Those who insisted on old values associated with newsprint were increasingly dismissed as outmoded 'Luddites' who did not understand the new realities. The young turks who were recruited to run the online edition became increasingly influential in the organisation, gaining the ear of the commercial department, which had been kept at arm's length from the editorial department during the reigns of Gageby and Brady. Kennedy's unfamiliarity with the new web-centred technologies facilitated the emergence of a new beast within.

A major shift was occurring also in the economics of newspaper and advertising sales. Increasingly, what had previously been regarded as 'quality' newspapers (like *The Irish Times*) were becoming more agnostic in their pursuit of readers. In the past, newspapers pursued the optimum ABC1 profile as the gold standard of readership demographics, vying to sell advertising space to the most upmarket customers they could reach. For online editions, what counted were 'hits' or 'clicks', and it didn't much matter who was doing the hitting and clicking. To provoke responses, opinion columns in the newspaper were opened up to the most noxious streams of abuse from posters, who had no apparent history of loyalty to or affection for the newspaper. My column and Breda O'Brien's became particular targets of highly personalised invective and ridicule, and all requests to have this moderated were rebuffed by senior editors to whom I complained. Hence, gradually but inexorably, the newspaper slid downmarket and into an ideological cul-de-sac, leaving many of its traditional readers behind and yet not making up the losses in new paying customers.

In 2007, the circulation of *The Irish Times* was kicking the arse of 120,000, just 6,000 of these being accounted for by bulk sales. At the time of Geraldine Kennedy's departure as Editor in mid-2011, the circulation had declined to 100,951. By 2013, the circulation had dropped to just over 84,000, with some 15% of this figure being bulk sales, which were sold at discounted rates to hotels and so forth. The average print circulation of *The Irish Times* from July to December 2017 was 61,049, almost 8% lower than in the same period in 2016. In its own report on the figures, *The Irish Times* claimed that the audited digital edition of the paper had recorded daily sales of 16,939 for the period, more or less cancelling out the losses. What the report did not say was that a digital subscription could be obtained for a small fraction of the cost of buying the newspaper across the counter every day of the week.

21

The Ballad of Billy Finch

Billy Finch died, as you hardly need me to tell you. I heard it at the last minute, on the day of the removal, and luckily was in Maugherow so I was able to get there in time to pay our respects and say goodbye. I told his wife Mary that he had been extraordinarily kind to you for many years and that's to say the least of him. I remember him as one of those people you seemed to depend upon intermittently and unpredictably but who were always there when you needed them – through sickness, mechanical breakdown or some other calamity. I remember more than a few mornings when the yoke refused to start in spite of all your efforts and entreaties, and you'd come back into the kitchen and say, 'I'll have to go and knock up Billy.' And knock him up you would, at 4.30 am or 5, and Billy would appear at the front door fully dressed and ready to go, jump leads and tow-ropes at the ready in case such were needed.

I remember more than a few mornings while I was still in school, when Billy would do the run in one of his small vans, because you were too ill – and that was fairly ill – and I would accompany him because I knew the stops and the paper drops better than he did. We would zip around the route as though it were Monaco on Grand Prix day, with Billy talking all the time about this and that, throwing his quirky eye over affairs of state and town. Because the schedule had been established to suit your rather slower pace, we would intermittently have to pull in to the hard shoulder to allow time to catch up with us, and Billy would do a quick review of the morning papers that was better than anything you might hear these days on *Morning Ireland*. He had a particular fixation with the Provos, I remember, hating them with a deep passion. It was only years later that I began to pick up around the place that Billy had a reputation for taciturnity and monosyllablism, and that came as a total shock to me. I found him consistently fascinating and entertaining, and we got on like a pair of chuckling twins, whizzing around as if we were in some kind of hurry.

From him I learned the knack of delivering newspapers without stopping the vehicle. He would line up the next half dozen drops in a jig beside himself and, as we approached each of the relevant shops, would slow down marginally, swerve in towards the shop doorway at the last minute and aim the bale into the corner of the doorway. He could do this on either side, being just as accurate when he flung the bale over the top of the van and stuck it in the corner of the net.

Sometimes, if Billy couldn't come himself, he would send his cousin, Declan Murphy, whom I liked and enjoyed equally well. Declan and Billy appeared to have a deep store of affection for one another but rarely communicated except through nods and gestures. I used to ask Declan about that and he'd say that Billy had no time for small talk, which was a bit like saying Hurricane Higgins had no time for the slow game. Declan died suddenly a couple of years after yourself, in January 1992, not yet out of his 30s.

When people talk about the much-vaunted 'changing Ireland' of recent decades, they invariably seem to think of prominent figures and personalities – Gay Byrne, Charlie Haughey, Gerry Ryan, Mary Robinson – implicitly discounting the role of anonymous figures like yourself and Billy Finch. Very few people likely know that for most of the last half century, Billy took care of the delivery of English Sunday newspapers all over the West, operating several trucks and lorries to transport them from Dublin airport to their final destinations in the doorways of shops all over the midlands, Connemara, Mayo and Donegal. It was thanks to Billy's capacity for getting out of bed that John McGahern was able to rely on picking up his Observer in his local shop in Mohill, and that, as McGahern would have been the first to tell you, was no small thing. There was something heroic about that Saturday night paper run – more so than could be said for the daily runs we did with the Irish papers – especially with the necessity for high speed on bad roads in sometimes shocking weather. Billy's father Ted dying in a road accident brought home that fact very starkly, and that risk was a constant feature of the job. I think Billy had a sense of subversion about picking those newspapers up at the airport and distributing them far and wide, shaking things up, as he'd like to say. (I'm talking here about the heyday of Harold Evans rather than the more recent Murdoch years.) There were those who looked down their noses at the very idea of allowing English newspapers in to contaminate the minds of the young, but at a time when things were probably a great deal more claustrophobic than we realised, having access to *The Observer*, *The Sunday Times* and even *The News of the World* was important in its way in keeping us sane. I remember you would come back from a quick visit to Finch's of a Monday with copies of the previous day's *Sunday Times* and the NOTW, which you would squirrel away for a precautionary perusal before sometimes – though not always – contriving to leave it lying around for the rest of us to read. I remember in particular *The Sunday Times*'s exposure of the thalidomide scandal in the early 1970s, but also have a warm recollection of reading many beautifully written and riveting articles in all those newspapers over the years.

Those days are gone now. The papers are full of effluent and lies and those who write for them are for the most part merely the hired guns of the ideologues who seek to remake the very fabric of our societies and lives. The last time I met Billy – less than a year ago, at another funeral – we talked briefly about the degeneration of the medium that both of us had, in different ways, served for close to a century between us. We agreed it was a dead duck.

Benjamin Franklin famously said that you should never fall out with a man who buys his ink in barrels. Anyone who has ever had the misfortune to be pursued in his personal life by journalists will know that there is no point seeking to intercede either with them or their editors in the hope of relief. Anyone who imagines they can negotiate with the media in order to adjust the public record to provide a more truthful version of publicised events involving themselves should know, from someone who has been on both sides of this fence, that by asking for mercy, you take your very existence in your hands.

At Billy's funeral, I met several men from those golden years of working and believing in the dignity of playing our small parts in the dissemination of a free press. I met Mattie Masterson on the way in and realised I hadn't seen him for 32 years – since the last time I stood with him in April 1984, waiting for the paper train in the Grey Castle – he to take his consignment to Claremorris, me to leave for the last time for Loughglynn, Ballaghaderreen, Frenchpark, Ballinagare, Mantua, Elphin, Cloonyquin, Tulsk, Castleplunkett, Lisalway, Ballintubber, Oran and Ballymoe. I remember not long afterwards, when I had been a few months in Dublin working for *Hot Press*, my niece Elaine, who was no more than five or six, asking me with great earnestness: 'John, which do you prefer – writing in the papers or delivering them?' Of course I chuckled at the time, thinking it a hilarious question, and retold the anecdote many times, with overtones of condescension at the idea that anyone, even a child, would think to make a comparison between the two functions. It was obvious – was it not? – that writing in the newspapers was an altogether more important and distinguished occupation than dropping them in newsagents' doorways!

Now I know different. Now, having spent three decades working at the frontline of modern media, I see that the decade or so I spent delivering mails and newspapers in the mornings had at least the virtue of innocence, as well as immeasurably more dignity, about it.

22

Omnipotent Victims

There's an essence of Ireland that does not reside in landscape, or institutions, that rarely manifests nowadays in formal culture. It's to be encountered chiefly in fleeting encounters with people – benign explosions of mirth and knowingness that leave you changed for the day. It cannot be communicated as a blow-by-blow account of an encounter. You had to be there. It speaks of a spirit devoid of claptrap, ideology or political correctness. It is gently ironic, mischievous, anarchistic. It sees through things without stopping to parse them. It is not cute-hoorism, or 'crack', still less 'craic' (awful makey-up word). It's astute and empathetic and deeply affectionate – a hug for the soul when you least expect it.

There was always the certainty of meeting it in the hours just before or after dawn – in a Spar or a filling station or a roadside café, or unloading newspapers on a railway station platform. I remember as a child being thrilled by the way you and the postmen and sorters would talk to one another about your lives, how you saw things. Or the way, when awoken abruptly by your rapping on the window, Mrs Moylan, the sub-postmistress in Tulsk would greet us with a weary resignation – like the prophecy of a Martin McDonagh opener: 'Wet again, Tom?' Of course, wet.

Something deep in me would be tickled at the way a deep condition of irony had risen up out of a murky history and vested itself in jibes and phrases: 'You have it solved!' (a Westport greeting meaning, 'You're on a soft number now'); 'Any sign of the lump?' (a perennial query about back pay or tax rebate, which for many working people represented the quintessence of hoping). The mainspring of the sensibility functioned as a casting off of pretence, or surface piety, to reveal a radical subversion underneath. We laughed at the exposure of our shared duplicities.

Immigration has driven this sensibility underground somewhat, the mixture of contemporary company almost invariably demanding more literal forms of exchange, a cultural Esperanto that leaves us lonelier and colder.

During my 'bother' of 2014 – under siege from toxic twitterati and the trendier end of the mainstream media – I often feared this Ireland had gone for good. It seemed that we had arrived somewhere that was not merely post-irony and post-reason, but that had also left behind the possibility of perspective, balance, fairness, truth or decency. In the depths of February 2014, I went to London and found myself walking around wondering if, what with the way things were going, I could live there now and start over, not caring about the public life of the place I lived in, privatising myself and emulating several of my peers by writing indifferent novels as though Beckett and Kafka had never bothered to burn the building. But I couldn't deny to myself that I loved something deeper in Ireland than what currently seemed to be available, belonged to it, shared its pulse. More recently I've begun a process of separation in myself, between Ireland and the people who have raped her. If I stay around Dublin more than a week or two at a time, a destabilising foreboding enters my soul, so I just get away, to Lislary or Spain or Italy or America. Nobody, not even a Dubliner, should stay in Dublin for more than a fortnight at a time. If you do, the nonsense closes in around you, a bubble of regurgitated cant that smells of staleness. You need to get out, beyond Lucan, beyond Leinster, beyond the Shannon. Even down there, listening too much to RTÉ or Newstalk, I'd begin to think they described the world as it is, but then I stopped listening to them and my country began to come back to me. Walking the beach at Lislary I could become certain that whatever they describe, it is not Ireland. Nowadays I listen only to Dylan Radio, and occasionally, when I think of it, to Start the Week on Monday mornings on BBC Radio Four.

In the very depths of the calamity, I would find myself thinking there was no safe place left to walk without the need constantly to avoid eye-contact. At a two-year remove, I can say that the only times I encountered negative personal responses were in Dublin – southside Dublin, as it happens – from people who seemed to have no more than slogans to work with and always hurried away after flinging their quantum of abuse. A couple of guys on bikes spat some toxic verbals at me as they passed me in the street; one young American woman walked up to where I was sitting in Starbucks and told me, without elaboration, that I 'ought to be ashamed' of myself; a guy at Dublin Airport muttered something sourly sarcastic about going off to get married as he scarpered past my table in Butler's Café.

There were others whom I pretended not to hear. Over the next couple of years there would be many other such incidents. Quite recently, a fat man with a red face approached me in Sandycove, clearly filming or photographing me with his mobile phone; when I asked him why, he replied: 'Because you're a national embarrassment.' It was like some kind of collective hypnosis had been achieved on a selective swathe of individuals who all happened to be either working in the media or fixated with what was being said on Twitter.

Even in Sligo, Mayo or Roscommon, I at first found myself hesitating about venturing outdoors. I made the mistake once or twice in company of bringing the subject up before someone else did, dropping in some reference to what someone had, eh, tweeted, what people might be thinking, what it all meant. Invariably, if people answered me at all, it was to pick me up all wrong, provoking exchanges that began at cross-purposes and petered out in embarrassment. Nobody I met had ever tweeted anything, or cared one whit what some drag queen had said about me, or what had happened afterwards. Had I been less sickened and unnerved by the experience, I might have become fascinated by the absolute determination of virtually all media outlets to keep on the agenda something that was exciting close to zero interest among the population at large. At first this realisation was difficult for me to arrive at, although some of my friends were telling me almost from the beginning that I was becoming deeply deluded if I imagined that Twitter, RTÉ and *The Irish Times* were in any way representative of Ireland as a whole. Most people I encountered beyond a narrowly defined Pale had registered nothing of it, and those who had were even more perplexed. One woman told me it was a shocking thing to be accused of being a queer! This is Ireland. I don't mean 'the real Ireland' – a phrase contaminated by kitsch and makey-up. I mean, rather, the 'true Ireland', where the historical personality of the Irish people might be located if you had a mind to look for it.

It's not that it's impossible to describe this place, but that no single statement on its own amounts to a truth about it. It's contradictory and paradoxical and Janus-faced – both/and, not either/or. This is why you hear this Ireland described less and less: because most commentators utilise an Anglo-Saxon viewfinder in which things are either one thing or another.

This Ireland, for example, is neither 'conservative' nor 'liberal'. To know what this Ireland thinks, you'd need to cross-examine each and every one of the human conundrums who populate it. The more you speak to these people, the more you realise that they don't fit into easy categories, that their outlooks on the world are carved out of personal experience – of sorrow and hoping and watching and listening. This is not an Ireland of received opinions, or fads, or right-on kneejerk stances. This Ireland observes and cogitates and judges by its own lights. And it delivers these judgments in the same way you used to, or Mammy did, in what seem like throwaway phrases but are really the sculpted pearls born of generations of observing and absorbing and not forgetting: 'Don't be annoying yourself'; 'They don't know what to do with themselves!'; 'I remember that crowd when they had the ass and cart'. This Ireland still exists, but it is diminishing, and, worst of all, is increasingly only to be located in the company of the old.

We've been talking a long time now about 'progress' without anyone remarking too loudly that we appear to be going around in circles. No one has ever postulated what the destination might look like. It's all very vague – abandoned to a process of mimicry that renders our destinies dependent on how things turn out elsewhere. It seems we're aiming to be something like Sweden, although most of us have never been there, and never wished to spend more than an hour in the company of any Swede we met. Moreover, by all accounts of recent times, Sweden is not necessarily the paradise it's been cracked up to be.

Our most intractable problems may be that our national personality is too complicated and ironic for the purposes of nation-building. Proper administration requires clarity, literalness and singularity, whereas our culture, at its deeper levels, tends to operate at the levels of doublethink and weightlessness. Our core personality is centred on an existentialism that arises from a sense of the transient nature of everything. This makes us wide and philosophical, but also devil-may-care. Our quandary is that we understand that to 'progress' we need to shake off our complicatedness, but we also know that, if we do this, we risk self-disintegration.

Most people out there nowadays tend to speak in code, to avoid pursuit by the guardians of the new orthodoxies. Others just play along, reserving their energy for battles about immediate things. There is this odd situation whereby a majority, or at least a sizeable minority of the population is appalled and scundered at the way things seem to be going, but dare not give any indication that they are dismayed. This generalised sense of confusion and disgust is a great secret, even between people who hold to the same view. At the level of the central conversation, the facts are denied or distorted to uphold the official line that only a tiny minority of recalcitrant throwbacks have any difficulty with anything that is happening.

Most people daren't even enumerate these current absurdities, but are dimly aware of the patterns: in the obsession with personal freedom expressed sexually, and the unrelenting emphasis on the 'rights' of nominated categories of person in the matter of doing whatever they please. They observe these agendas being driven in the media by what are termed 'human stories' – carefully selected sociological narratives, chosen and tweaked to indict the past and the way things used to be seen and done. There are the women who have been denied abortions and the women who have had abortions and seem to be proud of this..

< 244 >

Both are deemed heroines, or is that heroes? There are the men who are really women and the women who are really men, and the men or women who are men one day and women the next. What was a short time ago unheard of is now, it seems, ubiquitous.

At the core of all this is what appears to be an attempt to insinuate sex and sexuality as the centre of human existence, human happiness, human being. It is not possible to dissent from it, even to ask that you be spared the details. In the alleged new era of truth-letting, no one is entitled to claim an amnesty or immunity. Because the lie has been sold that everyone was involved in suppressing and oppressing those who have now 'bravely risen up', everyone must show up to salute their bravery and applaud their freedom. 'No thanks' is not an acceptable response, being likely to qualify as hostility, which invariably qualifies for a designation with an 'ism' or an 'obia' at the end of it.

This new culture has crept up on us, so that for a long time many people thought it was just a few isolated groups of soreheads demanding this and that entitlement they say had been denied them. Now, people are beginning to twig that there is a pattern here and that it is growing more insistent and pronounced. The escalation of this new culture has taken on an exponential character, to the extent that it often seems to be dictating the nature and significance of everything the media suggests as important. Chat shows are dominated with the stories of people who would once have been considered to have a bit of a want on them. These individual stories seem, moreover, to be connected, and plugged into the central grid of agenda-setting, which in turn appears to emanate from a lobby sector that commands the ear of government and instant access to the media. One story is crazier than the last, and tame compared to the next. But the weird thing is that nobody ever says – or at least not publicly – that the stories are crazy; instead, the subjects of them are congratulated for their 'courage' in speaking so personally about things that most people think should remain private. Anyone who dissents from this analysis is likely to be eviscerated – first on social media, and then in the mainstream, which is essentially the same people acting in, respectively, their anonymous and bylined manifestations.

Most people are simply perplexed by all this and confounded as to where it is coming from and going to. The idea that it is simply a series of isolated stories is starting to wear thin, and people are becoming more open to the idea that something fundamental has shifted in our culture, though they cannot even begin to say what.

'Political correctness' is a short-circuiting term that prevents people penetrating what is happening, keeping them on the surface of existing understandings and imposed definitions and agendas. They tend to think of PC as some faddish thing that's come in and will go out again, a silly and puerile way of looking at reality. But PC is more than a banal preoccupation with fashionable posturing. It's already clear that behind it lies a determined initiative to change the meanings of fundamental things and in so doing to render the world more in tune with the advances of consumerism and technological change, which essentially means uprooting reality from its bed in nature.

In truth, what is called 'political correctness' is actually a kind of force field thrown up around a phenomenon sometimes called 'cultural Marxism', a mutated version of the original, directed at changing fundamentally the way western societies conduct their everyday existences in the most intimate areas of their family and community lives.

Political correctness, the shield designed to protect these initiatives from attack, likewise infiltrated US academia and spread its tentacles across western societies, gaining a grip on the legal culture of many of these societies though institutions like the United Nations and the European Union. By the early 21st century it had radically infiltrated the collective thought processes of the English-speaking world through the assiduous lobbying of groups like Amnesty and UNICEF, which most people still think of as straightforward philanthropic organisations – in reality highly ideological movements operating with a common though unstated agenda. PC values rapidly gained ground through the efforts of

< 246 >

'liberal' broadcast media like the BBC and newspapers like *The Guardian* and *The New York Times*, enabling PC thinking to be transmitted as gospel to societal elites, political leaderships and innumerable institutions, including schools, civil service departments, political organisations, police forces, corporations and even armies and churches.

Far from being harmless and slightly comic, as many seem to think, the phenomenon of political correctness is a system of enforced cultural omertà calculated to advance a radical undermining of freedom of expression and the imposition of thought control – all directed at the inversion of the traditional social order and the creation of what would amount in effect to a totalitarian state. PC has its roots, not in some post-feminist prissiness, but in a hard leftist sect known as the Frankfurt School, which gained serious traction for its ideas in post-Second World War American academia. Although the Frankfurt School began under the influence of the Italian Marxist intellectual Antonio Gramsci, and had, to begin with, a clearly-defined set of intellectual leaders and thinkers – Theodor Adorno, Walter Benjamin, Wilhelm Reich, Eric Fromm, Max Horkheimer, Herbert Marcuse – it is no longer possible to identify a leadership that might plausibly be accused of prosecuting this agenda, which has become so diffused and bound up in culture that subversion is no longer necessary.

The term 'Frankfurt School' was an informal umbrella title used to describe the thinkers affiliated or merely associated with the Frankfurt Institute for Social Research. Marxist to begin with, they sought a synthesis between Marx and the works of major thinkers like Hegel and Freud. They themselves did not describe themselves as 'the Frankfurt School' and exhibited neither unanimity nor conformity, but they did generate a particular set of tendencies that are now immensely powerful in modern culture, in particular the culture of victimhood nowadays dominating the political agendas of every western society and the appropriation and frequent inversion of language in the cause of thought control and censorship.

< 247 >

The thinking of the Frankfurt School began as the pursuit of a kind of post-Marxist social analysis in Germany in the 1920s, later moved to the US to escape Nazism (all the intellectuals involved were Jewish), and was adopted by the 1960s counterculture, ostensibly to promote 'tolerance' of 'diversity' and alternatives to the 'conservative' values of the time. In the beginning, the Frankfurt School intellectuals focused on art and culture, on what they called 'critical theory': on the pervasiveness in society of propaganda, the use of the higher art forms to carry the insidious ideology of the oppressor, the banality of mass culture generated by what Adorno called the 'culture industry' and so forth. These ideas were fed intravenously to the mainstream as a result of the explosion of 'youth culture' that occurred in the 1960s.

The term 'cultural Marxism', much in use nowadays on the web, is something of an over-simplification. There was more to it than Marxism, especially its intellectual debt to Sigmund Freud. 'Cultural nihilism' might be more accurate. The context of the emergence of the label 'Cultural Marxism' was the belief of Frankfurt School ideologues – based on the failure of the working classes of capitalist societies to embrace their historical destinies by following the call of communism – that a Marxist revolution confined to economics would not succeed. Rather than exhibiting a passion for the victory of the proletariat, the working class seemingly wanted to improve their lives by becoming more prosperous and successful, showing little interest in tearing down the system and taking control of the means of production in accordance with Karl Marx's depiction of their historical role. The underlying agenda of the Frankfurt School was to identify and nurture a new kind of proletariat, one more interested in stepping into the historical role formulated by Marx. Hence, an array of victim groups has, via the promulgation of the Frankfurt School's ideas, become the modern, reinvented proletariat, now deemed to be the historically venerated inheritors of the Marxist remit to overthrow the oppressive classes and usher in a new dispensation of freedom. Hence, 'cultural Marxism', which begat what we now

< 248 >

recognise as modern feminism, the 'gay rights' movement and, latterly, the initiatives seeking to legitimise a multiplicity of gender types and cast doubts on the very validity of male and female.

The Frankfurt School intellectuals were preoccupied with the deconstruction of cultural totems so as to promote 'liberation', though for selected categories only. Whereas traditional theory sought to reveal the world as it was, 'critical theory' sought to expose the 'ruling understandings' buried in worlds of art, literature and music, which allegedly facilitated oppression of the victim groups by capitalist, authoritarian and patriarchal society. Adorno believed that both high art and mass-produced culture bore 'the stigmata of capitalism'. The two forms, he wrote, were 'torn halves of an integral freedom, to which, however, they do not add up'. He also insisted that beauty was a misrepresentation of reality, and that the idea that art was a language of the sacred amounted to a lie. Much of the later Frankfurt thinking tended to adopt Freudian ideas – in The Authoritarian Personality, Adorno defined attachment to family as a 'pathological' condition.

The foundation document of the 1960s counterculture, bringing the Frankfurt School's 'revolutionary messianism' of the 1920s into the 1960s, was Herbert Marcuse's Eros and Civilization, originally published in 1955 and funded by the Rockefeller Foundation. The school's ideas influenced a generation of feminist writers, including Germaine Greer, Betty Friedan and Kate Millet, and spawned the current contagion of women's studies, which demonises males, and Afro-American studies, which does the same to white people. The core ethos of the emerging, and increasingly convergent counterculture was alienation from pre-existing values and norms, repudiation of authority and the nuclear family, the reduction of the human project to the pursuit of sensual pleasure and consumerist adventuring, and the elevation of eros to the primary motivating dynamic of the human person. The Christian idea of the person as a uniquely dignified creative being, capable of impressing him/herself on civilisation was to be supplanted by the idea of the individual as heroic casualty of prior oppression. Thus identity rather than human dignity would provide the defining ethos of the human journey.

Among the Frankfurt School's most pervasive legacies are: a repudiation of the idea of verifiable objective truth – there is no such thing as universal truth or natural law; the belief that good and evil are subjective notions, which serve the interests of those seeking to define them, and that those who insist on such concepts are by definition seeking to subjugate others and therefore must be opposed; and the belief that the presence in a society of Christianity, capitalism and the 'patriarchal-authoritarian' family, has created a citizen prone to racial prejudice and fascism. The Frankfurt School advocated the fostering of alienation from mainstream society and its ruling ideas, using cultural forms designed to persuade society that only by embracing Marxism could this alienation be dissipated. The intimated solution included: that the patriarchal social structure be replaced with matriarchy; the belief that men and women are different be replaced with androgyny; and the belief that heterosexuality is normal be replaced with the belief that homosexuality is normal; and, above all, freedom be redefined as sexual freedom, including the right to contraception and abortion. All this, added together, becomes recognisable as the spine of the 'liberal agenda' of modern societies, and markedly that observed in Ireland in recent years. These ideas, having been refined in the halls of American academe, were fed into mainstream culture via the 1960s counterculture, and rapidly gained a hold on the thinking of journalists, artists, musicians and others with cultural influence over young people.

From the 1990s, with the ascent to power across Europe of left-leaning parties, the Frankfurt School programme, driven and camouflaged by political correctness, became the driving force of much of the mainstream politics of many western countries. Through political lobbying, infiltration of the education system, shifting the weight of public policy from parliament to court, and, above all, relentless censorship and cultural prohibition of contrary ideas – modern society has been persuaded to, in effect, turn its value system inside out.

The chilling effect of political correctness is felt as a result of the imposition on politicians, academics, journalists and citizens of a climate that conveys to them that it is forbidden to give voice to certain thoughts. Deviation from the principles of PC results in instant vilification and censure, with an increasing risk of loss of position and income. It becomes impossible to raise questions about urgent social questions such as the spread of a deeply damaging welfare culture, the exponential rise of single motherhood or the consequences of immigration policies that have changed the face of many western societies – not forgetting, in the most intimate realm, the marginalisation of fathers, the decoupling of biology from the cultural understanding of parenthood and the promotion under the guise of 'new rights' of radical notions of family diversity that remain untested in any social context. As these ideologies infect the legal systems of many countries, instances of people being investigated by the police and courts for 'breaches' of PC principles are becoming more and more common. Thus, in many instances, what passes for public debate no longer describes objectively verifiable reality, but an ideologically constructed pseudo-discussion in which certain matters become unmentionable and others utterly unchallengeable.

A 2014 essay, 'Microaggression and Mora Cultures', by Bradley Campbell and Jason Manning, published in *Comparative Sociology*, provides an analysis of what's happening in contemporary societies as a direct result of Frankfurt School thinking. The core point, according to Campbell and Manning, is that the western world is moving on from its previous moral paradigm, in which differences between people were seen in terms first of honour and later of dignity, to a new culture based on the primacy of the victim. This coheres with the concept of the Frankfurt School and had for me an immediate ring of truth about it, since it was almost 20 years since I coined the phrase 'omnipotent victim' to describe the personality at the core of the culture I then observed to be bearing down on straight white males in general and fathers in particular.

Disputes used to be negotiated between human beings – men, usually – through the medium of violence: gauntlets, duels, honour killings, self-immolations, wars and plain actual bodily harm. Honour cultures are strong where the rule of law is weak, or where there is a withholding of loyalty to the dominant system. Honour, incidentally, remained a strong element in the Brehon laws, the old system of law in pre-colonisation Ireland, which were underpinned by a tradition of imposing violence on yourself in the proximity of one who had wronged you – usually in the form of a hunger strike. Also, men protected themselves, their families, property and reputations by maintaining a reputation for retaliatory violence.

I've no doubt that residual memories of this way of seeing and doing were somewhere at the root of the thinking behind the Easter Rising – the idea of blood sacrifice as an instrument of shaming. But this was, to an extent, a dramatic throwback. A central element of the civilisation that spread through Europe in the wake of the Christian awakening was the creation of systems focusing instead on the individual dignity of the human person. In this system, you were discouraged from defending your own honour, and instead invited to offer disputes for mediation by the state. This took the form of courts and jurisprudence, whereby issues were adjudicated upon by uninvolved public officials, such as policemen and judges. At the centre of this was the idea that each human person had an equal entitlement to respect for his/her dignity. Thus, it was no longer necessary to be strong, or to personally risk your life to defend your honour: the state would do it for you. This resulted in an explosion of relative egalitarianism, whereby, under certain headings, all human beings were regarded as having equal rights and an entitlement to equal protection. One of the benefits of the shift was that, because the process of seeking retribution in a dignity culture could be slow and unwieldy, many disputes fizzled out before they got to the top of the queue. Thus, there was a slowing down of the tendency of human beings to take offence: only the more grievous offences went all the way.

What is happening now, the theory goes, is that this culture is dissolving into an emerging dispensation in which victimhood is the main element of negotiation and at the core of which is a quantity that might be defined as the moral value of historical grievance, whereby a category of humanity's claims of having suffered oppression under different headings can be calculated to increase the 'moral' claim of an individual member of that category. The increasingly close scrutiny of the remaining relative inequalities and discriminations that represents the late stage of dignity culture is leading to a kind of microscopic emphasis on remaining differences. The more 'equality' is attained, the louder the complaints of those who do not yet feel equal. And since equality is an impossibility, this situation can only grow like Topsy.

Hence this paradox: a revolution based on 'inequality' can happen only in a culture that has already achieved high degrees of equality. In this comparatively luxurious context, a new hyper-consciousness is developing about residual felt inequalities. This syndrome started to be talked up in American universities during the 1980s, rapidly spreading into the US media, whence it went global, via the academic systems and media culture of all western societies. At its core it involves the adoption of the residual grievances of recognised minorities: women, blacks and other ethnic groupings, homosexuals, disabled people etc. Exploiting the guilt implanted by ideological conditioning, these 'minorities' claim the backing of the ranks of pampered, idealistic youth attending universities and consume the products of an increasingly technologised and globalised media.

This culture is somewhat opaque to the outsider but appears to be constructed on an arcane set of rules that, though inconsistent, follow a general pattern of valorising victims and condemning those perceived as successful and powerful, now or in the past. The grievance issue is rarely as clear-cut as, for example, pure racism or outright homophobia, but tends to focus on nuanced hurts and offences that are very often decided subjectively, being identified, protested and prosecuted by the complainant. The more equal a society becomes, the more subtle and nuanced the complaints, so that even what appears to be an insignificant matter in the eyes of a casual witness may provoke outrage out of proportion with any objective assessment of the offence involved. Jokes, for example, are increasingly dangerous, as are compliments, chivalrous behaviour and sexual advances, or what seem like sexual advances to the 'victim'. Even a simple, apparently innocent question, such as, 'Where do you come from?' is capable of exciting accusations of racism or worse. The more elitist and privileged a setting or society, the more extreme the responses to ever diminishing levels of alleged offence. Those driving the culture constantly complain about 'equality', but, as evidenced by the fact that victim ideology is at its strongest in highly privileged settings like universities, it is precisely the existence of a relatively high degree of equality that creates the pressure for, in effect, perfect equality.

The way cultures shift from seeing something either indifferently or as an unequivocal wrong to seeing the same thing as a fundamental right is one of the most perplexing spectacles of our age. It is also the territory of escalating activity and warfare by actors with an interest, above all, in power. Intrinsic to the success of such initiatives is the abuse of language, the inversion of understandings and the relentless application of emotional pressure to the collective public consciousness. But even grasping the nature of such strategies is not enough to expose the true nature of what is happening; this requires a far deeper process of cultural excavation, to unearth the roots of the duplicities, the origins of the many necessary rapes of meaning and the shift from reason to emotion in public debate.

Whereas one can see a balance of merit in the evolution of an honour culture based on strength and violence into a culture where human dignity is respected, the same conclusion cannot (as yet at least) be reached in respect of a shift from dignity to victimhood. For one thing, how can it be deemed a gain for someone to achieve the denunciation of a slight or discrimination by presenting him/herself as weaker than some nominated opponent?

It is sometimes suggested that what is happening amounts to a kind of reversal of the evolutionary process. One of the unremarked problems facing the human species at the moment is that the divergence between its capacity for technological advancement and the development of an ethical paradigm in which to contain and control such progress grows wider all the time. This means that mankind is increasingly capable of discovery, innovation and technical dominance over the environment, but nowhere near as clever when it comes to formulating moral and ethical understandings that might prevent these progress projects leading to harm rather than good. There is also the problem that scientific progress is something that arises from the knowledge and understandings available to an elite, whereas the benefits can be dispersed to vast numbers of consumers, most of whom will, aside from being unable to do more than operate the technologies, lack the notional intellectual and moral scruples of the creators of the devices and systems they've been given. This means that these may, once handed down to the ground floor of a culture, have implications and consequences that were neither intended nor foreseen by their creators.

It is hard to say when I became aware of these tendencies in Ireland. If you pushed me I would say around 2007/8, though I cannot outline for you in any precise way the putative connections between these tendencies and the meltdown in the economy that occurred at the same time. I expect there is one, but the precise nature of it may not emerge with any clarity for a long time. Up to that moment, I would say, Ireland was advancing along a particular path. One could argue with different aspects of the changes under way, but by and large the feeling was of a positive advance. There were bad things as well as good things about the changing Ireland, but there was no single, central, immobilising factor that threatened to cause people to shrink into themselves in alienation and apprehension. This is no longer so. The change I have just outlined amounts, in my opinion, to just such a potentially immobilising factor. It is as if the civilisation of which we are part – perhaps under the tension of the disparity between its technological and ethical aspects – has turned around and started to retrace its steps. It returns, however, not to a culture in which honour is defended by physical violence, but to a condition in which differences between people arising from facts and circumstances and unresolved conflicts of interest are treated as gross and punishable affronts to the dignity of those claiming to be adversely affected. The disputes arising from these assertions of inequality are not to be mediated in neutral courts of law but in the gossip chambers of the worldwide web, where like-minded people, incapable of true empathy and driven by curiosity, idleness and a desire to be approved of, combine to create all-powerful convocations which can result in the evisceration and destruction of an accused party who is offered no real opportunity to mount a defence. Thus, the new culture, on its way back into history in search of solid ground to build its new edifice, bypasses the buildings that already exist – the courts, the parliaments, even the media houses – in search of a new seat of what amounts, in substance and in effect, to anarchy.

In this climate, nobody wants to say anything for fear of touching off one of the multiplicity of tripwires now booby-trapping public reality. People still have conversations, of course, but in the main they consist of material supplied by approved sources. They may mention the refugee crisis and avow that it is 'shocking'. If you ask them why it is shocking, they may add some tautological platitude about how terrible it is to see people displaced in this way, and an occasionally brave soul will make a comparison with the Great Famine, which has become a trope of public discussion of these matters. But again, if you delve into this comparison in a way that threatens to draw them out further, they will lapse into a silence punctuated by hmmms and haws.

Of course, the culture of 'whatever you say, say nothing' is not new. Ireland was always a place in which one of the most valuable talents was the ability to talk for a long time without committing yourself to a position. But it has entered a new phase in recent times. The 'marriage equality' referendum did not initiate this escalation, but it certainly made it clear that we have entered an era of privatised opinion: people are now so browbeaten by unreason and illogic that mostly they've decided to keep their positions and beliefs to themselves and opt out of expressing any view of what should happen in the public realm. It's quite amazing to feel the difference: people now ask questions but respond to your answers with vague noises and platitudes. It's as if everyone is terrified of being reported for holding unorthodox opinions. Better, then, to wait and see which way the wind is blowing.

< 257 >

23

Up for an Interview

Back in 2012, when I attended the Eucharistic Congress in Dublin as a speaker, I ran into many people who had been reading me, they claimed, for many years. Conducting a straw poll of such encounters, I found that about 60% read me in *the Irish Mail on Sunday*, 30% in *The Irish Catholic*, to which I occasionally contributed at the time, and just 20% in *The Irish Times*. Twenty years earlier, all of those people would have been reading me in the Times. As *The Irish Times* had became a colder place for opinions that did not conform to the dominant 'liberal' ethos, its relevance for people with 'minority' interests and divergent views had evaporated, and these people had spoken with their loose change. And the most dismal aspect is that these were the kind of people who still wanted to buy newspapers if they could only have found one offering the slightest affirmation of their lives and outlooks. Had it remained true to its own founding ethos, *The Irish Times* could have borrowed or bought for itself another decade or two of life at the centre of Irish affairs, simply by nurturing this constituency instead of chasing the online lunatics and extreme 'liberals' of its journalists' fevered imaginations. This would have given the paper some thinking time, and also time for the Internet revolution to settle down and reveal its settled patterns. Personally, I've always believed there would be a future for newsprint, once the novelty of the Internet had waned a little, as it inevitably will. but because of the approach taken by newspapers like *The Irish Times*, journalism will be out of business by the time the necessary distance is achieved.

With these trends and thoughts in mind, on Geraldine Kennedy's departure in 2011, I applied for the editorship of *The Irish Times*. I did so without the slightest hope or expectation of being appointed, but purely for the purpose of obtaining an interview and taking the opportunity to warn those in a position to make major decisions in the newspaper that its reputation in Irish society and the world was being severely damaged by a number of factors, including the tone introduced by the online edition – in particular the 'comment threads' now permitted at the end of particular articles, especially those belonging to the Opinion page – and the extreme and largely unmitigated 'liberal' and anti-Catholic bias that the newspaper had adopted in recent times. I was called for interview on 28 May 2011, my 56th birthday.

The interview panel comprised perhaps 20 people, including some members of *The Irish Times* Trust, *The Irish Times* Board, and representatives of the management and NUJ chapel. I answered their questions and made my pitch about the precarious state of affairs confronting the newspaper. I told them that the decision to concentrate the company's energies on the online edition, to the detriment of the newspaper, would prove disastrous. I used the analogy of a public house, in which beer was made available for free in the lounge but charged at full price in the bar. Where did they think the 'customers' would tend to go? And how long would they expect the pub to stay in business?

Essentially, I emphasised that we needed to go back to concentrating on the journalistic aspects of the organisation's business, rather than being obsessed with technological developments and chasing online poltergeists. I expressed the view that *The Irish Times* needed to reclaim its previous reputation as a fair and moderate newspaper, prepared to give all sides of an argument a fair hearing.

I also raised with the interview panel the odd circumstance that, whereas a paying customer who wanted to respond to something they'd read in the newspaper had to submit a letter complete with address and telephone number before it would be considered for publication, freeloaders could go on *The Irish Times* website and slag off its journalists in the most splenetic terms without even revealing their names.

I pointed out to the panel that, whereas they were the people who had

< 259 >

the future of *The Irish Times* in their hands, I – with perhaps a handful of other journalists – was the public face of the newspaper in the world. It was all too true: even I was unable to recognise more than three or four people around the table, and these were all senior but relatively anonymous players within the paper's editorial or corporate sectors. Going around the country as I did, people regularly told me what they thought of me and the newspaper, and I was therefore in a position to convey to the panel the broad attitude of the public concerning what we were doing. I recall pointing out that, whereas the ideological tone of *The Irish Times* was now such as to treat it as axiomatic that we had arrived at a 'post-Catholic Ireland', the fact of the matter was that an overwhelming majority of the population still considered itself Catholic. It was legitimate, I said, to pursue negative stories about the Catholic Church, and I had no particular gripe with the coverage of clerical sex abuse or its cover-up, but we should not forget that religious faith was far more than an institutional phenomenon, being rooted in the very psyche of the human person and the society. If they doubted this, I said, they should the following Sunday morning get in their cars and try to head in any direction out of Dublin, north, west or south – and they would surely find their passage impeded periodically by the volume of motor vehicles they would encounter outside churches along the way. The interview panel was courteous, but – I felt – somewhat patronising. In any event, I felt the exercise had achieved its objective, for what it was worth.

For a time I was somewhat alarmed in case I had made too much sense and might actually be offered the job, but I needn't have worried. It was only in the wake of the interviews that I heard rumours that Kevin O'Sullivan was the favourite to succeed Geraldine Kennedy. This shocked me. I would never have considered him editor material, although he was a good nuts-and-bolts man and seemed to be popular among the reporters. On 23 June, the announcement was made that O'Sullivan was to be the new Editor. I sent him a text that evening, saying: 'Congratulations, Kevin. The very best of luck. John Waters' He responded: 'John ... many

< 260 >

thanks for msg! K'. That was the sole communication I would receive from him as Editor until I left the newspaper nearly three years later.

Among the many strange aspects of this was that I had briefly, a long time before, been O'Sullivan's editor. While I was running *Magill*, he sent me an article on spec from Galway, where he was working as a reporter with *The Connacht Tribune*. The subject was unprepossessing – some arcane dispute concerning the future of a local mart – but I was on the lookout for a good stringer in the West and so decided I would try to tart it up for publication and see if he had anything more interesting to offer. O'Sullivan and I spoke several times on the telephone and I found him pleasant and keen. The mart saga, following the consumption on my part of several gallons of midnight oil, eventually made it into *Magill*, but very shortly afterwards I left the job and so had no future contact with O'Sullivan until nearly a decade later when he joined *The Irish Times*. We resumed on a friendly enough basis – occasionally stopping for brief chats in the newsroom – but did not really have much to do with one another.

At a superficial level, his appointment as Editor made no discernible difference. The paper seemed more and more to become a parody of itself. There was an early and ludicrous attempt to market O'Sullivan as the public face of the newspaper, with billboards of his head posted around Dublin; a waste of money, since no one had the faintest idea who he was, where he'd come from or what he stood for. As time went by, I became less and less a fan of his editorship, regarding the paper as increasingly rudderless: sloppy in its news values, unimaginative in its features and colourless in its analysis and opinion sections. I never expressed these views to anyone I even remotely thought might have repeated them to O'Sullivan.

After he became Editor, we met casually on two occasions, once by what appeared to be an accident when he happened along while I was meeting his deputy, Denis Staunton, in *The Irish Times* canteen. There followed a three-way, three-minute conversation about nothing. Some time later, in May 2013, I was with Róisín when she was among a group of aspiring writers being honoured by President Michael D. Higgins in the context of a writing competition run by Fighting Words, a Dublin-based centre for the promotion of writing talent among young people. The event was being sponsored by *The Irish Times* and O'Sullivan came over to congratulate Róisín. In a brief exchange between us, I suggested to him that he might consider introducing a New Irish Writing section to *The Irish Times* along the lines of the page edited for many years by David Marcus in the long defunct Irish Press. He said that some discussions were already in train with this in mind. (In January 2015, such a page was duly launched in *The Irish Times*, and as far as I know is still going.)

Otherwise, O'Sullivan might as well have been avoiding me. One night, not long after his appointment, I saw him two rows down, directly in front of me, in the Abbey Theatre. In between us were Gay Byrne and his wife Kathleen Watkins. At the interval, I spoke briefly to Gay, and noticed that O'Sullivan was standing up and looking backwards in our general direction. I nodded to him but he ignored me and started to talk to Gay. It was very strange and not a little ominous.

I found Denis Staunton, the new Deputy Editor, a likeable and genial individual, and we seemed to hit it off reasonably well. Very soon after his appointment, he called me and suggested we meet for a coffee. I went in to meet him in *The Irish Times* building on Tara Street, to which the newspaper had moved a few years before. I had long since ceased to visit the offices of the newspaper, since I was able to work remotely and send my copy in by email, and since the general atmosphere I encountered in the office could best be described as chilled. In fact, I had fallen into the habit of visiting the offices just once a year, to have my accumulated expenses endorsed by a senior editor. This was a rather comical ritual, as I was no longer able simply to walk in, as in the old days, nod to the security men at the desk, and take the lift upstairs. Now I had to fill out a form, receive a security clearance badge and wait for some senior member of staff to come down and escort me upstairs.

When we met (on a couple of occasions) Staunton appeared to be very enthusiastic about my column. He suggested that we speak every week before I decided on a topic, and I agreed that this would be a good idea. Some journalists bridle at the idea of an editor seeking to direct them in what they might write, but I have always valued such input as having the potential to open up my thinking both in terms of topics and in respect of angles on particular issues. Never in all my time as a columnist with *The Irish Times* had any opinion editor spoken to me in advance of writing my column, although this is common practice in other newspapers, including *The Irish Mail on Sunday*, for which I wrote a column for six years.

I found these conversations with Staunton very enjoyable and helpful, and he made very useful suggestions about topics and angles. He and I rarely met, but we spoke frequently on the telephone. In January 2013, we both participated in a seminar on journalism in UCC and had lunch together, with other speakers and Rita, and I found Denis very personable and entertaining company – and surprisingly indiscreet about the internal politics of *The Irish Times*. However, after a time, for reasons that are not entirely clear to me, our telephone conversations tailed off.

The new Opinion Editor, Chris Dooley, and I had a cordial enough relationship also, but occasionally he would send me abrasive emails about the content of my column, with which he frequently appeared to be in disagreement. This was in keeping with the long experience I had had at the newspaper, where journalists and editors seemed to spend more time disputing points of view than doing their own jobs or operating as editors are supposed to operate.

One of my developing bugbears was the recent shift to allow unmoderated comments from people described as 'readers' to be appended to the online version of my column. Even before this became a problem for me in *The Irish Times*, I had drawn attention to the disquieting trend in this direction in other newspapers. Back in 2009, I had written about such posts on an article in *The Observer* about Ethiopia 25 years after the famine that spawned Band-Aid, and including some analysis of the political activism of people like Bob Geldof and the U2 singer Bono. I had this to say about the comment thread at the end of the article:

Several contributors grasped the opportunity to vent their spleens about Geldof and Bono. One post called them 'an absolutely monstrous pair of fuckers who have made millions off the backs of the starving'. Another contributor wrote that he was 'relieved to learn that Bono isn't just a posturing, monstrous, tax-dodging cock who could write a cheque which would dwarf the original Live Aid fund – and then drop it in the street without bothering to look for it'.

'Let's start making poverty history,' declared a fairly typical post, 'by preventing people like Bob Geldof's and Prince Charles' offspring from pro-creating shall we? I really don't want another multi-millionaire tax-dodging mouth to feed, grabbing 99% of the world's resources whilst the rest of the world goes to hell in a hand cart, do you?'

I concluded with a summary of my general view of this new trend:

The most interesting thing about such threads is the mob mindset that seems to underlie them. They are not neutral conduits for spontaneous opinions, but channels dedicated to forms of disgruntlement with, for perhaps good reasons, no other outlet. Contributors appear to come to the process with a mindset possibly symptomatic of the isolationism involved in Internet relationships generally, and anticipating a certain group dynamic. The tone of a thread seems to be set by the early contributors.

Most contributors appear mostly to want to draw attention to themselves, seeking to convey an impression of strength, cleverness, cynicism or aggressiveness, while pre-empting the possibility of hostility or ridicule by pushing these responses in front like swords. Frankly, I am at a loss to perceive any intellectual or democratic distinction between most of this stuff and public urination.

Responses from readers is an essential element of journalism. But in my experience, the kinds of communications you get in the form of letters or even emails are quite different to what is to be found in these web threads. As well as abuse, traditional reader-to-author feedback offers constructive criticism, passionate and informed argument, useful information and sometimes even praise. I do not suggest that the new developments are not representative of something occurring in society, but I believe we should be looking more closely at what this trend might represent rather than unthinkingly absorbing its bile.

Within a short time I found myself having to contend with similar style posts on my own articles, many of them either anonymous or pseudonymous. I raised this with various senior people within the newspaper, arguing that it was as bad for *The Irish Times*'s reputation as it was for my soul. While Chris Dooley was Opinion Editor in 2012/13, I had a number of extended email exchanges with him on this topic, but found him extremely resistant to any proposal that the comment threads be restricted or moderated in any way.

In February 2013, I wrote to him:

> As I've told you, I long since ceased reading the posts at the end of my own articles. Occasionally I dip into the comments on articles written by others to see if the general tenor is changing in any way. Last night, noticing that Breda O'Brien had over 600 posts on her piece about the Magdalenes, I had a look and came upon the following (I quote from memory, but accurately I believe): 'Let's go back to bashing Waters for the last half-hour and then come back and finish off O'Brien'. Another poster supplied the rejoinder: 'Neither of them are worth the trouble of bashing them for half an hour'.
>
> Something snapped m'lud. For a long time I've felt that these comments add nothing to human knowledge or understanding and are actually bad for the image of *The Irish Times* in the world. I have also remarked upon the strange contradiction whereby readers, per

< 265 >

se, are subject to rigorous vetting of any comments they may seek to make in the Letters page, whereas anyone can write whatever they please on these posts free of charge. That we are prepared to subject our own columnists to such vitriol seems to bespeak some strange form of self-hatred.

As part of my submission, I cited several of the principles of *The Irish Times* Trust document, including inter alia those relating to the promotion of a 'friendly society' and 'opposition to all forms of violence and hatred'. I continued:

> It seems to me that the present policy of the newspaper in relation to its online edition drives a coach and four through all of these principles. I would therefore like formally to request that all reader comments on my articles be suspended until the present system is reformed in line with the principles upon which the newspaper was established.

Dooley responded initially in pretty desultory fashion, stating his views that the comments I referred to were 'ironic'. He said he had passed my email on to the Online Editor, Hugh Linihan, and his assistant David Cochrane, 'as they are the people more directly responsible for the comments system and ongoing efforts to raise the level of discussion, which are actually meeting with some (albeit) slow success.' Later he responded in more detail, albeit even more negatively in terms of addressing my request to look at the comments issue:

> I'm not prepared to recommend that we remove the comments option from any particular writer, for the reasons I'll set out here. We do occasionally close down a debate on a particular article if there is large scale abuse of community standards, and that option is always there, but it is the newspaper's policy now to open all oped articles

(and many others in the paper and on the website) to online comment, and I don't think it's a good idea to make exceptions.

I know you disagree with the whole thrust of the newspaper's approach to increasing its digital audience, but the reality is that we do now operate in a very different environment than used to be the case. The digital audience – many of them long-time readers of the newspaper I have no doubt – have developed different expectations in terms of how we interact with them. You draw attention to the difference between our treatment of letter writers to the paper and those who comment online. I think it's a reasonable point … but I'm afraid the day when a columnist can emit from on high, and then brook no dissent bar whatever responses are handpicked by an editor for publication perhaps three days after the column is published in the first place, are over.

Further on he added:

I hope you don't mind my saying that I find it surprising that you, of all our columnists, would ask that we prevent people from commenting online on your articles. You are the only one who tells me you never read the comments on your pieces, but you are also the only one who has asked me to suspend all comments on your columns. If you never read them why do you care what they have to say?'

This was a typically disingenuous response – typical, that is, of the culture of the senior *Irish Times* editors, most of whom were for obscure reasons drawn from the ranks of the newsroom staff rather than being columnists themselves. It was hard not to suspect occasionally that many of them had a deep and abiding disdain for people who write opinion columns for a living.

I responded:

Your characterisation of me as someone who seeks to 'emit from on high and then brook no dissent' is unreasonable and unfair. If that is what you believe, you have both misunderstood my point and bought into a version of me that bears no relationship to the reality. Since I joined *The Irish Times* 22 years ago, my articles have consistently been the subject of intense controversy on the Letters page and beyond. I have gone into every media bearpit in the country to defend my positions, and have never shrunk from the criticism or even the anger of readers. What I am seeking to draw attention to here is something rather new and deeply vile. It is true that I no longer read the online comments on my articles, but I sometimes read those on others. Moreover, my girlfriend and several friends continue to dip into the comments on my articles, and they all continue to report that I should continue to refrain from reading them.

The reasons I 'care' what posters are allowed to say about me and my work is that I believe the newspaper I have served for 22 years owes me a little more than to throw me every week to a pack of ravenous dogs. I 'care' because I have a daughter who I fear might one day have to read these poisonous attacks on her father. I 'care' because, oddly enough, I care about the direction *The Irish Times* has taken of late.

And so on and so on, wasting my time, banging my head on a thick brick wall.

The comments threads, whenever I did dip into them, invariably struck me in a number of ways. One immediate impression I gleaned was that the people writing on them, almost without exception, seemed to be doing so not out of any interest in the topics they were ostensibly discussing, but out of a need for interaction and banter with like-minded individuals. Most of the time they had but the fuzziest idea of the details of the topic of the article they had supposedly read and wished to respond to. I noticed certain patterns in their treatment of me: highly personalised comments about aspects of my private life, and a general tendency to amalgamate elements of my writing under different headings, twisting these a little to achieve a desired effect, and presenting the result as a summary of my position and my character.

For example, in a response to the column I wrote in the wake of the 2012 so-called 'Children's Rights Amendment', a poster calling himself Adam 19801 wrote:

> I do not want John Waters to be my children's social worker. As an atheist and a secularist John has described me in the past as a person devoid of hope and light. As a parent he thinks I would teach my child to be an incurious lump of meat devoid of natural curiosity. Clearly, by that measure, I am unfit and he would seek to have my children removed and adopted by a nice Catholic family.
>
> Would the amendment give him the power to do so? No, clearly it does not. Because of Article 42.3 John would have to prove that I am failing in my moral and religious duty. A very difficult thing to do because his opinion is extremist nonsense. Also because of Article 42.2 my children would be able to demonstrate that they were no more incurious lumps of meat than any other children. In fact, if you placed my children because [sic] two Catholic children of similar ages you wouldn't be able to tell which ones came from the atheist family and which ones came from the Catholic family.

This is such a farrago of outright nonsense that it feels a bit ridiculous to be making anything of it. I hope I need hardly say that there was no reference to lumps of meat in my analysis of the 31st Amendment. Adam 19801 clearly didn't understand the content of the amendment being proposed, or that it had been designed fundamentally to alter the meaning of Article 42. There wasn't then or isn't now anything in Article 42.3 about 'religious duty'. The amendment replaced the old Article 42.5, which provided for state intervention in families when the parents had failed in their duty to their children for 'physical or moral reasons', with a new article 42A which provided for such intervention when the parent had failed 'to such an extent that the safety or welfare of any of their children is likely to be prejudicially affected'. This was the nub of the issue, which had nothing to do with atheism, secularism, hope, light, natural curiosity or Catholicism.

Later, Adam 19801 returned to the fray:

> John Waters is not a person, given his views, who is fit to decide what a good or a bad parent is, since he thinks that people who don't fit his narrow worldview automatically make bad parents. That view alone should disqualify his opinion on children's rights, and any referenda attached to those rights in polite company.

For the avoidance of doubt, I had never set myself up as someone who is fit to decide what a good or a bad parent is, nor had I sought to suggest that anyone who did not fit my 'worldview' – narrow or broad – would make bad parents, 'automatically' or otherwise. These kinds of response, which were fairly typical of the general fare, were simply coined on the spot out of dollops of prejudice mixed with half-remembered, third-hand interpretations of things, taken out of context, that I might once have written on an entirely different subject altogether.

But this kind of thing was merely irritating. As I told Chris Dooley, I didn't, as a rule, read the comments on my articles, so most of the time this stuff was going down I didn't know about it and therefore didn't lose any sleep.

More troubling was when things got personal and people I ran into started to mention to me that, judging by the comments threads on my columns, things in the paper seemed to be getting out of hand. Again, stuff like comments about my appearance, the length of my hair, where I lived, were merely annoyingly gratuitous and invasive, like, for example, 'DamianCollins' observing: 'Waters would be even less insecure if he ditched his blatent [sic] hypocrisy. He lives a very liberal lifestyle in elitist Dalkey.'

But sometimes it became downright rancid, as for example in 2013, in the midst of a whole mess of venom that followed an article I wrote in response to reports that Pope Francis had performed an exorcism in St Peter's Square, a chap calling himself 'JayGee' had this to say:

> Jazus Corrigan I didn't know Sinead had had a child with JW. I love that girl and now I find out she was bedded by Waters. I'm sick to my stomach.

The reference is to Sinéad O'Connor, who is the mother of my daughter, Róisín. It's a strange thing: I had never written in *The Irish Times* about any aspect of my involvement with Sinéad O'Connor. Had I ever attempted to do so, it is likely that the newspaper's editors or, failing that, its lawyers, would have stepped in to forbid me. Yet, total randomers, who knew nothing about me other than the prejudices they picked up from the tabloids or one another, were allowed to come on *The Irish Times* website and make comments that were not merely intrusive but utterly obnoxious – and intended to be so. And *The Irish Times* called this 'debate'!

Very often, comments had little or nothing to do with what I had written that day, or at all. Underneath that article about Pope Francis and the 'exorcism', were a number of comments about something I had not written about in *The Irish Times* at all – which, as it happens, *The Irish Times* had never carried any mention of: the fact that, in 2013, not long after his election, on Saturday 18 May 2013, I spoke on a platform alongside Pope Francis in St Peter's Square in Rome, in front of more than 200,000 people. Although *The Irish Times* managed to avoid mentioning this occasion I had been on the radio talking to Miriam O'Callaghan about the experience of meeting the Pope, staying in the guesthouse where he lived and so forth. When, shortly afterwards, I wrote in *The Irish Times* about the 'exorcism' that newspaper reports, including in *The Irish Times*, claimed the pope had carried out the following day, I mentioned that, at the time this was supposed to have occurred, I was standing 20 yards away and saw nothing of the kind.

The posters, however, were not interested in whether the 'exorcism' happened or not, which is to say in the content of what I had written. Some of them just wanted to get personal. A chap calling himself 'PseudONym5' had this to say:

> The question left in my mind is … John was in Rome with his girlfriend, did they share a room? None of my business of course but when he's on here bleating about the poor old catholics getting a raw deal you have to wonder if he's sticking to all the rules himself. But maybe there's an evil spirit filling him with lust, sure you know how it can be … '

Someone calling himself John O'Brien rejoined:

> LOL – I just like pointing out the hypocrisy of our dear author. Don't have a holier than thou attitude when clearly your own lifestyle flies in the face of church doctrine. I think the Glass houses argument rings true in this case.

Later on PseudONym5 is visited by further comic inspiration:

> 'John, what's that pressing against my leg?'
> 'It's ahhh … just an evil spirit love … never worry …'

This kind of stuff, by all accounts, was par for the course, appearing every week at the end of my column. It's still there at the time of writing, if anyone wishes to look it up. To say it adds nothing to any discussion or debate is to invite weariness in the face of the proposition that any such intention lies behind it. It is intended merely to provoke more and more clicks, to add to the advertising revenues of *The Irish Times* and to contribute to the job security of the senior editors and executives who are responsible for the continuation of the policy that permits it, and, as a consequence, the continuing decline of a once great newspaper.

24

Engineering Consent

In the modern 'democracy', the right of a voter to express a subjective opinion at the polling booth is increasingly seen as problematic. It represents an unstable and uncertain element in the make-up of the modern state, which functions on the run-off from free capital movements and therefore depends for its functionality, even survival, on doing what its paymasters demand. The idea of allowing people to sit around having arguments, make up their own minds and possibly come up with an answer contrary to the wishes of the state's sponsors and custodians is obviously not one that can be given any serious consideration by those who are serious about power. It is obvious that the old style of politics, going back to politicians standing on butter boxes outside churches on Sunday mornings, shouting and roaring in their efforts to woo the electorate to whatever vision of independence or sovereignty they were purveying can no longer be contemplated. It is clear that there is no place in the modern political set-up for leaving things to chance, or public caprice, or democracy in the old sense. Things have to be taken in hand.

A key element in the armoury of the modern state and its rulers is propaganda, a concept which is often misunderstood as mere slanted information, when in truth the issue is the generation of public feeling.

The godfather of modern public relations, Edward Bernays, a nephew of Sigmund Freud, wrote in his 1928 book, *Propaganda*, that, even if every citizen had time to sift through data concerning every question, virtually nobody would be able to come to informed conclusions about anything. We therefore tend to farm out the sifting process to what he calls 'the invisible government', which we rely upon to tell us what things mean, which things are important and what are our options in considering them. By and large, we accept the verdicts provided to us by our media and political elites.

Universal literacy, Bernays recalled, was supposed to change these conditions radically, giving each citizen 'a mind fit to rule' – the core doctrine of democracy. 'But instead of a mind, ' he continued, 'universal literacy has given him rubber stamps, rubber stamps inked with advertising slogans, with editorials, with published scientific data, with the trivialities of the tabloids and the platitudes of history, but quite innocent of original thought. Each man's rubber stamps are the duplicates of millions of others, so that when these millions are exposed to the same stimuli, all receive identical imprints.'

It was Bernays who first experimented with applying his uncle's psychoanalytic principles to marketing by linking products to emotions in ways that tapped into people's inclination to behave in illogical ways. Intrigued by Freud's notion that irrational group-based forces drive human behaviour, Bernays set about harnessing those forces to sell products for his clients. In Propaganda, he speculated that it should be possible to manipulate people's behaviour without their knowing. Then he began putting his theories into action, firstly on behalf of George Washington Hill, president of the American Tobacco Company, which was keen to demolish the taboo that, insinuating a strong link between female cigarette smoking and sexual promiscuity, had until the late 1920s discouraged women from lighting up in public. Hill, seeking to promote his company's Lucky Strike brand, consulted Bernays, who in turn spoke to leading New York psychoanalyst and Freud disciple, Dr A. A. Brill, who gave Bernays a lightbulb moment when he postulated that cigarettes were symbolic of male power. Bernays developed a campaign aimed at convincing women that smoking in public would allow them to strike a blow for sexual equality. Hence, Lucky Strike's 'Torches of Freedom' campaign, launched during New York's Easter Parade on April Fool's Day 1929. Bernays had obtained a list of female models from the Editor of Vogue magazine and convinced enough of them that they could advance the cause of equality by lighting up on Fifth Avenue. The parade became an international sensation and Bernays dubbed his newly tested technique 'engineering consent'.

Later, another Viennese psychoanalyst, Ernest Dichter, further developed the idea of tapping into the unconscious to sell people things they didn't need. 'You would be amazed to find how often we mislead ourselves, regardless of how smart we think we are, when we attempt to explain why we are behaving the way we do,' he wrote in his 1960 book, *The Strategy of Desire*.

Dichter believed that human motivation was roughly one third rational, with the remainder governed by emotion. He referred to this syndrome as the 'iceberg' and developed the idea that people could be persuaded to buy things because of illogical associations implanted by advertising. He was a pioneer of focus group market research methods, which he used to great effect on behalf of clients like Procter & Gamble, Chrysler and DuPont. He was also an early practitioner of qualitative research, involving long, in-depth interviews, not unlike therapy sessions. To understand why people really bought certain things, he held, you had to talk to them at a deeper level. 'If you let somebody talk long enough,' he would say, 'you can read between the lines to find out what he really means.' Dichter tapped into people's desires – usually for sex, security or prestige. For him, shopping was a form of self-expression. He divined that certain people prefer cars that feel safe, whereas others like their steeds to speak of adventure and youth. He sold more typewriters by proposing that keyboards be designed to suggest the female body – 'more receptive, more concave'. He discerned that Americans preferred to borrow money at higher rates from loan sharks rather than patronise legitimate banking institutions, because they feared being judged. Using these insights, he helped banks to develop products and messages to get around such fears. He formed the view that people tend to buy things for other than utilitarian reasons – as extensions or reflections of their personalities, for example. Every product, he declared, has a personality, and the right

< 276 >

campaign will communicate this to people who see themselves in a certain way. He exploited neurosis and unfulfilled longing and was the first to understand that the choice of bath soap might have an erotic component. Through depth-interviewing he deduced that soaping while taking a bath was one of the few occasions when the average puritanical American felt permitted to caress himself or herself. The research showed that bathing was for many adults a pretext for auto-erotic experiment, a ritual that afforded rare moments of personal indulgence, particularly before a romantic assignation.

The most important thing about propaganda, Dichter asserted, is that it be universal and continuous, hammering home the same message by diverse means, again and again. The purpose is to 'regiment' the mind of a society in the same way that an army drills its soldiers. Propaganda is most effective in the hands of what Bernays had called 'intelligent minorities', by which he meant not minorities in the latter-day sense of victim groups, but intellectual elites seeking to guide society in particular directions. Bernays referred to these intellectual elites, without irony, as 'dictators'.

Co-opting the earlier work of the French philosopher Gustav La Bon, Bernays identified the 'group mind' as having entirely different characteristics from those of the individual mind. The group mind does not think, at least not in the conventional sense, and yet acts as if it had an intelligence of its own. The group mind, he observed, does not entertain thoughts, but instead has impulses, habits and emotions. It either follows leaders or, if forced to think for itself, does so by means of available clichés and supplied images relating to the common mentality of the group. By playing upon an old cliché, or manipulating a newly minted one, the propagandist can swing a whole mass of group emotions.

Bernays's and Dichter's thoughts were developed and added to by Jacques Ellul in his 1965 book, *Propagandes* (Propagandas), mistakenly translated into English as *Propaganda*. Propaganda was, he believed, the Siamese twin of the technological society, which uses it to integrate the individual into its ways and logics. 'In the midst of increasing mechanisa-

< 277 >

tion and technological organisation,' he wrote, 'propaganda is simply the means used to prevent these things from being felt as too oppressive and to persuade man to submit with good grace.'

Ellul refined and in some cases rejected inherited ideas, such as that all propaganda is lies and that its sole purpose is to change opinions. On the contrary, he observed, the best kind of propaganda is generated from half-truths and truths taken out of context, and its main purpose is to strengthen existing trends and perceptions and to promote action where appropriate, and – most importantly – to dissuade, with terror or discouragement, those of strong opinions contrary to the propaganda from interfering with its agenda. Ellul characterised conventional education as 'pre-propaganda', the conditioning of minds with enormous amounts of second-hand, disconnected, unverifiable, incoherent and/or useless information masquerading as 'facts', but intended to prepare the citizen for the planting of propaganda.

It is obvious from this outline that the fundamental conditions described by La Bon, Bernays and Ellul remain in place today, but have been subjected to exponential multipliers arising from the sheer pervasiveness of advertising, the ubiquity of technology, the power of the Internet and the 24/7 stream of information and responses in respect of selected events from around the globe. The chief impact of this has been to suppress further the possibility of independent thought. The brain has a finite capacity to manage and sort information, and when it is already overloaded by random, largely uninvited facts and opinions, it has little disk space for its own ruminations. Modern man, Ellul observed, accepts 'facts' as the ultimate reality. 'He is convinced that what is, is good'. He places facts ahead of values and unquestioningly applies the moralism of 'progress' to something to which he attributes value because it exists. Something dressing itself up as progress is therefore halfway to success.

Propaganda always addresses itself to the individual enclosed in the mass. The individual must never be considered as such but always, Ellul instructed, in terms of what he has in common with others, such as his motivations, his feelings or his myths. The individual is reduced by propaganda to become an average, thus rendering him amenable to manipulation. The propagandist addresses the individual – in newspaper articles, radio broadcasts etc. – as part of a group. The individual is never treated as if alone. This is the key to understanding how modern opinion polling works: it likewise treats individuals as part of a mass. When the pollster with her clipboard enters the room to canvass the opinions of those present, she brings the masses with her.

Propaganda, Ellul wrote, must be total. It must utilise all the available means of communication and at once: press, radio, TV, movies, posters, meetings, door-to-door canvassing. To use these media sporadically and without a propagandist intention is to achieve nothing. Each medium has a different line of attack, and all must be employed together to achieve a total surrender.

It is a symptom of the effectiveness of propaganda that people nowadays seem unthinkingly to throw up clichés in response to virtually every provocation. If you make a remark about the number of foreigners who have come to live in Ireland in the past decade or so, for example, you will be told that Ireland is now 'a multicultural society'. If you ask what this means, you will be told that it means having lots of foreigners living here. When you point out that this is precisely what you've just said, you may well be asked if you have 'a problem' with multiculturalism. In this way, a fixed, formulaic and tautological method for disposing of awkward questioning is spread by contagion and downloaded by every unthinking collaborator. Ellul noted this tendency of propagandised subjects to simply regurgitate the material they had earlier been fed, whose 'beliefs' are the direct result of propaganda. Such alienation occurs without conveying any sense of its nature to those affected.

Universal education bearing the characteristics described by Ellul has generated populations of citizens who provide easy meat for propaganda for at least four reasons: people who consider themselves 'educated' have a need to hold opinions on any and all matters arising in their purview;

they have access to large amounts of what might be called contextless information; they think of themselves as capable of judging all questions on their own; they are generally people who have left behind the kind of communities which in the past provided a kind of filtering for external propaganda, such as families, churches, villages etc. Hence, in mass society, the pre-programmed citizen, who becomes isolated and dependent upon his own resources to fulfil his conditioned needs, is a sitting duck for propagandists of all kinds. When you consider the present-day easy access to a certain kind of basic information about next to everything, it is not surprising that, on virtually every matter of public controversy, there is a ready constituency for the indoctrinations of propagandists among those who believe themselves educated because they hold a degree, have instant access to Google and other search engines and consider themselves to be 'entitled' to their opinions. Thus, what might be called the market for propaganda has expanded to include virtually every member of a modern society – everyone, that is, except those who understand the underfoot conditions and are prepared to seek their information from other than ready sources and remain determined to think for themselves. By Ellul's thesis, the citizen imagining himself 'modern' needs propaganda: to fulfil his sense of importance and involvement in the ostensibly prevailing democracy; to provide an outlet for his pent-up energies, to put on display his 'moral' disposition, and so forth. Seen like this, it becomes clear that a modern society 'needs' propaganda in much the same way, and for the same reasons, that it needs entertainment: to anaesthetise the population so that resistance to the wishes of the powerful is minimised.

It will be obvious to everyone but the wilfully blind that the outcome of the same-sex marriage referendum was almost entirely the consequence of highly organised and fluent propaganda. We can rule out from the outset the idea that any but perhaps a few of the main agitators for gay marriage were in the slightest degree interested in human or civil rights per se. For many years, as I have been repeating here, I had sought to raise the maltreatment of fathers in family courts, the marginalisation of fathers in Irish culture, the disrespect for the father-child bond displayed by legislators, judges, social workers and the like, but found my way blocked at every turn by a small coterie of determined ideologues – all of whom were to be observed on the front line of the same-sex marriage crusade. Similarly, politicians who for decades had brushed aside or ignored any representations to do with men, whether to do with the alarming rates of suicide among young men or the failure to recognise the status of an unmarried father in even the most rudimentary way, were to be heard trumpeting their commitment to 'equality', 'fairness' and even 'love'.

Although part of the propaganda was to persuade people that here we had 'the most important civil rights issue of our times', nobody with an ounce of sense could take such a claim seriously. In truth, the proposal was ridiculous, counter-intuitive, imported and trivialising of the real issues of civil and human rights facing Irish society. It succeeded because a concerted lobby group, taking its cues and energies from a determined international movement, and with access to vast amounts of donor funding, was able to tap into each and every one of the channels that must be utilised in a successful propaganda campaign. This lobby group was able to claim the support of most of the major transnational corporations on which the alleged 'Irish' economy depended, and in that way to put the hammer on politicians. The media provided a host of more-than-willing allies, many journalists turning into activists with microphones and laptops. The result was a virtual clean sweep of the channels of public debate – the Oireachtas, TV, radio, newspapers and, naturally, the worldwide web, which provided perhaps the most effective instruments of the campaign, via social networking sites like Twitter and Facebook, enabling a new form of quasi-democratic hyper-bullying by anonymous agents to promote and prosecute the message of the propagandists and punish those who dared to dissent.

Afterwards, in a rather typical instance of ex post facto revisionism, the Yes side started to put it about that they had won the 'debate' in what had been the cleanest and most civil public discussion in Ireland for many years. This was pure cant and lies. In all my working life, I had never witnessed anything as ugly as the tone and behaviour of same-sex marriage advocates in the course of the sustained campaigns of lies, intimidation and moral blackmail going back to the start of 2014.

Of course, the conditions in which propaganda is enabled to flourish are not confined to any specific issue, but now persist in relation to all things and at all times. Journalism has ceased to be such: it is now unabashed activism. There continues to be a degree of relatively dispassionate reporting of news, but this is really just an alibi for newspapers and broadcasting organisations, which exist for the sole purpose of promoting the agendas favoured by their operatives according to the diktats of their ultimate paymasters. Whether it's the relentless stream of stories about transsexuals who can't make their minds up, gay couples who are asked to leave restaurants because of lewd behaviour, non-Catholics who don't like crucifixes hanging from the walls of the Catholic schools to which they send their children, women who want abortions and can't have them at home, women who've had abortions and feel judged, and so forth. All these 'stories' belong to a common agenda for change: the rooting out from Irish society of all religious belief and the normalisation of every kind of eccentricity. Anyone who questions or objects to this becomes the subject of another 'story'. The point of such 'journalism' is to exalt and celebrate those who subscribe to the approved mentality and the regime promoting it, and to eviscerate anyone who goes against it. It has no other point.

It ensures that the Irish public is subjected on more or less a 24/7 basis to a torrent of propaganda and vitriol insinuating that everything has changed about Ireland because the people wish it so. The impression is consistently generated that everything being promoted is for the betterment – i.e. the enhanced modernisation – of Ireland and its peoples. Again, those who think differently are advised to keep their opinions to themselves.

< 282 >

Propaganda, Jacques Ellul believed, is 'a direct attack against man'. Although an advocate of democracy, he believed that propaganda rendered its true exercise 'almost impossible'. This is why those who persist in thinking for themselves, or even in expressing unapproved views, invite such opprobrium in modern societies. It's not just that they threaten the reach or influence of the propagandists, for in truth, because of their failure to achieve total saturation through media, dissenters rarely do this. It is that, by their very presence, they put at risk the whole edifice. Their dissent endangers the artifice that is essential for effective propaganda: the sense of naturalism, factuality, that accompanies it. For this to work effectively propaganda requires to be ubiquitous, universal. Propaganda, writes Ellul, 'does not tolerate discussion. It abhors contradiction. It must produce quasi-unanimity, and the opposing faction must become negligible, or in any case cease to be vocal.'

Once successfully propagandised, the individual ceases to be a passive recipient of the propaganda and becomes an evangelist. He takes vigorous stances, starts to oppose others on behalf of those who have successfully propagandised him. To submit to propaganda means to become alienated from oneself. 'Propaganda strips the individual,' Ellul declared, 'robs him of part of himself, and makes him live an alien and artificial life, to such an extent that he becomes another person and obeys impulses foreign to him.' This is achieved by suffusing the individual in the emotions and responses of the herd, dissipating his individuality, freeing his ego of all confusions, unresolved contradictions and personal reservations. It pushes the individual into the mass 'until he disappears entirely'. What 'disappears', actually, is the individual's capacity for personal reflection, independent thinking and critical judgment, these being replaced with ready-made thoughts, stereotypes and clichés.

One of the unnoticed consequences of propaganda, according to Jacques Ellul, is that it results in a gradual 'closing up' of the individual, arising from a growing insensitivity to repeated bouts of propaganda. Subjected to persistent repetitions of the same messages, he begins to

< 283 >

skim the headlines of his newspaper rather than reading the articles. In a more modern context, he uses the remote control to zap from station to station on his TV set, searching perhaps for some element of surprise, and always in vain. Radio becomes no more than background noise: he doesn't hear and doesn't care. This stage of the process does not signal immunity to propaganda, but the opposite. Deeply imbued with the symbols of propaganda, he no longer needs to absorb the detail. A splash of colour, a familiar logo, is enough to trigger the required Pavlovian response.

Once successfully propagandised, wrote Ellul, the individual 'can no longer judge for himself because he inescapably relates his thoughts to the entire complex of values and prejudices established by propaganda.' This leads to the atrophying of the capacities to judge, discern or think critically, and these faculties will not simply reappear when propaganda is discontinued or suppressed. Years of spiritual and intellectual reconstruction will be required to restore them. The victim of propaganda, deprived of one channel of opinion, will simply seek out another, like a junkie seeking a different kind of fix. Here, the 'fix' is the ready-made opinion that relieves the subject of the necessity of thinking for himself.

< 284 >

25

The Secret History of a Non-issue

Anyone observing the behaviour of *Irish Times* journalists in the wake of the Rory O'Neill interview might have been forgiven for assuming that their zeal, however excessive, was the understandable and natural consequence of having campaigned tirelessly and unapologetically for gay marriage for perhaps at least 20 years, over the course of which the newspaper and its key personnel had clamoured for the recognition of this wrongly withheld 'civil right' and demanded its full implementation. Thus, you might well imagine that their frenzy was born of an anxiety that all their great work might become frustrated by the interventions of people who had not been persuaded.

Such an apprehension of things would have been seriously off kilter. In fact, the newspaper had never campaigned for gay marriage by any conventional definition of the word 'campaign'. It had certainly joined the gay marriage bandwagon from about 2013, when the LGBT lobby began to get its pre-referendum campaign off the ground, but before that its commentaries in its leader columns had given little indication that it believed the issue of gay marriage was something that resided beyond controversy, or was axiomatically and unambiguously necessary in order to achieve equality for gay people.

There were occasional contributions to the newspaper that touched on the topic, but these tended to come from outsiders. In 1995, *The Irish Times* published an exceptionally thorough article on the topic of gay marriage by a gay Irishman, the late television comedy writer Gerry McNamara, who – dare I say it? – was a friend of mine. The piece was a review of *Virtually Normal*, a book by Andrew Sullivan, the then Editor of the New Republic, and himself a gay man. The book endorsed the gay agenda at its most radical and McNamara did not in any significant sense demur from its general thrust. However, he seemed lukewarm on the topic of gay marriage, which Sullivan advocated. McNamara wrote: 'Personally, I think Sullivan over idealises marriage. And perhaps (an Irish person might say) he's a bit too cavalier about divorce. Maybe he lists too much to the Right. He could have talked more about wedding presents.'

Another early treatment of the topic of gay marriage was in an article in the newspaper's 'religious' slot, 'Rite and Reason', on 13 December 2006 by one Jim Duffy, the academic who, as a student, brought to light Brian Lenihan Snr's inconsistencies concerning the notorious 1982 'phone calls to the Áras', during the 1990 presidential election. Citing research by Yale historian Professor John Boswell, Duffy claimed that the Catholic Church had, over the centuries, extended tacit recognition to gay unions, even suggesting that a type of 'Christian same-sex marriage' existed as recently as the 18th century.

The most noteworthy aspect of *The Irish Times* crusading on the question of gay marriage was its total absence. In the early days of the millennium, the paper was disposed to support a minor tweaking of the conditions relating to gay relationships, In 2004, for example, the paper welcomed in an editorial the announcement by the then Taoiseach Bertie Ahern that he intended to 'provide some form of legal protection for partners in long-term cohabiting relationships, whether gay or heterosexual'. It also praised a statement by the Catholic Archbishop of Dublin, Diarmuid Martin, supporting such a move. The leader writer noted: 'Mr Ahern, on RTÉ's *The Week in Politics*, made clear that what he has in mind is not the equating of gay relationships with marriage, but to provide a half-way house in the form of recognition of civil unions.' The leader expressed approval of Mr Ahern's remarks on the grounds that they eschewed 'the moralising that once was the staple of politics'.

'Dr Martin,' the leader continued, 'emphasising that his concern was

< 286 >

primarily with other kinds of caring, dependent relationships, was willing to encompass gay couples in such changes.'

The editorial continued: 'It is really time to grasp the nettle. For too many couples, the denial of spousal rights, from tax allowances to pension entitlements, the refusal of institutions to recognise next-of-kin, or the discretion which officials may exercise over recognising foreign partners, all may compound painfully the difficulty of living a gay life in a society still deeply prejudiced.' Here, not only was there no call for gay marriage, but there was no hint that it ought to be regarded as a fundamental human right. On the contrary, there was a hearty welcome for what was in effect a different course altogether: the creation of a new category of union for both gay and straight couples, falling well short of marriage. At the end of the leader, there was a call for the government to introduce legislation, on foot of the ongoing Gilligan and Zappone case seeking recognition for a lesbian marriage conducted in Canada, with a view to gaining recognition for such unions in the context of taxation equality.

In 2005, the paper ran an editorial in advance of the public hearings of a Joint Oireachtas Committee examining the possible reform of Article 41 of the Constitution, relating to family rights. The committee would, we were informed, be hearing arguments for change 'from, among others, one-parent families, the gay community, and advocates of children's and fathers' rights.' It was, the editorial mused, a measure of the change in Irish society that 'even the Catholic Church' seemed prepared to acknowledge that non-marital unions should receive legislative protection. Here again, there was no question of redefining or extending the prevailing definition of marriage. The rest of the leader was about the necessity to broaden the definition of family 'in light of modern societal changes'. It went on: 'And notwithstanding the cabinet's regrettable decision to contest a legal challenge brought by a lesbian couple seeking to have their Canadian marriage recognised in Ireland, Taoiseach Bertie Ahern has endorsed the need for a degree of recognition and protection of irregular unions, whether gay or not.' The issue was 'recognition and protection' rather than marriage.

< 287 >

Later the same year, on the occasion of the passage of civil partnership legislation in Northern Ireland, the paper ran an editorial welcoming
this development. Oddly, it appeared to muddy the distinction between
civil partnership and marriage, as in the following sentence: 'Britain's
new institution of civil partnership, like marriage, is firstly a mechanism
by which the community rightly acknowledges as important and pro-
tects the dependencies that arise in long-term relationships, whether in
terms of inheritance or other rights.' The editorial noted also that the
new law allowed for an extension of formal recognition of homosexual
relationships, regretting that intimate relationships had been 'until now
only solemnised by society for heterosexuals'. As regards the domestic
position – 'now lagging behind many of our fellow Europeans' – we
were informed that the Minister for Justice, Equality and Law Reform,
Michael McDowell, had been meeting with representatives of the gay
community and would be establishing a working group to examine this
issue. The minister was to be applauded for this, said the leader writer.
There was no mention of gay marriage and no suggestion that civil partnership might be in any way inadequate in extending equality of treatment to gay people.

In 2006, on the occasion of Pope Benedict XVI's first encyclical, Deus
Caritas Est, *The Irish Times* ran an editorial in which it managed to turn
the Pope's unsurprising affirmation of the 'traditional' idea of marriage
into a minor polemic of 'disappointment', allegedly on behalf of 'the
many Catholics who find deeply fulfilling, genuine love in other kinds
of relationships, whether unmarried, divorced or gay'. The leader writer quoted from the encyclical: 'From the standpoint of creation, eros
directs man towards marriage, to a bond that is unique and definitive.
Thus, and only thus, does it achieve its deepest purpose. Corresponding
to the image of a monotheistic God is monogamous marriage.'

This the leader writer found 'a cold, bleak view of human nature and
sexuality, which denies to many who fully share [Pope Benedict's] understanding of love as, above all, "concern and care for the other", the

comfort of a church that may mean so much to them.' The odd thing
was that Pope Benedict was not in the quoted passage outlining what
love is or is not, but what marriage is, which is to say that it means something that other kinds of relationship, however loving, cannot mean. The
passage had nothing to say about homosexuals or homosexual love, nor
did it in any sense withhold the 'comfort' of the church from either
homosexual people or heterosexual people who happened to be unmarried. The editorial was actually gobbledygook but, nevertheless, there
was nothing in it to suggest any particular interest on the part of the
writer in proposing gay marriage.

In 2007, *The Irish Times* published a leader headed 'Same-sex unions'.
In this the newspaper again praised the Taoiseach Mr Ahern for a speech
he had given at the opening of the new offices of the Gay and Lesbian
Equality Network, in respect of what the leader described as 'full equality
for gay men and lesbians'. Mr Ahern's remarks, as quoted, were: 'Our
sexual orientation is not an accidental attribute. It is an essential part of
who and what we are. All citizens, regardless of sexual orientation, stand
equal in the eyes of the law. Sexual orientation cannot, and must not, be
the basis of a second-class citizenship.' In light of these statements, the
editorial went on, it was disappointing that the government had recently voted down a Labour Party Civil Unions Bill 'and replaced it with a
worryingly vague promise to present the heads of a bill on the subject
by March 2008'.

'While the Labour Bill would have granted gay and lesbian couples a
status separate from but equal to marriage,' the leader continued, 'Minister for Justice Brian Lenihan promised no more than 'the establishment
of a system to allow same-sex couples to register their relationships and
thereby to subscribe to a variety of mutual rights and obligations.' The
editorial lamented that the intention of the government now appeared to
be 'to give same-sex unions a limited recognition that will not have a status equal to marriage.' Note that here *The Irish Times* appears to be equating the achievement of 'equality to marriage', not with the absorption

of gay couples into the existing constitutional definitions of marriage and/or family, but with a category of recognition defined as civil union but 'equal' to marriage. In other words, the leader writer appeared to be suggesting that it was possible for civil partnership to be seen as providing equality with marriage while still remaining separate from it. The government's proposed approach, the leader writer complained, would amount to imposing a form of 'second-class citizenship' on gay people. It stressed that the Labour Party proposal would not, according to constitutional experts, pose any form of constitutional problem and that to confine the recognition of gay unions to what Senator David Norris had called a 'dog licence' would be 'to entrench inequality'. The leader called on the government to produce a Bill that provided gay and lesbian couples 'with a degree of recognition compatible with the Constitution'. The government should start from the premise that 'those who are excluded from marriage by virtue of their sexual orientation are not excluded from love, from faithfulness, from citizenship and from respect'. (How long I wished and waited in vain for such a leader to be published about the rights of fathers and their children!)

In April 2008, the newspaper published an editorial in advance of the government's proposal on civil partnership. It signposted that the Minister for Justice, Brian Lenihan, was 'set to take a cautious approach by proceeding by way of legislation rather than through a referendum that might disturb the position of marriage under the Constitution'. It predicted that what was described as the minister's 'pragmatism' was likely to receive all-party support in the Dáil 'on an issue that still has the potential to be divisive in our society'. There were 'many reasons', the editorial went on, 'why the proposals in the new Bill should receive a warm welcome'. The leader went on to outline the by now familiar litany of 'diverse family' types in the state, all in need of 'a legal framework to cater for their financial and social needs'.

There followed what appears to be the first hint of an endorsement of a form of marriage, so named, for gay people: 'For some people – and particularly for campaigning gay couples, the legislation will not go far enough. They have sought to marry, to adopt children, to enjoy the same equality before the law as married, heterosexual couples. Why shouldn't they have such rights? These civil liberties should have a mature public debate. The deeply-held prejudices of previous decades have softened over the passage of time. It seems extraordinary, but sex between consenting male adults was only decriminalised 15 years ago.'

This is the first sign of a new tone and approach in *The Irish Times*. Still under the editorship of Geraldine Kennedy, the paper appeared to be shifting from its previous stance of calling purely for civil unions, while defining these, under certain conditions, as equating to marriage but established separately from it. Here, *The Irish Times* appeared to emerge from the closet on the marriage issue, while acknowledging the importance of finding ways of doing this without 'disturbing' the constitutional provision in respect of the Family.

Two months later, the newspaper appeared to backtrack somewhat, in welcoming the Civil Partnerships Bill with another editorial. Despite the reservations of 'some activists' at the absence of full marriage status, the editorial commented, 'the Bill represents a good balance between the legitimate aspirations of same-sex couples and intractable constitutional problems that would arise if an attempt were made to introduce same-sex marriage.' *The Irish Times* did not outline what these 'intractable problems' might be (and indeed has yet to say how, or if, they were sidestepped by the 2015 amendment), and seemed at that stage content to set aside the 'reservations' of 'some' gay activists. The leader went on to deal with the implications for co-habiting heterosexual couples arising from the legislation and, at the end, returned to issues affecting gay couples, raising the issue of what should happen when one partner in a homosexual relationship already has a child from a heterosexual relationship. This point, the leader stated, 'requires some clarification'.

The following year, the newspaper rehearsed briefly the general situation in respect of the changing nature of family life in Ireland and went

< 291 >

on to applaud the fact that there were two broad categories of relationship – cohabiting couples and same-sex couples – who would be catered
for by the Civil Partnership Act, when passed into law. It noted also that
the legislation gave protections to dependent partners in the event of
the breakdown of a cohabiting arrangement. It went on: 'For same-sex
couples who do not have the option of marriage enjoyed by heterosexual couples, there is much more comprehensive provision. The Bill,
when enacted, will confer "civil status" on registered partnerships, giving
explicit status to the relationship. This is of huge symbolic importance
and carries with it a range of rights and obligations, similar, though not
identical to, those enjoyed by married couples.'

The leader went on to note that the Bill was 'virtually silent' on the
issue of children who live with same-sex couples: 'Legal uncertainty sur-
rounds the position of such children at the moment, and this cannot continue indefinitely. These are not the only children whose relationships with
the adults in their lives need to be put on a firm footing. And it may be
better for the issue of gay parents and their children to be addressed in the
broader context of children's rights, looking at all aspects of guardianship.'

In 2012, the paper published a leader welcoming US President Obama's
declaration to a TV interviewer that, contrary to his previously expressed
opposition, he now thought 'that same-sex couples should be able to get
married'. In 2013, the newspaper similarly welcomed the announcement
that gay marriage was to be legislated for in the UK. Reference was made
in that editorial to a forthcoming meeting of the constitutional convention in Dublin Castle, at which the gay marriage question was due to be
discussed. *The Irish Times* had by now refined its position, as well as its
definition of the word 'equality'. 'Those who favour equality do so in the
name of justice and fairness,' the editorial outlined, 'arguing that only full
equality under the law can protect gays and lesbians from discrimination
and allow them to be full equal citizens of the State.' This somewhat tautological construction was followed by a brief lecture about the meaning
of 'traditional marriage', which readers were informed was an ambiguous

term. There was a vague nod in the direction of those who might object to gay marriage on grounds of religious conviction. The leader concluded on a catch-all piety, declaring that 'equal marriage should not come at the cost of freedom of faith, nor freedom of faith at the cost of civil rights'.

To summarise: *The Irish Times* did not, until months before the referendum of 2015, begin anything that could be described as a campaign for gay marriage. It barely mentioned the topic up until a decade before and after that carried at most one or two editorials per year touching on aspects of gay relationship and the alleged necessity to regularise them. By contrast, in what can undoubtedly be described as a crusade, I published at least 100 articles over the same period on the subjects of fathers, male suicide and other topics relating to men in the modern world, though not once was I given as much as a single shot of editorial artillery back-up.

None of the editorials I have listed above contained ringing exhortations in respect of gay marriage – only as the referendum campaign got into gear did this become an explicit element of the paper's editorial pronouncements. Of course, as noted already, the paper's commitment to defending the rights of gays might be described as fanatical by comparison with its interest in defending the rights of single fathers, or indeed any kind of fathers, but to put it like that would amount to faint flattery indeed.

And the fare on show from the paper's columnists was no better from the gay rights point of view. Fintan O'Toole, whose behaviour during the 2015 referendum campaign was such as to suggest himself as one of the world's foremost advocates of gay rights, did not start to suggest any great zeal, never mind urgency, for providing for gay marriage until about two years before the 2015 referendum. Indeed, he very rarely had anything to say about issues affecting gay people at all, and most of what he did write on the subject took the form of attacks on those who failed to live up to his own rather chimerical level of enlightenment.

In 2003, he published in his column an attack on the recently deceased former Chief Justice T. F. O'Higgins, and expressed puzzlement at the fact that obituaries had not referred to O'Higgins's role, 20 years before, in delivering the majority verdict in the David Norris case seeking a declaration that certain prohibitions on homosexual acts were unconstitutional. O'Higgins, O'Toole wrote, had rejected the case on grounds that were 'frankly theocratic'. His chief point seemed to be this: 'It is apparently impossible for the shiny new Ireland to acknowledge that, just 20 years ago, our chief justice could argue that some citizens didn't have rights because Jesus didn't approve of them.' There was no mention in this column of gay marriage, and no further ruminations on these topics from O'Toole for a number of years.

In 2009, he published a column headed 'Fear felt by gay people is to our shame', which dealt with the first open conference of lesbian, gay and bisexual primary school teachers, which had taken place a few days before. He also referred to the death of the former Boyzone singer, Stephen Gately, a gay man who had died over the same weekend as the conference. O'Toole applauded the fact that Gately's bereaved partner had been widely described as his 'husband', but appeared to lament the fact that the term was not technically correct since the couple 'were never given the choice to marry and were civil partners'. He also treated of the difficulties experienced by men like Gately, and the Cork hurler Dónal Óg Cusack, in coming out, which he described as 'not their shame', but 'ours'. The column contained no detailed argument for gay marriage, nor did it explicitly call for its introduction.

In March 2013, two years before the start of the formal debate on the same-sex marriage referendum, O'Toole made his first significant contribution. He recalled being on a TV show some years earlier which also featured a Catholic priest who was 'charmingly, delightfully camp'. The priest had made risqué comments in make-up and 'created self-consciously exaggerated gestures with his hands'. He was, wrote O'Toole, "for all the world like Mary O'Rourke in a dog collar". O'Toole recalled how he had watched on the TV set in the green room to see how this apparition would go down on live TV, but found that the priest's camp persona had vanished. 'The priest had performed an exorcism on himself.' He had slipped into a 'priestly demeanour – soft, asexual, unthreatening, controlled, precise, and he seemed to have slipped it on like a mask.'

Fintan didn't know whether or not the priest in question was gay, and it was none of his business anyway, hand gestures notwithstanding. "Being camp doesn't mean you're gay and most gay men are not camp." But, he continued, it was clear that the priest was quite comfortable, behind the scenes, with a version of himself that matched a certain kind of gay male persona.

O'Toole went on to deliberate upon how some such men had used the priesthood as a 'refuge' from the 'storms of doubt and guilt' which gayness might bring upon them. The priest's uniform, he hazarded, might offer 'a decent disguise'. There was 'no great shame' in this, but it was 'awfully weird'. It created an institution 'that is very like the priest I encountered in the TV studios: with one face for the public, another in private.' There were some strange consequences to this 'strange doubleness', O'Toole proposed: one, that it 'ups the ante on the game of homophobia'. The fact that many priests are gay does not result in tolerance and decency, but 'creates a perverse form of denial, that of protesting too much.'

All this was by way of introduction to Fintan's response to a running story of the time that a Scottish cardinal had been accused by a number of priests and former seminarians of having had consensual sex with them while he had been in a position of care or authority. 'It is, alas,' he wrote, 'not at all accidental that Cardinal Keith O'Brien, alleged by four priests to have "attempted to kiss, touch or have sex with them" has been the most hysterical denouncer of gay marriage, which he compared to legalising slavery.' He went on to criticise the Catholic Church's two-faced approach to homosexuality, which he said had also 'fed into' its appalling response to clerical sex abuse, serving to render all sexual offences equally grave as falls from grace or administrative problems to be managed. It was clear that he was condemning Cardinal O'Brien for the implied double standard of opposing gay marriage while being himself a homosexual. Still, Fintan did not go so far as to make a case of his own for gay marriage.

In April 2013, he published a column under the heading, 'Sayonara, Baby, our marriage is a sham' – a sarcastic demolition of a straw man argument attributed by O'Toole to those who oppose gay marriage. He described as 'stupid' the idea that gay marriage would diminish all marriages, because a marriage between two gay people had no implications for marriages between men and women. He wrote that he did not respect such arguments because they amounted to 'a pseudo-rational veneer on irrational prejudice', and were so weak that Fintan did not believe that 'any intelligent person would believe them unless he or she had already decided that gay men and lesbian women are not deserving of full human equality'. Such a conclusion, he wrote, was 'vile'. He also dismissed the idea that marriage is, as he put it, "about men and women making babies," an argument not long before put forward by the Catholic bishops. If the bishops believed this, they should "refuse to recognise the marriages of those who do not have children and those whose only children are adopted," he wrote. "For the only thing that rationally excludes same-sex couples from this definition is the begetting bit. Same-sex couples who have children, in fact, should be accorded a higher status than heterosexual couples who have no children at all." O'Toole continued with similar specious arguments for another 400 words before concluding: "Opposition to same-sex marriage is opposition to the proposition that all citizens are entitled to equal treatment by the state and its laws. And it's time we called that opposition what it is – not conservatism but prejudice. It is prejudice in the same sense that hatred of blacks or Jews or Catholics is prejudice. And it is no less shameful."

And yet, interestingly, Fintan still did not express an argument for gay marriage: rather, he expressed an argument as to why opposition to gay marriage – on, it seems any grounds whatever, is 'hatred' – as though this were the same thing.

In all my 18 years of writing articles about the rights of single fathers to have 'equal' rights with mothers and other types of fathers, Fintan O'Toole had never once expressed anything other than disdain and hostility for that argument. Did this hostility amount to opposition to the proposition that all citizens are entitled to equal treatment by the state and its laws? Did this also, by O'Toole's own logic, amount to prejudice? Did it amount, even, to hatred? Was it shameful? Or was this different and if so how?

Echo answers 'how?'

26

An Offer You Can't Refuse

Back in 1989, when Marshall Kirk and Hunter Madsen published *After the Ball: How America will conquer its fear and hatred of gays in the 90s*, it was still generally believed that changing the mind of a society was a slow, laborious process based on debate, persuasion, winning hearts and minds. Kirk and Madsen demonstrated the folly of these beliefs.

They were both Harvard graduates. In 1987, Kirk, a specialist in neuropsychiatry, and Madsen, writing as 'Erastes Pill', had published a seminal article in a gay magazine, *Guide*, entitled 'The Overhauling of Straight America'. Madsen, who had a degree in politics, was an expert in public persuasion tactics and social marketing, and had also operated as a consultant to gay media campaigns across the US. *After the Ball* was essentially a blueprint for the application of social psychology to the problem of achieving respectability for gay people and the goals identified by their leaders. This book is to be regarded as the single most significant factor in the escalation and success of the gay marriage campaign over the past decade, while other far more pressing issues were ignored or relegated by politicians in the countries where these demands were being processed and acquiesced in. A knowledge of the book and its content is vital to debunking the notion that what has happened is in some way a 'spontaneous' rectification by 'modern' society of some fundamental denial of human or civil rights. Both the ground-breaking 1987 article by Marshall Kirk and 'Erastes Pill' and the book that built on it employed the then most up-to-the-minute marketing, mass media propaganda and psychological-persuasion trickery to advance what actually amounts to a comprehensive blueprint for pushing pretty much any unpopular political idea to the centre of any society's public square.

After the Ball, written at the height of the global AIDS crisis, was conceived and marketed as a 'gay manifesto for the 1990s', a call for homosexuals to repackage themselves as mainstream citizens demanding equal treatment, rather than as a promiscuous sexual minority seeking greater opportunity and influence. 'As cynical as it may seem,' the authors declared, 'AIDS gives us a chance, however brief, to establish ourselves as a victimised minority legitimately deserving of America's special protection and care.'

The book demonstrates an easy familiarity with concepts like 'Direct Emotional Modeling' (the innate tendency of human beings to feel what they perceive others to be feeling); 'Associative Conditioning' (the psychological process whereby, when two things are repeatedly juxtaposed, feelings about one thing are transferred to the other); and manipulating the fight-or-flight responses of the human 'mammal'.

Gayness was to be normalised, and gays presented as victims so that 'straights' would be inclined by reflex to assume the role of protectors. Gays were to be made to appear good, and 'antigays' to appear bad. "Few straight women, and even fewer straight men, will want to defend homosexuality boldly as such," the authors hypothesised. "Most would rather attach their awakened protective impulse to some principle of justice or law, to some general desire for consistent and fair treatment in society. Our campaign should not demand direct support for homosexual practices, should instead take anti-discrimination as its theme." Free speech, freedom of association and equality were to be the issues brought to the public mind.

Kirk and Madsen proposed isolating conservative Christians by presenting them as "hysterical backwoods preachers, drooling with hate to a degree that looks both comical and deranged". ... "The public should be shown images of ranting homophobes whose secondary traits and beliefs disgust middle America. These images might include: the Ku Klux

< 299 >

Klan demanding that gays be burned alive or castrated; bigoted southern ministers drooling with hysterical hatred to a degree that looks both
comical and deranged; menacing punks, thugs, and convicts speaking
coolly about the 'fags' they have killed or would like to kill; a tour of Nazi
concentration camps where homosexuals were tortured and gassed."

The strategy, to be directed via tactical use of media and advertising,
was divided under three headings: 'desensitisation', 'jamming' and 'conversion'. 'Desensitisation' was defined by Kirk and Madsen as essentially the process of getting people more comfortable with gay ideas, gay
demands, the gay view of the world. The objective was to 'help' the
public to view homosexuality with indifference rather than strong feelings, to get people to the 'should-shrug stage'. Homosexuals as a class
must cease to seem alien, undesirable and other. 'Among the proposed
tactics was to flaunt homosexual behaviour to the point where it became
normalised, if not exactly acceptable. To win people over, they had to
persuade people that they had nothing to lose by being either neutral or
supportive towards gays, which would happen if homosexuality could be
made to seem less threatening.

Densensitisation did not need to be a coy or cautious strategy; the
main thing was to achieve a persistent presence, with constant talk about
gays and gayness giving the impression that pubic opinion was at least
divided on the matter and that homosexuality was practised or tolerated
by a section of the public. Even antagonistic debates could serve a useful
purpose if 'respectable' gays were fronting up for the cause.

The alleged 'anti-gay prejudice' of society was as a locomotive engine
that needed to be put into reverse. 'Desensitisation', they elaborated, 'lets
the engine run out of steam, causing it to halt on the tracks indefinitely. Jamming, in essence, derails it. Conversion – our ambitious long-range
goal – puts the engine into reverse gear and sends it back whence it came.'

Activists were urged to shift their attention from the upmarket press,
whose readers were largely among the already converted, and concentrate
on mainstream publications like *Time*, *People* and the *National Enquirer*.

< 300 >

Campaigns should concentrate in particular on the visual media – TV, film and advertising, which were to be used as a Trojan Horse to place the positive gay message in the centre of every living room in America. It was important for the campaign to be controlled and directed, and not left to the mercy of events. Daytime talk shows were identified as an especially useful means of exposure.

'Jamming' was defined as a form of intervention into the engine of societal prejudice to seize up the works, exploiting an identified inbuilt tendency of human beings to feel things they intuit others to be feeling. Jamming also attempts to blockade or counteract any sense of self-satisfaction the 'bigot' may feel by attaching to his 'homohatred' a 'pre-existing, and punishing, sense of shame in being a bigot, a horse's ass, and a beater and murderer'. In effect it involves a switching process whereby the emotions of the targeted 'bigot' are invaded by the kinds of responses he feels himself provoking in those who have evolved a little further along the path of enlightenment. In spite of himself, he starts to hate himself because he is not part of the herd. The authors hold that 'normal people' tend to feel shame when they perceive that they are not feeling or thinking like members of the pack. This shame was to be leveraged so that the 'bigot' could be confronted with the idea that his 'homohatred' was at odds with his persona as a well-liked person, offering him the 'reward' of being rid of it. Adverts were to portray such holdouts as homophobic, homohating bigots, crude loudmouths who use words like 'faggot and 'nigger', who are not Christian. Jamming depicts the hurt such homohatred inflicts on gays, linking the behaviour with attributes that even the bigot would be loath to possess. Peer pressure could be marshalled to pressurise him to see the error of his ways. The resulting emotional confusing of the bigot will result in 'emotional dissonance', leading to a change of behaviour and beliefs.

The book explains: "Note that the bigot need not actually be made to believe that he is such a heinous creature, that others will now despise him, and that he has been the immoral agent of suffering. It would be impossible to make him believe any such thing. Rather, our effect is achieved without reference to facts, logic, or proof. Just as the bigot became such without any say in the matter, through repeated infralogical emotional conditioning, his bigotry can be alloyed in exactly the same way, whether he is conscious of the attack or not. Indeed, the more he is distracted by any incidental, even specious, surface arguments, the less conscious he'll be of the true nature of the process – which is all to the good."

It is interesting that the *After the Ball* authors employ the word 'homohatred' almost interchangeably with 'homophobia' – interesting because use of the former word has since died out. The book also liberally uses the word 'bigot' to depict someone who opposes the homosexual view of reality.

The final section of the book is perhaps the most interesting and instructive in the context of reviewing what occurred in Ireland in the period running up to May 2015. It explains why gay activists seemed deliberately to engage in utterly illogical and casuistic argumentation – such as that surrogacy had no implication for marriage or family and the one about homophobia existing in a spectrum, from mild to severe, from which everyone 'suffers' to some degree.

The conversion stage utilises chiefly images of gay people who look like everyone else. This juxtapositioning of image and label in magazines and billboards presents the gay person as indistinguishable from the 'bigot' and his friends, or like any one of his other stereotypes of all-right guys, the kind of people he already likes and admires. This image must, of necessity, be carefully tailored to be free of absolutely every element of the widely held stereotypes of how 'faggots' look, dress, and sound. He – or she – must not be too well or fashionably dressed; must not be too handsome – that is, mustn't look like a model – or well groomed. The image must be that of an icon of normality. This creates a 'positive stereotype', which produces in observers, including the 'bigot', a rush of positive emotion.

Camp men and butch women were, as far as practicable, to be kept out of sight. "In practical terms, this means that 'cocky mustachioed leather-men, drag queens, and bull dykes' would not appear in gay commercials and other public presentations. Conventional young people, mid-dle-age women, and older folks of all races would be featured, as well as the parents and straight friends of gays."

The authors anticipated the objection that these tactics would distort the image of gay people, and in effect present a deceitful version of the gayness. "But it makes no difference', say Kirk and Madsen, "that the ads are lies; not to us, because we're using them to ethically good effect, to counter negative stereotypes that are every bit as much lies, and far more wicked ones; not to bigots, because the ads will have their effect on them whether they believe them or not."

Lies could be justified, because the objective was a good one. "We argue that, for all practical purposes, gays should be considered to have been born gay – even though sexual orientation, for most humans, seems to be the product of a complex interaction between innate predisposi-tions and environmental factors during childhood and early adolescence.

"To suggest in public that homosexuality might be chosen is to open the can of worms labeled 'moral choices and sin' and give the religious intransigents a stick to beat us with. Straights must be taught that it is as natural for some persons to be homosexual as it is for others to be het-erosexual: wickedness and seduction have nothing to do with it."

After the Ball amounts to a manifesto for moral revolution. By portraying themselves as mainstream Americans seeking nothing but liberty and hap-piness, homosexuals could redefine the cultural equation to lay claim to a different kind of morality by way of defining their place in society.

After the Ball urges gay activists: 'Please don't confuse Conversion with political Subversion. The word "subversion" has a nasty ring, of which the American people are inordinately afraid – and on their guard against. Yet, ironically, by Conversion we actually mean something far more pro-foundly threatening to the American Way of Life, without which no truly sweeping social change can occur. We mean conversion of the average American's emotions, mind, and will, through a planned psychological attack, in the form of propaganda fed to the nation via the media. We mean "subverting" the mechanism of prejudice to our own ends – using the very processes that made America hate us to turn their hatred into warm regard – whether they like it or not.'

In their 1987 article Kirk and Madsen had made themselves even more plain. 'In the early stages of any campaign to reach straight America, the masses should not be shocked and repelled by premature exposure to homosexual behavior itself. Instead, the imagery of sex should be down-played and gay rights should be reduced to an abstract social question as much as possible. First let the camel get his nose inside the tent – only later his unsightly derriere!'

Only by achieving these conditions of public receptivity, whereby peo-ple would volunteer to remove themselves from the realm of 'prejudice', could the underlying message of 'gay rights' be transmitted correctly. The phenomenon of 'prejudice' was to be identified as capable of infect-ing anyone and everyone. 'Haters' were to be treated as victims of a kind of cultural virus that could strike the unsuspecting at any time: 'These folks are victims of a fate that could have happened to me.'

A glance back through the fine print of this strategy is sufficient to convey just how deliberately and systematically the gay movement ad-vanced its cause by following the Kirk and Madsen plan. The success of the tactics outlined in *After the Ball* is the principal driving factor in esca-lating the demand for gay marriage from being a matter of consequence to a tiny minority to being hailed the 'primary human rights issue of our time'. Kirk and Madsen's strategy has been pursued with ruthlessness worldwide and has swept all before it, leaving conventional left-liberals breathlessly surveying its effectiveness and consistency.

The agenda set out in *After the Ball* led to nothing less than social transformation throughout western societies. By portraying themselves as mainstream Americans seeking nothing but liberty and self-fulfilment, homosexuals redefined the moral equation, enabling themselves to switch from the minus to the plus side of the equal sign. Issues of right and wrong were isolated as outdated, repressive and culturally embarrassing.

Instead, the assertion of 'rights' became the hallmark of a global public relations strategy. The resulting cultural changes could be seen in particular in the treatment of gay issues in the communications media and in popular culture – in the explosion of gay characters in American movies, soap operas and sitcoms, the generally quiescent, often enthusiastic reception given to gay issues in the media generally, right up to the almost overnight success of the 'marriage equality' agenda. Together it amounts to a breathtaking victory of public relations, propaganda and moral inversion.

The techniques outlined by Kirk and Madsen have been married by LGBT campaigners with other methodologies owing more to guerilla warfare than democratic discourse, creating an irresistible social revolution. These methodologies include the use of 'availability cascades', 'informational cascades' or 'opinion cascades', identified and defined a decade after the publication of *After the Ball* by two Americans analysts, Cass Sunstein and Timur Kuran, in a 1999 article in the *Stanford Law Review*. An 'availability cascade' is defined as 'a self-reinforcing process of collective belief formation by which an expressed perception triggers a chain reaction that gives the perception increasing plausibility through its rising availability in public discourse'. People are propositioned and asked to support a particular cause, to make themselves 'available' as supporters, or to decline and face the consequences. The process is propelled by 'availability entrepreneurs' – volunteer activists in positions from which they can manipulate the public discourse – who employ radical crusading tactics and techniques to persuade high profile figures to endorse their agendas and to demonise those who decline. The potential of these methods has increased exponentially in the era of the Internet and social networking. Needless to say, this is in no way a conventional form of political activism, but depends greatly on the involvement of psychologists, social scientists, opinion manipulators and other communications witch doctors who remain prudently out of sight. The purpose is the manufacture of consent and the chief methods are intimidation and scapegoating. The engine of the process is the offer of an implicit choice between social acceptability or social isolation. Supporters will be deemed progressive and compassionate, and dissenters made to look backward and unsophisticated. Opinion cascades can overnight induce previously freethinking individuals to change their minds and 'apologise'; to affect a particular stance or opinion and benefit from increased standing as a result, or face the prospect of sometimes quite extreme negative consequences if they demur. Those who refuse to endorse the cause risk becoming outcasts in their societies, communities, workplaces, sports clubs etc. – sometimes even in their own families, especially their teenage children who are expressly targeted by the cascades. Thus, critical thinking is disabled by a fear of repudiation. The laws of the herd rule. People affect particular opinions knowing that this is the way to social approval. Usually the issue is not central enough to their personal interests to involve any negative consequences for supporting the agenda. In a sense, it's a no-brainer, since, at an individual level, the individual stands to lose nothing in the short term.

Here, then, is the 'deal': You want to support us? That's great. If you do, then we'll put the word about that you're a cool, compassionate, enlightened and progressive kind of guy. If you don't – if you threaten to question our agenda in any way – we'll do you. We won't just call you nasty names – we'll hang you out to dry in a way that you won't believe. Calling you a homophobe is just the start of it, because that's a word we created, and therefore a word that we control absolutely. It means exactly what we say it means, no more and no less. We've chosen it, honed and twisted its meaning, and launched it into society precisely to load onto it any meaning we choose, any degree of diabolical connotation you care to imagine. We decide. We'll turn you into Public Enemy Number One. We'll make it like the word 'homophobe' is synonymous with your name. We'll have people walking up to you in the street to tell you that you ought to be ashamed of yourself. We'll make you wake up with a start in the night, wishing you'd taken the chance we're offering you now. We'll make your children regret you are their parent. It's not worth

< 306 >

going against us. What's in it for you, anyway, being opposed to us? It doesn't matter what you think, or how subtle or complicated you think your views are. Unless you say you agree with us, we'll write your script for you. We'll tell you what your views are, by telling the world what your views are. People won't really care what you think – all they'll care about is not ending up like you. So they'll do whatever it takes, which is to say they will support us and everything we say, in order to avoid that fate. Do you understand? The window of opportunity is still open. You can still do the right thing – by which we mean the right thing for you. We promise you: you don't need in your life the kind of heat we're capable of generating and directing at you. But hear this also: We don't really care. When we get going with your life and your reputation, you'll think we really hate you. But really we won't. You'll just have happened to walk into our parlour. We're asking you now, real nice, to support our cause, but if you say no, believe it or not, we'll be even happier, in a way, than if you say yes. Because then we'll have a scapegoat to make an example of. The fact that you'll have offered yourself up as an object of the kind of treatment we've perfected for people just like you will mean that we can fuck you so bad in every way that everyone who beholds it will say, 'Not me! Not me! Not me!' Everyone else, at least everyone of good sense – will say, 'Where do I sign?'

27

Mired in Depression

After I'd resigned from *The Irish Times* in March 2014, I worked for about 10 months with Independent News and Media, writing for both *The Irish Independent* and *The Sunday Independent*. Gradually I had been coming round to a decision to knock journalism on the head. I was being well paid, but I had never been interested in writing just for the money. The point of the kind of polemical journalism I'd been involved in for three decades was that you participated in public debate on the basis that different opinions were vital to the health of the society, and that therefore there was a presumption, indeed an imperative, that the very articulation of a different perspective was some kind of public service. This was all gone now. The only way to survive in journalism was to keep your head down and mimic the prevailing consensus when you wrote or spoke. I had no interest in doing that.

Although my heart wasn't in it, I decided to continue in journalism until after the same-sex marriage referendum on 22 May 2015, not least because I did not want to hand an instant victory to those who had set out to bury me to prevent me from articulating the nature of the smash-and-grab they were proposing to conduct on the rights of Irish parents and families.

Over my years with *The Irish Times*, I had received periodic approaches from *The Independent*. There had been times when the offers were pretty tempting, but I opted each time for the devil I knew. Now – seemingly entirely coincidental with the Rory O'Neill assault (the first approach had been made just days before) – they were chasing me again. I put them on hold for a while to let things settle down and then entered talks about talks. As the post-Panti event rumbled on, I had several meetings with senior INM executives, and eventually, as summer approached, hammered out the deal under which I would write one article per week for *The Irish Independent* and another for *The Sunday Independent*.

I started in early July. I expected a choppy period and I wasn't disappointed. Brendan O'Connor, the presenter of *The Saturday Night Show*, was himself a senior editor at *The Sunday Independent*. I knew he was sore on account of having screwed up with the O'Neill libel and that our previous good relationship was likely to be at an end. So it proved. I met him briefly the first day I went into the office and we shook hands, had a civil if somewhat strained conversation and discussed the possibility of me writing long pieces for Life magazine, which was part of the notoriously varied Sindo package. We agreed that we would discuss this further when I got settled in.

There was other history to contend with also: my continuing war with another of the Sindo's journalists, Niamh Horan, who had conducted a peculiar interview with me in the wake of my *Village* article, failing to mention anything at all of the content of that article and throwing me to the wolves again on a whole new front.

One of the most striking things about the offensive mounted by the LGBT lobby was the way they changed the nature of the charges at the drop of a hat. When one argument lost its traction, or began to show its holes, they would simply shift the ground to something new. When it began to emerge that the things Rory O'Neill had said about me on *The Saturday Night Show* were off the mark, the issue became that I and others had threatened to sue over what they repeatedly described as an instance of 'robust debate'. The charge here was that we had breached one of the cardinal rules of free speech – 'journalists shouldn't sue'. They then demanded that we hand back the money (licence payers' money, we were reminded with great sanctimony). I'm charitably paraphrasing here – in truth, these demands were issued to the accompaniment of quite unbelievable vitriol and invective.

Journalists, of course, were delighted to join in with this onslaught, and

< 309 >

succeeded in giving it serious legs. Anything to do with libel actions tends to mobilise journalists on both their paymasters' behalf and their own, since, in most cases, their ideal situation would be to publish lies every day without any possibility of consequence or sanction.

It didn't appear to matter that nobody had 'sued' anybody. Actually, all that had occurred was that a number of people who had been seriously defamed on a prime time TV chat show had requested the TV station, through their lawyers, to put the record straight. (A small number of journalists had the decency to point this out.) The TV station, instead of acting on the objective facts of the situation, started to prevaricate and dissemble, seeking to tap into the escalating outcry being orchestrated by allies of the individual who had launched the libellous attack.

I don't 'do' Twitter – never have and never will. Twitter is like a court without a judge or jury, in which there is no possibility of a defence. The prosecution states the charge, announces the conviction, pronounces the sentence and then starts looking around for a sturdy tree from which to hang the accused. The only way to confront the things that are said on Twitter appears to be joining up and getting down in the gutter with the rest. Since I had no intention of doing that, I had to sit and watch as they essentially rewrote the facts to suit their sense of the exigencies of the moment. Panti Bliss was, of course, their hero, incapable of being wrong. The fact that he was demonstrably wrong about me simply added more fuel to their injection systems, rendering it necessary to squawk all the louder to drown out the facts.

It is strange to be at the centre of such a storm. You find you care in spite of yourself. You tell yourself that it's just a bunch of cowardly toe-rags talking to themselves – which is actually what it is – but the torrent serves to unseat any prospect of rationalising things. You also feel a countervailing and somewhat irrational sense of panic at being pilloried without the possibility of mounting a defence. I think of it as being set upon by a swarm of wasps: you are unable to fix on a single adversary, and have no way of knowing where the next sting is coming from.

< 310 >

Human beings have a congenital need to justify themselves before the world. Mixed up with this is the idea of the self-image, pride, the sense most of us have of seeking to do good. There are few things more radically disruptive to the human psyche as when this is questioned, especially when questioned unjustly. When an accusation is justified, the formerly upright and compliant citizen is reduced in the eyes of his fellows. But an unfair accusation in a situation where there is no voice to speak the truth loudly is far worse. A familiar image from TV news is that of the prisoner being taken into court with a coat over his head, which is bowed in shame. To successfully imagine yourself in such a situation is to experience what may well be the worst that social life is capable of inflicting. To be accused, convicted and sentenced in the wrong adds an entirely new dimension of horror to the mix.

We tend to think of the things we do, say and stand for as having merit that is demonstrable if not manifest. One of the characteristics of life as a commentator is that you are persistently challenged to explain and justify yourself – this is what, in effect, public debate amounts to: one protagonist responding to the challenge of another, and bringing a total stake of personality, character, reputation and experience to the encounter. It isn't just that you stand up and deliver yet another opinion: you are the argument; your bones and the marrow of them are the guarantee you offer that you speak the truth and care about the outcome. This can sometimes be a bracing experience, but it is also part of educating yourself to the limits and weaknesses of your own positions. Often, you get to the real meat of a debate only when you're hit with an unexpected question and you find yourself having to revise or recalibrate your arguments, sometimes actually stumbling upon a part of the picture you had missed. In my experience, whereas this can be a little hair-raising, it almost invariably results in your arguments being strengthened or rendered clearer. This is why a real debate between two people who are actually present as people carrying the weight of their entire experience can be so exhilarating. It is where the heartbeat of democracy is most likely to be found.

< 311 >

When these conditions are suspended – as they were in the Panti Bliss affair – and there is no court of appeal against a verdict that obliterates all your good intentions, all your sense of your own uprightness, all your knowledge and experience and certainties, you are left standing naked in a desert of meaninglessness. It must be something like being involved in a football match and finding that the referee has decided to suspend the rule book in favour of the opposing side. A punt goes wide but the ref awards the other team a goal. The goalie holds the ball up several yards behind the net with a quizzical grimace and the ref books him for insolence. In no time, in such a situation, the players and supporters would be in a state of insurrection, but here there was a virtually continuous silence, broken occasionally by fresh accusations.

Over the years, especially in my advocacy on behalf of men and fathers, I'd found myself in some dirty corners, where the fur and teeth were flying pretty thickly. One of the features I noticed in those debates was that, whenever people were unable to respond to one of my arguments, they just called me names: 'misogynist', 'reactionary', 'male chauvinist' etc. I came to see this as coming with the territory, but what was happening now was a whole new level.

Of course, this is why libel laws were conceived. The point of compensating someone for reputational damage is to acknowledge the wrong and communicate some sense of public revulsion at the fact that untruths have been spread about the wronged person. Money is the measure of this process, so to question the fact that someone is paid damages arising from defamation is in effect to deny the validity of the complainant's case and therefore tantamount to repeating the slur. (Indeed, a characteristic of the Twitter 'debate' on these matters was for contributors to loudly repeat the central allegations made by Panti Bliss and then holler 'Sue me!', deftly sidestepping the fact that in almost all cases they were hiding behind pseudonyms and were therefore untraceable.)

A new element entered three months later after I published my 7,000-word account of the saga in *Village* magazine. Niamh Horan from *The*

Sunday Independent had first contacted me in late January, at the height of the controversy. I took her call and she asked me to speak to her on the record for *The Sunday Independent*. We had a conversation, in the course of which I told her that I did not trust any element of the Irish media on this topic, since it appeared that virtually every journalist was ideologically committed. She insisted that she would give me a fair interview, but I said that the situation with regard to *The Sunday Independent* was especially problematic because of Brendan O'Connor's role as both a Sindo senior editor and presenter of *The Saturday Night Show*. We had an extensive off-the-record conversation, during which I criticised the role of the media in stoking the controversy in order to undermine the very concept of defamation law. Horan was quite combative in this conversation, persistently talking about the terrible things that had been suffered by the gay community and sidestepping my challenges as to whether she was insinuating that I had some responsibility for this. She also repeatedly referred to the 'public anger' about the RTÉ settlement, and I expressed scepticism about this on the grounds that it was journalists and the LGBT lobby who were 'angry' and who were stoking a controversy about which most people couldn't care less.

Three months later, in the wake of the publication of my *Village* article, she texted me as follows: 'Greetings from the English countryside where word of your village [sic] article has reached! So I'll be damned … Patsy McGarry?! Will you talk to me this week John? N' I texted back asking if she had read the article and she said that some people had read out some paragraphs over the phone. She was waiting for an emailed copy. After a few more exchanges of text, we agreed to do the interview that Saturday morning. Big mistake. In the course of a three-hour meeting in Sligo, Horan subjected me to another sustained process of interrogation and accusation. She first objected to the presence of Rita, whom she took to be a PR consultant! I insisted and, realising her mistake, Horan started to apologise to Rita as we went upstairs to a quieter lounge area.

The atmosphere was at first civilised enough, if a little strained. I didn't trust Horan. I found her somewhat fawning while at the same time given to snide insinuations and leading questions. She seemed always on the lookout for a salacious angle, or some confessional moment. She seemed largely uninterested in merely giving an account of the available facts, or even the viewpoint she purported to be interested in obtaining. It turned out that she had not the slightest interest in the *Village* article and, whenever I sought to bring it up, she asked me if I had a 'victim complex'. She repeatedly harked back to the events of January and sought to bring up a number of issues I believed I had adequately dealt with in the *Village* article. She cited, for example, some of the quotes from the transcript of the interview I had given to UCD's *College Tribune* in 2012. I said that the quotes she was referring to were highly selective and taken out of context, and asked her if she had read the entire transcript. To my astonishment, she admitted that she had not read the full transcript, but only a short card, with four or five half-sentence extracts, compiled by LGBT activists. I told her that it was outrageous that she was seeking to raise this matter when she had not made even the most rudimentary attempt to inform herself as to the total context. I said it was clear that, as I'd suspected, she had come to the interview with a pre-decided agenda. I said that I had made a mistake in agreeing to the interview and that I wished to withdraw. She rather ominously at this point asked how this was going to look – implying thereby that she intended to write her piece whether I co-operated or not. Rita intimated to me her view that I should continue, which I reluctantly did.

Shortly afterwards, however, the problem resurfaced when Horan started to press me concerning my alleged 'career' as a litigator. She referred to several defamation actions I had taken. I asked her if she had looked up the details of the cases in question. She said she had not. I asked her if she knew what any of the cases had been about. She said that she did not. I suggested that, before she condemn me for taking a legal action, she might at least try to find out what it had been about. I instanced one of the cases – in which I had successfully sued *The Sunday*

< 314 >

Times after the gossip columnist, Terry Keane, had suggested I would make a poor father to my daughter because of views I'd expressed in a speech in the Abbey Theatre in Dublin about the play Medea by the ancient Greek playwright Euripides. I asked Horan if she thought that, attacked in the most personal and dishonest terms because I had expressed a position on a literary work, I should have engaged in a public debate with the individual who had scurrilously attacked my relationship with my daughter. Horan said she knew nothing about the cases but was merely repeating 'what people were saying'. I asked her who these people were and she refused to say.

After perhaps three hours, we got to the *Village* article. I showed her the comprehensive evidence I had accumulated concerning various allegations I had made in that article, and she appeared to be shocked and impressed by this. She took photographs on her phone of several tweets by Thomas59. As the interview proceeded, the tension began to evaporate a little, although I remained wary of Horan's agenda.

She repeatedly sought to focus on my state of mind, having apparently decided in advance that I was suffering from some acute emotional distress and perhaps angling for a sensational headline for her article. I had a sense that she had been told some kind of untruth on this score by an individual with a malignant agenda to settle an old score with me.

At one point, Horan asked me repeatedly: 'Are you depressed?', 'Are you suicidal?' I said that there was nothing the matter with me, that she might be better examining the facts. Horan repeated her questions: Was I depressed? Was I suicidal?

How do you say convincingly that you are not 'depressed'? Should any person have to deny publicly that they are suicidal? What I said was: 'It's bullshit. There's no such thing, it's a cop-out'. I repeated the reasons I had agreed to the interview and told her the questions were invasive and irrelevant.

The following morning, I received a phone call from a friend who told me that *The Sunday Independent* had made a major issue of my comment about depression. I was stunned, since this had nothing to do with the

purpose of the interview and since I had merely made a throwaway remark and had not expanded on it. My friend warned me that already the
interview was trending on Twitter and the depression comment appeared
to be the main focus. She read the remainder of the interview to me and
immediately I realised that Niamh Horan had completely omitted any
mention of *The Irish Times*, of my resignation, of the Una Mullally episode and the Thomas59 tweets. She had made no mention whatever of
the content of the *Village* article which had been the supposed reason for
the interview. I couldn't believe it. Immediately I began getting calls from
relatives and friends telling me that I had again got myself in hot water
with my remark about depression.

For several days after this, I was inundated with media inquiries about
my position on depression. I also received numerous emails from people
who told me they were suffering from depression and felt hurt by what I
had said. Some of these verged on the poisonous. I do not follow Twitter, but I am reliably informed that the controversy raged in that medium
for several days, aided by the efforts of several of my former 'colleagues'
from *The Irish Times* who did not under-utilise the opportunity to kick me
again. Among those who lined up to kick me were Rory O'Neill and one
Paul Kelly, founder of the 'suicide charity' Console, which would go bust
a couple of years later when it emerged that Kelly had run up debts of
more than €300,000, partly as a result of his use of company finances to
fund his own extravagant lifestyle.

There are a number of things that might be said about my response to
Horan's intrusive questioning. One is that, clearly, my attitude to depression, whatever it might be, had nothing whatever to do with the context
or subject matter of the interview. What I said was not a considered
answer to a relevant question, but a rhetorical device to convey to the
interviewer that these were inappropriate questions and that she should
move on. Had I been giving an interview about depression and/or suicide, I would certainly have couched my responses differently and gone
on to explain precisely what my views on these topics happen to be.

< 316 >

When the media got this new bit in its teeth as a way of hounding me into silence, it occurred to me that, although I had been writing about the topic of male suicide for 25 years, none of the researchers, producers or so-called journalists who were now laying siege to my own phone and sanity had ever once shown an interest in anything I had to say on the subject of human misery. It was convenient to become interested here because the occasion afforded an opportunity for my journalistic 'colleagues' to assail me again and, at the same time, elide the fact that none of them had made the slightest attempt to make public a single sentence of my 7,000-word article in *Village*.

What was striking about the coverage of this matter, apart from its total disproportionality, was the moral fervour that accompanied it. It was not simply that I had supposedly uttered something impulsive, stupid or uninformed (why should that be a story?) but that I had 'offended' countless people and even possibly put lives at risk. Psychiatrists were rolled out to condemn what I had said as ill-informed and irresponsible.

The funniest aspect of this saga was to do with the fact that, for nearly three months, Niamh Horan had been ringing me up taunting me with what she said were the views of what she called my colleagues. 'People say you make your living from suing people,' she would coo, ignoring that at the time I was writing two columns per week for national newspapers and had published nine books, several of which were runaway bestsellers. In the wake of the 'depression' episode, after I sketchily described some of her behaviour in my own defence in a couple of radio interviews, she hired a high-powered 'celebrity lawyer' and ... had him send me a demand for damages and an apology on the grounds that I had suggested she was 'unprofessional'! Rita and I compiled statements and I gave them to Kevin Brophy, who sent them to Horan's celebrity lawyer. That was the last we heard of that.

Actually, if I'd intended to describe unprofessionalism on Horan's part, I might have been a little more emphatic. On one occasion, during a break in the interview, when I went to the bathroom, she said to Rita – in reference to several heated exchanges in the interview earlier –'John is a very passionate man'. At this moment I returned to hear the punchline. Rita, detecting an agenda of some kind, responded to this remark in a non-committal fashion, and Horan mused: 'The sex must be great!'

I knew the Sindo's Editor, Anne Harris, also, and, although we'd had a somewhat mixed history, I respected her. Though I hadn't always liked everything about her style of journalism, there was no doubt that she was by far the most talented and, along with her late husband Aengus Fanning, most successful editor of her generation. I didn't get the impression that she was extra happy about me joining the Sindo in the circumstances we found ourselves in. Understandably, she would have had a loyalty to Brendan O'Connor – and also to Niamh Horan. We had a couple of meetings in which we had rather strained conversations about this and that, but once I started writing things started to settle down. Within a short time we were working together famously and I found the weekly conversations I had with her to be invaluable in pushing me in directions I might not otherwise have taken. I began to enjoy myself.

My weekly column with *The Irish Independent* was going well also. The page editor there was Liam Collins, whom I'd also known from his own days as a *Sunday Independent* writer and reporter, a gentleman in every sense and a writer himself.

At the end of September, I was looking forward to the publication in *The Sunday Independent* of a piece of mine about the monks of Mount Melleray monastery in County Waterford. I'd been invited down to lead the annual retreat for the monks, the first time in the history of the monastery that this had been done by a layman. I spent a week there and wrote an account afterwards of which I was sorrowfully proud, having felt throughout that week that I was witnessing the dying breaths of pure Irish Christianity. On the Saturday evening, about 9 o'clock, I did something I hadn't done for more than two decades: I drove into Dublin city centre to pick up the early edition of *The Sunday Independent*. In my years as a magazine editor and my early days as a journalist with *The*

< 318 >

Sunday Tribune, this had been one of the great buzzes of the job: getting the first papers hot off the presses and fingering and flittering through them with a sense of excitement that is on the point of becoming un-imaginable. Before I found the Mount Melleray article, however, I saw a headline underneath a photograph of Brendan O'Connor on one of the supplements that named me and referred to some kind of self-justifica-tory statement by O'Connor about his role in the Rory O'Neill interview. The interview inside contained a full-frontal attack on me, utterly gloss-ing over the fact that a grievous defamation had been perpetrated on O'Connor's watch, and seeking to rewrite history to take advantage of the version generated by the Twitter mob and LGBT lobby. The tsunami of hatred generated against me eight months earlier, together with the almost total corruption of the mainstream media's coverage, had made it easy to peddle this self-serving and utterly contorted versions of events, and now here it was again, plastered all over a paper I was writing for. I contacted Anne Harris to say that I would cease writing for *The Sunday Independent* forthwith. She tried to dissuade me, but I held my ground. My biggest fear was that O'Connor was among the favourites to succeed Harris after she retired as Editor at the end of the year, and I knew that I would have to resign anyway if that were to happen.

I continued to write for *The Irish Independent* but had by now resolved to quit once the referendum was over. I was determined that the bullies who had sought to bury me would not succeed in their most immediate objective at least, but I'd had enough of the cesspit that journalism had become.

In early 2015, a new Editor was appointed to *The Sunday Independent* – a surprise choice, Cormac Bourke, who had previously been working in various roles across the daily and Sunday titles. He called me and pro-posed that we meet. I found him personable and keen to have me back on board. He proposed that I resume writing for *The Sunday Independent*, exclusively this time, and offered me a decent enough deal. Things had changed since my original agreement, as a result of my decision to depart the Sindo in September, and a two-title contract was no longer available. I wasn't bothered about that. I enjoyed working to Liam Collins, but I had found the Sunday, which offered more space and scope, preferable to a boxed-in column in the daily. The Sunday also offered a more effective platform for the campaign I intended to mount in opposition to the proposed constitutional amendment on marriage, which I had now, as a result of the events of the past year, become determined to oppose.

For the year or so since the Panti Bliss interview, I had vacillated about getting involved in the debate. Given the state of the Irish media, I was deeply sceptical about the chances of obtaining a fair hearing, but I didn't want the vermin who had tried to silence me to have it all their own way. I decided that I would use my slots in *The Sunday Independent* to set out my position on whatever the amendment proposal might be, and leave the outcome in the lap of the gods. Win, lose or draw, I would quit journalism the day after the referendum.

28

The Splash

The way the country currently does its business is like if our grandparents left us a shop with a flat overhead and we took a quick look and decided that, rather than bothering our heads working out what to sell in the shop, we'd just rent it out and live upstairs. In good times and bad, we find reasons for overlooking the need for deeper development and longer-view thinking.

Despite these conditions, we continue to behave as though we are the authors of our own destinies. We talk a great game – about politics, for example, as though what happens in the future depends on the actions of people grinning down from the lamp posts now. When things are good we tell ourselves, sure there's no need to be worrying now, aren't we on the pig's back? And when the pig dies, we rant and rave in search of the culprit but still do nothing to change anything fundamental. We blather on about progress and create shitstorms of bogus transformation, but it's all part of the self-deception. In reality, the failure of any generation of Irish leaders since independence to tackle the question of how Ireland might live by its own lights has delivered us to a condition of learned dependency, in which, while claiming autonomy, we have merely replaced the ancient overlords with a new kind. And this, in turn, has fostered a particular type of politician: one who lacks any talent for envisioning an autonomous future for Ireland, but is equipped only to carry out the wishes of the new colonists, which he is more than willing to do in return for a comfortable lifestyle supplied by the unwitting taxpayers of Ireland.

Ireland is now not a republic, or even a functional democracy, but a corporatocracy. On the tidemark between the post-imperial and post-colonial worlds, we luxuriate in a tepid tidal wave of chemicals, IT and social network prattle – tapping into the creativity and entrepreneurship of the wider world to avoid having to overheat our own mental hard drives. Our existence owes little to our ingenuity or forward seeing. Our tragedy is that we're too scared of letting go of our dependencies to investigate what we're capable of becoming.

We live off what my late friend Billy Brown used to call 'the splash'. There was a time, maybe 40 years ago, when Billy Brown was as well known throughout Ireland as, say, Bono is today. Anyone who ever stood in an Irish dance hall in the 1960s or 1970s will know who Billy Brown was. He sang, played piano and saxophone and functioned as musical bandleader for the Freshmen, the 'showband' for which I worked briefly as a roadie in the late 1970s.

After the Freshmen's second coming of the late 1970s had petered out, Bill retired from the music industry to paint, read, fish, breed wildfowl and shoot the odd duck. He became known to a whole new generation as the voice on the nature slot on the Saturday morning children's show *Poparama*, on the station then known as RTÉ Radio 2. His postcards from the woods and fields were mesmeric, stammer and all. He gave up listening to rock 'n' roll and invested his creative energies in painting representations of the natural world where he was happier than anywhere else. Art, he told me one time, was just like the music biz: 'You have to have a sort of a hit, and then you can do whatever you want.' This 'hit' eluded him. His landscape painting, he would say self-deprecatingly in later life, was 'very representational'. I think he meant that he was still doing cover versions and still wanted to break free. I have one of his watercolours on my wall in Lislary, of a thrush lurking in grass. It reminds me of him in that it's the way he saw things, casting a sardonic eye on human activity but with an extraordinary tenderness that really only came into focus for most people when they heard him speak about animals.

Whenever I would run into him in the years after the showband days were over, I would gingerly ask him how he was surviving. Along with his painting, fishing, shooting and work for *Poparama* – for which he'd also written the signature tune – he played piano in a restaurant off Dublin's Lower Pembroke Street and hired himself out as a producer/arranger for other artists and bands, including one recurring hush-hush project, 'the annual Daniel'.

Invariably, Bill would respond to this question by declaring that he lived off 'the splash', which he explained in this way: 'There are animals who live in the sea, and there are animals who live on the edge of the sea, and there are others who manage to live on the land but are actually sea creatures. They survive for months on splashes up from the waves. That describes the operation succinctly.'

He was ahead of his time. Now Ireland lives by the same method, though perhaps without the bounty of ingenuity and resourcefulness that Bill brought to the question of his own survival. We live off the 'splash' of the global economy, totally dependent on the ebbs and flows of the tide.

The most vital element in our economic armoury is neither a product nor a service, but a tax regime: the 12.5% corporation tax rate that we offer to multinational industrialists to set up here and generate a few oul' jobs. As with many a showband head, our existence owes nothing to our ingenuity, other than under the dubious heading of self-destructive cuteness. This is the culmination of an unacknowledged history and a historical abdication by our political leadership which, decades ago – while Billy Brown was a dance hall superstar – offloaded the responsibility of generating the means of Irish survival to external agents. Bill's tragedy was that he stumbled into a showband explosion that made it too easy to become a superstar by a process of mimicry, so he didn't have to bother letting his unparalleled genius off the leash. Our tragedy, similarly, is that we're too scared of letting go of our dependencies to discover what we're really capable of becoming.

The essential shape, structure and outlook of the Irish economy is now much where it was in 1996/7 – our pores totally open to the global economy, which we hope will continue to smile upon us. We survive

< 323 >

by selling the essences of ourselves and our countryside, trading irreplaceable riches for transitory survival like proud but broke aristocrats burning their Chesterfields and walnut bookcases and sitting around on the stacked-up books.

In part it has to do with the delusion of independence that we cling to in the face of all facts. We talk non-stop these days about reforming our political culture, reinvigorating our public realm, restoring democracy to our institutions, but it's really an elaborate pantomime. In truth, if tomorrow morning everyone in Ireland stopped talking about politics altogether, and our politicians took to their beds for good, nothing fundamental would change for better or worse. Political reality would continue much as it has, to the beat of entirely different drums. It hardly matters a jot what we do, what we say, what we decide, whom we vote for. We become, by turns, apparently rich or undeniably poor, but either way it has little or nothing to do with ourselves. We insist, of course, on attaching credit or blame to the personnel we elect to 'lead' us, but this is no more than self-flattery. It doesn't matter who we put in 'power' – provided they don't make any sudden moves, or cheek their doms and dommes in 'Europe'. There is really but one significant policy with any relevance for our survival: the continuance of the 12.5% corporation tax rate – our way of converting nods and winks into euro and cent. Ireland's world-infamous corporation tax rate has become the great sacred cow of our recent political discourse, defended by everyone from taoiseach to taxi driver.

We're a nation in hock, and not just economically. Everything we do or propose is mimicked from somewhere else. We pretend to be a modern democracy, but it's really all a performance. We long ago waived the option of living by our own genius, in favour of prostitution: selling our national ass as 'the best small country in the world to do business in'.

For as long as the situation remained entirely hopeless, there remained an outside possibility that some man or woman might, in Pearse's words, arise to do a splendid thing in virtue of which all might be forgiven. But,

< 324 >

in the nature of our debased condition is the tragic circumstance that, as soon as there's the slightest possibility of the splash reasserting itself, we lose our appetite for radicalism and adventure.

The awful truth is that, since independence, Ireland, fundamentally believing itself incapable of self-sustenance, has constantly scanned the horizon for someone new to take 'responsibility' for our destinies, some-body who might be willing to provide the wherewithal for a half-decent existence in return for anything they might see about the place that might take their fancy.

Although the present corporation tax regime dates back to 1998, our record low rates of corporate tax have a much longer history. The policy of seducing foreign direct investment (FDI) as a silver bullet solution to the Irish economy dates from the 1960s when it was first pursued as a last-ditch effort to lift Ireland out of the stagnation that had af-flicted her through the 1950s. Since then, governments have pursued a relentless strategy of encouraging foreign-owned transnational operators to establish here high-skilled, labour-intensive, high value-added, strong growth-potential manufacturing industries. The 'bait' was that relatively high labour costs would be offset by other factors, including an expand-ing technologically literate workforce, high-quality infrastructure and the 'assimilative capacity' of the Irish landscape. This latter factor was of special interest to pharmaceutical industries, on the run from their in-creasingly environment-conscious home territories and on the lookout for places where they could pollute with impunity. Economists refer to 'assimilative capacity' as a 'natural factor endowment' in the area of in-ternational resource allocation. The argument is essentially that beggars can't be choosers, and that governments desperate for employment op-portunities should not get too precious about offering up their coun-trysides for the absorption of industrial waste. The factors taken into consideration by nomadic polluters in making these decisions include: a relative lack of regulation, high social tolerance to pollution and the un-used capacity of the landscape to absorb effluent. Ireland ticked all these boxes and, above all, had a sufficiently craven and desperate political class willing to seal the Faustian bargain. These policies were described by H. Jeffrey Leonard in his book, *Pollution and the Struggle for the World Product*, as 'a dustbin strategy for development'.

The Telesis Report, published in 1982, criticised this trend towards dependence on foreign industries, particularly those producing chemicals and electronics, on the grounds that it had failed to meet expectations. Contrary to the claims of the Industrial Development Authority this strategy was failing to produce even one third of the jobs that had been promised, but, moreover, was failing also to feed back into the wider Irish economy and likely diverting scarce resources which might be better used in stimulating indigenous industry. Coming in the middle of perhaps the most politically unstable period in post-independence Ireland, these findings and warnings were ignored.

The 'success' of the 'dustbin' policy escalated through the 1980s and early 1990s. By 1985, some 850 subsidiaries of foreign corporations were operating in Ireland, employing one third of the manufacturing workforce. Much of this activity was in the electronic and chemical sectors, accounting for more than half of Irish manufacturing exports. These firms were able to reach levels of profitability twice what they could achieve in the UK or Japan, and three times what was possible on the mainland of Europe. Because of profit repatriation, however, they were not contributing to Irish economic growth to the extent suggested by their healthy export figures. In 1986, £1,346 million was repatriated; by 1995, the figure was in the region of £4 billion. It was the start of the cuckoo-in-the-nest economy that has been the core characteristic of Irish economic reality ever since.

The early 1990s, however, brought signs of an awakening around Ireland to the environmental damage being done by some of these cuckoos. People's minds began to focus a little in the wake of a high-profile court victory by the Hanrahan family of Tipperary, overcoming the might and money of chemical giant Merck Sharp & Dohme, after their lives and livelihood were destroyed by emissions from the local Merck factory. Gradually, people began to mobilise against the imposition of unsuitable industrial development, to the irritation of the politicians who had no better ideas for running the country. For a time it appeared that governments might have to start rethinking the policy that had been their salvation.

Then came the Celtic Tiger.

At the end of 2013, I travelled up to Moville in County Donegal to meet some residents there who were trying to fight a comprehension-defying proposal by the local council to impose a sewage treatment plant on the edge of the Foyle estuary, with the certain prospect of desecrating one of the most beautiful places in the north-west. When I arrived, these good people reminded me that I'd been there more than 20 years before, when I wrote an article that helped them to overturn a plan by the multinational chemical manufacturer DuPont to build a chemical waste incinerator on the banks of the same estuary. They still had my article from *The Irish Times*, dog-eared and faded, its headline just about legible: 'The Promised Land'. That headline, which for once I'd chosen myself, had been intended to carry multiple meanings: Ireland, promised by its rulers to the highest bidder, or any bidder; Ireland, a haven of stupidity and ignorance to be exploited by foreign polluters; Ireland, once a paradise, now an indentured industrial dustbin. The protestors had aged 20-odd years, but, virtually to a man and woman, they were the campaigners who'd opposed the incinerator. Now, just when they thought they might be putting their feet up, they had to take to the barricades once more.

I remember Ireland as it was back in the early 1990s: a hopeful place for all its faults, buoyant with optimism and energy, mad as hell and not going to take it anymore. People were on the march to make things better. They had spirit, hope and resolve. But it all came to nothing, because the destination point of prosperity that had been placed before us by our leaders, and already signed up to by the majority, appeared to have been achieved virtually overnight and could not be challenged or questioned.

The Celtic Tiger, then, did much worse than simply raising hopes and setting us up for a fall that was to floor the country for the best part of a decade. It destroyed the idealism and radicalism of our people and left those of us who warned of the dangers of what was happening without a leg to stand on. Once we'd become 'rich' it became impossible to raise any issue about how Ireland was being run. All you could do was join in the raucous celebration of our new-found prosperity.

And, once the Tiger had crept in, the politicians upped the ante. It was Charlie McCreevy, in the 1998 Budget, who introduced the legislation – the Finance Act 1999 – for a new regime of corporation tax that led to the introduction of the 12.5% rate from January 2003. Before that the rate of corporation tax was set at 32%. Over time, the new regime came to amount to a virtual zero tax rate for many companies.

As a result, we have long had a two-speed economy, if not two distinct and separate economies. On the one hand there is the highly efficient, hugely successful transnational industrial sector, producing computer components and pharmaceuticals, as well as a thriving international financial sector and, latterly, the European headquarters of several of the arriviste internet giants. On the other hand, there is the indigenous economy – struggling and limping behind, and relatively neglected by government because of the much higher levels of employment afforded by the multinational sector.

We have yet to compute the total consequences of this situation, not least because we have yet to admit the truth of it. For all our cuteness, we've never actually managed to use the transnational corporation (TNC) economy to steal workable ideas and put them to use for ourselves. We're happy to leave the thinking to the outsiders, who'll let us do the fetching and carrying for them between drinking binges. Ryanair and, in their own way, U2 showed it was possible for Irish people to build global businesses from Ireland, but it all seems like so much trouble when we can simply live off the crumbs from the transnational table.

Whenever anyone refers to elements of the Irish economy as 'high-per-forming', it is the cuckoo-in-the-nest, foreign-owned phenomenon, accounting for roughly two-thirds of total output, they have in mind. The foreign direct investment (FDI) elements of the economy have broken all records in the past two decades, delivering about 85% of Irish GNP, compared to 35% in Spain, 20% in Italy and an OECD average of 25%. Foreign firms account for two-thirds of our exports, a share that has grown by 50% in the past decade. In the same period, total national exports grew by just half that figure, underlining the sluggishness of the indigenous economy. In recent years, yields from corporation tax of between €2 and €2.5 billion accounted for about 10% of total tax take, and FDI firms put another €1–2 billion back into the economy in wages and other expenditure. We are now more vulnerable than ever before. Details published by the Revenue Commissioners indicate that some 2,000 foreign-owned multinationals, employing a total of 336,000 people, generated €12.3 billion in employee wages in 2015, compared to €18.8 billion in wages generated by a total of 36,000 Irish-owned companies, employing between them roughly three times that number of people. These figures indicate the nature of the dependency and its disproportionalities. In 2017, ten foreign-owned firms paid nearly 40% of Ireland's corporation tax, continuing a surge starting from 2016 and amounting to a total corporation tax-take of €7.35 billion.

Despite the ostensible health of the headline figures, it is by no means clear that the 12.5% tax rate achieves the best balance for the Irish economy. Indeed, it is arguable that the FDI model of industrial development pursued since the 1960s has passed the peak of its usefulness, that what the Irish economy needs now is not the continued expansion of its transnational sector, but concentrated development of the indigenous elements so as to reduce Ireland's dependence on external forces.

For years, a blind eye has been turned to the many creative devices employed by FDI companies to use our hospitable tax regime to avoid taxes in their home territories. Two decades ago, a survey of American TNCs operating outside their home territory found that two out of three of them were keeping two sets of books – one for tax purposes, the other for evaluating performance by their subsidiaries around the world. These practices have spawned many creative devices, employed to max-imise profits. For example, many Irish-based FDI subsidiaries import their raw materials from their parent companies at significantly understat-ed prices, and export the finished products at overstated rates. Thus, a far greater proportion of the production costs of such products qualify for the low Irish tax rate than should properly be the case. This little fiddle is known as 'transfer pricing', and has long been deemed a necessary evil of Irish economic life. In 2013, for example, one multinational corporation announced revenues in Ireland of €3 billion, out of which €7.29 million was deemed to be profit. On this it paid taxes amounting to €2.3 million. Among the many interesting items on this company's balance sheet are royalty payments to companies that are part of the same conglomerate for 'licence expenses', 'management fees' and marketing and support services.

Our low corporation tax rate, then, has not come without moral cost, arguably contaminating our ethical groundwater and damaging our rep-utation in the wider world, where Ireland is increasingly seen, first and foremost, as a tax haven. It seems nonsensical to run tribunals to ex-amine locally based tax evasion and other minor corruption when we encourage outsiders to locate in Ireland in the expectation that a blind eye will be turned to their chicanery. These, after all, are not victimless crimes, but result in significant losses to the exchequers of the countries to which these multinational companies belong.

Several generations of wholly inadequate leaders have turned Ireland into a fiscal strumpet. Our bargain basement corporation tax rate is our red light to the world, a wink to the wise designed to seduce multina-tional tax-avoiders and obviate the necessity for deeper thinking among our ruling e-listers. Accordingly, it has also delivered to us a particular class of political leader: craven, unimaginative, visionless, clueless – suit-ed to the role of messenger, but singularly ill-adapted to lead a nation of independent-minded people, proud of their own history, heritage and culture, desiring to live in a country capable of controlling its own fate, fortunes and future in the world.

Most galling of all is that our tax-avoiding 'benefactors' have now started to tell us how to run our country. For a while, they remained quiet, content to milk the system, but latterly, especially since the 2008 downturn, have started to let it be known that there are things about Ireland that will need improving if they we expect them to remain. And the type of leaders our historical situation has thrown up are, unlike even their predecessors of the 1980s and 1990s, definitively not the types to tell these interlopers where to jump off. Instead, as we observed with increasingly frequency, it is the so-called Irish leaders who ask how high they might be expected to jump – and this purely for the purpose of ensuring that their jumping is pleasing to their true masters. This is fundamentally the context of the new and utterly changed Ireland, explaining the upsurge in naked propaganda, the ceaseless bullying of dissenters, the mysterious new laws that almost nobody was heard to ask for, and the sequence of constitutional amendment after constitutional amendment until there is almost nothing left. And all the while our so-called leaders constantly talk down Ireland Past, so as to convey to the outsider that they are prepared to do anything demanded to ensure their own survival, beguiling the foolish young with their 'liberal' crusades against the Christian Taliban of the fevered 'liberal' imagination.

29

Gaelic *Autobahns*

Do you remember those overhead devices they had in E. J. McDermot's drapery shop for sending money from the various counters to the office and getting back the change? It was like a mini cable-car system, which connected each of the different departments to the cubicle over in the corner from which the bookkeepers and Eamon McDermot kept a close eye on things. I remember as a child staring up open-mouthed at the little round boxes stuffed with cash and dockets zipping back and forth, for as long as it took Mammy to do her shopping. When a customer tendered money for a purchase, the assistant would wrap the cash up in the dock-et, pull down one of the boxes and shove the whole shoot in, then send the box skimming over to the cubicle in the corner. It always seemed that there was about to be a terrible accident – that two or more of the boxes were going to collide, causing an explosion of change and confettied pa-per; but, as if the whole thing were controlled by a battalion of invisible controllers in some unseen signal box, such a calamity never happened.

Back in 1993, I wrote a column in *The Irish Times* in which I remarked that, every time I heard a politician talk about 'drawing down' the next tranche of European funding, the image of those whizzing containers would pop into my mind. The connection, I speculated, was to do with the purpose of the cohesion or structural funds (I could never tell the difference and who cares anyway?): most of the money went on roads. The overhead cash transporter in E.J.'s, I observed, was obviously a la-bour-saving device designed without irony to cut down overheads. To my childish eyes, it seemed to exist for the convenience of the shop as-sistants, to save them walking over and back to the cubicle in the corner. In reality it was designed to save time, and therefore to assist in maximising the profits of E.J. McDermot Ltd. Although the assistants were appearing to obtain the benefit of the cash transporter, it was simply a way of regulating things so that more of their time was dedicated to the service of their employer. The focus of the technology was neither the assistants, nor the customers, but the office in the corner. 'Without this rather basic insight,' I wrote, 'the childish observer could not but conclude that the machine was some kind of high-class retailing toy which helped to pass the time in an enjoyable fashion for the assistants as they went about the work that had been made so much easier by the benevolence of their employer.'

So it was, too, with roads, the most visible element of EC-sponsored munificence (it was still the 'European Community' back then) on Irish soil. In the previous four years, since the year you left us, one third of all funding received by Ireland under the European Regional Development Fund, a sum amounting to three quarters of the total allocated to transport infrastructure, had been devoted to road-building. This was not the kind of roadworks you'd have been familiar with from the 1970s and 1980s – a lash of tar here, a bit if widening there – but massive excavations, flattenings, blastings and diversions to construct new dual carriageways, motorways, bridges, flyovers, hard shoulders and bypasses. In a column published a few months earlier, I had proposed that we might consider renaming the country The Tarmacadam Republic.

It ought to have been obvious already that this transference of funding was not about us, but about the use of the Irish countryside for some as yet unannounced purpose. I am certain it would have been obvious to you, who never had a good word to say about the EC or the Common Market all your life.

At that time, however, most people remained convinced of the availability of the free lunch. All this 'development', as we called it, was part of the bounty of reward for our being 'good Europeans'. Roads, we were assured, were an essential element of the modern infrastructure that would help us 'catch up', or 'achieve equalisation between periphery and core'.

< 333 >

But, as with the overhead cash transporters, the benefits of the roads were not necessarily to be conferred on those in closest proximity to them.

To the naked eye, I noted, a road gives the impression of bestowing benefits equally in both directions, whereas, like the overhead cash-shuttle, 'a road is actually part of an apparatus which draws benefits overwhelmingly in one direction'. Each road within a system (in this case the EU) ought to be seen not as a separate piece of infrastructure benefiting its immediate hinterland, but as part of a network that is actually of the core – extending outwards towards the margins rather than as something that belongs to the periphery. 'A modern road,' I wrote, 'is an instrument of economic colonisation.' To talk of roads enabling us to 'catch up' on the core was like saying that the overhead cash conveyor allowed the shop assistant to catch up with the draper.

But, whereas the kinds of roads we were seeing being constructed all over the country might bear the same name and basic technical description as those that had hitherto connected our towns and villages, they related to a different concept entirely. I cited Milan Kundera's novel Immortality, in which he outlined two different 'conceptions of beauty': roads and routes, which should not, he cautioned, be confused: 'A route differs from a road not only because it is solely intended for vehicles, but also because it is merely a line that connects one point with another. A route has no meaning in itself; its meaning derives entirely from the two points that it connects. … 'A road, on the other hand, is a tribute to space. Every stretch of road has a meaning in itself and invites us to stop.'

I think you'll know immediately what he means. I remember the way you used a road, and that summation reminds me of it. I only very rarely – when you had delayed yourself gossiping to someone – remember you rushing along a road as though its purpose was purely to take you from A to B. That was a scary experience: the few times in my life I experienced you driving fast! Well, ish. You would crank her up an extra 10 mph and put your head nearly out the windscreen in your determination to concentrate. On all other occasions, the van seemed to be given its head and treated as though it had a mind of its own, capable of making its own way between the ditches as you turned half around to talk and laugh with the people sitting on the mailbags in the back. The road was an event, a location (almost in the sense of movie location), a playing field in which your life was taking place. I remember still the personality of many of those roads we traversed: the tunnel of trees near Granny's house in Cloonyquin; the barren, be-heathered drive between Frenchpark and Fairymount, the bog extending to infinity on both sides, with just a couple of houses along its several miles; the magical transformation of the section outside Castleplunkett when the rains came and brought the turlough to life – suddenly a banal stretch became a lakeside trail. These were not routes, not a resource to be used expediently, but places with names that blurred into one another like the hawthorns along the way as we trundled along. The roads were, as we used to say, 'bad'. That was the extent of the technical description extended to the mess of bumps, dips, sharp curves and potholes, but we noticed this only when we hit a serious rut and the whole van would vibrate and you would go 'tsk, tsk', which frightened me a little because it signaled something slightly beyond the scope of the ordinary. I feared the world only to the extent that you did not seem able to accommodate it, the extent to which, in a given moment, it might seem beyond your tolerance. I remember those places, those roads; I remember their smell and the precise lurch in my stomach of every degree of bump. I loved them, as did you. I miss them now that most of them have been widened and upgraded out of meaningful existence.

Of course, such a sentiment is automatically written off as 'nostalgia' in this modern Ireland of ours. 'Nostalgia' has become a pejorative word, denoting a hankering after past moments without taking cognisance of their negative aspects. But it is not that at all. Nostalgia is transcendence in reverse gear, the full engagement of the senses with the continuity that I know as and call my life to this moment. Without nostalgia I would have no memory for anything but abstractions. I might as well Google myself.

< 335 >

'A route,' Kundera elaborated, 'is the triumphant devaluation of space, which thanks to it has been reduced to a mere obstacle to human movement and a waste of time.'

Yes. That is how I feel nowadays about taking the motorway from Dublin to, say, Mullingar. The nature of the journey has changed fundamentally, to the point where you wonder if 'journey' is the right word anymore.

Thirty years ago, driving west, especially on a Friday, was a nightmare business, and we complained so much about it that we became compromised when it later came to reacting to, and correctly judging, the way that problem was resolved. To go West in those days, you had to leave via the centre of Dublin and then head out via Chapelizod. Unless it was the middle of the night, you were stuck in a traffic jam until you cleared Enfield, usually two hours or more later. Then, thanks to the endless generosity of our European partners, the M4 opened up and you could be across the Shannon in less time than it used to take to clear Lucan. The toll was expensive – it's currently €2.90 – but seemed worth it for the time you saved, and you could additionally persuade yourself that you were saving maybe the equivalent in petrol.

After a couple of years of mindlessly absent driving, it occurred to me to try out the old N4 via Enfield and Kinnegad, which, due to the M4, was by then virtually traffic free. In the course of a number of controlled experiments, I discovered that, staying within the speed limits on both options, you saved about six minutes by using the M4, the mileage being almost exactly the same. It seemed a modest gain for the amount of tarmacadam involved, so we went back to using the old road. Not yet having read Kundera, Róisín started to call it 'the scabby route', even though we invariably spent far more than the toll tariff on tea and muffins in the Hilamar Hotel in Kinnegad, or even a full Irish in Mother Hubbard's roadside diner, which, if anyone is interested, is still there. (In the interests of methodological transparency, I have to concede that, whereas almost nobody using the M4 observes the speed limit, and since the N4 is single-laned and rather windy (to rhyme with 'behind me'), it takes just one literal-minded

Yaris-driver travellng at 57 kph to reduce the benefits spectacularly. On the other hand, since queues tend to build up at the tollgate at peak times, the overall probability comparison balances out overall.)

Back in the 20th century, before Mammy died and I was still driving to the Grey Castle, the way that suggested itself was Kinnegad, Mullingar, Ballymahon, Lanesboro, into Roscommon town and on to home. But the changing 'infrastructure' of the midlands proposed a new route: Kinnegad, Edgeworthstown, Longford, Strokestown. Going to Sligo, you swung off at Longford and proceeded via Newtownforbes, Carrick-on-Shannon, and on, bypassing Boyle, to Castlebaldwin and Collooney. Once you cleared the vicinity of Mullingar, something happened – not a going back in time so much as a stumbling on a place you remembered but which you had temporarily mislaid in your memory box.

What happens, of course, is that you have left the route and are back on a road. The interesting thing is that, whereas the new Gaelic autobahns are in many ways emblematic of 'modern' Ireland – with wide, straight lanes, foreign-looking road markings and even, bless the mark, gasoline stations – the way to Sligo from Multyfarnham, just beyond Mullingar, and the 'old' way to Roscommon via Ballymahon, retain many of the qualities of Ireland Past, which remains nestled deep within the being of the new, like some secret room at the heart of a house. To drive between Mullingar and Ballymahon is to collapse three or four decades and rejoin again your continuous self, the one with a history and a consciousness through time. For me it is to be travelling again as though from a Roxy Music concert in the RDS in 1982, or rushing to the *Hot Press* offices in 1983 with my Big Tom interview.

In that 1993 column, I identified the new EC-sponsored 'routes' as a line of demarcation between two categories of citizen, operating in the currency of time. The dividing line I intuited was between those with too much time and those with no time at all, those with 'time 'to kill' and those for whom 'time is money'. The two groups proceed in opposite directions, one possessed by a loyalty and an affection that are no longer respected, the other moving towards a destination that is illusory. One group has been pushed to the margins, literally into the ditch, as the new route was ploughed through their home place, sentenced to a life with time on their hands, to await instructions as to how they are to redeem themselves of their sin of sub-modernity. The other group flashed past them without seeing anything or anyone, regarding the very fields they cut through as impediments to their progress.

I think I may have understated the problem. The issue is not, or not merely, the violence inflicted on the man standing in his field as the Volvo passes him by, but also the violence the Volvo driver acquiesces in being visited on himself by his inability to 'visit' the place he is passing. This loss is to his soul and to the possibility of his understanding his life as a true journey.

What this portends is a population divided into two: those who fly so fast they are never actually anywhere, and those who, as with you and Mammy, remain in the same essential places virtually all your lives. We tend to think of travel as good, as 'broadening the mind', but there is a difference between travel and mere movement from place to place, the kind of movement that requires photographic evidence to confirm to the voyager that he was actually where he 'remembers' being. This suggests also a divide between those driven by a particular notion of 'progress' – one fixated on escaping from where they are rather than actually moving towards any concrete place, the other present in the landscape he happens to be manifesting in. Progress, by this definition, is not merely restlessness – it is also a hostility to the now, and motivated primarily by that hostility. This hostility manifests itself in many ways: impatience with the reticence of those who have been 'left behind' by the juggernaut of progress; contempt for the 'outmoded' perspectives of those whose minds, and the pathways within them, have remained allegedly unbroadened; economic strangulation of the lives lived in this way on the basis of a bogus calculus of worth and viability.

It manifests in other, more visible ways also: the 'modern' phenomenon of actual, physical violence that manifests periodically around Ireland arising from a combination of improved roads and the entirely foreseeable consequences of the disproportionate engorgement of Dublin and other cities. The failed policies of densification and ghettoisation, and the alienation they have spawned, impose a tariff on the unwitting, to be paid in blood and tears every time a gang of Dublin gougers scoots down the M4 to terrorise people in their homes in Loughglynn or Williamstown or Maugherow, certain of being back again in their social welfare ghettos before a Garda can be woken from his slumber in the Grey Castle or Tuam or Grange. Here we encounter a collision between two categories of those victimised by the progress project, one unrecognised and disregarded, the other talked up by the left-liberal intelligentsia as the casualty of 'inequality'. They also represent two distinct and irreconcilable types of modern human existence, both with 'time to kill'. One lives, dreams and reminisces in the now little more than metaphorical heartland of what was once unambiguously Ireland; the other lives within a literalness as sharp as the knives he wields. In your day, an old person waking up in Mantua or Moyne might look forward to a visit from the local postman, or know she could stand out on the roadside at 8.35 in the morning or 4.50 in the afternoon and that you would come along and, having heard and conveyed all the relevant newses, taken her list of messages to be fulfilled in Duffy's of Ballaghaderreen and delivered the following day. No more. Now, if she's lucky, she might get a weekly visit from an overstretched 'home help', the State seeking to achieve the very definition of the impossible: bureaucratic love.

Before roads could be disappeared from the landscape, Kundera observed, they had already to be banished from the human soul. Man had ceased to see his own life as a journey – a road rather than a route. Time and distance had become obstacles to something else, which involved the necessity to cover as quickly as possible the distance between two points.

The new 'routes' bequeathed us by our European 'partners' strike us, unbeknownst to ourselves, as the motorways of a foreign country. We feel we are abroad in the place we once thought of as 'our' country, a feeling that chimes with the instantly suppressible realisation on walking through the streets of an Irish city and realising that you are the only Irish person in sight. Both feelings are forbidden by the laws of modernity: one because desiring some lost idyll is tantamount to ingratitude for the bounty of modernity; the other because what is really the fruit of the listed demands of the globalised operators who rule us has been dressed up as 'openness' and 'generosity' – and who wants to be 'closed' and 'mean'? Another effect is that they stop us noticing, at any given moment in the landscape of the place formerly known as Ireland, where we are; in fact, we are nowhere, other than adrift between two points. We are 'lost' between Dublin and Sligo or Roscommon and Dublin. It is as though we have been catapulted into space and must wait to read our location from the configuration of planets and the position of the Sun.

Heisenberg's uncertainty principle states that the more precisely the momentum of a particle can be measured the more difficult it is to know its position. If I doubt this, I need but look at the speedometer anywhere between Enfield and Mullingar on the M4 one day and ask myself: where am I? This 'uncertainty' is emblematic of a deeper feeling of alienation, not just from the place we pass through but from the country to which we superficially imagine ourselves to belong.

Very often in the past, when I wrote about the effect of colonisation on Ireland, the taunt would come back: 'Dublin would have no great buildings had it not been for the English!' I would respond: 'Yes, it would – just different great buildings. They would be our great buildings.'

And just as the Georgian buildings of Dublin are one mark of the old form of colonialism, the motorways that criss-cross Ireland are a mark of the new. The Georgian buildings are beautiful in themselves and they are part of Ireland as it is now, but they will never be Irish buildings. Similarly the motorways will never be other than impositions on our speculations about what we might have become. Perhaps, left to ourselves, we might have built our own motorways, but that would have

< 340 >

been at the end of a long time of thinking about things. The motorways of Ireland arrived without as much as a moment's thought in an Irish mind, and the signs are on them: you drive from Dublin to any of the major cities and will not see as much as a café or a public convenience along the way. These are not merely mere routes, but inhospitable routes that exist for purposes to do with the rendition of Irish geography to the global marketplace. They are not there for the use of actually existing Irish human beings.

If we were ever to begin to undo the harm that has been done to us in this phase of colonisation, the motorways might not be a bad place to start. They are all we have in return for our fish, our gas, our seaweed and three-quarters of our collective soul. It would be a brave but welcome leader who would arise from among us and say to those who have looted our bank of riches: 'Roll up your motorways and pull the gate behind you! Leave us be with our own bad roads!'

30

Sleight of Hand

We have fallen into an odd way of dealing with referendums, and do not seem to consider that it is odd. Instead of seeing a referendum debate as a contest between two equal and legitimate positions – the status quo versus some new proposal – we tend to see it in terms of the virtue of the new confronting the obduracy of the old. I have in mind here the general tenor of such discussions in the media, which tend to divide the field between 'conservatives' and 'progressives', seemingly unmindful that this characterisation is likely to slant the discussion from the beginning. And, of course, the 'progressives' get to say Yes, while the 'conservatives' are wedded eternally to No.

When a new proposal is tabled to change the Constitution, it is generally presented in much the way you might propose to an unkempt and eccentric uncle that he ought to treat himself to a new suit. His old suit – he has but one – is threadbare and patch-bedecked. The arse in it is far more transparent than the windows in his bachelor dwelling. It is well past time he visited the tailor.

But changing the Constitution is not like that. A more faithful analogy would be with a proposal to modernise a historic building, which retains most of its original features but might be improved by some minor alterations. It is beautiful and beloved, but a little draughty, and someone thinks it a good idea to introduce underfloor heating and double glazing. Are you for or against? In such a discussion, it is vital that the discussion be enabled to occur in conditions of neutrality between two coherent but different ideas. The issue is not 'conservatism' versus 'progress' but conservation versus change in this single instance. It may seem a subtle distinction but it is not a minor one. You know this at least as well as anyone, having long defended de Valera's Constitution as 'the only decent thing he did in his life'.

This tendency to see constitutional amendments – and much else besides – in the 'conservative' versus 'progressive' way has infected much of our public culture. Of course, it is permissible for advocates of an amendment to present their positions in line with the 'scruffy uncle' scenario. More worrying is that media, generally speaking, have tended to treat certain kinds of referendum question in this way as well.

But a constitutional amendment, no matter how apparently unexceptionable, should not be given a free pass. If we are to maximise our chances of avoiding adverse consequences, it behooves us to thrash out everything. That means a contest between those who think the Constitution will be improved by the amendment, and those who insist it is better left alone. The pro-amendment side is entitled to its say, but it is not entitled to be treated as though right were unequivocally on its side. Opinion polls are neither here nor there – otherwise why bother having referendums at all?

A proposed amendment is simply that: a proposal. Until it wins a majority of electoral support and is installed in the Constitution, it remains a proposal, and the outcome an open question. If the amendment is not accepted by the people, it becomes nothing, meaningless words on paper, and the Constitution continues in all its splendour and majesty. Those citizens who wish to defend the Constitution as it stands have as much right to be heard and valorised as those who wish to change it, and are equally vital to the life of our democracy.

The modern journalist is incapable of accepting or even comprehending this, because he is almost invariably not a journalist but an activist committed to the achievement of whatever fashionable causes he thinks his adherence to will make him look better to his peers. In the 16 months or so before the same-sex marriage referendum of 2015 we observed this syndrome at full flood – media activists deploying their power and influence to impose changes on Irish society that nobody had been permitted

< 343 >

to discuss in any depth or with respect for the good faith of their dissent.

Following the attack on me by Rory O'Neill and its fallout, I had been in two minds about becoming involved. Two factors made my mind up for me: one was that it became clear that the impact of the constitutional changes to be wrought by the specific amendment being proposed, as well as further changes contained in legislation hurriedly passed to clear the way for same-sex adoption, would destroy permanently the chances of achieving any kind of basic rights for fathers, especially, but not solely unmarried fathers. The other factor was that I had seen at first hand what the LGBT lobby was like and was determined, in as far as I could, to prevent them demonstrating that thuggish and undemocratic tactics could succeed in bullying an entire country into submission. I resolved not merely to continue writing about the issues underlying the referendum question, but also to take an active part in the campaign.

The problem with the amendment, from my perspective, had very little to do with the principle of gay marriage. I had no great enthusiasm for this concept, believing it to be a makey-up 'right' that was objectively overblown and superfluous to the true and urgent concerns confronting the institution of marriage and the rights of existing parents and children. However, on its own, I wouldn't be bothered opposing it. I had no issues with gays being given a right to enter into civil unions and to avail of the protections pertaining thereto, provided things were allowed to remain there. And, if gay people wanted to upgrade their relationship by appropriating the word 'marriage', I wasn't going to lose any sleep about it.

Nor had my concerns about the kinds of change that would arise from opening up to gay adoption/gay parenthood been of the conventional 'conservative' kind, which tend to focus on the relative merits of heterosexual versus homosexual couples. I had seen some persuasive research in this regard that might have bolstered the anti-amendment cause, but did not seek to make this argument in public. I did not say, with many allegedly 'conservative' opponents of gay marriage and adoption, that 'a child needs a father and a mother'; what I said is that that 'a child needs his or her father and mother'. I believe, in other words, in the all but indispensability of the genetic link between a child and both his/her parents, which I say should be maintained wherever possible. I had noted a disquieting tendency of self-styled 'progressives' to denigrate and downplay any idea of the primacy of the blood link. I have sought to oppose this also, wherever possible.

Since the concept of gay marriage was in Ireland being coupled to adoption rights and would come with the highest level of constitutionally guaranteed parental rights – I believed there were legitimate grounds for fearing that this risked a radical undermining of existing family rights. In fact, I saw some real problems with the specific amendment being proposed. At the core of this difficulty was the fact that a gay couple, of either sex, is incapable of generating a child of its own capacities. For a gay couple to be deemed the 'parents' of a child, one or both of that child's parents may already have been sidelined or eliminated, and I was keen to ensure that this could not happen without also introducing some balance of protections in respect of both those natural parents and their child's entitlement to a continued relationship with both of them. I had seen too many grotesque injustices over the previous 20 years to stand idly by while such a dispensation was given the explicit imprimatur of the Constitution.

Together with Kathy Sinnott and Gerry Fahey, with whom I'd campaigned during the 'Children's Rights' Referendum of 2102, I set up an organisation to oppose the amendment on these grounds. Thus, First Families First (FFF) entered the 'Marriage Equality' referendum campaign primarily to direct public attention at the amendment wording. We also wished to highlight the potential consequences of this change in legal practice, working in tandem with other instruments, including the recently enacted Children and Family Relationship Act and the Children Amendment, which had been approved of by the electorate (58–42%) in 2012 and finally passed for inclusion in the Constitution in April 2015 following an extended but ultimately unsuccessful court challenge in which I was again centrally involved.

Most of the other anti-amendment groups were arguing on the basis of what might be called 'traditionalist' positions: the sanctity of family life, the importance of 'a father and a mother', the gendered basis of the institution of marriage, and so forth. First Families First did not express any view that might reasonably be construed as emanating from a religious or traditionalist position – not because we considered such positions invalid but because we detected a serious lacuna in the debate and also identified an attempt by media operators to suggest that the only objections to the amendment came from 'traditionalist' positions. We zeroed in on the actual effects the wording might have within the ecology of the Constitution, and as a result on actual families who, for whatever reason, might in the future find themselves before a family court.

On the face of it, the actual amendment wording appeared harmless. It read: 'Marriage may be contracted in accordance with law by two persons without distinction as to their sex.' This innocent-looking formulation was in harmony with the tactic of the gay lobby to present the issue as a simple 'human rights' matter – identical, it was claimed, to the historical campaign for equal citizenships of black and coloured people in the US. This was superficially plausible but actually bogus. The extension of full citizenship to the black population of the US was a matter of genuine 'equality', because it could occur without any diminution of the legitimate rights of other people. There was, therefore, no good or just reason why such equalisation should not be effected, in turn confirming that there had indeed been a gratuitous and disgraceful denial of human rights. The same circumstances did not obtain in relation to gay marriage, which really amounted to a sleight-of-hand – the usurpation of an institution that had belonged exclusively – and for unimpeachable reasons – to couples exhibiting the normative probability of intrinsic procreation. Moreover, it was not the case that gay marriage, when accompanied by adoption rights and the authentication of claims over other people's children, could be deemed as having no consequences for other categories of citizen. By extending full constitutional parenting rights to

< 346 >

gay couples, Irish society would be acquiescing in a radical dilution of the parenting rights available to normative families and actively setting out to discriminate further against the parents of children who remained deprived of such recognition – for example, unmarried fathers – as well as those children themselves.

One problem arising from the corruption of the media sector was that the wording was being debated purely in isolation, without reference to its potential, once inserted in the Constitution, to alter the meanings of existing provisions. The government was claiming that the amendment was simply an add-on to the existing form of marriage, and had no ramifications for children or the constitutional definition of Family. First Families First disagreed. The inclusion of the wording into Article 41 of the Constitution, which was headed 'The Family', was bound to impact upon the meanings of other clauses within that section, and this potential impact on both explicit and unenumerated rights was likely to be unpredictable even for experienced lawyers. It could hardly be denied that any individual change in the constitutional treatment of marriage and family opened up the potential for profound implications for the future interpretation of all related provisions. One had only to consider the mess made by the Eighth Amendment in 1983, on the rights of the unborn child, to see the potential for chaos that might be generated by an inadequately considered change. It is interesting that, for the entirety of the campaign, not one lawyer emerged to stake his or her reputation on contradicting what we were saying.

Our case was simple and in a fair contest would have been devastating. We focused not on sexual preferences but on constitutional law.

Article 41 began: 'The State recognises the Family as the primary natural and fundamental unit group of society and as a moral institution possessing inalienable and imprescriptible rights, antecedent and superior to all positive law.' Did anyone seriously imagine, we asked, that a Yes vote would not change the constitutional meanings of the words 'natural', 'primary', 'fundamental', 'moral', 'antecedent' and 'superior'?

< 347 >

The word 'natural' in that context obviously referred to the fact that, up to that point, a family had been defined as a mother, father and child/children, the children having been born as a result of the complementary biological functions of the mother and father. If you diluted this concept with the idea that a couple comprising a man and a man, or a woman and a woman, must be treated the same under the law, you could not avoid abolishing the legal force of the biological connection between parent and child as a criterion of parenthood. Parents who were the natural parents of their children would have no special rights on this account over others, and, in the event of disputes, would not be able to plead such a special right on the basis of biology. There was, in other words, an unseen and unacknowledged constituency whose rights were greatly threatened by the amendment.

We also believed that the Children's Referendum of 2012, the Children and Family Relationships Act of 2015 and the same-sex marriage amendment needed to be seen as three linked instruments that together mounted a radical onslaught on the constitutional definitions and protections relating to the normative family. We believed that this combination might in future family court proceedings lead to a radical and unjust advantage being extended to second or subsequent 'families' over first or earlier families. Hence, 'First Families First'. In the context of break-ups of relationships involving children, marital or otherwise, the Children and Family Relationships Act shifted the balance of protections from prior parental relationships to favour the claims of subsequent relationships involving whichever parent would be deemed the primary carer of the child or children. The Act would also make it possible for same-sex couples to adopt children, extending high degrees of protection to the parent-child relationships thus defined. Allied to this, the change to the definition of marriage implicit in the 'marriage equality' amendment would expand also the definition of family, and extend to same-sex couples the premium level of constitutional protection in respect of parental rights. As a cumulative effect of all these changes, the ability to marry would enable a couple (there would be no distinction as between same-sex or opposite-sex) to access significantly stronger parenting rights than single, separated or divorced parents seeking to rely upon biological connection or rights presumed to derive from a dissolved marriage. Post-divorce in this new dispensation, many parents and children could stand to lose the rights that bound them together in what previously appeared to be secure (being 'natural' in Constitutional terms) and legally protected relationships.

The risks no longer applied exclusively or mainly to single fathers or even merely to fathers. Suppose a (biological) father were to leave his non-marital family and enter into a same-sex marriage with another man. This couple, once married, would – in the event of the father entering a legal dispute over custody with the left-behind parent, the children's mother – find themselves with greatly enhanced rights compared to that mother. This scenario might seem less likely than the converse case whereby the mother left the unmarried family and entered a lesbian relationship, leaving the father at a disadvantage. But that remains to be seen. In either case, the left-behind parent would be in a position of serious disadvantage if the amendment were passed. The Children and Family Relationships Act also gave unprecedented powers to courts to resolve such disputes in an opaquely pragmatic manner. For example, a divorced father or mother, or an unmarried father, deemed to be a source of 'conflict' because of, for example, taking a dim view of the child-rearing practice of the new co-habiting spouse of the other parent, could have his or her guardianship rights revoked because the alleged climate of conflict was liable to be deemed contrary to 'the best interests of the child'. That the new spouse had no biological relationship to the child would be an irrelevant factor.

Hand in hand with this catastrophe was its most glaring cultural connotation: that the 'marriage act' – the coming together of a man and a woman in sexual unity – would no longer have any legal significance. The idea that there was a core category of marriage, defined as an exclusive commitment between one man and one woman, built around the idea of their conjugal union, being open to new life and genetically committed to the nurturing and protection of its own children, would be banished to a legal graveyard. For ever.

Although the government claimed that the Children and Family Relationships Act would legitimise all kinds of families that had hitherto been excluded from constitutional protection, the Act did nothing to change the most fundamentally discriminatory aspects of Irish family law. What it did, rather, was extend the categories of adult that would be entitled to legally call themselves parents, while perpetuating discrimination in respect of parents who were not married to, or in a formal relationship with, the other parent. For example, the act stipulated that, in order to qualify for automatic guardianship of his own child, an unmarried father would have to show that he had lived with the mother of the child for one year, including three months during the life of his child. For most such fathers, this would prove impossible, and in at least some instances where the conditions had been met, the father would be dependent upon the mother verifying his position. Because family courts tend to operate on informal principles, it was not long before this became the favoured question of judges assessing the question of whether fathers should be given guardianship at all.

Hence the new law perpetuated existing categories of marginalisation and created several more, and thereby promised to exacerbate the situation whereby at least one in every three children would continue to be excluded from full constitutional protection. And since it would mean that children whose parents fell into unprotected or less-protected categories stood to be treated differently by the courts, 'marriage equality' would inevitable result in further child inequality.

A short time before the referendum, UNICEF published a document which stressed that its use of the term 'parent' now referred to a child's 'caregiver', and was not limited to biological or legal parents – 'or, indeed, even to parents'. The word 'family', likewise, would refer to 'the most significant intimate group, which can be defined either by kinship, marriage, adoption or choice'. Similarly, the net effect of the several changes being effected in the Irish legal framework in respect of families, including the 'marriage equality' amendment, would be to shift the legal protections from natural parents to a newly defined concept of parenthood, defined not by biology but by a legal instrument – guardianship – which would be entirely in the gift of the state and could be withheld from a parent – and its benefits, by extension, from that parent's child – for no clear purpose in a process occurring in a secret court. Thus, parenthood would become a matter for dispensation by the state, which would in effect require to 'ratify' each parent/child relationship as entitled to legal status before the parties could be deemed parent and child. One of the effects of this change would be to place what was being called 'psychological parenting' – the roles of nurturing, caring for, daily contact and interaction, companionship – far above that of biological parenting, and, indeed, rendering a biological nonentity capable of trumping the claims of a natural parent simply by virtue of having gained proximity to a child in circumstances such as, for example, embarking upon a sexual relationship with one of the child's natural parents. The net effect would be such as to demolish the existing protections accruing to children in respect of their relationships with their natural parents and siblings, and shift the emphasis to the interests and alleged rights of often unconnected adults.

Another of the effects of the Children and Family Relationships Act was to give extraordinary powers to judges to remove a parent from the lives of his or her children. In seeking to establish a workable set of rights for a tiny minority of new categories of family, the act seriously undermined many existing rights and failed to make the kinds of changes that had been indicated as urgent long before the push for gay marriage began. This was likely to result in denials of natural justice, unwarranted interference in vital relationships and lifetimes of emotional trauma for many people, including children. Under assault from the bullying power of LGBT activists, the now chronic dishonesty and abdication of journalists, the say-so of multinational corporations and the craven self-in-

< 351 >

terest of politicians, virtually the entirety of family protections was being dismantled and rewritten.

The idea that there was no connection between adoption/family/parenthood and gay marriage was one of the many disingenuous refrains of 'Yes, Equality' campaigners. But it is obvious that gay marriage, in the form it was being demanded by gay activists – and has now been acquiesced in by the Irish electorate – must, as a matter of law, involve rights equal to those applying to heterosexual couples, and that this would sooner or later arrive at the idea that they have an 'equal' right to children. Because gay couples are intrinsically incapable of procreation, and gay male couples are especially disadvantaged by virtue of not having access to a womb of their own, a question arises: where are the children going to come from? Aside from the fact that the spouse of a previously married person with children from that previous marriage will be entitled to claim 'parenting' rights over those children, there are three possible sources of children to meet the demands of 'equality' in this connection: egg or sperm donation, surrogacy procedures and old-style adoption. Hitherto, for example, high-profile male gay parenthood has tended to arise as a result of surrogacy arrangements, but these are expensive and in the future likely to be subject to increasing legislative controls in other countries.

The concept of womb-rental ought to offend under several 'liberal' headings, including that it is exploitative of impoverished women, a category that 'liberals' otherwise claim to be protective of. Surrogacy is a contract arrangement by which a woman agrees to carry a gestating child in her womb for, usually, an infertile heterosexual couple or a gay male couple, and undertakes to abandon the child to that couple once he/she is born. Sometimes the woman carries a child that is genetically her own and hands it over afterwards for money; in other instances the child is the genetic offspring of at least one partner of the couple for whom the child is carried. In some cases, the process involves two different women – one to provide the egg, the other to carry the child. In Ireland and other western countries, these arrangements sometimes occur between friends or relatives, but in other situations they involve the exchange of money, exploiting economically disadvantaged and desperate women, usually from Third World countries, where baby farming is becoming one of the fastest growing industries, with much of the demand coming from male gay couples. The conditions in which the babies are gestated and born are almost invariably primitive and dangerous, but we hear little protest about this from the self-appointed guardians of 'human rights' in 'progressive' western societies. This is a classic case of the operation of the senselessness and incoherence of left-liberal ideology leading to contradictions that impose a profound silence on self-styled 'human rights' enthusiasts. The reasons for disquiet should be obvious, even to liberals: since it is illegal to sell a child after birth, why should it be different if the transaction occurs before the child is conceived? The women who carry the children are usually black or coloured. The client couples are almost invariably white. There should be all kinds of opportunities here for liberals to decry such arrangements under all kinds of headings – racism, economic exploitation, patriarchal oppression – but self-styled liberals have so far had very little to say on this topic. Usually, too, left-liberals are death-down on demands made by men on their own behalf, but if the men in question are gay … well, that's different, isn't it?

In all these circumstances, it is unsurprising that pro-amendment campaigners in the Irish 'marriage equality' referendum dishonestly sought to dismiss all talk about surrogacy as a relevant issue to the discussion. It is manifestly unconscionable, and therefore unsustainable, that governments which preach about the rights of children can countenance their citizens being involved in child trafficking of this kind. Despite liberal shiftiness on the issue, even some 'left-liberal' governments are already beginning to look askance at these arrangements, which frequently occur on a cross-jurisdictional basis. It is therefore only a matter of time before most of civilisation pulls down the shutters on the surrogacy window, leaving only adoption as a source of babies for gay couples. The problem for Ireland is that the precise amendment that Irish voters have now acquiesced in inserting into the Constitution may actually have rendered unconstitutional the outright banning of surrogacy, since gay couples will be able to argue that, because they are intrinsically incapable of procreation, surrogacy represents their only hope of achieving family 'equality'.

It was also a strong element of the First Families First agenda to highlight again the increasing pursuance by western governments of policies that served to weaken the ties between parents and children. This, we believed, would lead inexorably to the creation of a culture in which the removal of children from what are nowadays ominously described as their 'natural parents' becomes easier and more common. Already there were signs from behind the thick veil surrounding such matters that social workers in both Ireland and the United Kingdom were using economically and educationally based criteria to justify seizing children, usually from vulnerable single mothers. Again, 'liberals' had remained silent about this, and indeed had hushed anyone who sought to raise it. The resulting silence added a new piquancy to the historical failure of left-liberals to support any extension of parental rights to single fathers: it is as if they saw all this coming and realised long ago that to support that particular claim to 'equality' would have queered the pitch in advance.

The Yes, Equality campaign responded to all such arguments with bland assurances or vitriol, but failed to answer any of the questions raised about the architecture or substance of the changes. For example, if, as they claimed, there was no linkage between the Children and Family Relationships Bill and the amendment, why was it necessary to introduce the bill before the referendum? The reason was clear: the Government wished to deny the people the right to decide on the question of gay marriage and adoption together, rendering the more contentious issue of same-sex adoption a fait accompli and ostensibly confining the referendum to the question of gay marriage alone. Anyone who dared even to raise this possibility was ipso facto a homophobe, even if what they were seeking to point out was that the question being addressed to the people was not whether or not they favoured gay marriage, but whether they agreed with the constitutional provisions in respect of family life being dismantled under cover of a fog of obfuscation, dishonesty and intimidation. It was clear, indeed, that the government had cynically sought to capitalise on the emotive power of LGBT claims and methods to install in the Constitution a measure which, in effect, removed from the definition of family all criteria to do with natural procreative capacity, biological connection and sexual complementarity. In other words, 'marriage equality' was to be achieved in Ireland not by bringing gay couples up to the level of existing couples, but by bringing 'straight' couples down to meet the gay couples halfway. It was 'equality' at a new level for everybody: for some (gays) a radical elevation, but for male/female marriages a radical degeneration of the rights and protections that had been available hitherto. Nobody on the Yes side refuted this charge, which was simply ignored or dismissed out of hand.

There were disingenuous attempts by certain forces among the gay lobby and in the media to dismiss our arguments as trumped up and irrelevant to what was a very simple question about whether or not to extend the existing definition of marriage.

I was gratified to see that one commentator, albeit belatedly – the former *Irish Times* Editor Conor Brady, writing in his *Sunday Times* column the week after the referendum – called out this tendency to barge past arguments, bundling them out of the way. 'Not a few of those campaigning for a "yes" vote,' he observed, 'displayed a disturbing, not to say frightening tendency to arrogance and intolerance. There was also a lack of intellectual rigour in much of the polemic; a know-nothing, kneejerk dismissal of fears and concerns expressed by others. Not unreasonable issues raised about unenumerated rights that may flow from the amendment were slapped down as irrelevancies or intellectual conceits.'

It was true – and First Families First made this clear – that, once the amendment was passed, all these altered conditions would in the future obtain regardless of whether the 'new' family was straight or gay. The point was that, without the same-sex amendment, the rights of the original family would have remained contestable on the basis of the robust provisions of the existing Article 41, now dismantled to accommodate an entirely unreasonable demand.

But in the newly defined 'rights' culture, it was all but forbidden to speak of the rights of those who stood to be affected, on pain of being dubbed a bigot. The LGBT lobby was highly voluble, visible and articulate about its own rights, and, having a free run of the media, had all but convinced the public that the changes being proposed would come at no cost to anyone apart from a few bitter traditionalists fixated with Catholic dogma. People were being persuaded that there was nothing at stake except some outmoded sense of 'family values', a meaningless cliché in the Ireland of 2015. Voters were also being reminded that they all knew or were related to gay people. What they were not permitted to hear was that they also knew and were related – or potentially related – to people in the invisible constituency of the future that would be at risk from the amendment. This included an enormous future constituency of children who stood to be adversely affected by the changes.

When we talk of 'marriage' and even of 'the family' we are to a degree dealing in abstractions. Many legitimate families are unprotected by marriage, and many such families did not qualify under the prevailing constitutional provisions. But acknowledging this was a long way from saying that, as an act of redress, the state should undermine biological connections in the interests of promoting eccentric (meaning 'outside the centre') models of family. A family doesn't need a marriage to be a family; a family doesn't even need to be called a family to be a family. But a family emphatically does need the protection of the law if it is to withstand the kinds of ideological and legal forces currently bearing down on families coming to judicial notice on account of relationship break-up or other difficulties.

The really shocking thing was that a form of gay marriage could have been introduced without risking any of these consequences. The government could have chosen to introduce gay marriage by means of a statutory

< 356 >

instrument, as had already been done in a number of other jurisdictions, including the UK, creating a dedicated category of marriage that did not intrude on existing constitutional definitions and building a firewall to safeguard the rights and protections of the normative family, while also protecting gay relationships and, where applicable, the children dependent upon them. This, however, was not enough for the LGBT lobby and its allies, who wanted the prize of 'equality', even if this concept had no meaning in the context in which they were insisting upon it. Neither was it enough for their powerful allies in the transnational industrial sector, on whose good favour the Irish government was now entirely dependent for its survival and capacity to continue running the country.

At the core of the deception was the sinister sleight of hand by which the government was implying that the 'people' – the electorate of 2015 – had the ultimate and absolute right, under the 'guidance' of the government of the day, to give and take away rights willy-nilly from present and future citizens. In fact, many of the rights outlined in the Constitution – including natural parent-child rights – are not extended by the Constitution but simply recorded there. By advancing its 'marriage equality' amendment, the government had effected a trick akin to a conman seeking to sell someone else's coat. Requiring the people to demonstrate their 'progressiveness' by passing the amendment, it insinuated that these rights existed by the gift of the state, and that they were accordingly open to being radically rewritten or even abandoned if the electorate so decided. This was entirely bogus. The rights of parenthood, as the Constitution makes clear, cannot be abandoned by a parent – either personally or in his capacity as a voting citizen – because they are 'inalienable' and 'imprescriptable', which is to say they cannot be given up or taken away. The people were therefore being tricked into believing that the state had the right to oversee the reallocation of such rights by organising a supposedly democratic vote of the people. This raises an interesting possibility: that the gay marriage outcome is capable of being overturned by a future Supreme Court, sufficiently alerted to the damage that has been done to decide that the result of the 2015 referendum ought to be vitiated by reason of disinformation and duress.

I had, to an extent, seen all this coming. Over the previous 20 years I had gradually come to the conclusion that the attacks on fatherhood, which I've been resisting for two thirds of my working life as a journalist, were really not down to simple bias, but represented the advance march of an ideology now hitting its full stride. It was by now clear that the agenda did not end with the evisceration of fathers, but was really concerned with ultimately disintegrating all normative ideas of family. By marginalising fathers, the system had been nurturing a culture of vulnerable mothers, highly dependent on state largesse, who would in turn become vulnerable to the reconstructive energies of the regime.

The brutal nature of family courts was a central element of the furtherance of this agenda. The last thing the 'cultural Marxist' ideologues wanted was the emergence after divorce of co-operative versions of the fractured family: fathers and mothers, albeit living separately, raising their children in relative harmony. That's why governments had resisted a serious, legally recognised mediation option for family disputes and refused point blank to permit any enhanced rights for unmarried fathers, while promoting far more tenuous 'family rights' claims from other quarters. Indeed, in framing the Children and Family Relationships Bill, Minister for Justice Frances FitzGerald had in effect double-crossed single fathers by indicating that she would 'look at' the question of automatic guardianship for them in the final stages of redrafting the legislation, but in the end she introduced even more hoops for them to jump through, in effect placing guardianship rights outside the reach of most of the fathers so implicated. (I now, however, had a new proposal for such fathers who might come to me seeking help and advice: I began to ask them if they had ever thought of meeting a nice young man and settling down, because then I could virtually guarantee that they would be given every conceivable right to love and care for their own children.)

We in First Families First were fully aware that we were up against

< 358 >

not merely a formidable coalition of opponents – the LGBT lobby, all parties in the Oireachtas, several of the most powerful operators in the transnational corporate sector, innumerable NGOs masquerading as honest brokers and a former president trampling all over the established protocols of that office – but also a deeply corrupt media that would do its utmost to prevent the discussion being broadened as we required it to be and would try to spike our guns at every opportunity. So it proved.

Observing these bizarre and baneful developments and their implications, we suggested underwriting the legal protections that had grown up around parenthood over the centuries, and were noted in the Irish Constitution simply to catalogue the natural state of affairs. Our objective was to prevent this bedrock of rights being dug out and replaced with a new relativist concept of family, which would include a nod to biology only insofar as this, in any particular instance, was in tune with the requirements of the governing ideology.

Our proposal involved the addition to the ballot paper of a second amendment, to Article 40.3.1, as follows (proposed new section in italics):

40.3.1
The State guarantees in its laws to respect, and, as far as practicable, by its laws to defend and vindicate the personal rights of the citizen. *In particular, the State shall respect the right of the child who is separated from one or both of its biological parents to maintain personal relations and direct contact with both parents.*

This addition to Article 40.3.1 was a direct lift from Article 9 of the UN Convention on the Rights of the Child. It would copperfasten the rights of existing parents and their children and render a great deal less dangerous the changes being wrought in law and the Constitution in the hurried attempt to make Ireland a haven of gay rights.

Journalists and debate moderators, seeing precisely what our amendment signified, why it was essential to protect normative families but would in some instances stymie gay couples from achieving 'equality' as parents, deliberately avoided the issue and repeatedly sought to bring discussions back to the safer territory of the 'sanctity of marriage', the comparative merits of gays and straights as parents, and so forth. The crux of the matter was that, from the beginning, the gay lobby wanted not merely gay marriage but 'equality', an entirely different thing. Even though gay couples were incapable of the intrinsic generation of new life, the LGBT lobby wanted same-sex couples to have the same claim to children as a man and/or woman who had caused a child to be conceived. This was outrageous, and media people could not help knowing this, which is precisely why they glided over the core of the First Families First argument and, time and again, tried to force us back into traditionalist territory.

31

Autonomous Automatons

I think I may have mis-stated things in the beginning. It is not true that Ireland has 'gone mad'. That's the way it seems but it's actually not a very helpful or useful way of seeing what's happening. The deeper truth is that we have ceased to be ourselves – have, at some point in the quite recent past, crossed a line and entered a new kind of human collectivity, experiencing a rupture that made no sound and left no visible trace. This is probably true of all western societies, and quite a few further afield as well. It affects us in ways we are unaware of, but, even more worryingly, it threatens to affect our children, who are growing up in this as yet un-diagnosed new reality.

There are so many new things and few, if any, of them bear any of the hallmarks of the kind of 'progress' we have been promised. We appear to go deeper and deeper into ugliness and incoherence. I feel all these diverse phenomena we've been talking about as a single event, as some-thing outside not just our experience but our imaginations. Contemplat-ing what I observe to be happening, and what I sense it to mean, I am struck by the redundancy of the available constructs and understandings. We need new mechanisms, analogies and metaphors if we are to achieve any grasp of what is happening.

It has, of course, to do with technology, with screens and clicks and 'likes' and posts and the constant babble that pushes all thought out of every thinking space. But we need to desist from thinking of this as mere catastrophe, in terms of the damage that is being done to culture and education and belief and so forth. It is much worse than anything we could dream up in that context. This is a new event in the history of the world, whereby mankind becomes more and more subservient to the

< 361 >

machine of his own creation, and the things they could do for but also to him, having trusted them with tasks as diverse as forecasting the weather and keeping his children occupied. The result of it all is that reality has been recreated as a metaphor and now we are moving into it, crossing the road with all our bags and kit, sleepwalking through the night to find our new homes in the virtual and waking up in the morning with just the vaguest sense of having moved from some other place. We enter the metaphor and becomes its citizens, have walked out of our bodies, away from ourselves, to look back and consider ourselves – as voters, taxpayers, consumers, even as citizens, but not as human beings. We are as facsimiles of ourselves, standing outside our selves and moving our beings about as though pieces on a chessboard.

The change has its roots in shifts in the structure of the human, which are themselves due to the action of technology, corporations, cultural forces such as propaganda, and other processes deep in the organism of society resulting from these. Many thinkers, writers and artists have stabbed at definitions and descriptions of what is happening to the human person, but the closest I have seen anyone come to nailing it in a single paragraph is Jean Baudrillard in his book, *Impossible Exchange*, in a passage about the modern 'subject', an entity he places in opposition to the 'object', which he credits, at least metaphorically, with having a mind and a life of its own. He talks – ironically, one hopes, but perhaps not – of the 'liberation' of the subject through technologies, networks, screens, which cause him to become fractured, 'both subdivisible to infinity and indivisible, closed on himself and doomed to endless identity'. The 'perfect' subject is an individual who has also a mass status. He is 'the dispersal of the mass effect into each individual parcel … Or, alternatively, the individual himself forms a mass – the mass structure being present, as in a hologram, in each individual fragment. In the virtual and media world, the mass and the individual are merely electronic extensions of one another.' This may very well mean that the 'person' is no longer the norm of the human form – that mass communications is in the process of converting the human race into a single intelligence, or absence thereof.

For the past couple of years, my stepdaughter Sarah, who's a fluent Irish speaker, has been going around the gaelscoileanna talking to kids and parents about the potential for serious damage as a result of the escalating fixation with technological connectivity. She talks to them about stuff like Nicholas Carr's groundbreaking 2010 book, *The Shallows*, which outlines in stark detail the scale of the catastrophe facing humanity as a result of the uneducated way we have come to see the Internet and the screens we use to access it. Carr's thesis is that the web is changing how we read, and therefore how we think, feel and remember. He takes us into the workings of the human brain and then departs on a tour of the written word in human culture. He outlines how the distraction-ethos of the web may be rendering impossible the process of 'deep reading' by which the unfathomable sensibility of man has been nurtured since the invention of the printing press. These tendencies have already started to short-circuit the processes whereby deep reading has functioned to fill our memory banks with the profound understandings and complex connections that enabled us to empathise and understand things intuitively. Instead, we are being taught to memorise and think mechanistically, to shift rapidly from one thing to another, to regard the Internet as an external memory bank. This, says Carr, is reducing us to 'pancake people', flattened-out versions of our ancestors, whom, on account of our technological advancement, we regard with condescension. Unless we begin to understand our new condition and deal with it, he warns, we may yet find that the period in which human understanding was defined and informed by deep, solitary and uninterrupted book-reading will have been an aberration of human culture. History and civilisation may already have gone into reverse.

This is another way of describing what I have called becoming citizens of a metaphor. It sounds like a different problem but really Carr's diagnosis is a more plausible, concrete way of saying the same thing.

With the primary schools, Sarah encountered a degree of openness for the first while. The kids all seemed to be spending frightening amounts of time on their laptops and smartphones, but they were also interested in reading and talking and, above all, listening to someone who, like Sarah, can weave a good story. When she ventured into secondary schools, she found a far bleaker picture. The students sat sullenly in their seats, fiddled with their phones while she was speaking and treated the whole subject as if it was self-evidently a joke. Most kids were spending four or five hours per day on various pieces of technology and, as far as they were concerned, that was the way it was going to continue. They didn't expect grown-ups to get it or approve. And the teachers mostly couldn't be bothered. The young of Ireland have now become, as the hills and fields and rivers became before, a 'natural endowment factor', their minds having 'spare' absorption capacity for all kinds of toxic nonsense, designed ultimately for the enrichment of corporations and their shareholders

In a January 2013 article for the *Financial Times*, April Dembosky interviewed Jaron Lanier, Silicon Valley writer, philosopher, technologist and author of *You Are Not A Gadget*. 'We have been designing a paradise for people with Asperger's syndrome,' the report quoted Lanier as saying. 'I don't think we're making ourselves stupid or inferior, but I do think we're making ourselves more narrow.' Today's dominant Internet programmes, Lanier claimed, reflect the minds of the engineers who built them and fail to capture the 'humanistic' elements of everyday existence. He outlined also a fear that the increasing use of screens is eroding or remaking the emotional and empathetic pathways of the human brain. In other words, humans are starting to think like machines.

One of the problems is that online culture, and social networks in particular, are oriented towards outer rather than inner lives. These ways of engaging with the world favour objective, quantitative thoughts over subjective, qualitative feelings. This is why people who may otherwise be kind to their cats tend to turn into monsters when they go online. Social media, for example, is not capable of communicating the full range of emotions – fear, fascination, admiration, exhilaration, compassion – that comes from encountering a real place or person in reality. And the constant exposure to such reduced forms of feeling may already represent a serious threat to the quality of human feeling available in society.

Lanier compares what is happening to human cognition to monocropping in agriculture, where the cultivation year after year of one massive crop on the same land reduces the diversity of soil nutrients and results in a weakening of the plant stock. 'We're creating a mono brain,' Lanier told Dembosky. 'We are losing a little bit of empathy for other people's internal lives. We're substituting ethics for empathy in more and more situations. In other words, we have logical reasons for being nice to each other rather than emotional reasons.' Experiments with book-reading, he said, indicate that the areas of the brain that light up during close reading are not just those associated with attention, but also those involved in movement and touch. People who read books seem to locate themselves as though physically in the story. This could mean the more people read superficially, as on a screen, the less they put themselves in other people's shoes. But, because the brain is capable of reconstructing elements of missing information, it may be building into our responses a false empathy based on learned ethics and approved reactions, a kind of virtual empathy devoid of actual emotional content.

A friend of mine, Joe Foyle, a former economist and journalist who nowadays teaches people to speed-read and also assists those with reading problems such as dyslexia, diagnoses the problem in a very precise way. He says the issue is 'pixel-reading', the accumulation of knowledge via the millions of minute dots that make up screen images and texts. Billions – particularly young people, he says – have for years been unwitting guinea pigs in a global experiment, the outcomes of which were unforeseen by those who initiated it.

In the 1960s, Foyle was friendly with the Irish-Canadian media theorist Marshall McLuhan, and has reinterpreted some of McLuhan's theories for application to the Internet age. He says: 'The powerful subliminal effect, foreseen by McLuhan, of a heavy daily diet of interaction with the billions of fast-moving pixels of the screens of TV, computers, smart-phones and similar devices shows up in a predominance of lethargy interspersed with short bouts of activity. Those of us who must read much quickly, to have material for writing, are utterly untypical of the generality.'

Foyle read Carr's book when it came out in 2010, and, while admiring it, felt that he had missed something – that, though Carr acknowledged a debt to McLuhan, he failed to get his essential reading-related point. 'As a result he failed to prescribe the McLuhan-based solution, and even admits at the end that he had reverted, addict-like, to the Internet use that had alarmed him.'

Foyle says the distinction between 'pixel reading' and 'paper reading' needs to become the key perception if educational values are to be pulled back from the edge. The trend towards paperless education, he believes, is disastrous, for all the reasons Carr outlines – and others too.

The work of dealing with pixels, Foyle says, entails colossal, exciting speeds for both eyes and brains, which cause disorientation and lapses in concentration. There are now trillions rather than hundreds of dots on screens every instant, and the addictions arising from pixel reading are even more intractable than addictions like alcoholism or gambling, because the Internet is now such a ubiquitous tool of most people's everyday life. The world has so far tended to see the question in 'either/or' terms, and frequently plumps for screens if a choice seems to be called for. The solution lies in 'both/and': as well as Internet use, we need also to make space for paper reading every day, to counteract the pixel-damage. Pixel reading, Foyle says, is now, with massive government, media, academic and commercial backing – taking over at all education levels and, increasingly, the related homework hours. 'It is pushing paper reading out to the margins as a bitty thing. If my analysis is correct the opposite should be happening.'

'The fact is many now function well despite using TV, the Internet and other forms of pixel reading, because daily they also use their eyes enough for paper reading,' Foyle wrote in a letter to the editor in response to Dembosky's *Financial Times* article. 'It's true that many eyes are so adversely affected by pixel reading that their minds find it difficult – some find it extremely difficult – to sustain paper reading enough. But things can be done to rectify that difficulty quickly for everyone so affected.'

Whereas these are vital understandings to enable us to grasp what is happening, they tend to root our thinking in the technology, which leads us astray because it draws us into the false idea that the issue resides somewhere in the intricate mess of wires, keys, buttons, circuitry etc. that make up the 'problematic' devices. But the true problem is in the head of the user and cannot be understood technologically. It has to do with the effects of reliance on these devices, not just on the brain, but on the hopes, expectations and understandings of the person attached to them as though umbilically.

Technology is breeding a new kind of human. If the word 'breeding' seems inappropriate, it's because we don't quite realise what's happening, which is unprecedented and not just in the obvious ways. There is in train a remaking of the human that appears to be 'merely' a technological revolution.

But technology is no longer something remote from the human, a tool. It becomes, in different ways, an extension of the human, invading the mind, soul and imagination of those who think themselves the manipulators of sophisticated toys. Technology of the sort we're talking about here, for example, collapses time. It also eliminates, for example, the process of maturing, and delivers a passable imitation of maturity that is really just an outer shell, inside of which grows nothing at all. The technology delivers articulateness, cleverness, sophistication, knowingness, jadedness, wryness, exhaustion. It delivers these even to a terrified 11-year-old who has seen nothing, known nothing, experienced nothing, felt very little but fear and anxiety and, where he is lucky, a little hope that all the things that seem to be true will one day dissolve and be replaced by order and guidance and – whisper it – values. He has searched in himself and in the world for the ideals that he intuited from the stories his mother or older sister read to him as a boy, but cannot find anything to begin from. Reality is disappointing: slow and unresponsive, incapable of delivering anything like the feelings he has encountered on screens since before he could read. He has delved into the depths of his fantasies and known everything that human sexuality is capable of delivering, but without the human element. He wants to feel something but feels only victimhood and loathing and a flimsy kind of hoping that seems to have no evidential basis in anything he encounters. He has had no childhood, because childhood is simply something to be prated about by politicians while it is being stolen by corporations. What he has had is something akin to the ghost of a chemical addiction, which has frozen his heart in terror and chilled his soul into hiding. He has cowered in his room with his Gameboy and taken this existence for life. He has discovered the worldwide web, which seems to be a place where you can live without being alive. His body has grown, his vocabulary has grown, his penis is hungry and prone to an iron hardness, but his heart has shrivelled for want of sustenance and his emotional life exists purely as a virtual reality. This, tentatively, is the beginning of what we are talking about.

The person so conditioned is ripe for manipulation and hypnosis, for propaganda and lies. Because the world is something that comes to him through the thing in his hand, he has no reference points besides. He cannot touch or hold or seize or dismantle something in an attempt to understand how things work, what things mean. He walks out of his bedroom with the outward appearance of a teenager resembling the hordes who have preceded him. But he is nothing like those who have come before: he has no heart worth speaking of, and no memory of anything other than the things he has seen, which are confused between those he has actually seen with his eyes in reality – he thinks – and those he has simply come across on his screens. He doesn't know for sure if there's a difference.

We have a society now that wilfully, enthusiastically eradicates memory, as a matter of principle. Our elders are banished to old folks' homes and fathers have no longer the words to speak to their sons. Masculinity is demonised and our education system impresses upon adolescent males that their fathers are inappropriate role models. We sit around 'debating' whether the demands of 'parenthood' require the presence of parents. Robert Bly wrote about the creation of generations of young men who become numb in the region of the heart. The umbilical cord has been severed, but no more than that. The father can find no way of protecting or guiding his son, who remains tied to his mother's apron. Still, deeply aware of his maleness, he shies away from adopting the emotional life of the female, choosing to have no emotions at all. He does not know what it means to be a man. There are no men to mimic in his vicinity.

His sister has issues of her own, different but related. She lives as an image created on the technologies that she imagines to be like mirrors, still within her control. In reality they have stolen her soul and kidnapped her identity, giving her back to herself as an avatar of what she imagines to be her own design. The technology gives her the only life she now recognises as her own. Face-to-face relationships have become secondary to technologically situated friendships. Her self becomes as though a screen onto which the technological projector flashes images, impressions, opinions, information which form the whole of her being and subjectivity.

The information and communication society has supplanted production as the central logic of economy and the organising form of society, and virtually every action carried out under this dispensation is ontologically pointless. In the metaphor in which we now live, the worker is no longer a pivotal figure, but one of a dying species, soon to be extinct. Social constructs and ideas have no meaning other than as theory. Culture descends into self-referentialism in which the idea of external or absolute meanings is literally unthinkable. Everything succumbs to randomness, because it is impossible for the human person to keep up with, and thereby comprehend, the factors that impel his thoughts or actions. The self dissolves into a blur of sensation and activity, overcome by objects and images and movement, and is reconstructed as a projection of the culture it inhabits. An unfathomable algorithm dictates the thoughts, identity and fate of the person without presence, the subject without subjectivity, and this projected individual lives in a state of barely suppressed terror, which is his sole expression of a true humanity.

More difficult to grasp – even while we are still theoretically capable of grasping an idea rooted in the former world of the real – is that three-dimensionality itself is disappearing from everything but the decaying edifice of the entity formerly known as the world. And this is a place we simply move through on the way to the next act, scene or tableau of the metaphor in which there is neither dimension nor depth to penetrate, perspective to observe nor essence to divine.

There is – literally, again – no time for meaning, even if meaning could be located. Images are bounced from screen to screen and finally on to the screen of what is left of the human mind. Everything is justified by itself, refers to itself, and knowingness resides in being able to negotiate this circuitry of meaninglessness without falling off. We have attained a state of existence in which nothing surprises us and nothing is not boring. We literally do not know what to make of ourselves, do with ourselves, because we are not making ourselves, are not in control of our lives, are mere flotsam on a current that is generated by nobody and takes us to no place.

And with this has occurred also a retreat into our heads. Because we have ceased to use our hands, we have lost contact with the grit and weave of reality, and have therefore given to the ideas of the Cartesians a substance they did not necessarily have when formulated. It is likely that most of the content of the thought of René Descartes and other thinkers retroactively credited with launching the Enlightenment remained at a fairly remote and abstracted level until well into the 20th century. On the face of things, it might seem mildly preposterous that the ideas of a man who has been dead for more than 350 years could be having a decisive impact on what happens on Twitter in an age of which he made no claim to prophesy. For centuries his thoughts about thinking were the stuff of the dinner parties and melancholic ruminations of other philosophers, artists, writers, theologians, teenagers, perhaps the odd politician and, most crucially for a very long time, teachers. Nevertheless, at the street level of culture, it is doubtful whether these ideas had any real impact. They affected the thinking of the governing classes, to be sure, and in this way served to shape and mould society in particular directions – especially in scientific thought – but they did not become common property or enter the thought patterns of the generality of people until relatively recently. In the second part of the 20th century, however, the thinking of the Enlightenment, which in a sense might be said to have incubated for three centuries, suddenly went mainstream. There were four core elements in this transformation: the revolutions wrought by technology, the rock 'n' roll explosion that erupted from the mid-1950s and unleashed the 'freedom decade' that was to follow; the advent of mass media society at around the same time, with TV at the cutting edge; and the student uprisings that swept through Europe and the US in the late 1960s.

Born of the entirely legitimate desire to escape the stifling diktats of priests and princes, our retreat into Cartesian subjectivism has cut us off from the facts we need to verify anything. We have gone up into our heads, withdrawing our attention from the world, removing ourselves from the evidence of things and other people, convinced that truth and understanding are subjective phenomena which will erupt willy-nilly in our heads, with a little prompting from outside. This threatens our capacity to think straight, but, deeper than that, places a question mark over our ability to develop a true individuality, which, in the age of individualism, would amount to quite a turn-up.

The logic goes something like this: The reflex of retreating into our heads, apart from depriving us of evidences, unleashes a sense of loneliness, alienation and solipsism that destroys self-confidence and renders us even more amenable to a mentality that is actually that of the mass. Thus, individualism destroys individuality, creating a form of autonomy that, as Matthew Crawford has observed, is closer to automatism. Having recreated our identities as individuals in the privacy of our own heads, we have to invent different personalities for external use, and these we formulate on the basis of conformism and mimicry. We subject ourselves to a form of what Søren Kierkegaard called 'levelling': we surrender to being members of 'the public', with all this entails. In our public manifestations, we become more and more indistinguishable, in effect third parties to ourselves, entering a limbo where neither reverence nor rebellion is possible. Thus, the modern Internet: cynicism mixed in with ersatz dissent, albeit largely behind the cloak of anonymity, where the unself-confident self exercises autonomy by imitating all the other automatons, hopefully while doing or saying nothing to attract their negative attention.

The modern citizen, more and more, exists in a state of 'freedom' in which, like a bullock in a gated field, he thinks he has the run of the whole world. In reality he is penned in on all sides in his technological bubble, exploited for what labour or tithes he can contribute and what he can consume, dumbed down by a cynical education system for that express purpose and thrown scraps of diversion and provocation to keep him misdirected from the true sources of his situation. He opts out, while being convinced he is opting in, being totally engaged, contributing, influencing, making his mark. In truth he has surrendered his sovereignty in return for a relatively comfortable existence, but without true meaning or the possibility of a truly hopeful gaze on the future. It is easy to convince him to hate anyone he is told to, because he needs some target for his pent-up aggression.

In the modern world, freedom has become a double bind: the freedom afforded by technology starves the user of the satisfaction of a true freedom that flows from the capacity to make a real impression upon reality. The culture tells him that this mark of his uniqueness is vital to his continuing identity. The ideology of the technological society tells him that he was never freer, but he cannot escape the sense of limits that the technology imposes. He feels autonomous, but it is the autonomy of the automaton. The frustration arising from this paradoxical experience of freedom has him reaching, again and again, for his keyboard, laptop, smartphone, in the confused hope that he will this time break through the pattern, and in the paradoxical comfort of knowing that he will not. Its like a game of World of Warcraft: he knows he'll never beat the house but something tells him that the next time he might just do it. We are all, increasingly, in the situation of the addicted gambler standing before the machine in the small hours, determined to remain until we have lost everything.

For Jean Baudrillard, the catastrophe has already happened. We have entered a kind of paradise, or at least crossed the line into the future. Baudrillard's later work seems to balance on a thin thread between nostalgia for a lost paradise and nihilism predicated on immersion in the illusion of the simulacrum of reality he believes we now inhabit. As he grew older, his tone moved beyond didacticism and exposition to a kind of celebration of the chaos, as though certain that in comprehending it we might learn to live in it. In much the way that he describes the world as having passed a point of rupture, Baudrillard himself crosses in his work an invisible line between sociology and philosophy into art and metaphysics. His insights can sometimes seem close to impenetrable, but they are worth pursuing, if only because they sketch out the territory in which we must all henceforth consider ourselves. He takes a perverse view of human nature, deciding on something close to masochism as a remedy for man's postmodern condition. Instead of fighting the world of images and objects, we should simply embrace its rule as a quasi-metaphysical absolutism, seek out its essences and mysteries and become conversant with it. We should surrender to the object and the screen because we have no future independently of them. The eradication of the transcendent is a 'perfect crime', which imprisons us in a manufactured metaphysical world.

Where I part with Baudrillard is when he insists that reality can have no meaning and that this is something we ought to embrace, that affirming meaninglessness is actually liberating: 'If we could accept this meaninglessness of the world,' he wrote in Impossible Exchange, 'then we could play with forms, appearances and our impulses, without worrying about their ultimate destination.' Citing the Romanian philosopher Emil Cioran, he declared: '[w]e are not failures until we believe life has a meaning – and from that point on we are failures, because it hasn't.'

The problem is that it is nowhere demonstrated that human beings can survive long without meaning unless they rush for refuge to chemical assistance and soon after that towards self-destruction: first madness, then premature death. At an earlier stage of the mass media society, we identified the early stages of the present condition as ironic non-involvement, detachment, cynicism, anti-authoritarianism and ennui. These seemed like appropriate responses to a ridiculous or inhospitable reality, but that was when there were still some adults left to run things. The promulgation of cynicism about all existing sources of authority carried the implicit risk that, in creating an authority vacuum, a new kind of authority was being facilitated which, being under the radar, could acquire immunity from scrutiny or criticism. Media, especially TV, and the paymasters who called the tunes, become the new authoritarians, but invisibly, irreproachably. The corporations who paid the piper had grown wide to the idea of manipulating the ironic sensibility of the modern young rebel, to make him feel that it was on his side against the dark spectres summoned up in the technology. Meanwhile, the same corporations sold him, in the guise of emblems of his individuality, the same stuff they sold to millions of others who luxuriated in a similar sense of individualism while enjoying also the fellow-feeling that comes from belonging to a distinctive culture or tribe. TV, and later the Internet, inculcated a sense of superiority that kept the viewer/user passively spectating in a state of increasing loneliness while imagining himself one of a select and knowing crowd. These technologies soon become the chief source of his sense of worth, while actually undermining that worth by filling him with trepidation about the conditions in the world 'out there'. Ridicule became a kind of language by which to negotiate a hostile and defensive world of people just like himself. The last thing he wanted to do was betray real feelings, real concern for anything real, a craving for values, truth or meaning, naivety or vulnerability, faith or hope in the future or in the species to which he ostensibly belonged or to any notional concept of an originator who might care what happened to him. TV taught people to laugh at everything and everyone, and to hold themselves in such a way that the laughter of others didn't hurt as much as it might. The Internet enabled them to feed the same process while imagining they were answering back.

More and more, human beings took refuge in irony, which is fundamentally about ambiguity. It passes itself off as a pose, a strand of identity or a quality of character, but it's essentially a defence, an evasion or a postponement of judgment. On the credit side, irony is capable of burrowing into the layers of contradiction that comprise our cultures, allowing us pain-free means of negotiating them. At its best, irony is a guise employed by human beings in the project of negotiating culture – a way of operating without necessarily understanding fully the underfoot conditions, of dipping a toe in the pool of public attitudes and sentiments so as to test the reliability of your instincts without committing yourself.

Irony is also a kind of insulation against the self-imposed meaninglessness of a seemingly total cultural knowingness. It seeks to insert a studied indifference as a precaution against despair. But it also seeks to evade the great questions, for fear an attempt to put words on the answers might expose the raw centre of the wound of meaninglessness. Irony is a way of creating deniability. It greases the wheels of modern freedom-seeking and consumerism, protecting against the disappointment that arises as the inevitable outcome of seeking satisfaction where it's ultimately unavailable. And so everything is both serious and not, camp and real, kitsch and culture.

Irony is really a studied front to deflect the aggression of the world. Seemingly arising from a jaded knowingness, it may, on the contrary, be the product of fear and uncertainty and a desire to somehow fill in the gaps in the hypotheses the world offers. In a world that educates its young to know innumerable things without a proper map, irony becomes an increasingly necessary tool of survival. For how else might the human person deal with the confusion of having abundant information but no real knowledge of what the totality of it means or amounts to, or the means to express it if he had? In such a world, some technique of detachment is essential.

And yet, there is a sadness behind the irony, symptomatic of a kind of neurosis – a public repudiation of something that is secretly longed for, or, conversely, a pretended attraction to something that is publicly despised. This derives from a questioning of sincerity, conviction and principle generally. Irony is safe ground – where you can appear not to care what happens, and so avoid at least the outward appearance of disappointment.

Irony is ultimately the way we live lives that are unknowable as to their purpose or destination. We suspect that we are the butts of some cosmic joke but must go on anyway, having no realistic choice. To this end the functional human being acquires through irony a lightness towards reality that really doesn't touch it at all, that disregards it except for the purposes of getting by, that sees through everything and yet sees everything for its immediate usefulness. The complete human is the ironic human, because he or she accords everything just the weight it merits in the functional matter of survival – very little – knowing that the ultimate destination, or the absence of an ultimate destination, renders everything humorous.

But irony is a bad builder, a handy weapon of self-defence that was never intended to become an entire armoury of responses to the world. It denounces but does not announce. Irony is not constructive. Irony is technically not coterminous with cynicism, but increasingly, in our societies, they converge. The problem with the cynic is that he can't win – literally, he refuses to stop being on the losing side. At the slightest sign of imminent victory, he sabotages everything so he can stay in his detached comfort zone. It becomes obvious, then, that generations steeped in cynicism and irony will be pretty useless when it comes to constructing systems of government and conceiving new ways to make the world work.

Ultimately, sincerity is essential, for both the private life of the individual and the collective life of the community. You cannot, for example, run a state or society in an ironic fashion. Irony belongs to the bystander, the non-involved, the irresponsible and the apathetic. Sooner or later, everyone has to swallow the smirk and get real.

The ironic approach to reality is the most serious position you can take – provided you don't take it too far. If it is merely a pose, or a mask, it becomes useless. If you take it too seriously it becomes deadly. As C.S. Lewis says in *The Abolition of Man* of a slightly different phenomenon – 'seeing through' things: 'You can't go on "seeing through" things for ever. The whole point of seeing through something is to see something through it. It is good that the window should be transparent, because the street or garden beyond it is opaque. How if you saw through the garden too? It's no good trying to "see through" first principles. If you see through everything, then everything is transparent. But a wholly transparent world is an invisible world. To "see through" all things is the same as not to see.'

While he wrote, the American playwright Arthur Miller always had a card in front of him with a single word on it: forgo. It was a reminder to him that he should not arrive at a resolution too soon, that as much as possible he ought to postpone the moment of revelation or climax so as to keep the audience interested. In a way we're all like that now. It's the way we live, holding in abeyance any thought of an idea of what our lives might signify, or where their drift is leading us. It's one of the core symptoms of a world without meaning, a world in which there is no possibility of agreement upon where reality resides. The problem of existence is postponed beyond today, beyond the hour and the moment, always moving ahead like a carrot hanging on stick from a donkey's bridle.

It's a trick that takes some time to develop. First you have to learn about the proffered or constructed meanings of things, and then you have to allow these meanings to dissolve in you, to become ironic or purely functional or both. Our educational systems used to be good at the former; now they pretend to still be about the former while becoming increasingly adept at the latter. Even the churches have lost faith in themselves, and so preach with a postmodern twist that allows a free pass from tradition under headings of 'mercy' and 'compassion'. This seems to imply not so much that the rules don't matter (a minor, collateral aspect), but that the whole thing may be made up.

It is possible, dimly, to conceive of a world, perhaps a future world, in which the human being might slide from the beginning into a state of indifference to meaning, to see life in this world as a kind of holiday from nothingness. In such a world there would be no need for churches, and schools would exist primarily to teach people why they ought not to kill themselves straightaway. But for the moment this is neither feasible nor imaginable, so we need to learn a version of the world that we will later grow to become ironic about. One of the consequences of this is that we inhabit a species, a structure, a consciousness that is not (yet?) able to bear the thought of life without meaning. Some of us may claim to do so already, but this is almost always a badge of defiance. The trick of 'forgoing' is essential to survival in a world like this, in which meaning is evaporating but in which we have not yet learned how to walk upright without something to look towards. This may come, or it may not. It may be possible, or it may not.

We do not speak of these wonders, only of their symptoms. We speak of technology and use it to gossip, but we do not gossip about the shift in human culture and nature that it implies. While we are waiting for such a world to evolve, we distract ourselves from the absence that has actually already arrived – the absence of meaning, that is. In a sense, we are already in the state of 'holidaying from nothing'. And, of course, it is not 'we' who conduct the distracting of ourselves – this is done by a cadre of operatives who belong to our number and yet do not. They are the entertainers, the celebrities, the actors, the artists, the writers, the journalists, the TV personalities who fill our consciousnesses with things that leave no place for thought, because thought must ultimately lead to

< 378 >

despair. These are the holiday camp 'redcoats', who prepare and present the entertainments that deflect people from the absence of anything remotely identifiable as reality. Put another way, the only way for the consumer society to protect itself from its own ultimate logical destination is to create 24/7 diversion and distraction aimed at arresting thought at the moment of conception. There are those for whom these precautions are ineffective, who are unable to keep their eyes off the absence in the sky, the hole in the future, where meaning used to be. These casualties suffer from what is called 'depression' and are treated as malfunctioning.

The logic of your time, the now barely remembered past, is no longer relevant to us. It is important to state this, and other such observations, with as little judgementalism as we can muster, lest we short-circuit into moralism or are accused of courting nostalgia. Of course, we still speak, more or less, as though nothing has changed. This is the most spectacular element: that even though nothing is in the slightest as it was not long ago, that even though we have experienced a rupture of culture possibly without parallel in human history, we continue to speak as though we had travelled through a continuum of time. In fact, even more so: our language becomes more and more clichéd with moralism and sentimentality and positivism. We imagine, for example, that we can understand the totality of a person through access to one detail of his outlook. We reduce all possibilities to two and set them in conflict: future and past, progress and tradition, good and evil. Everything becomes binary, as though in imitation of the foundational logic of the technology. But the world is utterly different and the beings inhabiting it – the human ones at least – are unlike anything that you, after just three decades of absence, would be able to recognise.

If you ask me to identify the moment at which this rupture occurred, I would point my finger somewhere between 2004 and 2008. Don't ask me exactly why: the usual explanations – Celtic Tiger, pervert priests, Internet, cappuccinos. Symptoms all, of course, but indicative all the same.

I have described what has been happening in terms I thought you would at least be able, approximately, to follow. In doing so, I have flirt-ed with moralism, nostalgia, sentimentality and traditionalism. So be it. Now I come to the sting: It is all irrelevant. The world we are moving into now, the one that Róisín will inhabit as an adult, would be unrecog-nisable to you and will most likely become unrecognisable to me if I live another 20 years. I do not say it will be a 'worse' world than the one that is evaporating, any more than I would say that it will be better. Better and worse are not appropriate concepts, because they imply a meaning that, as we have noted, no longer exists.

The events I have described belong to this world rather than the one that was yours. If you think they make nonsense of everything you be-lieved and worked for, then I suspect you are beginning to get the pic-ture. If you think they promise a world going to hell in a handcart, I confess to forebodings along those lines of my own. But there is no other world now, and no other world is either conceivable or achievable. You wouldn't be able to live in a world like this. I am – just about and for now. I have tools adapted to both worlds. I understand the language of both and am able to lapse into either tongue at will.

You might say that such a society has no future and you would be right – by definition. No future is precisely what it has. It has only the ideology of progress, which carries it along in a kind of continuous present. A future is something that lies ahead, and the citizens of this world can no longer look too far ahead for fear of looking at the hole in the sky, which they now fear more than looking at the sun, or even the hole that used to be in the ozone layer.

Notwithstanding our fashionable ideologies and deadpan nihilisms, we are primed to believe in the essential need for meaning. Even when we do not acknowledge the need for meaning, this remains true. Even when meaning is absent and is not lamented, this remains true. It ceases to be true only when the absence of meaning is acknowledged as a straight-forward fact of life, which may not even be possible for a whole culture to achieve for more than an instant before disintegrating. We have been

< 380 >

primed to look for meanings in everything: history, stories, the hopes of our children. The absence of meaning is unbearable for us, though this does not mean that it is definitively unbearable in the context of the human condition. The jury will remain out on that question for a long time, and will be sent to a hotel for the long weekend of the present possibly transitional century before the ghost of Friedrich Nietzsche comes knocking on its door to say the judge is impatient for an answer.

This is the true explanation for what I have been calling the madness. Forget progress. Forget equality. Forget all you may have picked up about a craving for justice. Forget even cultural Marxism. The reason these things are happening is because they are ultimately all part of the distraction apparatus. So I suppose the more we are in need of distraction, the worse things will get. The young of today need – far more than even we did, and certainly far more than you did – to latch on to things that fill the spaces in them that open up as a phantom projection of the hole in the future. This is why they crave values that ignore the structure of values they have inherited, follow pied pipers who have neither maps nor direction and latch on to progress projects even though there doesn't appear to be any place to go to. And Ireland is no longer merely the passive victim of such developments. Because of our association with tech and social media companies, we are (again) both hare and hound in the new colonialism. A culture that can claim to have constructed the foundations of modern civilisation through the contribution of the monks and scholars of ancient Ireland is now to the fore in its demolition.

It goes without saying that there is no possibility of rehabilitating elements of the old world and its thinking and using them to restore order. The best we could hope for is to try to understand anew the essential make-up of the old order and its relationship with the reality of its time, extract the most fundamental lessons from this and apply these, in essential form, to the conditions we now find ourselves in. I'm thinking here of Matthew Crawford's encapsulation of the losses incurred as a result of no longer working with our hands: what might this mean in a world without meaningful work of any kind for human beings? Perhaps we need to construct some metaphysical equivalent of the gym, which evolved to supply a new set of machines to work the human body that had grown obsolete and feeble as a result of its activities being usurped by an earlier generation of machines. This analogy has its difficulties, not least the problem that we now appear to be reaching the end of the gym explosion, at which human beings will tumble to the understanding that they cannot replace with calculated exercise and measured exertions the spontaneous interaction of a human body with reality. Why? Because the process is necessarily too self-conscious, and therefore draws attention to the body itself rather than the activity that once had the effect of body-building as a collateral consequence of its primary purpose. Hence, obesity, anorexia, bulimia, OCD, gym addiction. The same principle will undoubtedly apply to any application of Crawford's thesis to the dissociated mind of man. A mind developed for itself, rather than through the action of healthy curiosity, will tend also to forms of obesity and bulimia: heads stuffed to the gills with nonsense and starved of truths. There is no substitute for the innocence of the past, except the past, and the past has no future now that it has been tried, convicted and is awaiting a mandatory sentence of death.

< 382 >

32

Cloud Cuckoo Land

On 11 May 2015, a Monday evening, 11 days before polling day, I was scheduled to launch a magazine for the transition year students in a school down near home. I'd been doing these kinds of events for many years, always pro bono and with a heart and a half. I remember when I was in school myself, dreaming of being a writer or a journalist and longing for someone to come in and tell me how it worked, what I needed to do to begin the journey. That afternoon, though, my car broke down within an hour of my destination, so, in the tow-truck to the garage, I called the school principal to see if someone might collect me. She was relieved to hear that I was close at hand and immediately dispatched a posse to fetch me. Then she told me something else – it was only fair to warn me: that morning, she had received some calls from activists on the Yes side in the same-sex marriage referendum asking her why the hell I was being allowed to speak in the school. Did she not know that I was opposed to the amendment? The principal told the callers in turn that I had been invited as a journalist to speak at the launch of a school magazine. It was a private gathering and had nothing to do with the referendum. Unappeased, the callers intimated that they might have something to say if the event went ahead. The principal told me that she was determined not to be intimidated, had already been in touch with the Guards and would call them if any attempt was made to disrupt the launch. It briefly occurred to me that, since elements of An Garda Síochána had already declared their support for the Yes side, this might not necessarily be the best advised option. As the event kicked off at 7.30, I scanned the audience for the familiar hate-filled faces I had learned to spot over the previous year or so. I saw none and proceeded to give my talk and reading as arranged.

The event passed off peacefully. Afterwards, discussing with the principal what had occurred, she pleaded with me not to mention the name of the school in anything I might write about it.

The stories I came across during the campaign of intimidation and hate-mongering were for me unprecedented in over 30 years of writing about politics and another 10 to 20 poring over every detail of the public life of Ireland. I met people whose children begged them not to let anyone know they were thinking of voting against the amendment, lest they, the children, be ostracised by their classmates. I met gay people who had been targeted and abused because they had chosen to speak in favour of the status quo. There were countless other examples of illegality and blackguardism: the widespread tearing down of No posters; a gloating ISIS-style YouTube video posted by the perpetrators, boasting of same; the intimidation of a hotel in Galway to the extent that it cancelled an anti-amendment meeting under assault from Yes campaigners.

The amendment had been sold through bullying, moral blackmail, scapegoating, the twisting of meanings and misuse of words. The most degraded word of all was 'equality'. The Irish Constitution already provided that all citizens should be deemed equal before the law, but also allowed for differences of capacity and function, which were axiomatically germane to the question of fairness. Is a bus equal to a train? Is an apple equal to a banana? Are two men capable of being defined as 'equal' to a man and woman with children under the same family provisions of the Constitution? Page 194 of the report of the 1996 Constitutional Review Group gives a definition of equality that touches on the issue of how the concept can be mangled into its opposite. It acknowledges that 'equality', properly understood, 'endorses the recognition of pertinent differences and requires that persons be treated differently to the extent that there is a relevant difference between them'. This passage exposes the central lie of the 'Marriage Equality' referendum, a trumped-up 'rights' issue with no basis in human nature or reason. In this unprecedented assault on the public consciousness, 'equality' was employed as a blackmail word – and

< 384 >

with extreme prejudice and venom, in order to force changes on people that would inevitably result in the siphoning off of many of both their own rights and the legitimate rights inheritance of their children.

Afterwards, there were attempts by Yes, Equality campaigners to re-write history and claim that the debate had been civil and fair. It was anything but. I would say that, even if you leave out the appalling events of 2014, the 'debate' was almost entirely one-sided, ugly, and complete-ly rigged in favour of the Yes side. A few months before the referen-dum, a journalist with *The Guardian* asked me for an interview about my positions on the issues involved. I told him that the lobby behind the amendment was the ugliest and most venomous mob to descend on Irish public life since Independence. 'They make the Blueshirts look like a boyband,' I said. Strangely, or perhaps not, that highly quotable quote didn't see the light of day in an article that went big on the victimology of the LGBTers.

For months on end, and right through until polling day, newspapers carried pro-amendment material at a rate of two to three times their coverage of the other side of the argument. This was blatant and un-apologetic. In the broadcast media, which were bound by requirements for balance during the campaign proper, No campaigners were treated in the manner of chewed mice that the cat had dragged in and deposited on the living room carpet. For the final couple of weeks, the measure of 'balance' required of broadcasters was delivered – to the extent that it was – reluctantly and with ill grace. Virtually every debate I participated in exhibited the same characteristics: a presenter whose sympathies were clearly with the Yes side, who interrogated or twisted every point the No campaigners made while gently nudging the Yes activists to make sure they made the best of their airtime. Some broadcasters were actually actively campaigning for the amendment, one day taking part in debates and appearing on pro-amendment platforms all over the country, the next chairing debates between other protagonists with a feigned and al-most sardonic neutrality. At least you could, in a sense, call this honest,

< 385 >

unlike the sneaky obstructionism offered by other ostensibly objective chairpersons. In one debate in which I participated, the four panellists on either side were to be allowed to make opening statements – Yes, No, Yes, No and so on. When it came to my turn, the presenter, instead of calling on me – the sole No speaker who had yet to contribute – allowed a Yes campaigner who had already spoken to come in and make another point, which the presenter then put to me. Thus, I had to abandon my opening position and instead bat on the other side's agenda. When I made a quizzical gesture in his direction, the presenter smirked back. This kind of ankle-tapping by the supposed referees was common practice through the two to three final weeks of the alleged 'debate'. Other so-called journalist/presenters sought to derail any argument I sought to make about parenthood by asking me moronic questions like: 'So this is all about fathers' rights, is it?', seeking to tap into a prejudice already planted by years of journalistic sneering.

Constructed confusion had been an integral component of this campaign from the start. The LGBT lobby deliberately set out to put people at sea so that would be easy meat for emotive arguments and moral bullying. Prolonged use of advanced propaganda techniques had cast the electorate under a spell of sophistry and emotive misdirection. Every time you opened your mouth to dissent, you were in effect playing into their hands by acting out the role they had allotted you.

The climate of intimidation to which those objecting to the amendment were subjected was, in my experience, unprecedented. Everywhere I went, I was set upon by groups of LGBT activists, barracking, harassing and bullying. Most of these, it turned out, knew almost nothing about the Constitution, or even about details of the proposal being made to change it – they just wished to intimidate anyone who might be even thinking of opposing any detail of their demands.

We in First Families First had had no call for funding, but that was just as well, since the few people who came to us offering donations were mostly concerned to ensure that there was no possibility of their gesture being made public. Although the legal position was that donors up to a certain limit were entitled to privacy, in all cases we thanked them and politely declined their offers, since, due to the widespread corruption of public entities, it was no longer possible to guarantee that the law would be either obeyed or enforced.

These were the bared fangs of a new dystopia. Its logic – and what it portended – had been creeping up on us, in all the talk about 'new rights', 'new family types', 'children's rights' and the blank refusal of liberal intellectual establishments to answer questions about the selectivity of their agendas – why, for example, they were interested in gay marriage and gay adoption, but not in the rights of natural parents. This was Ireland 2015 – a very different Ireland from the one I grew up in, an Ireland where bullies held sway, where reason was alien, where the truth rolled itself into the foetal position against the all-pervasive climate of hatred, demonisation and lies.

What I had experienced and observed in the 16 months prior to the vote of May 2015 had chilled me to the marrow, and alerted me to the fragility of our democracy. In effect, a baying mob had acquired the free run of Irish society's media apparatus. The drag queen who had baselessly demonised me had, more or less as a result, become a national celebrity, himself given the run of the so-called 'National Theatre' and of radio and TV chat shows coast to coast. In due course he would be given an honorary degree by Trinity College.

It was clear that our deeply corrupted media had in turn achieved the almost total debasement of our public culture. I mean 'corrupted' in two senses: degraded, firstly, by ideology, agenda-setting and a mixture of hostility and condescension towards the greater part of its potential audience; secondly, corrupted by money, since the 'Yes, Equality' campaign had access to virtually unlimited funding, most of it provided by an American-based 'philanthropic' organisation, and it was clear that those who pulled the strings in many media organisations had decided, quite cynically, to exploit the financial possibilities of the gay marriage issue at the expense of truth or fairness. The business of media had clearly

< 387 >

ceased to have anything to do with informing and educating, and was now directed at bullying, lecturing and converting listeners and viewers to a more 'enlightened' way of seeing the world.

Towards the end of the campaign, I met an elderly man who declared that, in imposing the referendum on Ireland, the Taoiseach, Enda Kenny, had provoked in Irish society a 'mental civil war', which he believed could have ramifications in their way comparable to the civil war that occurred 93 years earlier. He was right. This had been the most comprehensive betrayal of democratic principles by a political establishment in living memory. And it was not that most politicians actually cared one whit about either rights or gays – they have simply either caved in to the bullying of the gay lobby and the transnational industrial giants who mainly supported them, or were playing to a deluded sense of the 'cool' vote, perhaps imagining that they'd be safely over the line to their pensions before the chickens came home to roost. And, like the politicians, many citizens appeared to be willing to let others do their thinking for them, deciding the issue on the basis that the outcome was unlikely to have any negative effect on themselves. 'Live and let live,' one man said to me in the street and walked away when I tried to engage him in a deeper exchange. For the first time in Irish political life, we were witnessing a kind of anti-citizenship, in which the civic impulse of the citizen, under pressure of intimidation and mendacity, tended increasingly towards outright privatisation.

I noticed that, in the run-up to the vote, many people I met were both confused and certain at the same time. Many clearly did not know what they'd be voting Yes to – only that if they voted No they were exposing themselves as 'homophobes'. Others, especially young people, wanting to be seen as enlightened and compassionate, to enjoy the buzz of being part of a movement rooted in solidarity and what felt like idealism, and were easily persuaded to sign up.

For several months in the run-up to the referendum, the public was pummelled with non-stop propaganda, including the persistent insinuation that biology was a random or inconsequential aspect of parenthood.

< 388 >

Politicians, commentators and so-called experts repeatedly explained that what matters in child-rearing is solely the quality of the 'love' on offer. The public was subjected to a public conversation in which it was seemingly reasonable for people to be asking each other things that in a million years nobody ever imagined they'd hear anyone asking – like, 'Does a child really need his father and his mother?' Suddenly, it was as if nature had been abolished. 'We have to move beyond,' they told us, 'this obsession with biological parenthood'.

An article headed 'Does it matter to a child who their "real" parents are?', published in *The Irish Independent* on 10 March 2015, was typical of this tendency. The clinical psychologist, author and self-described 'television personality', Dr David Coleman, questioned the importance of biological parenthood in the development of a child. In support of his thesis, he cited the fact that children of the same parents who grow up in the same house and go to the same school 'still grow up to be different'. This, as far as can be divined, means that the fact that a man grows up to be distinguishable from his brothers and sisters means his parents are to be regarded as interchangeable with others adults. This about sums the whole thing up.

I had come to recognise such formulations as codes for something ominous: the redefinition of parenthood so that it becomes a function occurring by state appointment. As a parent, a citizen and – actually – a human rights activist of many years, I was determined to resist this idea with every fibre of my being. I had yet to obtain a convincing justification from self-styled liberals as to why they were happy to champion the rights of gays to adopt children, but had said nothing at all about the failure to provide any form of rights to children and fathers unprotected by a marriage contract. But, far more worrying, I believed, were the implications arising from the context of 'equality' which would attend the new constitutional concept of gay marriage, which I believed, and still believe, might yet bear out the fears of those gay people who feared the proposed changes might one day lead to a backlash.

Most people hadn't delved into the issues but were still going to vote Yes 'for love' or 'for equality'. These were the classic symptoms of a propagandised society, its head clotted with clichés that kept all thought at bay. People went into a kind of tizzy of irritation and hostility if you prodded them with questions: Where did this come from? What is it about? Why is it happening now? How did a tiny minority of a tiny minority manage to impose its will on the entire political establishment, when most causes have difficulty getting as much as a Dáil question? Why are we being required to accept things nobody even mentioned until three or four years ago, and treat as suddenly controversial things that always seemed obvious? Few wanted to explore such conundrums because the implications were too ominous. Better to stay in the emotional zone, where a 'Yes Equality' badge was an emblem of moral integrity and love conquered all.

This was Cloud Cuckoo Land. Far from becoming more 'progressive', Ireland was being driven backwards along the corridor it had tentatively and awkwardly negotiated over the previous half century. The core impulses and values of the Ireland that had survived past tyrannies were being trampled underfoot by a new one.

The Yes vote of 22 May 2015, giving an apparently democratic imprimatur to all of this, amounted to the drawing of a crude line across the path of human journeying in Ireland. Beyond this line, some of the most fundamental things we had so long taken for granted would no longer have any meaning. That Yes went much further than the redefinition of marriage or the demolition of normative family protections. It was also a green light to any group of bullyboys in Irish society with an agenda to peddle. Here, now, they had a blueprint to follow: threaten, demonise, intimidate, smear – and you will get your way because most people will fear to stand up and be counted. In effect, that Yes amounted to leaving the keys of our democracy lying around for any group of extremists to pick up and take what they pleased. My fear in this regard were borne out three years later, on 25 May 2018, when what was essentially the same mob of agitators applied that successful blueprint to eviscerating the rights of the most defenceless of human creatures, the child in his mother's womb.

The issues for Irish society raised by the saga that began with a drag queen know-nothing on *The Saturday Night Show* were in themselves considerable and equally disquieting. For one thing, they revealed that the media platforms operating at a national level – and most of those operating regionally – were wholly inadequate to the requirements of a modern democracy, being largely operated by activists disguised as journalists who had more or less identical outlooks across a wide range of the issues having implications for society and human beings. From the potential consequences of this could not be excluded the possibility of an imminent climate of prohibition of certain forms of thought and speech, a reign of intolerance towards those who dissented from the prevailing consensus, the censoring of unapproved opinions, attacks on Christians and other believers, an Orwellian revisionism directed at texts and memories that might bear witness to the old dispensation, the extinguishing of questions directed at a rethink of the direction we were taking, and so on and so on. This is not 'scare-mongering' – that trivialising and patronising term so beloved of politicians seeking to avoid giving answers or discussing actually existing problems – it is pure prophecy.

For more than a year afterwards, I continued to attract abuse and taunting in public. Sitting in a café, minding my own business, walking down the street, I seemed to offer an irresistible target for some hero to have a go at.

One evening around the middle of November 2015, six months after the same-sex marriage referendum, I was in the Starbucks on Dublin's Dawson Street with Róisín, having a cup of tea and a chat. We would meet there sometimes when I would pick her up after her lectures in Trinity – one of those great moments of joyousness for me when I have occasion to reflect on how miraculous is my life to take me to moments I once might have thought unattainable. We were talking about Cartesianism: I remember that. One of the challenges of having a smart child is that you have constantly to up your game; one of the benefits of no longer being a journalist is that there is no necessity to allow my brain to remain clogged with cliché. We were continuing our conversation as we made to go, I on the left, Róisín on the right as we made for the door, walking slowly and stopping every few steps to face one another in order to state or catch something. I no more than barely noticed the three young people sitting at a table on the right-hand side: two of them, a male and a female, sitting with their backs to the wall; a third, male, with his back to us. This guy was in his early 20s, with curly, sandy hair and the red face of a budding dipso. As we came abreast of their table, he suddenly swivelled round in his chair and, looking me straight in the eye, put the forefinger and middle digit of his right hand to his temple, mimicking a revolver, and went 'Phuuucchhhhh'. His message seemed clear enough: either I needed to shoot myself or someone else should do it. I can't think of any further variations of possibility.

I took this in without really fixing my gaze on him. I'd grown used to being accosted by the neurotics, nasties and smartarses who seem nowadays to proliferate around Dublin and who appear to think that they have a duty to accost someone like me who says things they have disagreed with. Or, rather – most of the time – someone who they have heard may have said such things, since none of them is ever able to back up his rantings with either evidence or argument. I have therefore developed a technique of 'looking through' such people, as though I am lost in thought and therefore unaware of their presence in front of me. Whether as a result of this non-reaction or otherwise, the red-faced young man rapidly whirled back to the way he had been, and with a hint of what could even have been embarrassment, continued his conversation with his friends. Neither of the others reacted in any way to what had occurred, and I noted no sign that either had even been aware of what was going down.

Róisín and I continued towards and through the front door, without any break in our conversation. I wasn't really bothered; my main concern was in case Róisín had seen what had happened and been fazed by it. She hadn't, and wasn't, as she had been turned to face me at the moment our hero made his move. When I described the incident to her as I had observed it, she merely grimaced: we had by now become used to such capers. As a child, she had solemnly explained to a teacher that her Daddy 'argues for a living'.

The weird thing is that, as far as I've been able to divine, Róisín most likely voted Yes in the referendum. I've never asked her, nor do I regard it as in the slightest degree relevant to our relationship. My sense is that, even though she disagrees with my position on this matter, she is pretty appalled by what occurred in the course of the 'debate'. Unlike most of her contemporaries, and more than a few of her elders, she gets the idea that democracy can only work if there remains a capacity to express differing perspectives in public.

But I know this too: If I were to be seen making to a stranger a gesture anything like the one this young warrior made in my face, there is a high probability that it would be regarded as a police matter. I could certainly see the point: In these generally menacing times, to make a gesture aping summary execution in the face of someone you have no reason to share a sense of humour with might well be thought to take you into the realm of threatening gestures. Were I to do the same thing in the face of, say, a gay person, the chances are that, within an hour or so, there would be an account, possibly with pictures, going viral online. But I've got to 'suck it up', because that's the way things are now. Were I to make anything of it, the Garda officer to whom I might make a complaint would most likely look at me patronisingly and ask if I had said or done anything to merit such a response. If the media happened to get hold of it, they would turn it into a joke. Outrages are perpetrated against one side only; everything else is a storm in a teacup. I don't lose any sleep about what gobshites might say or act out in front of me. If I did, there are enough of them walking around Dublin these days to keep me awake for the rest of my life. Nevertheless, if the term 'hate-mongering' has any meaning at all, the red-faced young man's gesture has to qualify. Indeed, it conveyed not merely hatred but also the possibility of violent – no, lethal – intervention to silence someone who says things the red-faced mime artist does not agree with.

Ireland used not to be like this. I cannot imagine such a thing happening 20 or perhaps even 10 years ago. Of course, it's possible that such a gesture might still be made, half in jest, in a public house in the late evening, when the 'crack' is edging up beyond the 80 mark. I'd be the first to acknowledge that such a manoeuvre as was executed by the red-faced hero in Starbucks might well have a different meaning in such a context. But to make such a gesture in a café frequented by the general public, in the face of a man walking along with his teenage daughter – that seems to me to be something new and unhealthy.

If I wished to be kind, I would describe this incident as an example of the importation into reality of the culture of cyberspace. For a moment, the young man forgot that he and I were both physically present. He made his gesture almost in the way that he might press a 'dislike' button on an online platform, and then, catching himself as actually present, staring his quarry in the face, retreated into something I would describe as a kind of virtual embarrassment at the emotional shock of having done in real life the kind of thing he does all the time online. I don't say that his capacity for empathy suddenly returned – rather, it was as though he suddenly awoke from a happy dream and realised from the faces of people around him that he had been talking, acting out, in his sleep.

In spite of these episodes, and the possibility that they may well continue for as long as I live, I remain glad that I participated in the campaign, if only to be able afterwards to say that I had spoken out and left behind a record of my fears. And, for the same reasons, I took to the trail again in the referendum on Article 40.3.3 in the horrendous spring of 2018.

I regret nothing of this. Over the previous 10 to 20 years, there have been a number of moments in Irish life when we confronted revelations concerning certain events of the past – institutional abuse, clerical sex abuse, banking madness – and asked in incredulity: why did nobody speak out? Did nobody see this disaster coming? Why did nobody blow the whistle? This time at least a record of dissent would remain. Those who promoted and supported these measures, calculated to tear, firstly, the heart out of the normative family, and then the fledgling child from his mother's womb, would not be able to escape the judgment of history. And, in these cases at least, nobody would be able to say that no whistles were blown.

33

Driftwood

I am sitting here in my house in Lislary, one of your great gifts to me. As I don't need to tell you, it was never your house, but I think of it as ours. The old house fell in and drifted out of the clan. A long story, hardly worth telling. The point is that I bought this place as a replacement. I think of you every time I open the front door from the inside. I think of you looking out, on rain or shine or fog or snow. I cannot describe the exhilaration I feel to be here, as though on the final stages of a journey (it does not escape my notice that I am to be the last male Waters from our line of the clan). As I write, in mid-September, the sun is shining, one of those bonus summer days that we seem to be able to rely on more than on the summer itself. I've just been out picking blackberries, and will make some more jam later on. There are lorries from the county council along the road, preparing to tar it. I talk to one of the drivers and point out to him that, if they tar the road the way it is, it'll be washed away by Christmas because of what seems to be an overflowing spring in a field up the hill. He says I should talk to someone in the roads department and gives me a name –'But don't say you were talking to the lorry driver'.

I spend 20 minutes trying to get through to the roads department. No answer at all from the county council offices. I leave it for 20 minutes and try again. This time the phone is answered: tea break over. I ask for the name I got from the lorry driver and get through to a guarded man who sounds like he's only picked up the phone because there's no one else in the vicinity and now wishes he hasn't. I say that I see council lorries out fixing the road, but that there's no point unless they stop the flow out of the field up the hill, from which the water has been flooding out the gap for three winters now, coursing down the hill, cutting a French drain into the side of the road. I tell him I've rung several times already (true) and spoken to various people whose names I can't recall. I tell him that they will need to locate a culvert under the road – they appear to exist at regular intervals along it but have become blocked or overgrown over the years. He hmmms and haws, probably thinking: 'Why didn't I just let it ring?' Then he says: 'I think I might have been talking to you before.' Probably, I say. I had to spend a small fortune a year back clearing out a culvert on the road outside my garden to stop the water flooding the septic tank and making it useless. Because the main house is rented to local authority tenants, it's subject to an inspection by the council, which withheld my certificate of approval, or whatever they call it, because of the problem with the septic tank. When told the problem was essentially their responsibility, the council issued the clearance but did nothing about the water. Although I'd rung the roads department several times, nothing has been done to address the problem. This time, the man on the other end of the line gives me the name of the foreman, and seems almost as surprised as he seems relieved that I take the bait and leave him in peace.

I've left the door open, to hear the noises of the lorries and diggers and the shouts of the workmen. I think I am you in these moments, in a different, parallel time. You are still here – I mean in Sligo. You never left. There are few moments in the rewind of my life that I look back on and find an equal degree of peace or pleasure in as I find here in moments like this. Later, I might go to Drumcliffe and maybe buy some scones for the morning. Later on I might go to the beach to get some kindlin', although I think I've more or less exhausted things there for the moment. But you never know, and in many ways I'd value the walk even more without having to look out for sticks and stakes. I'll carry the bag as a prop but give myself the day off from beachcombing.

I had another chat with some of the men working on the road. They were aware of the water problem but I don't think they were planning any urgent action. They made some placatory noises in my direction, but I won't be holding my breath. They'll be coming back, they said, to do

< 397 >

in front of the houses, so they'll have a look for the culvert then. Yeah, right, said I. Actually, they've scooped out a makeshift drain right down to the corner of our garden, which means the water will get there much faster than it did before, which I think is probably bad news for us.

I've loved the smell of freshly spread tar from when I was a child. Watching the men tar the roadway on Main Street was a source of unexpected fascination: the way they firstly broke up the old tar, then covered the road with chippings. After that, the tar lorry would come along and pour the tar in an even layer across first one half of the road and then the other. Then they put on more chippings, left it to settle for an hour or two and finished it off with the steamroller. But the thing I remember most vividly is the smell of the tar mixed with the smell of strong, sugary tea, which the men would make in billycans on a big primus stove. Then they would eat their sandwiches made of pristine sliced pan, which they would grab sacrilegiously with their blackened hands and swallow hungrily, tar and all. The paradoxical nature of the smells made it unforgettable for me, and I credit it still with my liking for strong tea.

Some people I know have a thing about country roads: they prefer then with a strip of grass growing up the middle. This type generally comes from the city, where a grass strip in the middle of the road is a rare enough sight. Our road was like that until yesterday, but it never meant much to me. I prefer a newly done road with an even camber, offering minimal threat to exhausts. It's funny how those who demand modernity in all things up beside themselves tend to want things to be old-fashioned in the distant places to which they travel purely for recreation. It's a bit like the way Aunt Nora(h) long ago was put out because she couldn't have the indoor rest room as well as the thatched roof, the fitted kitchen along with the kitsch.

I have a wood-burning stove in Lislary, which has changed my life. Actually, it burns both wood and turf, and also, I suppose, coal, though I experimented but briefly with this possibility, fearing that the intensity of the heat from the coal might crack the metal or break the glass of the stove. I don't like coal anyway: it's too easy, like shooting fish in a barrel.

All you have to do is pull into the garage or fuel store, load up two or three bags and take them home.

I've taken to collecting kindlin' on the beach at Lislary. I don't entirely understand what it's all about, but it feels pretty fundamental. I go there every day if it's reasonably dry, and never come home empty-handed. When the weather is rough or the tides high, I take a big plastic bag and a small woodsaw. Sometimes I fill the bag to the point where I'm barely able to put it on my back. In calmer times, I bring a short piece of rope tied around my waist, and bind together whatever bits I find and throw them over my shoulder, carrying whatever big stuff I find in my spare hand to cut up when I get home.

I leave little or nothing behind, taking little twigs, fence posts, planks, branches, briars, boxwood, bits of furniture, handles of brushes or spades, even sometimes dried seaweed. With the bigger stuff, if I have the saw with me, I cut it up on the spot and take it home in the bag. I have a supply of netted bags back at the house in which I store the kindlin' so that it dries in the shed. My favourite kindlin' is the small dry pieces of timber, white as bones, moulded by the sea from months or years of swishing about. I've often noticed that they seem to lie around in twos, like nurses at a dance years ago, waiting to be picked up. With a handful of these and a wad of paper, you can light a fire with a single match and no recourse to chemical assistance. Rita thinks this kindlin' thing is some kind of addiction, and I'm not sure I disagree: an addiction, perhaps, to the idea of a frontiersmanship that, being impossible in a modern technocratic society, exists as a deep craving in the male spirit.

I've fallen in love with the word 'kindlin'' too, with its irony and warmth. It's become the name of something that amounts to more than a useful commodity or resource. For me, the kindlin' patrol on the beach is actually not just a thing I do but a way of being in the world while I am doing it that is quite different from other things I get up to. It has something to do with throwing yourself at the mercy of the elements – heading out in hope rather than confidence, which seems to act as a kind of antidote to the consumerist sense of entitlement that takes all the fizz out of everything. If I go to a certain garage, there's a high probability that they'll have logs, but when I head to the beach I have no idea what I will find. Some days I have to stash some of the driftwood away to pick it up later; on others I can carry my spoils in one hand. There's something about this process that I need, that satisfies me, that connects me to – I don't know what: Ancestry? History? Nature? Providence? It's the unpredictability of it, I think, that hooks me in, the fact that I set out each time with no sense of expectation, and then find myself either struggling to fill my most modest quota or stumbling upon treasures beyond my wildest imaginings. The other day I found a massive hunk of timber that will just about fit into the stove. I had a suspicion it was part of the prow of a ship or something and was keeping it for some day in the depths of winter when I planned to build a fire around it and stay by the stove all day, maybe even Christmas Day, in honour of the fact that it was the size of a medium-sized turkey. Then I came across a newspaper report about pieces of the Armada wrecks which have been lying off the coast near Streedagh for the past 430 years, so I thought that maybe I'll leave the timber aside until I get to talk to someone about it.

This kindlin' obsession may go back, yet again, to the Swiss Family Robinson, those tales of small victories over the elements. Or it might be to do with the elemental nature of fire itself, the satisfaction of supplying an appetite that is not mine but which warms me and mine. Perhaps it's the idea that, when you take the kindlin' pickings home, you're only at the start of a much deeper process of meditation that is a hard-wired inheritance from the mountainy men we come from. Or maybe, because of this mysterious connection or memory, when I'm stalking up the road with a bundle of sticks on my back I'm in a similar state to the way I once was as a young man, heading to the pub along Merrion Row on a Friday evening, skipping towards the buzz that lies ahead.

I have invented a way of building a fire that allows it to last for three or four hours. I had noticed that, when I left the doors of the stove open,

< 400 >

which I liked to do, it was eating up the fuel, necessitating constant trips between the fire and the fuel basket by the front door. By putting a single large log at the centre, and enabling the fire to lap around it, I can make a fire that lasts half the day. The only one alive I bow to when it comes to lighting fires is your granddaughter Róisín, who learned from watching Mammy, her Nana, when we came for the weekend to the Grey Castle when she was a tiny girl.

The workmen made such a racket all day that, when I passed the house down towards the beach with the mad dog he didn't bark at all. He was probably exhausted barking at diggers and lorries and steamrollers since he woke up. Before, on the smoother tar between the central grass strip and the ditch, I used to tiptoe past the house, never fully trusting the fence and the hedge to keep him in. I had visions that one day he would slip out through a gap and savage me. Now, since I can't avoid making a noise on the new, stony surface, I've discovered that it was probably my surreptitious approach that set him barking. When I walk naturally and loudly he doesn't bother his head.

Naturally, without my kindlin' bag, I found no end of driftwood on the beach, but I gathered up as much as I could and brought it under my arm. Then I found an old rope and tied it together and flung it over my shoulder. I think I'm turning into one of your brothers, and you know which one: the one who stayed home. I have just a couple of pictures of James Patrick, which were taken in Mount Edward not long before he died. In one of them you can just see his silhouette in a poor light, probably dusk, scooting across the garden, like a small animal, his body bent towards the ground, picking up sticks. He has an unkempt grey beard and a cap, a long overcoat and wellingtons. In the other photo he's with another man, probably 20 years younger but still old looking, who is also wearing a cap but more respectably, and a Columbo-style raincoat, like it's Sunday and he's coming from Mass. He and James Patrick are caught in some strange and ambiguous movement, like they're conceiving or rehearsing a dance of some kind. They're facing one another and watching each other closely, but clearly also in the act of a movement. To say that it's a photograph from a different era would be to undersell the situation pretty radically. It's like a photograph from a different era before the last different era. If you wanted to be pretentious, you might say that it's like a still for an undiscovered Samuel Beckett play, but of course this would be to see things the wrong way around. The point about Beckett, of course, is that he based his works on people like James Patrick. Because his plays, in particular, have acquired the label 'absurdism', it is assumed that the characters are in some sense akin to cartoons. In fact, the men Beckett depicts are ones he actually observed, refugees from a catastrophe that became a slapstick. We natives watch them with two sets of eyes: the eyes of the outsider, contracted by dint of literary education, and the eye of the insider, which sees also – or used to see – what is actually there. That's probably all but gone now – not just the James Patricks but the capacity to see them for what they were and to celebrate their immortalisation in the work of one of the greatest writers the world has ever read.

The one downside of the kindlin' patrol is that I become so fixated on searching for driftwood that I sometimes forget where I am. Half an hour will have passed sometimes before I look up from the hunt and catch sight of the inlet shrouded in a yellow glow, Inishmurray sleeping diffidently in the mist and the waves lapping against the rocks below me. In these moments I have that feeling that no part of me is equipped to take in everything there is to love and know in this world.

I think I'm turning into James Patrick. If you'd seen me coming up the road this afternoon with a bundle of sticks on my back, you'd never have taken me for that boy that used to be writing in the paper above in Dublin. I looked more like the man on the cover of Led Zeppelin IV (don't worry about it), who Jimmy Page described as a man at one with the land, taking from it, and giving back to it, the true and proper cycle of life. I'm not sure what I'm exactly giving back as yet, but I'm working on it.

I used to think of a life such as Uncle James Patrick's as wasted by peripheralisation, but now I think he was probably right at the centre of everything. Those of us who tried to escape his fate are the ones who've been wasting our time, chasing rainbows and tilting at windmills. All pointless and enfeebling.

I suppose what I've been describing is a two-way journey from the West to Dublin and back again, a journey vibrant now with paradoxes and contradictions: the dream of being free in Dublin turning into a dream of being free of the nightmare that Dublin became, for me and for itself. Now I see that this is just one tiny part of a journey involving you and me both. More than three quarters of a century ago, you left Mount Edward and headed east. Along the way, you came to the village of Tulsk in County Roscommon, and got a job there as a mechanic. You stayed, got married, moved to An Caisleán Riabhach, the Grey Castle, This journey has its own unquestionable dynamic – it needs no other justification. What is odd is that you never came back down here, indeed refused to. I remember the night of my sister Marian's wedding in the Great Southern Hotel in Sligo town, when your best pal in the world, John Burke, and I ganged up on you to get you to take the extra 10 miles to Mount Edward. Your 'no' was unequivocal, and to this day I cannot fully comprehend it. John was in a unique position between us, being both your friend and mine. That afternoon we all but pleaded with you to come with us to visit your brother, but you refused to the point of being willing to fall out with us both.

I know almost nothing about how you grew up apart from a few out-line facts and the legends you fed us with. I know there were eight acres to be divided between five brothers, so something had to give. I suspect it must have broken your heart to leave this place, and that would seem reason enough not to want to return. With all due respect to the town I grew up in, its charms would be no match for those around here. From time to time since I discovered where you came from, I have wondered how you could have come to live with such an exchange.

It is possible that there was some lasting difference between James

Patrick and yourself, but I don't believe there was. I remember the careful way you used to supervise the annual sending off of his Christmas box – a cake, a bottle of whiskey or rum, a plum pudding, 40 Players, and a letter you spent two nights in the writing. And I remember reading his misspelt replies, in large spidery writing. They were formulaic letters, to be sure – 'I hope all is well with you as it is with us … ' – but brotherly and affectionate for all that.

Now, with you both gone, here I am, and happy to be here. It's as if I have undertaken, by some unconscious route, the journey you refused to take that Sligo evening in 1975. Our lives have gone full circle, but as though we were one person rather than two. It has taken two generations and eight decades for the journey to be completed, but now we are back home. And now, your granddaughter, Róisín, has announced her desire to settle here also. Could you ask for more?

Never in my life have I been in a place that has such resonance for me. Much of the year almost nothing happens, no one comes, and yet the place is full with a constant sense of expectation. It is like a fictional place, the setting for a novel in which I have a significant part and which is in train right now, being read by someone, God knows who or why.

I rarely go back to the Grey Castle now. No more than yourself, I have an ambivalent view of it and probably always had. I wrote a great deal about it in *Jiving at the Crossroads*, and still go there occasionally to funerals when I hear about them. I love and hate it, as you do with things that are, or have been, central to your life. Castlerea is the town in my head, the one that inhabits that archetypal space left aside for towns. I think the nature of the town – streetscape to the front, wilderness to the back – has been a key element in the formation of my thinking. But I'm not in the least sentimental about it. I used to drink when I lived here and have since given it up, so I rarely mix with the locals any more. I have some childhood friends, but our relationships are a bit stilted and nostalgic. My life is mainly outside and, to be honest, I prefer coming down here.

< 404 >

How do I feel about all this? Wholly different from what I might have expected if you'd predicted it for me as I set off from the Grey Castle in my green Ford Fiesta on 1 May 1984. Back then I would have thought of you being (rather typically) Jeremiah-like, not understanding what was happening, where I was going and how it was going to end. What was happening, I was certain, was the achievement by me of a total break with the past. I was going to the heart of the capital city to work with a rock 'n' roll magazine. I was going to continue on a full-time basis the work I'd made a tentative start at breaking into about six and a half years before, and which I'd been doing part-time for the previous three. I was about to enter the new world, the one my generation had taken it upon itself to midwife in, a world of personal freedom, peace, equality and love. I couldn't have told you then what my new life would be like, but I could certainly have told you that I had no intention of ever looking back.

But no sooner had I embarked on this new adventure than it seemed to me that I had no way of judging the shape of the future other than by measuring it against the past. And the only past I knew was this one: you and Mammy and where you came from, your histories, griefs, hopes, trials, labours and joys. While I was there, in Castlerea, in the West, I could rail against the way things were, oppose and snipe at everything and everyone, including you. I was a rebel, a leftie of sorts, a potential revolutionary, and now I was off to the capital to continue the fight. But there I found that the first call upon me was on my loyalty to where I came from. Encountering the condescension towards culchies that was then ubiquitous in Dublin – and most of all from culchies denying their beginnings – I confess I reacted badly. Rather than apologising for my origins, I started to play them up – my accent, my ignorance and my reactionary opinions. At first this was a game, but later I began to see how serious it was. The condescension of those towards the place I'd come from, and other places like it, told me that there was an absence of sincerity in their commitment to fraternity and egalitarianism. I started to pay attention to the things they stood for, which up until then I had taken to be self-evidently idealistic and derived from higher forms of think-ing. Then I started thinking for myself: a fatal error. Gradually I began to dissent from the orthodoxies that I'd bought into before, and which had in effect been responsible for bringing me to Dublin. The tendency worsened after 1991, when I joined *The Irish Times*, where I found the condescension towards the greater part of the country to be of the full-blown variety. Only by going native could you continue to be tolerated, but tolerance was never something I craved from anyone.

It became clear to me that the 'project' being undertaken in the news-paper, and which I was expected to throw my weight behind, was the transformation of Irish society according to an imported model that had no place for pretty much anything of the Ireland then existing – by which I mean its traditions, value system, faith, ways of remembering, language, music, pretty much everything about it apart from the scenery and the clean water, although these were expendable also, depending on the price. So it came to pass that I turned tail and crossed the road in my head, back to stand alongside you and men and women who were like you, who stood for things other than self-obsession and freedom defined as the right to do whatever you liked whenever you wanted to do it.

In Dublin, the nature and definition of my revolution altered funda-mentally. I identified a previously unnoticed oligarchy intent upon usurp-ing the democratic rights of the people I belonged to, and turned what firepower I had in that direction.

I may have gone too far; I confess it. There is a tendency when op-posing something to imitate the dynamism of your opponent in order to match and then exceed his strength and energy. There is also an element of glee that enters in when you find you are winding people up. My late friend Derek Dunne and I used to have a catchphrase between us that was drawn from an article Gene Kerrigan wrote in *Magill* one time about informal interrogations being conducted by extra-enthusiastic officers in a certain Garda station up the country in the years of the Heavy Gang. It came from a remark from one of the cops in the station, referring to the back room where the action reputedly took place, who confided to Kerrigan: 'I do love to hear them roarin'.'

I, too, enjoyed hearing the roars of the prim and patronising as I deconstructed their nonsense and groundless superiority complexes. They couldn't believe that one of themselves had turned and was going against them.

But in the end they won. It was inevitable, I suppose. They swept all before them, eradicating not just the country's faith, traditions, values and memories but most of its spirit also. I'm not talking grandly here about some inherited coherence of Christian values. I'm thinking more of priorities, perspective, balance, common sense and, above all, the entitlement to hold your own opinion and give voice to it when you please.

As I grew older, I began to see that there was more to what I was saying and doing than taking the piss out of a bunch of self-important assholes, that the things I was fighting for were worth fighting for on their own terms, and that the only things that mattered were to be found back where I – or, rather, you – had started out.

So, I return defeated. But I also return happy – happy that I did all I could and happy to have understood that what I went off chasing on 1 May 1984 was a will-o'-the-wisp. At the time, I suppose, I wanted something else as well as the realisation of the revolution. I wanted also a life worth living and fancied that I wouldn't be able to achieve that if I stayed where I was. I wanted to get away and I presumed that that meant permanently. I carved out a life worth living: I have a wife, a daughter, a reputation in certain quarters I can work like a mine, if I'm willing to, a couple of properties to fend off the winds of want in old age. And I was right that I wouldn't have been able to do all that if I stayed where I was. My own guess is that, had I stayed, I'd be dead long ago, from alcohol and frustration in no particular order.

So, here I am, back again where we started out, more or less. Or, to be more precise, back where you started out, half a century before I started out on completing the journey you began eastwards. I see our journey now as one journey. It's like together we amount to a man aged 114. It's not that we were seeking the same literal things, but that we both understood that, in the circumstances we found ourselves in, we had to move east. But we moved east holding the West in our hearts, and, although we never found what we were searching for, together we came to the understanding that what we needed had been right there in front of us all the time.

< 408 >

34

Trophy Country

What has happened to Ireland, when you spell it out, is almost beyond belief, but the evidence that it has happened is overwhelming. Ireland in 2015 was targeted by the international LGBT lobby as a 'trophy country'. For all kinds of historical and cultural reasons, it presented as a country that might easily be rolled over. Those within Ireland who might present an obstacle to that agenda were targeted to ensure that the trophy could be carried off.

There were two exceptional factors relating to Ireland that made it desirable, if not imperative, that gay marriage be passed here – and not just passed by means of a compromise form of marriage for gays being introduced by statute – a discrete category of marriage for gay people that would not have encroached upon the existing, normative form. It was vital that it go into the Constitution.

The most concrete reason had to do with the concept of 'equality' being trumpeted as the main point of the referendum, which changed utterly the nature of the demand – no longer just 'gay marriage' but, immediately and in one fell swoop, the collapsing of all distinctions between marriage of straight and gay couples. When civil partnership was being teased out by the politicians prior to legislation in 2010, the LGBT lobby claimed that it would be content with such a provision provided it catered for a number of adumbrated issues. Once civil partnership became legal, those purportedly speaking for gays began to ask why they were not entitled to be married. It was almost as if the extension of civil partnership represented some kind of provocation, since, by their logic now, it suggested an improper lack of equivalence between gay and heterosexual couples. Thus, civil partnership was never anything more than a stepping stone to

< 409 >

full marriage, underwritten by the Constitution, or 'equality' as they would have it. By 'marriage', the gay lobby meant marriage in the precise same sense as marriage was available to heterosexual couples, even though gay couples were manifestly different in that they were intrinsically incapable of procreation, and therefore incapable, in constitutional terms, of founding a family. It also meant equality above everything else, including equality over marriage as it had hitherto existed: it did not matter that marriage was being reduced, so long as, in the end, gays were 'equal' to straights. Yet these matters were not even permitted to be discussed. The point of putting gay marriage in the Constitution on the same basis as heterosexual marriage – however that ended up – was to claim for gay couples the right to children, to become parents of, in many cases, other people's children. The consequences involved the diminution of rights and protections long conferred – by nature more than by any law or constitutional provision – on male-female couples married and rearing their own children, and also on the children who might in various ways themselves become implicated in this new dispensation.

Apart from adoption, children could become available to gay couples by the use of eggs or sperm donated by others and by the use of 'womb rental' from surrogate mothers, usually in exchange for money. During the referendum 'debate', the Yes lobby insisted that surrogacy had nothing to do with the gay marriage amendment, but of course this was nonsense: surrogacy was by far the most obvious means by which gay couples could obtain children. With the passage of the amendment, gay couples acquired precisely the same constitutional entitlement to 'found a family' and to acquire children as male-female couples, which means that the Irish state would in the future face a difficulty should it try to outlaw surrogacy or to control any reproductive technology that makes it easier for gay couples to achieve their constitutional entitlements. This is why the government dropped the surrogacy provisions contained in the draft of the Children and Family Relationships Bill which preceded the same-sex marriage vote: by fraudulently removing the most potentially divisive element, it was able to get the same-sex marriage amendment passed while kicking the surrogacy forward to be dealt with in legislation later on.

A more culturally centred reason why it was imperative that Ireland put its gay marriage provisions in its Constitution was that Ireland had been seen as a beacon of Catholic faith in the world, so that the news that it had acquiesced in the demands of the LGBT lobby would represent a victory that could be trumpeted around the globe as a challenge to countries already believing themselves more secular and liberal. By not merely passing a gay marriage provision, but elevating gay couples to the same constitutional level as male-female couples – and not just in marriage, but parenthood as well – Ireland would become big news around the globe, and this could be used by the LGBT lobby to advance its agenda elsewhere. After all, if backward little old Ireland was prepared to go that far to accommodate its demands, how could any country professing to be 'modern' possibly resist what in most cases would be far more modest and restrictive provisions?

Ireland was also a small, relatively unitary country that could be propagandised and controlled much more easily than a larger, more fractured country. We had a tiny media sector, already pretty much in the grip of pseudo-liberal hysteria, and most of our newspapers were struggling to retain audience share, especially among the young. These were ideal conditions for the carrot-or-stick approach favoured by the LGBT strategists.

There was also a more technical and legally important reason why it was vital that Ireland insert its gay marriage provision in the Constitution. This had to do with the stipulations of a protocol achieved by the Irish government in 2009 when it sought to put the Lisbon Treaty to the people for the second time. This protocol served to protect not just Ireland but all EU countries seeking to preserve their autonomy in the face of encroachment from the EU Court of Justice on matters relating to family and marriage. In advance of the referendum, Anthony Coughlan, whose name may be familiar to many Irish people from the 'Coughlan

Judgment', which deals with balance in broadcasting during a referendum debate, explained the issues as follows:

> One of the many unconsidered consequences of voting to change the Constitution is that it would alter the legal-political effect of the first Lisbon Treaty Protocol, which the Government used to persuade Irish people to ratify the Lisbon Treaty in 2009, after they had rejected it in 2008.
>
> The Lisbon Treaty, which establishes the EU Constitution, gives the EU the power to lay down human rights standards as a matter of supranational law across its 28 Member States. Article 9 of the EU Charter of Fundamental Rights allows for same-sex marriage and the right 'to found a family' on that basis. As it stands, Ireland's Lisbon Treaty Protocol is an insurmountable legal barrier to supranational EU law on marriage, the family and education across the EU.

Coughlan's argument received minimal attention and fell on stony ground. The implication of what he said – and in advance of the referendum – was that the legal effect of changing the Irish Constitution of our own volition would be to vitiate the protocol we had insisted upon in 2009, thus removing the barrier that prevented the EU legislating across the union on 'human rights' issues like gay marriage and adoption rights and imposing these over the heads of national governments. Hence, in voting Yes to inserting what was generally believed to be a simple provision for gay marriage into our Constitution, we cleared the way for EU laws on same-sex marriage to be imposed in due course on all EU countries by decision of the EU Court of Justice.

And here Coughlan's analysis becomes most interesting indeed: 'Ireland would thus become a bridgehead in the EU for the powerful pharmaceutical companies that make up the donor-assisted human reproduction industry and the accompanying lucrative surrogacy business in America and Europe.'

< 412 >

'Bridgehead' means 'a strong position secured by an army inside enemy territory from which to advance or attack'. Ireland was already the number one European location for international pharmaceutical investment, and one of the largest net exporters of pharmaceuticals in the world. As we were already playing host to eight of the top 10 global pharmaceutical and biopharmaceutical companies, we would be in a position to attract lucrative new inflows of investment in the areas of surrogacy and donor-assisted human reproduction. This would mean more jobs in the Irish economy and better job security for the politicians who made it possible. As Anthony Coughlan put it a few days before polling day: 'If voters change the Constitution on Friday the Irish State will become an ideological flag-bearer in the EU for the powerful economic interests involved in the donor-assisted human reproduction industry and the lucrative international surrogacy business that is its complement.'

In other words, Ireland's Constitution had now become a 'natural endowment factor' – something that could be offered up in return for the continuing goodwill of the fiscally footloose corporations of the world.

With such stakes being played for, it was unsurprising that all parties with intentions with regard to future involvement in the running of the country would row in behind such a political no-brainer for politicians whose bag-of-tricks did not stretch far beyond the tugged forelock and the begging bowl. Now would it be difficult to convince a media sector largely struggling to make ends meet of the wisdom of doing as we were told. The only potential obstacle – and it was a real one in view of the near defeat of the 2012 so-called 'Children Referendum', was that a bunch of 'right-wing headbangers' might stir up enough doubt and anxiety to overcome the best efforts of the gay propagandists and their media allies. This was why it was vital that John Waters, Breda O'Brien and the Iona Institute be disabled or taken out at an early stage. This was the meaning of the Rory O'Neill intervention. If it had not happened on *The Saturday Night Show* on 11 January 2014, it would have happened a month or three or six at the most later. It was not an accident; it was not a random schmozzle. The dogs of war – the 'availability cascade' of will-ing agents of scapegoating and demonistation, were waiting, straining at their leashes for the signal, and when it came they were let loose.

Beyond the central knot of orchestrators and manipulators, what hap-pened to Ireland in 2014/15 can be characterised as the eruption of a kind of national madness, all the more disquieting because it could not be discussed. Three years later, most people still clam up when you raise with them matters to do with the sudden phenomenon of interest in gay rights, transgender rights and so forth. Several people to whom I spoke in the course of writing this book – mainly for the purpose of clarifying things I was likely to deal with concerning the aftermath of the Rory O'Neill assault – made it clear that they didn't want to be mentioned for fear of incurring a backlash from the LGBT lobby.

It remains the case that, over the past four or five years, questions that were never before regarded as having any urgency have been pushed to the top of the political agenda, mainly through the persistence of a relatively tiny group of indigenous lobbyists and the acquiescence of the media in placing and keeping them at the top of their list of priorities. To call this bizarre is seriously to understate things. It is not that there might not be some merit in seeking to extend proper protections to homosex-ual relationships, or to make things easier for people who see themselves differently in sexual/gender terms from how they have been regarded by society all their lives. The difficulty arises because of the suddenness with which these issues descended on the public realms of virtually all western societies, and the insistence of those pushing them that societies were not entitled to conduct comprehensive debates before making the kinds of changes being demanded.

The most shocking thing about these developments has been the strange acquiescence by the mainstream media, which have gone along with these agendas to an extent that, notwithstanding the supposedly 'liberal' ethos long known to permeate media circles, is remarkable in its blatancy. What is difficult to understand is not that the media were by and large in favour of these changes, but that they became so readily convinced that they needed to happen immediately, without question, as soon as the LGBT and other lobby groups so demanded. Consider, for example, the following question: How many of the Irish newspapers, newspaper columnists and radio or TV presenters who became so agitated on behalf of 'gay rights' during 2014 and 2015 had been taking stances on these issues prior to, say, 2010? The answer, as we have seen in the case of *The Irish Times*, is virtually none, and the same is true of politicians. Yet now, all of a sudden, these same people were assuring us that gay marriage was the most obvious and pressing human rights issue of our time, and that anyone failing to share this opinion was a bigot.

Part of the explanation may be the state of turmoil that had enveloped in particular the newspaper industry over the previous decade. This, without doubt, rendered the industry susceptible to imitating online tendencies and methods, and in effect seeking to compete with Internet operators in creating shock value to attract more hits and clicks. Whatever else you might say about the LGBT agenda and methodologies, it has the power to excite controversy, and this was likely to be seen as manna from above by those managing an industry with all the signs of being in its death throes. Another factor is undoubtedly the increase of yellowpacking in the day-to-day running of media organisations. Many of the journalists manning the national newspapers these days are young, wet-behind-the-ears graduates who have come through one of the handful of third-level journalism courses now available, and the same applies in broadcast media. These courses are, almost without exception, delivered by radical, left-leaning and ideologically motivated former journalists, who appear to be agreed that the point of journalism is to push society in certain directions, regardless of what the citizens may think or desire.

The culmination of these and other contributing factors is a media sector radically and dramatically changed – out of all recognition – from the kind of media we had even a decade ago. Undoubtedly, this, as much as any competition from the worldwide web, had contributed to the decline of newspapers in the same period, since, while some people may be unperturbed by what is happening – or even approving of it – others are likely to be puzzled and disoriented by the sudden change in priorities of newspapers bearing the same mastheads that they bore through years of staid and measured reportage and commentary on Irish society.

It is interesting that, within days of the 2015 referendum result, a change appeared to come over the media, which seemed immediately to begin pushing transgender issues in the way they had previously been pushing gay demands. Three months after the gay-marriage referendum, the country awoke one morning to find itself besieged by reports that an RTÉ news reporter had announced that he was unable to decide between being a man or a woman and had decided to be both. It seemed that another 'most pressing human right of our time' might be in the offing.

Three months later, *The Irish Independent* carried a report (i.e. not a column, a report) headlined: 'I do not want to be an adult right now - Transgender father (52) leaves family to live life as six-year-old girl'.

The report went on to relate that a 'Canadian transgender father' had left his wife and children to start a new life as a six-year-old girl. There was nothing in the presentation of the article to suggest that it was a satire or a spoof of any kind.

It went on: 'Stefonknee (pronounced 'Stephanie') Wolschtt is now living with an adoptive family and says she does not "want to be an adult right now". The father-of-seven had been married for 23 years before she identified as transgender.'

Note the way the pronoun referring to the main subject of the story alters after the first paragraph from 'he' to 'she', even though this usage is challenged by the semantic context.

Online, the report was accompanied by a video featuring an interview with Mr Wolschtt, conducted by an organisation calling itself The Transgender Project. The report more or less co-opted the content of this video without amendment or qualification.

< 416 >

The man said: 'I can't deny I was married. I can't deny I have children. But I've moved forward now and I've gone back to being a child.'

The report continued: 'The 52-year-old admitted that her wife found it impossible to accept her as a transgender woman and told her to either "stop being trans or leave".

"To me, 'stop being trans' isn't something I could do," she says. "It would be like telling me to stop being 6ft 2 or leave".'

The report continued: 'Her family's rejection of her new identity is what prompted Ms Wolschtt to find an adoptive family, who she says are "totally comfortable with me being a little girl".'

Indeed the video contained photographs of Mr Wolschtt, dressed in feminine clothing, in the company of an elderly couple whom he referred to as his adoptive parents. Wolshett explained that, at first, he had been an eight-year-old girl but, at the request of the youngest grandchild of this couple – his 'adoptive sibling' according to the *Irish Independent* report – he had decided to be six. 'A year ago I was eight and she was seven. And she said to me, "I want you to be the little sister, so I'll be nine." I said, "Well, I don't mind going to six." So I've been six ever since.'

The report continued: 'Ms Wolschtt explains that the two children have a "great time".

'"We colour, we do kids stuff. It's called play therapy. No medication, no suicide thoughts. And I just get to play".'

The report elaborated: 'In an earlier part of the series, Ms Wolschtt spoke of how she became suicidal after taking part in the first Toronto transgender march in 2009.

'She spent some time in hospital and after she was discharged, Ms Wolschtt's wife accused her of harassment and assault. She later pressed charges against her husband to achieve a restraining order.

'In 2012, Ms Wolschtt was invited to her eldest daughter's wedding but on the condition that she "dress like her dad" and sit at the back of the church without addressing the family.

< 417 >

'The day of her daughter's wedding, Ms Wolschtt attempted suicide for the last time, and was unsuccessful.

'She now receives support from the Metropolitan Community Church of Toronto where the congregation is mostly made up of LGBT people.'

The point I wish to make about this has little or nothing to do with Mr or Ms Wolschtt. It takes all sorts. As far as self-description goes, whatever gets you through the night is all right by me. I can't help, though, noting that, normally, newspapers tend to be unforgiving of fathers who abandon their families, but in this case, obviously, *The Irish Independent* was willing to make an exception. I don't think Mr Wolschtt is a very responsible gentleman, but that's just my opinion on the facts as presented above.

My point has more to do with those pronouns, the way they follow an ideological course through the article rather than a semantic or culturally attuned one.

Once it is established that Mr Wolschtt started out by being a he, he is immediately permitted to become a she, because that's the way he sees things, and, because he does, no one is entitled to dissent from this description. The, at best, ludicrous idea of him befriending a seven-year-old girl, with the approval of that child's legal guardians, is treated as un-exceptional and unexceptionable, when in fact it is the kind of thing that used to be on the front page of the *National Enquirer* not that long ago.

What is most disturbing about these recent tendencies is not that they seek space for the eccentric or the unusual, but that they seek to displace the normative world, in effect asking that it collapse itself, to make 'amends' to those who claim to have been excluded in the past. But this dispensation of compassion does not appear to extend to other categories of discrimi-nated-against citizen, only to those who are identified as 'victims' of some prior oppression. What would it take to persuade newspapers to carry a pro rata volume of reports and commentaries relating to the family courts' treatment of single fathers in the way it carried 'personal stories' for the LGBT lobby over the previous two or three years, and was now seemingly intent upon replicating on behalf of the trans and fluid lobbies?

It did not, for example, appear to have occurred to any of those responsible for this exercise in what can only with the utmost charity be called journalism that, were Mr Wolschtt's 'human rights' to gain the same foothold as had latterly the 'human rights' of 'gay families', there would no longer be any way of protecting children from predatory paedophiles who happened to find Mr Wolschtt's success inspirational. The fact that Mr Wolschtt was not one of these would be irrelevant to this danger, since all protests against the risks involved would be swept aside as representing some kind of 'phobia' by the kinds of people who pushed the gay marriage agenda, and before long the 'right' of such people to access children on demand might very well trump the right of those children to be protected. If you think this implausible, ask yourself this: at what point did you begin to think that gay marriage was an overdue adjustment and self-evidently a good thing?

It was clearly insane that such rubbish was being foisted on the Irish public simply because newspapers wished to ensure their own survival and the best way they could think of doing this was to hitch their wagons to whatever freak show happened to be passing. It was shocking beyond belief that Irish people were being subjected to this, that they were required to contemplate such headlines and such drivel as though it made perfect sense, on pain of being regarded as old-fashioned or daubed as a hate-monger.

Such 'journalism' is clinically insane. And it is a measure of the insanity that had gripped our country that almost nobody is willing to stand up and say so. Behind the screen of propaganda provided by this and similar articles, the Irish government had in 2015 brought in the Gender Recognition Act – just two months after the 'Marriage Equality' referendum' - providing for people over the age of 16 to change their gender, though specifying that teenagers aged 16–17 must go through a medical and psychiatric process before changing. The Gender Recognition Act allows all individuals over the age of 18 to self-declare their own gender identity. This meant that any citizen over 17 could reverse their given sex by a simple written declaration. I could overnight become a woman, and one of my sisters become a man, simply by filling out a form. What this meant for gender quotas was unclear, but it was noticeable that none of the political sponsors of this madness had anything to say on this aspect.

In July 2018, it was announced by the Minister for Social Protection, Regina Doherty, that the government proposed to amend the legislation to remove the restriction on children under 16 accessing a therapy that had yet to be properly tested, and the long-tern consequences of which had yet to be observed.

A provision that, no more than five years previously, would have been regarded as bonkers had, through the machinations of invisible actors supported by ideological bullying and with the aid of covering fire from a corrupted journalism, become as though an unexceptionable proposition, beyond public discussion or professional reservations. While genuine issues of discrimination and injustice were ignored or treated with political contempt, a thoroughly crazy proposition, opposed by countless medical experts, had been adopted and processed in a matter of months, and was already being refined in accordance with the demands of its invisible proponents. This is Ireland 2018.

35

The Road to Infinity

On my window in Lislary I have a sepia-toned photograph of you, taken perhaps 80 years ago, pulling a broken down Model T Ford in which several children are sitting delightedly. You are pulling it with your bare hands, using a rope tied to the axle.

For more than 25 years I have looked upon that photograph, wondering why it struck me so powerfully. It was taken in Tulsk, so most likely dates from the 1930s, shortly after you first arrived in those parts. Your hair still has its colour. You would have been in your early 30s.

The engine of the Model T has been removed. It looks like you've recently acquired the car, perhaps from somebody's back yard, and are taking it back to the workshop.

I don't know the names of the children. There are at least five of them in the car. I asked Mammy one time and she could name them all, but to my shame I didn't write the names down.

The children look happy. You look serious. It's almost like they've climbed into the car without your knowing, though I presume the 'driver', a boy of maybe 13 or 14, is acting under instructions.

Looking the spit of Tom Waits circa Heartattack and Vine, you pull the Model T like the carcass of some proud animal you have slain and brought down in the wild and now triumphantly drag home, the children of your tribespeople on its back. I note again how serious you are, how intent on the effort of pulling, and yet you are not in any respect thrown out of your equilibrium by the effort involved. The task at hand appears to require no going beyond how you would normally be. You are not posing. You do not succumb to, or even recognise the possibility of, showing off. There is no larking for the benefit of either the camera or the onlookers. The children are giddy, but you are not. They are at play, you are at work. They are laughing, full of joy to be in this moment, but you are solemn-faced: the one who supplies the energy and direction for the entire enterprise but also stands as the sole protector of the children against the possibility of their moment of fun going out of control.

In this photograph you appear to personify a time in which technological progress was of necessity in the control of the human person – not some remote member of a dissociated elite, but the man, literally, in the street. To imagine you with an iPhone is impossible. What would you do with it? Not to tweet or 'like', that's for sure, but perhaps open its back and take it apart in the hopes of finding a way to check the timing on the Model T.

The day we buried you, your great friend Kevin O'Grady told me about one morning many years ago when he was travelling with you from Ballaghaderreen to Mantua and, just outside Ballanagare, the vehicle came to a lurching, catatonic halt. You got out to investigate, did your usual roll underneath for a look-see, and eventually resurfaced to say that the driveshaft had broken. For virtually anyone else, this would have been a terminal calamity, but not you. You told Kevin you'd be back in a few minutes, negotiated the fence of a nearby field and disappeared. About ten minutes later, you reappeared carrying a timber stake and a rolled up section of rusty barbed wire. Kevin asked no questions, but you again rolled underneath the vehicle and, by his account, reunited the broken pieces of the driveshaft using the stake as a splint and tying it in place with the barbed wire. In a few minutes you resumed your place behind the wheel, started up the engine and gingerly proceeded to Mantua, on to Elphin, Cloonyquin, Tulsk, Castleplunkett, Lisalway and home.

You are not looking at the camera. Many modern photographs represent attempts at 'relationship' with the notional person who may look at the photograph later, a relationship projected through the person of whoever is behind the camera. But you do not recognise this person's existence, not, I guess, due to any incivility, but because it doesn't occur to you to think that you are actually going to be 'in a photograph'. The

< 422 >

photograph will have been taken with a camera obscura, the 'darkened box with a convex lens or aperture for projecting the image of an external object on to a screen inside', which preceded the modern camera. The photographer may have been underneath a 'cloak of invisibility', which would explain why neither you nor any of the children appear to acknowledge his existence. Head down, you are concentrating on the job in hand, on summoning up the strength to pull the car full of children behind you.

The car, which is in a rather serious state of undress, seems to be one of the early versions of the Model T Touring Car, possibly even a 1914 edition, which would make it among the first cars to be built on Henry Ford's moving assembly line. It might well have been a slightly later version. It's hard to tell, given its decrepit condition. Ford called his Model T 'the car for the great multitude'. The first production Model T Ford was assembled at the Piquette Avenue Plant in Detroit, Michigan, on 1 October 1908 and was nicknamed the 'Tin Lizzie'. Ford's first car, the Quadricycle, produced in 1896, had a one-cylinder petrol engine in a chassis that was essentially a frame fitted with four bicycle wheels. From the time he started the Henry Ford Motor Company in 1903, they had been producing each car individually. In 1908, he launched his automatic production line, based on the methods of Frederick Taylor, pioneer of the 'one best way' of mass production. Ford's ambition was to produce a car that was straightforward, versatile and, above all, affordable, and which one of his own factory workers could manage to pay for. He achieved this within a couple of years of launching the Model T: the first cars cost close to $1,000, but, by 1915, the price had come down by two-thirds, and remained at or below that level for the rest of its lifetime, reaching its lowest level in 1925 when a Model T could be bought for $260.

Ford and his team identified four principles that would further their goal: interchangeable parts, continuous flow, division of labour and reducing wasted effort. During the Model T's 19-year lifespan, between 1908 and 1927, Ford produced 15 million of more than a dozen different varieties: the Model T Roadster, Coupe, Coupelet, Runabout, Roadster,

Torpedo, Mud Buggy, Town Car, Touring Car, and the Fordor and Tudor sedans. All of these body styles were furnished with the same engine and essentially the same chassis. Only the Volkswagen Beetle achieved a longer lifespan. Both cars feature in the top 10 best-selling cars of all time. The average Model T achieved less than 20 miles per gallon.

Contrary to the legend based on the apocryphal line attributed to Ford about painting the Model T 'any colour so long as it's black', the early Model T's came in a variety of colours. Between 1914 and 1925, though, the Model T would be sold in black only. The reason was that the particular kind of black paint used by Ford dried more quickly than other paints.

In his biography, *The Legend of Henry Ford*, Keith Sward wrote of Ford's travails in introducing his production line: 'So great was labour's distaste for the new machine system that, towards the close of 1913 every time the company wanted to add 100 men to its factory personnel, it was necessary to hire 963.'

Why? Because men like you, who had been used to being the masters of their own hands and creativities, couldn't bear the idea of doing just one tiny job, like tightening a nut on a cylinder head, over and over again. It represented a metaphysical affront to real men, real republicans. Can you think of any more telling statistic of what is lost to us?

In this modern, postmodern or pre-apocalyptic moment, the human and the technological have become so intertwined in the space formerly identified as the human psyche that they can no longer usefully be treated separately in this context. Man has ceased to be a purely organic species and has become a kind of cybernetic organism or cyborg. The argument about whether man will become capable of producing 'intelligent machines' is therefore redundant: the answer is that man himself is becoming an 'intelligent machine'. As the very concept implies, this means a trade-off: man trading down to adapt in order to couple with the machine, which is elevated to the level of optimum functionality and compromise. This involves some gains, which we need but ask the nearest numbskull to list, and many losses, which for the most part we will try to keep from ourselves. One of these is the loss of particular forms of creativity. In his book *The End of the Modern World*, Romano Guardini describes the downside of the perfection of machines: the intimate relation between the artisan and his work, 'in which his eye, hand, will, sense of material, imagination and general creativeness cooperate', can no longer be accessed and 'disappears', leaving man much the poorer for all the ease and connectivity he may have gained. Man loses his individuality and succumbs to the will of the machine, becoming its servant even as he imagines himself its master. 'In place of the artisan, we have the worker, servicer of machines.'

In reality the machine allowed for a while for the kind of creativity that Guardini attributed only to artisan work. This may be because he failed to grasp that machines of the early kind exhibited a simplicity and a vulnerability that made them like children to men like you. The picture of you and the Model T may well have been taken at or close to the last moments of this possibility, for its repair allowed for the same creative care as its conception and design. There was as yet, therefore, no diminishment of creativity.

In the photograph, Ford's magnificent vehicle is broken, its designers humbled, tamed by bad roads. You have rescued it, lifted it up. You are taking the vanquished vehicle home to be healed, as heal it you will, with your own hands, the hands that are now upon the rope, calloused and lined from the experience of grasping the world. The offspring of Henry Ford and Frederick Taylor, humbled and defeated, has surrendered to you, but you are not in the mood for triumph. There is a job to be done and you are heading hard for the workshop. You move ahead of the technology of locomotion, in the driver's seat in every sense except literally.

You are no 'worker' in Guardini's sense here, no 'servicer of machines'. You acquiesce in no diminution of personal creativity and therefore in no loss of satisfaction, no sacrificing of individuality. In your tangling with machines you retained the capacity for organic creativity that Guardini identifies with the pre-technical age. Your relationship to the machine remains as that of the craftsman to his tools, and also akin to that of the drayman to his horse. You are a craftsman in the last moments of craftsmen, the midwife called to the sick bed. This may be the last relic, the last photograph, of these moments as they glimmered in history. This may be the last moment before technology's full breakthrough, a fleeting glimpse of the short span of time between the pre-technical epoch and the technological totalitarianism soon to be born. You stand with one foot in each era, for you are still capable of experiencing personally the essential reality of the conception and realisation of Henry Ford's automobile, of seeing it in its simplicity and vulnerability, but also of respecting and comprehending the power of the machine and its internal combustion engine, over which you preside like a priest over the Eucharist. For you, the world still contains both mystery and knowability, but your attitudes to these are almost precisely the reverse of what obtains today: you insist on knowing how everything works, we insist only on a guarantee that it does; you believe in the limits of your man's capacity to grasp total reality; we believe that it is only a matter of time before everything will be known – but largely by others, symbolically on our behalf.

In a fundamental sense, there are two types of photograph. There is the kind generated by a camera that simply captures what is in front of it: not quite a random vista but certainly an objectified one that relates to something particular in man's artifices, a social realism that provokes no response except a kind of politicised engagement. This is the everyday kind of photograph we come across in our newspapers. These photographs tell us things but do not move us, because they exist merely for the purposes of information, of confirming that the known world remains as it was yesterday. They operate to a logic derived from man's machinations in a world he has come to take for granted, from his self-ordained sense of having already mastered his environment and created his own meanings. Such a photograph merely records man's movement around his own world, and often comes as an accompaniment to descriptions of man's enactment of his own arrangements.

< 426 >

And then there is the kind of photograph that stops you in your tracks, that draws you into itself, into some story that you intuit to lie there as a testament to something pre-existing man's manoeuvrings. This type of photograph seeks to penetrate reality, to see and record the nature of man's true relationship with matter, space and time, and always, explicitly or otherwise, to observe man's own nature in this situation. The first category reduces everything to appearances, agreed understandings; the other subjects the viewer to an impact, a shock, causing him to vibrate in an unaccustomed harmony with the truth about himself and his fellow man. A true photograph of the exterior world speaks to us of the interior, awakening our sense that the scale and scope of nature is actually an externalised drama of the internal seeking, desiring and hoping that define us. Similarly, a true portrait of a human being seeks to penetrate also to the created entity rather than the socially described or ideologically apprehended. Thus, a photograph of a man, woman, child, offers these two possibilities: either it depicts a political being, a functionary, passer-by, consumer, commuter, young person, old man, citizen; or it depicts a human being caught in the act of Being, stretched taut between his origin and his destiny, like the rope with which you pull the car full of children. It depicts man's struggle and surprise, his waiting and wonder. This is what I see in the Model T photograph.

It is easy nowadays, perhaps unavoidable, to remain unaware, when we look at a photograph that accomplishes this, that this is what we are observing, because our cultures seek to waylay us into ruts of received understandings: aesthetics, composition, structure, personality, technique, 'art', nostalgia. But these critical criteria are merely post-rationalisations for something that speaks to us more directly, at the very core of our selves. Such an image defies the descriptions and explanations that man has arrived at, implying their inadequacy and smallness but also hinting at immense further possibilities. It shows, simultaneously, man's tininess and his grandeur, insinuating his intrinsic connectedness to the world but also summoning up the configuration of a world before he arrived.

Thus, a great photograph abolishes time, condensing eternity into itself. Such images are a witness to something that happens continuously but has been rendered invisible by virtue of reinterpretations of an untruthful kind, and the ubiquity of images now.

I don't have many photographs of you, but I am glad I have this one and I would not trade it for a thousand selfies you had taken of yourself on an iPhone. Of all the things I have of yours and of you, this photograph is to me the most precious. It is not just a photograph of you. It is, in a sense, *you*. It is the you I knew through the brief time our two lives intersected on the road to Infinity.

< 428 >